The Squatting Age in Australia
1835-1847

New South Wales up to 1835

THE SQUATTING AGE
IN AUSTRALIA
1835-1847

STEPHEN H. ROBERTS

Formerly Challis Professor of History
University of Sydney

MELBOURNE UNIVERSITY PRESS

LONDON AND NEW YORK: CAMBRIDGE UNIVERSITY PRESS

First published 1935
Reprinted, with corrections, 1964

Printed and bound in Australia by
Melbourne University Press, Parkville N.2, Victoria

Registered in Australia for transmission
by post as a book

Text set in 10 point Juliana type

PREFACE

This book was first published in 1935. It therefore affords me great pleasure to have a new impression completely reset and published by the same firm nearly thirty years later. The text has been retained in the original form, except for obvious correction of misprints, elimination of errors, the redrawing of the maps by Miss Joyce Wood, and the modernization of the bibliography. Nothing has occurred in the intervening three decades to make me change the original thesis, although differing interpretations of the importance and place of the squatting age have been made by some later historians, especially as affecting the general evolutionary flow of the Australian life story.

Sydney   S. H. R.
March 1964

CONTENTS

Preface   v

1   Australia in 1835   1

2   The Wool Trade   35

3   The Origin of Squatting   49

4   The First Regulation of Squatting   69

5   The Early Policy of Sir George Gipps   93

6   The Squatters' Tracks   127

7   The Great Crisis: 1841-1844   186

8   The Struggle with Sir George Gipps   214

9   Leases and the Locking of the Land   263

10   The Squatting Life   272

11   The Transformation of the Squatters   350

Appendices

   I Position at beginning of this survey, 1836   359

   II Annual wool exports   359

   III Position after the great expansion, 1840-1841   360

   IV Position in the first elected Legislative Council, 1843   361

   V Position at end of this survey, 1848-1849   362

   VI Indentures of labourers imported for squatters   363

Select Bibliography   365

Index   373

MAPS AND DIAGRAMS

New South Wales up to 1835   *frontispiece*

The position of Australian wool in the thirties and forties   45

New South Wales: the move to the west   130

The squatting occupation of New South Wales   139

The squatting occupation of Victoria   151

Victoria, 1834-1847   161

The squatting occupation of Queensland   174

1

AUSTRALIA IN 1835

IT IS NOT UNUSUAL in the history of organisms for the protoplasm to remain in a state of retarded development—almost quiescence —for some considerable time, and then suddenly to commence growth at practically a forced rate, as if to make up for the delay previously experienced. So it was with the early history of Australia —so much so that the observer may point to a single year and say that *then* commenced the real story of Australia's progress. This point when the graph suddenly took its upward curve was the period of 1835—when the protoplasm began to indicate what form of organism it was developing into, when the infant community began to assume its distinguishing characteristics.

It was altogether a fascinating stage. Free immigration was commencing in earnest, and the old predominance of the convicts was threatened. The capitalists and yeomen of England, hitherto merely tolerated in a land that was primarily for felons, were asserting their supremacy in no measured terms; and the Government was beginning to make its policy conform to the changing conditions. New settlements were springing up round the Australian coast, and the whole interior, looked upon up to this time as a huge dead sea or a swampy morass, was beckoning. From Bass Strait to the Pandora Pass, cattle and sheep were moving onwards; everywhere, the lowing and bleating invaders were showing themselves a more relentless force of occupation than regiments of red-coated soldiers, and were passing over plain and mountain alike.

It did not need much prescience to forsee the whole of Australia united by settlement—so much had it, at a single bound, outgrown the coastal stage of Sydney and Hobart Town. It was a new Australia —a land of free settlement and progressive occupation—that was there, and the old convict days were drawing to an end.

Both human and monetary capital were pouring into the various colonies and transforming the nature of their population and problems. Canary-jacketed convicts no longer set the tone; even the autocratic Governors in Macquarie Street belonged to a day that was passing; and, instead, the country was in the grip of a strangely buoyant, and equally optimistic, race of free men—men who sounded the new note by a myriad bush camp-fires and chanted:

> So it's roll up your blankets, and let's make a push,
> I'll take you to the country and show you the bush,
> I'll be bound you won't get such a chance another day,
> So come and take possession of my old bullock-dray!

So the sheep pattered onward in the dust, and the drays creaked their complaining way, and a new Australia broke on a thousand horizons.

I   The Extent of Settlement

Until this time, settlement had been very circumscribed. New South Wales, for long hemmed in by the mountains, had gradually expanded from Sydney, but very slowly. Before 1817, Windsor and Camden had marked the extremities of occupation, with one isolated offshoot at Bathurst across the range. A few cedar-cutters were down the coast at Lake Illawarra, and stray 'black sheep' among the convicts scratched the earth of Port Stephens for coal, but, in general, the emphasis was on restriction of settlement rather than any undue increase. Oxley was at that very moment somewhere in the New England plains, but this was judged the hazardous venture of an unsettled spirit and it was thought that the County of Cumberland, round Sydney, was quite sufficient for the settlers' needs. A few men of the 46th Regiment were quartered at Cox's River to guard the stock going to the frontier-post at Bathurst, and already cattle had been coming out from beyond the mountains for two years; but still official Sydney frowned. New Holland, save for the subsidiary convict-settlement at Hobart Town, meant the home county; and the element of control, so rightly stressed in a penal colony, clearly demanded that this limit should not be lightly passed.

But the increase of the troublesome *Horned Cattle*—a phrase that Governors Macquarie and Brisbane must have cursed!—could not be so easily dealt with, because Cumberland, after all, was so limited and so poor. Cattle were toiling out along the old Bathurst road, past Mount Blaxland and over the Hawkesbury at the bottleneck of Emu Plains—and these superbly fattened creatures, so different from the mediocre beasts of the settled districts, represented a force that no official disapprobation could check. The stock-owners pushed out in all directions and, though this movement was infinitesimal as compared with the migrations of the Heroic Age of the thirties, it was the nucleus which made the later stage possible. The convicts and Oxley had revealed some of the riches to the north; now, Throsby and Hume went far to the south, to Jervis Bay and the Goulburn country (1818), and it was these two areas, rather than the early Bathurst outpost, that became the 'New Country' of promise in the twenties.

Owners concentrated for a time on the south, and, in a few years, dotted settlements all over the country from the old cedar-huts of Illawarra to Lake George and the Lachlan, even sweeping round the mountain-edge to connect with Bathurst. By the close of 1822, though only five years had elapsed, herds of cattle had reached Lake Bathurst, and settlers, having cursorily exhausted the south, were turning to the Hunter River, the key of the north, the banks of which had been opened to selection in that year. This region absorbed most attention for the next ten years or so, especially when the Australian Agricultural Company, a millionaire English venture, received a million acres of land in Gloucester County, just north of the Hunter.

The bounds of the colony were thus more or less set. The Lachlan and the Goulburn plains seemed to impose a natural limit on the south; the Hunter region served for the north; while, to the west, the inhospitable lands beyond Bathurst indicated Wellington Valley, the offshoot since 1823, as the outermost post. The lands between these points became known as *The Nineteen Counties*—from the Manning to Moruya, from the coast to the Lachlan. Here, official Sydney took its stand. These were the limits of colonization, and only within them would settlement be tolerated. This kidney-shaped area of nineteen counties would be surveyed and thrown open as circumstances developed, but any settler who crossed the Lachlan or the Manning must be quite clear in his mind that he was deliberately abandoning Government protection—more: that, in a fashion, he was opposing the constituted authorities.

The Nineteen Counties, to all intents and purposes, meant Australia, and the Government decreed that they should be viewed as if the sea flowed all round, and not merely to the east. Oxley and Mitchell, the successive Surveyors-General, had mapped out the counties, and five million acres stood open for a population of 70,000. Surely, it was argued, this offered all the land that reasonable men could desire, especially since most of the population were convicts debarred from settlement, and since the few free men or expirees who could settle were allowed a virtual right to graze as many stock as they pleased on Crown lands. Mitchell was planning great trunk-roads as *points d'appui* of settlement, and the Government held it only logical that these should direct the course of agricultural occupation. But, if there should exist persons sufficiently unreasonable and disloyal as not to be satisfied with the Nineteen Counties, and if they should deliberately seek to embarrass the Government by extending the settled area, then they should be visited with the full penalties of the law ! To cross the Manning or the Lachlan would be viewed as a dereliction as grave as scaling the walls of Buckingham Palace and grazing sheep on the King's lawns !

In short, the Government erected a huge non-trespass sign over the interior. The Counties were proclaimed in October 1829: already the southern flock-owners were at Yass and looking down the big river flowing to the west, and already their northern colleagues were dreaming of New England and Oxley's lands! It was a curiously irresistible urge, which made the mandates of the Government seem very remote. The settlers could see only the new lands, only the purplish horizons and the plains stretching away from the tableland of the south and the sharp ranges of the north: and nothing else counted, when each dawn broke on the Great Unknown. Soldiers could not have stopped them, and certainly not the feeble proclamations of a Sydney Government.

By 1835, then, the thick black line of the Nineteen Counties remained as solid as ever on the map as the legal limit of settlement, but, actually, it had been crossed in all directions. Apart from the old nucleus of Cumberland, the largest alienated areas were round the Hunter and Goulburn, with a less progressive group at Bathurst; but most emphasis was on the Murrumbidgee and the Liverpool Plains.

The actual limit at that moment can fortunately be set out. To the north, occupation had been hemmed in by the main sweep of the Liverpool Range up to 1832, though in that year the Australian Agricultural Company received its huge estates at Peel River and Warrah, on the other side of the divide. Cunningham, five years before, had pushed directly through this land, on his way to the Darling Downs, and the flock-masters thus knew of the Liverpool Plains and the even better lands to the far north. Hence, they were at Tamworth in 1834—almost up to Oxley's old northern line of march—and thus on the fringe of the Namoi and the New England tableland. But this was difficult country to traverse—a land of razor-backs and seamy ridges, of hidden gorges and huge rock outcrops—and the march wavered on a line between Tamworth and Kempsey. This was the position in 1835, when stockmen were waiting to see what the great Company would do with the Liverpool Plains, and were indisposed to move across the mountain-barrier to the north.

By some curious *volte face*, attention had once more returned to the south, and the term, *The New Country*, was generally taken in these years to mean the line of the Murrumbidgee—from Yass to Wagga, with the drier plains on both sides of the river. Stockmen were realizing (though slowly, it is true) that the sun-baked plains, with their dry crisp air, were better for sheep than the more richly grassed country and were looking somewhat askance at the wetter portions and the cold hill-lands of Monaro. Hume had formed a station at Lake George in 1821—only thirty miles from the Murrumbidgee—and soon the stockmen swept, fan-like, up to the river, and past Yass to Gundagai. This was the terminal point in 1835, and, owing to the filling-up of the country already passed over, remained so for some time.

Both streams of settlement had thus halted—the northern before the avoided land of the Namoi, and the southern somewhat daunted by the unattractive country out from Gundagai. The Government said that settlement was confined between the Manning and Moruya: actually, it spread from Tamworth to Gundagai—from New England to the Murrumbidgee, but nobody thought either of these positions final.

From this point, the great age of pastoral occupation—SQUATTING, as it was called—set in. Stockmen looked far out and started to connect the isolated spots on the map. The central belt was viewed as already consolidated, a mass from which new feelers could be flung out to various regions round the coast.

Far to the south, on the western extremity of what afterwards became Victoria, the Hentys had occupied Portland Bay in the previous year, and were considering driving sheep inland. Major Mitchell was preparing for that overland expedition which was to take him over the plains of *Australia Felix* to link the settled districts with the rough camp at Portland Bay, and incidentally to mark out the line of pastoral occupation for all Victoria. In June of 1835, John Batman had marked out the site of Melbourne as suitable for a township, and, two months later, his bailiff warned off another party arrived from Van Diemen's Land—Fawkner's. The basis of Melbourne's settlement was laid before the year was out, and various sod-huts built on the higher levels. Sydney knew of this venture in August, and the Hentys had been in correspondence with the officials for some time, so that it was the obvious way of expansion to link Portland and the infant Melbourne with the Murrumbidgee settlements, and to occupy the pastoral lands between.

But this should not be exaggerated. The stockmen were not vision-

ary Empire-builders so much as peripatetic farmers seeking a permanent home as near a market as possible, and, in 1835, before the
return of Mitchell's party, were rather inclined to look for spots that
had been passed over nearer home than to pin too many hopes on
the south coast. Both ends of Van Diemen's Land, it is true, were
ringing with the prospects of Port Phillip at the close of the year, but
it was not looked upon as a Sydney-side issue. There was little public
excitement, and only one article in the *Sydney Gazette* for the whole
year—even that transcribed from an English journal! Despite this,
the stockmen were eagerly awaiting the return of Mitchell and
dreaming of virgin sheep-runs to the south. Wyse had crossed the
Murray before the year was out, and Mackillop had penetrated from
the Monaro uplands to a lonely outpost tucked away in the Omeo
hills. The edges of the rampart that shut in Port Phillip were being
attacked; it needed only Mitchell's return late in 1836 to change the
isolated ventures into a tumultuous frontal onslaught.

Further west, another new settlement was being created—the
famous South Australian colony, embodying the principles of the
Wakefield reformers, the 'systematic colonizers'. This was formally
set up by an English Act of Parliament of 1834. At the end of 1835,
after interminable delays and confusions, the first emigrant-vessels
were being fitted out for the new site, but were not to arrive at the
wastes of Kangaroo Island until the following July. Sydney-siders
were even more sceptical over this than over Port Phillip. At the
beginning of 1836, they had heard little of the project for some time,
and spoke scathingly of what they knew. The *William Lockerby*
brought them the final news in May 1836, but the old settlement
could not be thrilled, and was far more concerned with the scheme
of an 'Eastern Australian Company', which was to colonize all of the
Darling Downs and New England with a million pounds of capital.[1]
The previous year had closed with the colony concentrating on this
new scheme, and, as compared with the settlement of the always-
favoured north, what mattered a few land-raiders at Port Phillip and
a paper-colony at Port Lincoln?

The rest of Australia was unsettled in 1835, save for the two old
failures of Van Diemen's Land and the Swan River. The former consisted of some 40,000 people, as many bond as free, and, though
its cramped pastures ran almost a million sheep, barely limped on
from year to year, its energy submerged by a flood of criminality.
Over three million acres of land had been quite wastefully alienated,
but apart from the huge Company in the extreme northwest, effective

[1] *Australian*, 20 May 1836.

settlement was confined to a belt along the rivers from Launceston to Hobart, concentrating on the County of Monmouth in the south. The chartered Company had held half a million acres since 1826, but had done little except squabble with the Administration and run a few sheep on Woolnorth and cattle in the colder Surrey Hills. Its efforts seemed to have failed woefully, its £200 shares were down to £16, and, until the opening of new settlements on the coast of the mainland, its very survival seemed a matter of doubt. Beyond this, the island was depressed—its sheep-walks overcrowded, its agriculture extraordinarily unscientific, its great Company tottering, and convicts being flooded in as fast as the transports could arrive. The long depression—one destined to linger for sixty years—had set in.

Nor was its twin-colony—Swan River—in any better plight. Isolated from the other colony by 1,500 miles of untrodden desert, this venture of 1829 appeared to exist only as a target for the shafts of the new colonial theorists in England. It seemed a striking example of how *not to colonize*. Land was so recklessly granted to absentees that the actual settlers could obtain none: even its founder lived in a stone-hut covered with rushes, and the colony dragged on a listless life of prostration. By 1835, Perth was a meagre township of 600 persons, King George's Sound was a backward outpost for ships of call, and the only feature of interest in the entire colony was the opening of the land *over the hills*—the York country found five years previously. A few tentative settlers were being introduced to the new plains, or, further south, to the Hotham and the Williams, and a track had been marked out in this year to connect King George's Sound with Perth, but nobody thought of taking stock over it. A coma was over everything, so much so that even the good coastal lands south of Perth were left untouched. Defaulters held the easily accessible lands, and no incentive remained to occupy the interior when settlers could so easily take advantage of the far greater opportunities offering on the other side of the Continent. What could be clearer? People were flocking away from Swan River, and, if dalliance there had atrophied their activities too much to pioneer in the new settlements on the south coast, there was always the parent-colony of New South Wales!

It was thus obvious that, at the end of 1835, Australia really meant the occupied portion of New South Wales from Gundagai to Tenterfield, and that attention centred on expansion outwards from that centre. That was the problem already confronting the Government: it was so obvious and immediate that some policy had to be outlined. The old theory of the Nineteen Counties was now worked out. With stock roaming hundreds of miles beyond the limits, it seemed absurd to waste time on further theoretical bans. All that remained was to call the counties the 'settled' land, refer to the new regions as 'unsettled', and enunciate a practical policy. Even in 1835, to speak of driving back the stock within the legal bounds of settlement was utterly chimerical: not all the military forces available could have kept them there, even had such an outcome been desirable. Faced with this problem, the Government had to answer a question—whether it would frankly acknowledge how obsolete its former mandate had become and devise schemes of control and regulation, or whether it would rely on an ostrich-policy and foolishly refuse to notice the new movements taking place?

Everywhere, people were dabbling in sheep, and all thought was in terms of flocks and herds. Their talk was all of runts and heifers— Dr Johnson had said deprecatingly of a certain community: certainly, this was the case in the New South Wales of 1835. The whole colony had one idea—to use that surplus money which came from the wool-sales and the whale-fisheries, that excess of capital which so much troubled Governor Bourke, in buying sheep and cattle. They had the experience of the bubble of 1827-9 in their memories, and most of them still remembered how it burst; but the years had softened the reckoning, and now the colony once more tripped gaily towards an orgy of over-speculation. As a writer of the time said, 'The soldier unbuckled his belt to become a keeper of sheep, and the priest forsook his altar to become a herdsman of cattle.' *Put everything in four feet*, was the advice given to the newcomer; and men spoke of secret pastures on the Namoi and the 'new country' to the south, and looked dotingly on the spindly legs and collie-dog faces of the improved Saxon sheep as providing a rapid way to wealth. The colony was unbalanced. The Government could not cope with the specie it had in hand, the financiers could scarcely find employment for the private wealth coming to the colony, and anybody could sell stock hundreds of miles away, 'sight unseen'—and that at fabulous prices!

The year had opened with a depression in wool-prices, owing to German competition, but the answer was to move on to new pastures. Was not one firm already purchasing for the American market, rich with possibilities and with all the allurement of the unknown? And was not even the Chief Justice, Forbes, a sheep-farmer and wool-speculator? What could stem this resistless tide? Australian wool, badly tended as it was, could realize 2s. 11d. a pound, even with the existing German pressure: there was plenty of new land and stock in abundance; and, from January onwards, the brigs and barques were riding the tide in Sydney Cove straining to set out for the London market: and what else was needed?

Everybody thus turned to wool. Expirees naturally battened on the life in the remote bush, where *clear-skins* and wandering animals could be pounced upon to enlarge small flocks: and shop-boys and teachers, soldiers and merchants all joined the rush, which was every bit as pronounced as the later exodus in search of gold: and emigrants, almost to a man, especially the newly demobilized army-officers, swelled the stream. Men changed their black-drab beavers for cabbage-tree hats, their coffee-coloured *tails* for dungaree shirts, and set off for the inland—to some remote spot dimly hinted at in the gossip of a Sydney pothouse. Nobody minded being called a 'squatter' now, bitter reproach though that term had been even a year before, and rational persons thought of the 'squatters' now as persons to be encouraged. The mania was in full swing, and every able-bodied man thirsted for the bush and pined to ride in the dust behind masses of smelling sheep and live on an unchanging diet of mutton-chops, unleavened damper, and *post-and-rail tea*. It was something in men's blood, like the emotional patriotism of a war-period or the unnatural stimulus of a gold rush, and this particular gamble was thought to have the special feature of presenting no blanks! Thus the little community of 70,000 dreamed and speculated, and thus sheep, too often ridden with scab and catarrh, set the tone of everything. It was a curiously topsy-turvy time, with men's perspectives strangely blunted. The bush, sheep, the clipper on the tide —the process ran almost like a refrain in men's minds, and the community sang their song of the western waggon and turned towards the interior.

II The State of the Community

The community itself was a curious one. Practically for the first time, strata in society could be discerned. Before this, New South Wales had been a gaol—there were convicts and their keepers, with a sprinkling of freemen who, for some freakish reason or other, chose to live in a convict-land. But this simplicity of structure disappeared with the twenties. The rise of distinctions within the penal section and the opening of the colony to free immigrants changed the situation, and society came to know classes.

At the top stood the Governor and his personal staff—birds of passage, and, in the case of Darling and Bourke, far from being the social leaders of the community. Under them, came the *pure merinos*

—*la haute société*, such as it was. Since about 1829, emigrants of good social position and possessed of considerable means had come to form the nucleus of a society—retired officers, and merchants, and younger sons sent out to swell the family fortunes or to work off their energies in a new and distant land. This species of emigration had been stimulated by the endeavours of Sir Wilmot Horton, the Under-Secretary of State, and was now bearing fruit. Intensely aristocratic and with all the arrogance of living in a community organized on a slave-basis, such persons tried to keep the convicts in their proper place. *Once a convict, always a convict*—they claimed, as they bitterly fought the advance of the emancipists. A convict, and his children to the furthest generation, were supposed to be separated from them by an impassable gulf; and he who had the temerity to propose that anybody of convict-stock could be deemed a sociable being was at once outside the pale. It was these pure-blooded aristocrats who had harried Darling and were now causing Bourke endless trouble (though a curious thing was how 'colonial' their gentility seemed and how unknown they were in Old World annals!): it was they who were directly responsible for those aggravated caste-struggles which wasted so much of the colony's strength in the mid-thirties.

The Macarthurs of Camden headed the roster, closely followed by Sir John Jamison, 'the hospitable Knight of Regentsville', who had certainly founded the Turf Club, but whose political principles seemed a trifle dubious to his social equals. Also within the sacred light, but tarnished by his association with Darling, that Darling who had even sought to dine with ex-convicts, was Alexander M'Leay, the Colonial Secretary—disloyal head of a disloyal Civil Service, whose idea of his oath was to embarrass as much as possible that Governor whose right-hand man he was supposed to be. When such people set the running, the condition of the field is best left to the imagination. Dull beyond conception, proud with the inordinate pride that rests on no basis, and resentful of the land which gave them their living, the *pure merinos* represented a cause which was dying.

The second element in the population consisted of the ordinary free immigrants, as distinct from the *pure merinos* or those 'lordly settlers' of the Hunter River who afforded so much copy to the local journalists. Before about 1830, these had had no place in the community. Society resolved itself into the few gentlemen-settlers, most of whom came out with specific recommendations from the Secretary of State for the time being, and convict-labourers, either emancipated or assigned. There was nothing between them: anything in the nature of a free labouring-body or a peasant-proprietary was completely lacking. With the thirties, however, a new element wedged its way into the gap. A few hundred freemen had trickled in since 1828, but it was not until 1831, when the new sales-regulations made money available for emigration, that the stream really set in.

New South Wales at that time was decidedly prosperous, and there was a steady demand for mechanical labour. In England, these were the years of distress. The financial panic of a few years before had run its course, but its traces remained, and both agriculture and pasture were in a very depressed state. Rick-burning and machine-breaking were prevalent, and many an oppressed labourer looked with relief to the convict-hulk as a way out of his sufferings. Naturally, when an Emigration Commission was appointed in 1831, and such people learned that they could get to the promised land without first infringing the penal law, the outlook was changed, and from that moment may be dated the real commencement of Australia's free population.

The position had become clear in a moment. Up till then, various influences had been working discordantly and effectively preventing any unity of action. A Select Committee of 1827 had offered a nebulous report on Malthusian lines, but appeared to think that to speak categorically of New South Wales would have been as reprehensible as postulating the colour of the Martians' hair. They made not the remotest suggestion, beyond stating that only permanent paupers would be sufficiently ill-advised as to forsake their village inns. Against these, the Wakefieldians were urging that emigration meant the selection of the best elements of the English lower classes, and, indeed, that emigrants could be of any social or economic status. Dr Lang, the Scottish cleric who had temporarily transferred his many activities from Sydney to London, was hammering at the gates of the Colonial Office and collecting fifty mechanics from north of the Tweed to take out in the *Stirling Castle*.

Out of these arguments came the plan of 1831. The Earl of Ripon, at the moment Viscount Goderich, and formerly that 'Prosperity' Robinson who had helped Huskisson reform the finances, reduced the problem to simple terms. The colonies were prosperous and wanted mechanics and women: their newly-instituted land-sales would provide money not required for purposes of ordinary administration: while England, racked with distress, had labour a-plenty. Therefore, if the excess revenue of the colony went to remove the excess labour of England, both participants in the exchange would benefit. Goderich enunciated this plan as part of the Whig policy early in 1831; an Emigration Commission went to work in June; and, four months later, the first emigrants under the plan sailed.[2]

From that time until 1835, the period at which survey is being taken, 7,221 emigrants went to New South Wales, including the 300 who managed in some way or other to cross the ocean in the year the new plan was being evolved. This does not seem a very large number, especially when one considers that 16,289 convicts were sent in the same years, but the point is that, for the first time, a consistent effort was being made to send freemen to Australia.

It is true that there was much confusion—that the whole of the land-revenue was not systematically appropriated to emigration, that the emigrants had to pay varying amounts themselves, that private ventures like Lang's were subsidized from time to time, and that undue emphasis was laid on young women and mechanics; but emigration towards Australia had set in, despite all of these. Goderich did not know whether he wanted Government or private or bounty efforts, he was not certain whether the rural distress of England should first be considered or whether only mechanics should be sent out, and he was dubious if the penal colony offered more than the much cheaper America: but, as long as Lord Grey's Ministry survived, he persisted in some way or other, the point, of course, being that the Government negotiations and the accompanying publicity were far more important than the actual shippings of human cargo.

A point of view favourable to emigration was being slowly inculcated in the rural English mind, and this of itself was quite a new factor. Thus, before Goderich gave way to a lesser man, he had hit on the key of the situation: that what Australia wanted was a new race of free men, a 'hardy peasantry' who were to occupy a fresh niche in the social structure of the colonies and not simply, as with the first mechanics and maid-servants, to buttress the existing divisions. Now, to the contrary, by sending out Midland yeomen-farmers or Sussex shepherds, he was implanting new classes.

Within the colony, similar moves had been taken. A Committee of the Legislative Council reported in 1835 that from four to five thousand free labourers and mechanics were urgently wanted, and the sheep-farmers were crying aloud for shepherds. There was a steady demand for both rural and urban labour, but Governor Bourke, in the whole of his term of office, did nothing beyond issuing his scale of bounties in October 1835, and offering £30 to any settler

2 Correspondence is in Goderich-Darling, 23 January 1831.

who brought out an immigrant-couple. Only a fifth of the land-revenue went for this purpose, however, and Bourke must be accused of neglecting the importance of immigration at this crucial moment.

Yet, under him, the position was changing. With his two prede-cessors, Brisbane and Darling, the free immigrants had been but a drop in an ocean of convicts and emancipists; whereas Bourke, in his years, saw them become a clearly marked element in the body social, one which, though far from predominant, was more important in its influence than its numbers would have supposed. It was the next Governor, Sir George Gipps, who was to see the immigrants and the native-born absolutely in the ascendant, although the transition was obvious even in 1835.

Once in the colony, the free emigrants quickly assumed a distinct place. They satisfied the demand for town-labour and were quickly attracted to the bush by the inducement of higher wages. Their feel-ing of fellowship against the felons was so strong that a Committee of Emigrant Mechanics was formed as early as 1835. This was one of the first cases of industrial combination in the colony and served both to safeguard the interests of its members and spread information as to how a newcomer was actually received. The Government reports and the Wakefieldian dreamers at home might speak of boundless opportunity, but this local Committee told of fluctuations of demand and of the real wages that might be expected. Blacksmiths and car-penters, for instance, could earn from five to seven shillings a day, but the rest—ploughmen, shepherds, shearers, and all agricultural labourers—had to rest content with £10 or £12 a year and rations. A dairywoman ranked as high as any man in the colony, and fencers had the advantage of a weekly wage, but, beyond this, the flat £10 rate, advanced to £12 in the remoter parts, applied to all.[3]

It must be confessed, however, that the town seemed the natural haunt of the free men. There, they could foregather and receive the benefits of group activity and that strengthened *morale* which comes from a feeling of being with one's own kin. In the country, even in the timber-districts around Sydney, ex-convicts evinced 'a general disinclination to work with a free emigrant'; the check-shirted cedar-men were more likely to greet a freeman with their long lace-up boots than in any friendly fashion, while the lazier convict-shepherds thought the average emigrant either a *lag* or a spiritless person. Having escaped the brotherhood of crime, they had no right to the masonry of experience, especially when, as not infrequently hap-pened, their desire for progress led to a marked frugality in the

[3] *Sydney Gazette*, 10 February 1835.

matter of the multitudinous *nobblers* of gin which absorbed an emancipist's pay. Confronted with this hostility, an average freeman had to come down to the convict's level and ingratiate himself with them by joking of being 'a free object' and of '*lagging* myself for fear the King should do it for me'. The alternative, if the newcomer wished to keep to the bush-life, was to be a lone wanderer—not a very healthy prospect in a country of convict-gangs and deserters.

One such emigrant, Harris, has left a remarkable account of his life under these conditions,[4] wandering about the country from cedar-splitting to doubtful cattle transactions, and in constant fear of convict outrage at the wayside inns or at work. Most labour at the time was migratory and paid for piecemeal, so that the most emphasized feature of a freeman's life was wandering along bush-tracks and stopping at settlers' huts or *cribs*. His lot was not an enviable one, with the country plagued by bushrangers from Two-fold Bay to the Hunter, and with employers both perforce and by inclination favouring convict-servants. Too often, especially when driven from the towns by the distress that set in after 1835, the newcomers stole cattle and took to predatory life in the bush— 'duffing and going in plant', to use the *argot* of the time! Then they either justified themselves as successful squatters in some distant spot or were rounded up in one of the periodic cleansings by the mounted police, as in the Twofold Bay district early in 1835. But, mainly because they kept what was called 'a carpet-bag mind', at least two-thirds of the freemen, according to the *Sydney Gazette* of 1835, congregated within the boundaries of the County of Cumberland, the region directly around Sydney.

Far more important from every point of view were the convicts— the 'canaries' who made the colony a very cesspool of humanity. Various apologists have attempted to make out from extreme instances that these were largely apple-stealers, or innocent rick-burners and the like, but, though the rigour of the penal code must be taken into account, it cannot be denied that, up to 1835, 75,200 convicts had been cleared from England's gaols to Australia, and that all who were not hanged were sent out. There may have been thousands of men and boys transported for trifling offences, there may have been hundreds of completely innocent persons, but the fact remains that, with the wronged ones, came the very worst of Britain's felons—the scum of the land. Convictism, by its nature, was a corrupting cancer, spreading its influence over all with whom it came into contact. It mattered little what human material, young

[4] A. Harris, *Settlers and Convicts*, 1847, republished 1964; very useful.

or old, villain or mere tempted man, went into the machine; the result was the same.

One does not have to fall into the lugubrious sentimentalism of a Marcus Clarke to perceive this, or to react too far from painting the lily-white breasts of the convicts beneath their canary-jackets: a simple deduction from human nature, together with a little intelligence, is all that is needed. The total free population in 1835 was about 45,000, and this included all convicts who had been freed or who had served their sentences (it must always be remembered that only 8,000 free men had ever entered the colony, and their colonial-born progeny could not have been numerous, even if they refrained from dipping into the convict-factory for their females!): of these free men, probably 15,000 were adult males, and half of these were in menial capacities! Against them was a bond population of 28,000, restricting the term to those actually serving their sentences. If the adage, 'Once a convict, always a convict', be accepted, it is thus clear that far and away the majority of adults in the colony were felons—a conclusion with obvious results. Yet Dr Lang and others wanted a representative body of fifty members![5]

It is not proposed at this juncture to go into the details of the convict-system; it is sufficient to outline the place the convicts occupied in the society of 1835. The system was delusively simple. From the moment of sentence, all received equal treatment, whether the individual had knocked down a squire or was a triple murderer. Forgers and poachers, drunken ploughboys and Cockney pickpockets were thrown together indiscriminately on hulks and started in the direction of Sydney. On arrival, their complaints (the irony of it!) were heard by a deputy from the Colonial Secretary's Office, the females were at once sent into private domestic service, and the males packed to the Barracks, where the principal superintendent classified them. The incorrigibles would go to one of the outer penal settlements—the gaols of the gaol, so to speak—and the remainder would be drafted for Government service or private assignment.

The latter was the crux of the whole system. Simply stated, assignment meant that convicts provided the labour-supply for private settlers. Any settler could obtain convicts from the Government, so long as he gave them fixed amounts of food and clothing. For a weekly ration of twelve pounds of wheat and seven pounds of meat, and a few slop clothes a year, a settler acquired the body of a man, and kept his soul in pawn by means of the lashes any magistrate (almost always a neighbouring settler) could inflict!

[5] *Sydney Gazette*, 24 January 1835.

There were no rules, except that one mechanic counted as two labourers. Each settler received as many 'assignees' as his position or influence with the Government warranted, and no regard was paid to the convict's crime or record or attainments. Sentence, age, character, nature of offence mattered not in the least. If a man had been a mechanic, he received a better position, that was all. 'To make the punishment fit the crime' seemed to be unknown in these days before Gilbert and Sullivan; and equally beyond the scope of imagination was any attempt to secure uniformity of treatment, once the man was assigned. It was bad enough to place them all on one dead level on reaching Sydney; but to make the punishment depend entirely upon the caprice of a bush-settler removed it from the realm of reason. To speak about the end of punishment as the reformation of the individual was so much cant: there was no attempt even to punish uniformly. A murderer might be assigned to his wife, and a boy who had stolen sixpence be flogged to death by some up-country monster !

It was this uncertainty that was so bad—this was the feature that seemed so odious to the Commons Committee on Transportation in 1838. They spoke of 'the lottery of punishment', of 'the drawers of prizes and the drawers of blanks in this strange lottery', and there could have been no more apt summary of the position. 'As the lot of a slave depends upon the character of his master (*a very significant analogy!*), so the condition of a convict depends upon the temper and disposition of the settler to whom he is assigned.' This was the element of capriciousness in the system, making punishment not only something apart from offence or conduct, but dependent on elements uncertain and variable by their very nature. As long as 20,000 convicts were assigned in New South Wales, and 6,500 in Van Diemen's Land, and as long as they were viewed as mere economic material, it was either delusion or deep hypocrisy to speak of transportation as a system, and still less a reforming system !

Convicts assigned to respectable settlers, as the Committee reported, were in much the same condition as servants in England : they may even have been better fed and better clothed than the average rural Hodge, but this was by no means universal, or even usual. The fundamental fact was that transportation was slavery as well as exile, as the Committee reported in so many words—and slavery with all the caprice and uncertainty of any such system ! The Committee said

that transportation is not a single punishment, but rather a series of punishments, embracing every degree of human suffering, from the lowest, consisting of a slight restraint upon the freedom of action, to the highest, consisting of long and tedious torture; and that the average amount of pain, inflicted upon offenders in consequence of a sentence of transportation, is very considerable.

There was never a system so divorced from any element of responsibility and control, never one so systematically degrading humanity and placing a reliance upon human frailties. There were probably about 7,500 adult males in the colony who were their own masters (freed felons included), and to these, irrespective of any factor, either in the master or the servant, the entire custody of 20,000 human beings was consigned. A man could treat an assigned servant as a petted son or could flog him to death, with the connivance of his fellow-magistrates, and, whatever he did, he was virtually uncontrolled. Extreme cases were, of course, investigated, but, society being constituted as it was, the word of a master could not be gainsaid, and those cases when convict servants were withdrawn were almost invariably due to personal frictions.

In the New South Wales of 1835, therefore, some 7,000 convicts were in gaols, 1,000 ironed in road-gangs, 20,000 scattered under private control throughout the country, and from 3,000 to 4,000 arriving yearly. One convict in four was flogged every year and, by the nature of things, the official return must have been incomplete and restricted to the serious cases. Even then, it admitted that 304,000 lashes were inflicted on raw backs every year, and not a police post but had its separate flogger! The terrible 'flogging return' called for by the Commons in 1837 does not bear analysis, so consistently dreadful are its annual figures and so stamped are they with the impress of merciless cruelty. The official record of floggings fixed the average number of lashes at 45. A cat-o'-nine-tails, a man tied bare-backed to the triangles, and a flogger liable to take the place of his victims if inefficient—the picture is complete, if the observer once more remembers that, up to 1835, any magistrate could inflict any number of lashes on a convict not assigned to himself. As if this were not sufficient, 1,200 convicts were re-transported yearly to the final place of punishment at Norfolk Island!

Under these circumstances, it was fair to say that assignment meant taking a ticket in a lottery of cruelty—a fact that was very obvious to so humane a Governor as Sir Richard Bourke. He was the first administrator to regulate assignment in any way at all: such human cattle had been beyond the interest of the naval Governors. Bourke, on the contrary, tried to place the system on an orderly basis. He could not, it is true, dispose of it, though he made it known, as his private opinion, that the settlers would be much better off without convicts in any form. All that he could do at the moment was to publish the assignment-code of May 1835, making the distribution of the convicts conform to some fixed rule. He wanted to dispense with the existing favouritism and treat all applicants alike, whether in dungaree or fine-cloth. A settler was to receive one convict for every 160 acres he held, and one extra for every 40 acres cultivated, but under no circumstances, not even with the privileged Australian Agricultural Company, could anyone take more than 70 servants from the Government.

This seems a fair and unquestionable settlement, yet it is difficult to imagine the stir it created in the young colony. To place the poor and the rich on an equality seemed an unheard-of thing—what the *Sydney Herald* called 'a Whig attack upon the property of the country', so clearly did 'the bull-frog farmers of the Hunter' monopolize assignees 150 at a time! Despite this attitude and some absurd mutterings about a boycott and the use of force, Bourke insisted, and threatened to use all the power of Sydney to achieve his results. He resisted the monopolistic Company even to the desk of the Colonial Secretary and, difficult though the task was in so circumscribed a community, allowed no exceptions to his fixed rule. When he completed the task by limiting magistrates to sentences of fifty lashes and by allowing certain emancipists to serve on criminal juries, the way was opened for some kind of order in the system and a certain degree of hope for the convicts' future; but the opposition at every step made progress slow and incomplete.

His reforms, all in all, were not so important in themselves as in forecasting the development that was likely to take place in the future. The signals of change were becoming obvious, even in the Sydney of 1835. There was no longer either the brutal nonchalance or the *laissez-faire* attitude of a few years before. The system was questioned, and, being questioned, commenced to crack. It could not bear analysis, and its fall was delayed only until the various forces of criticism united in one movement. Both transportation and assignment were on the wane. Their inherent faults and the clamour of the new freemen were combining to make the position untenable, and the colony was wresting itself free from the heavy pall of penal life.

Every reforming agency was pointing the moral. Abroad, Archbishop Whately of Dublin was showing how transportation had failed to prevent crime, and the Commons Committee were preparing that report of August 1838, which was so grave an indictment of the whole system. In the colony, the agitations of Bourke and

Chief Justice Burton were bearing fruit, and, already in 1835, the popular movement against transportation had started with the formation of a political society to watch over colonial affairs and correspond directly with an agent in the Commons. So obvious were the disadvantages of the system that Colonial Secretaries of every political opinion—Glenelg, Normanby, and Lord John Russell in turn—were urging its abolition. Convictism was already doomed, Norfolk Island was now viewed as the receptacle for the gaol-birds of England, and everywhere in the colony, the turn was to free immigrants. Those drab figures in Parramatta frocks and canvas trousers who laboured in road-gangs or slaved from dawn till dusk on settlers' holdings belonged to an age that was going. It was the Cockney labourer and the stolid men of Norfolk and Durham who were henceforth to attract attention, and, with their coming, the bad old days of the triangles and of limited rations were to go.

A peculiar feature of the transition was the manner in which attention focused on certain more or less spectacular evils in this very year of 1835. This was the year when convicts and deserters joined the blacks in terrorizing the prosperous Hunter River, when armed gangs down south plunged the new Yass settlements into chronic fear, when Twofold Bay demanded military protection against the persistent raids, and when the settlers had to form vigilance associations for mutual protection. Bushranging was growing everywhere, there were riots of assigned servants on the large estates, and the whole colony was ringing with the murders that convicts had committed on the ill-famed Mudie estate at Castle Hill. An outburst of outrages in every direction threw a flash of interpretation on the real nature of the convict system, just at the moment when the Governor's laxity was the subject of so much complaint. The periodical crimes had resulted in the appointment of a *Committee on Police and Gaols*, which, in a lengthy report, showed how every part of the colony was insufficiently protected. Nor, the public were not slow in adding, had the Governor's favours to emancipists or the new assignment code been deterrent factors!

Bourke, for his part, asserted that 'a degree of liberty superior to that of a Gaol or Penitentiary is essentially incident to the system of this Colony, and the evil and the good of this partial freedom must of necessity grow up together.'[6] But the suffering people were not concerned with generalizations and merely pointed to the constant trouble over road-gangs and mutinous servants, and the leniency of the Governor towards such unscrupulous emancipists as Watt, who,

[6] Bourke-Glenelg, 18 December 1835.

under Government patronage, had become editor of the leading paper. The opposition carried this particular case to the courts and, though the attempt was mainly a political move to embarrass Bourke, it certainly showed how the Governor's leniency worked in the direction of encouraging unrest among the convicts.

At this moment, came the famous charge of Sir William Burton, a Puisne Judge of the Supreme Court—a charge which attracted much notice both in Australia and England.[7]

On 18 November 1835, before proceeding to the strict business of the Court, Burton vigorously criticized the existing state of the colony. With more than a fourth of the population convicts still in servitude, and an indefinite number expirees or ticket-of-leave men,

the picture presented was one of the most painful description : it would appear, to one who could look down upon the community, as if the main business of all were the commission of crime and the punishment of it; as if the whole colony were continuously in motion towards the several courts of justice : and the most painful reflection must be, that so many capital sentences (399 in three years) and the execution of them have not had the effect of preventing crime by way of example.

The figures are abundantly clear, though the English Committee would have made a far more telling case of its report had it relied less on emotional diatribes and analysed the statistics a little more.

A single analysis suffices to show the actual situation. The gross figures tell little, but an analysis shows that, in November 1835— the time of Burton's charge—New South Wales had 29,202 adult convicts to 18,478 free men. Eight times as many convicts as free men continued to come in, or, in Burton's words, 'the tide of convict population still sets strongly here, while that of free emigration appears feebly to reach our shores'. Tendencies apart, New South Wales was still preponderatingly a convict-community and, it would appear, one in which the criminal traits were becoming more marked in those years.

The outlook was certainly not very pleasing, and the numbers were such that it rested with those years whether convict or free influence was to be in the ascendancy. This was the struggle that paralyzed the periods of Darling and Bourke and that absorbed most attention in the years immediately before and after 1835. The issue, though difficult to settle, was simple in its essentials. Most of the population were actual or past convicts, but the census-figures showed 49,265 free persons to 27,831 bond; and the argument was whether the former or the latter position was to be recognized as

[7] Elaborated in his *State of Religion and Education in New South Wales*.

normal—whether, in a word, a man, once freed from the lien the law had over him, had his past wiped out at a stroke and could mingle in society without discrimination or hindrance, as if that past had never been? The mass of the immigrants naturally stood for the gap between their class and the convicts, in which division they placed all expirees or ticket-of-leave men : and the *pure merinos* left no doubt as to their exclusiveness. The difficulty was whether the successive Governors would take the easy line of acquiescing in the ban on ex-convicts or insist on giving them an opportunity in this new land once they had been punished.

The Governors had varied in their attitude. Macquarie, the last of the despots, had insisted on viewing the colony as a gaol, with free emigrants living there only on sufferance; and Brisbane, his successor, was too busy with his astronomy to worry over the matter. The real trouble commenced with Sir Ralph Darling, the Governor from 1825 to 1831. He was a typical soldier, immersed in the details of military routine and recking little of literature or law. A Horse Guards man, he was known as 'one of the school of the Duke of York'—not, as was observed at the time, that the Duke was energetic enough to found any school, but simply because he gathered round him the highest of the high Tories. Such a man naturally consorted with the exclusives, and, through the instrumentality of his friend, Alexander M'Leay, the local Colonial Secretary, opposed all emancipists and ordered a strict *régime* for the convicts. He refused to receive emancipists in society and wanted to deny them political rights, on the ground that, once convicted, they were perpetual felons. This attitude had the effect of consolidating an opposition to him and making him one of the most unpopular Governors the colony ever had. The prosperous emancipists at once took their stand against him, and—what was the significant point— were joined by the liberals amongst the colonists, especially the reformers, led by Wentworth and Wardell, who wanted more representative political institutions. Even some of the landed gentry, under Sir John Jamison, joined for this reason, and the Chief Justice, Forbes, a republican born in Bermuda, added his power, both because of his principles and because he hated Darling personally. The Governor therefore left the colony amidst an unprecedented wave of contumely and expressive, though somewhat uncouth, demonstrations of hostility. He had reduced the rights of the convicts to zero, had prevented the effective emergence of expirees, and had pandered to the licence and unjust demands of the larger settlers—thus being directly responsible for the crop of convict outbreaks before 1835.

His successor, Sir Richard Bourke, who administered from 1831 to 1837, was of a different stamp. He was an Oxford man with a good record in the army and with service in Holland, Buenos Aires, and the Peninsula, before going to the Cape as Governor of the Eastern District. A frank cordial Irishman, he was noted for his general urbanity and comprehensive outlook. He had none of the bigoted smallness of Darling's sergeant-major mind and was fitted to take wide views of State policy, both by his superior intellectual attainments and the range of his experience. He was clearly the ablest man who had come to the colony and, it was said, 'equal in zeal, energy, and common sense to Macquarie, and superior in the liberality, humanity, and statesmanlike far-sightedness of his views'. His striking intelligence could not be gainsaid. One had only to concentrate on the face of this otherwise quite ordinary, middle-sized man to perceive his alertness: he had a remarkably well-defined profile, the old wound across his face emphasizing his humour and quickness of outlook. But he was no paragon, as the colonists soon perceived. It was quickly obvious that, if he were willing to listen to all sides in an argument and bring a certain cosmopolitanism and common sense to bear on its solution, he was very firm, and even obstinate, in his opinions. He arrived at his conclusions by a process that was usually well-informed and just but was unduly tenacious in adhering to them, once he had decided on them.

On the other hand, he was the creature of no class or interest, and would consider each question—convicts, squatters, or constitution—irrespective of the demands of factions. He thus resisted the small official clique of civil servants in their untoward demands, yet would allow no concessions to their opponents. He relentlessly fought the monopolistic claims of the landed proprietors, but would tolerate no licence from the unauthorized squatters. He opposed the advanced claims of the theorists in the colony, yet incurred the displeasure of Downing Street by insisting on a separate colonial viewpoint and opposing the Wakefield plan. In short, he commenced by being 'no man's man', and if, in his later days, events forced him into a partisan position, he still retained independent views on the wider issues that were really to decide the colony's fate. And yet he had all the Irishman's capacity for hating, as the M'Leay faction at once found, and he would allow no nonsense even from his allies. Bourke was, on the whole, a very sagacious and determined Governor—a Governor with wider views and a more enquiring spirit than most administrators in his position, but with the distinctly human faults and the peculiar mixture of good and evil these assume in a Limerick man of world-wide experience.

At first, he was very popular, largely as a reflex from Darling's great unpopularity. Moreover, the colony was just recovering from a long drought and the years of aggravated speculation after 1825, and was looking forward to a period of quiet optimism. In addition, the new system of selling land relieved him of charges of favouritism, and his obvious determination to help settlers of all classes soon gathered various sections around him.

But, though he always insisted on an independent attitude in connection with the problems of settlement, he at once fell into the hands of the liberals in dealing with the great social question. Almost superciliously refined himself, he yet favoured the convicts and emancipists, reacting directly from Darling's policy of repression and discrimination. He held that the future of the colony lay with the freemen and that any man who had discharged his bill to the King was once more entitled to all the privileges he had formerly enjoyed.

Having these views, the new Governor inevitably fell into the arms of Wentworth, Chief Justice Forbes, and the other opponents of Darling, and as naturally, both from principle and by the force of events, rallied against those civil servants, under M'Leay, who had been made into an omniscient oligarchy by Darling, and those large landed proprietors, who looked upon the entire colony as a reserve for their own interests. Given a Governor with liberal tendencies, this division of forces was inevitable; and Bourke, even had he tried to prevent it, would have been forced by the very pressure of facts to acquiesce in such a partisan position. As it was, his every inclination drew him there, and he was convinced that the claims of the smaller privileged sections could not be held with advantage to the community.

As stated above, most convicts were released from gaol almost immediately on arriving. Some were kept in the penal settlements and about 2,240 worked on the roads, but most were scattered throughout the colony. They were assigned as labourers, and thus became farm-hands and shepherds. Moreover, many were pardoned, others served their sentences and became expirees, and still others ticket-of-leave men, that is, after a certain amount of sentence, they received permits to work for themselves in any given district, provided that they reported to a magistrate every Sunday. A *lifer*, for instance, received a ticket after eight years, others from four years onwards, according to the gravity of their offence and their conduct in gaol or as assigned servants. All of these classes made up the emancipists, and it was their problem that so convulsed the colony. The Commons Committee of 1838 showed how such 'old hands' were often preferred to free immigrants, and how they rose to occupy all positions. The ranks of the police and the overseers of road-parties and chain-gangs were filled by them: they became clerks, tutors, and managers of estates: two were editors of leading journals: and not a few became pioneer squatters and large landed proprietors: one, a man unable to read or write, received an income of £40,000 a year from his Nepean estates and founded a business-house that became the largest in the colony, and that, falling, precipitated the big crisis of the forties.[8] It was these people whom Bourke admitted to his table and allowed on the jury-lists: it was these to whom he offered an unprejudiced place in the whole structure of colonial life, and it was on their behalf that he stood firm against the hitherto privileged classes.

Society naturally viewed the Governor's activities with alarm, for it must be remembered that, in this community of 70,000 souls, 20,000 were convict-servants, whose obedience had hitherto been secured by methods which were undoubtedly terrorist and based on the assumption that classes of convict-origin were destined to occupy inferior positions in the body politic. In support of this stand, three elements combined, strangely assorted comrades though they were!— M'Leay and the mass of the civil servants, the magistrates who were the spokesmen of the landed gentry, and Dr Lang, who, through his organ, the Colonist, vociferously collected the new emigrant-classes against what he termed the menace of convictism. Aiding in that singularly low standard of journalism, with its crude revilings and coarse personal criticisms, were the Sydney Herald (which had for-saken its earlier moderation for unrestricted opposition to Bourke), the Monitor (an emigrants' paper conducted on Cobbett's principles), and several minor sheets.

These miscellaneous forces were opposed by the official sections. Bourke, supported by the Whigs at the Colonial Office, stood at the head and was aided by elements as diverse and as irreconcilable as those grouped under the opposition. Wentworth and the reformers who had attacked Darling, and who now wanted political reform, in general supported the Governor—or, at least, when he was fight-ing the M'Leay faction. More numerous were the emancipists, solidly

[8] 1838 Committee on Transportation, p. xvii: Martin, The British Colonies, Vol. II, p. 414.

in favour of the new Governor and marshalled by the tactlessly over-
zealous Roger Therry, the Commissioner of the Court of Requests,
who was as much Bourke's favourite as his enemy, M'Leay, had been
Darling's. This faction carried with them the two leading journals
of the day, the *Sydney Gazette* and the *Australian*. The *Gazette*,
which had been the official paper until Bourke started a separate
Government Gazette, had strongly supported Governor Darling, but
now, strangely enough, had come under two ex-convicts, the emancipist O'Shaughnessy and the 'ticket-of-leaver' Watt, and had swung
round to Bourke. The *Australian*, founded by Wentworth and the
clever barrister, Dr Wardell, had sprung into fame by its bitter per-
secution of Darling, and, though always the opposition paper *par
excellence*, now aided Bourke, because he was fighting the aristocratic
minority and standing for liberal reform. For their immediate purpose, these papers, especially the *Gazette*, which was facetiously
known as 'the Prisoners' Journal', declared that there was no distinction between an emigrant and an emancipist, and that any dis-
criminatory acts were illegal. They denied Burton's tales of the
increase of crime, opposed 'the Hole-and-Corner' petition of the
Macarthurs and the M'Leays and the Bowmans as illiberal, and
themselves petitioned Parliament for a better Council, more juries,
and a representative legislature.

With all of these quarrelsome elements, unrestrained by any
effective libel law or any standard of decency, the New South Wales
of 1835 was a pestilential little place overridden by a spirit of faction
—a spirit that must be emphasized, because it was against this background that the squatting expansion took place, and because it was
the existence of this spirit that caused the men outback to spurn the
Government at Sydney.

The first trouble was in connection with the juries, to which all
men not actually under penal servitude had been admitted two years
before. Any householder of a certain rate could become a juror without any selection, a tolerance that was farcical in a colony of emancipists. In April 1836, for instance, the *Sydney Herald* reported that
the cases of cattle-stealing before the criminal session almost exceeded
belief, and cited the case of one man who had been a juror in 1835,
though himself at the time out on bail for a charge of cattle-lifting,
and who had stood out for acquittal in the face of the clearest
evidence.[9] So obvious was the evil that, after impanelling a jury on a
cattle-stealing case in May 1836, the Attorney-General, Plunkett,
addressed the Court thus:

[9] *Sydney Herald*, 9 May 1836.

In the absence of almost all the special jurors, he would not go on with the case of the Deans for stealing cattle. The names that had been called were almost all publicans (that is, emancipated convicts), and, in the absence of the merchants, he would not risk the administration of justice in their hands!

No commentary on this is needed, save to add that, time and again in these years, the most flagrant cases of cattle-stealing—a vastly increasing offence in these days of squatting expansion—could not be sheeted home, owing to the attitude of the juries. Magistrates and the respectable citizens chose to pay fines for non-attendance rather than associate with jurors who had been convicts, and so reduced a theoretically admirable practice to the gravest farce.

In answer to this charge, Bourke held that the outcry was unjustified. All the judges except Burton, he said, favoured the system, and, after all, Burton's analysis of the jury-lists was irrelevant, provided that the verdicts were satisfactory. But the sting lay in the qualification, and Burton's figures were more reliable than the Governor's assertion that only 116 emancipists could be found on a jury-list of nearly 800 persons. Nor was it adequate to explain away the opposition as a pretext of the Conservatives, nor to argue that the qualifications were higher than in England, because what mattered was the effect such a system would have on a society mainly constituted of persons of convict-origin.

The free classes were further disgusted when the Watt matter became one of public comment, and no better commentary on the degraded state of public life is possible than the fact that such an issue could become so important! Therry had defended the convicts and attacked the magistrates and masters in general in the Mudie murder case, and now defended Watt when the magistrates stooped so low as to charge him in the public courts with immorality.[10] The charge, true enough as it was, was a petty piece of political chicanery —a movement of the magistrates, the civil servants, and Burton against the Governor. In itself, it was not of the slightest importance; whether the convict whom Bourke had allowed to become editor of the *Sydney Gazette* had a mistress or not, could scarcely be said to have been a matter of State: yet its echoes reached Downing Street and ultimately led to Bourke's recall.

Bourke, to put the matter in a nutshell, was attacked for relaxing the convict-laws, for favouring individual convicts of the Watt stamp, and for omitting the names of certain of his opponents from

[10] The details are in Bourke's despatches, Mudie's *Felonry of New South Wales* (1837), and the press.

the list of magistrates. What happened in the sordid story was this. Bourke certainly gave undue concessions to the convicts, O'Shaughnessy and Watt; co-operated with them (implicitly but none the less effectively) in the *Sydney Gazette;* knew that the vindication of his Government by *An Unpaid Magistrate* was by his henchman, Therry; and must have realized that all together were working for the confusion of his adversaries. It was rather an infamous combination, as the *Sydney Herald* and the other papers did not hesitate to point out. Perhaps never had a Governor been so violently associated with a partisan set in a colony, and yet it is difficult to see how much was due to the machinations of his enemies. These were the years when class-rivalries were at their very apex in New South Wales and when there was no vestige of a community-spirit. The convicts in charge of the Government paper and their scurrilities, Roger Therry and his dealings with criminals, Mudie of Castle Forbes and his fellow 'merino' magistrates, and the harried Governor with his feelings pulling him entirely on one side—all of these went to make up a mass of petty futilities and grotesquely exaggerated personal rivalries. Nobody seemed to think of the colony: the questions of the day were whether Mudie should be flogged for not being quite a gentleman, or whether the Governor would abandon Watt when his mistress was discovered, or whether Therry could be forced into the open.

Yet it was against this vulgar background of Sydney that the sheepmen were pushing into the interior and building up the country's staple. There might be massacre in the Liverpool Plains, the Murrumbidgee might run dry in its bed, and squatters be frozen out in Monaro, but all that mattered, even in the Governor's despatches, was that Watt had been caught *in flagrante delicto* with a convict-woman! The pastoral advance might seem to be breaking before the cordon of menacing natives, and the new road to Port Phillip red with the war-wrack of the tribes who were 'out'; but Sydney was concerned with the dismissal of certain partisan magistrates, and the Governor, perforce, had to spend most of his time refuting calumnies directed against himself or contriving pitfalls for his social and political enemies. The life of the colony was on the frontier—on the Ovens and the Murrumbidgee—and its welfare was being wrested from the flocks: but its Governors and its successful men were striving to keep it back in the puerile quarrels of a convict-stage that was going. They were back in the twenties, when New Holland was a gaol, but the march of the sheep and the dust of the cattle-herds were stamping in the new age of the free pastoralists!

In light of this, what mattered the trivial machinations of a few expirees and ticket-of-leave men, and the anomalous prestige of a handful of exclusives who had nothing to be proud of?

As for Bourke, perhaps he could not wrest himself free from the pettiness of the old counties, but at least, he could have stressed such matters less, and forced the tone of the colony into different directions. He aggravated the arid quarrels by becoming a partisan. Perhaps he was too conscientious to overlook charges against his administration, perhaps he was not sufficiently strong to override them: he may even have liked the quarrel and the fight, since he himself spoke with gubernatorial prestige; but, whatever the cause, he did not emerge unsmirched, and certainly neglected tendencies that were evolving to change the whole future of Australia. Against this, however, it must be remembered that he finally established the principle that a man, once free in Australia, should be untrammelled in his activities and know no degrading social or legal distinctions: and this, after all, Australia being in the transition stage in which it then was, was the outstanding feature in his administration. The quarrels were temporary, but this decision was permanent—as permanent as the existence of the new pastoral industries that were spontaneously raising themselves in the outer lands at that moment.

III   The Political Situation

While the social problem was thus being solved, the political question was just emerging in its complexity; and, if it was important to the squatters that the colony was entering on a period when the social distinctions of the convict age were going, it was none the less vital to them that political concessions were coming.

In 1835, New South Wales was under the Governor, who was aided by a Legislative Council, entirely nominated but with a small unofficial element. There was no election and the Governor could override the Council on any point. Indeed, up to Bourke's time, the Council had been viewed simply as a species of wider Executive Council, deliberating in secret, and merely a gesture to the more important landowners. But events were rapidly changing and the Legislative Council was becoming assertive. Its *Votes and Proceedings* suddenly turned into registers of complaints, and some of the members spoke of representative, and even responsible, government. Blaxland and Macarthur inside, and Wentworth outside, were pleading the cause of the legislature against the executive officials. All of this involved a striking displacement of power within the community, coinciding as it did with the commencement of free immigration and the approaching fall of transportation.

In 1834, for instance, *The Australian Patriotic Association* had been formed to demand a Parliamentary Agent in England and to make known the real state of colonial affairs. They had even appointed H. Lytton Bulwer, a very vain and foppish man who was said to plagiarize other people's books on France; but the Colonial Office looked askance at their efforts.[11] More important were their demands to control part of the revenue. Bourke, in his first session of the Council (January 1832), had promised the innovation of laying estimates before them and, by some misapprehension, had allowed the Council to think that a *Compact* of 1835 gave them the right to appropriate land-revenue. Such a claim, clearly erroneous though it was, was grasped eagerly by the newly insistent Council and caused much trouble all through the squatting period. The land-revenue was now anything between £90,000 and £130,000 a year, where four years before it had been negligible; and the Council, despite Glenelg's clearly-worded despatch of 10 July 1835, insisted that all of this lay at their disposal. Whether they were right or wrong mattered not at all; all they cared about was their privilege, as they chose to call it, so that what had been quite beyond the scope of practical politics a few years before had become a burning question in 1835.

Apart from this matter, the colonists were demanding a wider and better Council. The existing Government Act had expired and was being renewed from year to year, while the Colonial Office was slowly making up its mind which form of constitution would best suit the peculiar conditions of this changing convict-colony. That an improved Council was imperative, practically all admitted. Bourke himself, speaking freely in a communication to Under-Secretary Hay at the commencement of 1836, reported that

the great subject of interest amongst our Colonial Politicians at this time is the new Colonial Act . . . In a country containing now at least 50,000 free inhabitants; with a press totally unrestricted, a prevailing intelligence, increasing wealth, and a quick temperament, it is not possible to govern with advantage by means of such a Council as is here established. With a total income of £273,000 surely the expenditure of such a sum requires not only due deliberation, but the consent and approbation of the People from whom it is collected, expressed under some form of Representation.[12]

Bourke even went too far in the direction of Whig liberalism in

[11] Bourke-Glenelg, 13 April 1836: sketch in *Australian*, 24 May 1836.
[12] Bourke-Glenelg, 28 December 1835, 1 February 1836.

this regard, as in his optimistic interpretation of the despatches purporting to give the Council control of land-revenue. He wanted a
Council that would have been too powerful for the existing conditions. Late in 1835, he had forwarded Chief Justice Forbes' proposed Bill for the Government of the colony. This advocated a
Council, with two-thirds of its members elected, and with power to
appropriate certain revenues. Indeed, it was more liberal in these
regards than the actual Act passed in 1842. In his covering despatch,
Bourke intimated that he would deny emancipists the right to sit
but, as in Canada and Newfoundland, would offer them the franchise. This stage represented the position Bourke ultimately reached
in political matters, and it certainly cannot be characterized as
illiberal. If not quite as far-reaching as the demands of the Blaxland
section of reformers, it was considerably in advance of representative
official opinion. It showed how a moderately liberal Whig could be
dissatisfied with the existing political machinery and, above all (and
here his successor, Gipps, at once concurred), how the existing
Council was inadequate; how it did not help the Governor in legislation, and how it could not be said to give Government Acts the
support of the people.

In 1835, then, it was clear that some form of representative body
was needed but that, under the existing social conditions, a purely
representative Council would be a foolhardy experiment. Events were
rapidly tending in favour of some form of mixed Council, with a
strong advisory right over most of the appropriation and perhaps
a positive right with regard to a portion, and it was simply a matter
of time before this would be achieved. The Constitution Act was on
every landholder's tongue and, as soon as the system of licensed
squatting commenced, the flockmen demanded that they too should
participate in its benefits. The Act was due any time after 1835, and
every year that passed saw the squatters more powerful, more
organized, and more insistent on their political rights. It seemed a
singularly happy stroke of fortune that, just as they were rising as a
new element in the economic body, the constitution should be in
process of adaptation to the new conditions.

With the social problem thus being solved and the political issue
assuming definiteness, Bourke was confronted by a further grave
issue, the solution of which was fundamental for the future of the
colony but the achievement of which involved his own personal fall.
This was the question of the executive officials who had hitherto
co-operated with the land-owning magistrates in dominating colonial

affairs. They were really a self-constituted oligarchy who had come even to challenge the Governor: if they remained in control, development would be along class-lines and the freemen in the cities and the stockmen on the boundaries would be virtually of lesser castes.

At this time, Bourke was faced by the concerted opposition of the Legislative Council and the civil servants, led by the Colonial Secretary who normally should have been his right-hand man. Alexander M'Leay, who had rather ingeniously combined the office of Colonial Secretary with leadership of that 'official clique' which had ruined so many Governors, was a tenacious Scotsman of over sixty-five years of age at the time of his conflict with Bourke. He had always enjoyed varied activities, combining in some way or other the Secretaryship of the Transport Board during the Napoleonic War with that of the Linnaean Society, of which he was an original charter-member. When already an oldish man, Bathurst selected him to be the Colonial Secretary of New South Wales in 1825 and, from that time until his resignation twelve years later, he had been a local tyrant. He conducted all local correspondence and was really the permanent head of the Government until events forced him to quarrel with Bourke. Darling had not questioned his paramountcy, but a quarrel with Bourke was a foregone conclusion because this testy old man could not brook a rival, even in the Governor. He made no secret of his antagonism and openly opposed the Governor on four important matters in the Council in 1836 alone. Yet he had sworn to be the first officer in the local ship of State!

Naturally enough, Bourke frequently protested against this impossible state of affairs. At intervals, he complained to the Secretary of State of 'public servants professing without restraint and frequently without respect, opinions at variance with mine upon important Colonial Affairs', of 'the difficulty I experienced in carrying on the Government of the Colony through the agency of Public Servants, many of whom openly professed opinions hostile to the principles of my administration', and, in particular, of M'Leay's 'constant intercourse and intimacy with the principal opponents of my Government'. M'Leay took an especially awkward stand in opposing the emancipists and in favouring the pretensions of those disaffected magistrates whom Bourke was compelled to omit from the commission of the peace in 1835. Indeed, when the entire colony was troubled by this act of Bourke's and when he needed every ounce of support, a petition in favour of the magistrates issued from the very office of the Colonial Secretary!

Reporting this, and complaining of the extremely factious spirit within the Colony, the Governor explained the situation in moderate words which remain the vindication of his acts: [13]

They are inclined to lead and not to follow, and would dictate measures to Government rather than forward those which happen to be opposed to their opinions. The opinions of the greater number in matters of local concern are generally opposed to mine. Theirs are of an exclusive tendency, whilst my object has been to introduce a strict impartiality of administration. Your Lordship is well aware that in this colony party feelings are high, and that the Government, with every endeavour to steer a middle course, has not been able to escape a good deal of hostility. This hostility has, beyond all doubt, been fostered and increased by the adverse spirit of many of the Civil Officers.

In overthrowing this incipient revolt of the executive officials, Bourke was clearly fighting for the future, though for the moment his cause seemed submerged.

In 1835, he had dispensed with four magistrates for sitting on the Mudie case and attacking the convict Watt, on the ground that their object was 'to elicit something which might cast a slur on the Government'. Glenelg, the Secretary of State, approved of this, but became dubious when Bourke went further. The Governor had run his favourite, Roger Therry, for the position of Chairman of Quarter Sessions, an official elected by the magistrates. Had he succeeded, he would have triumphed over the landed proprietors, but the opposition secured the election of Riddell, whom Bourke described as the open and avowed *frondeur* of the Government and who was obviously a weak but respectable man of no outstanding abilities. The complication lay in the fact that he was actually the Colonial Treasurer at the moment of election and, though he disavowed any knowledge of his candidature, was clearly lending himself to the purposes of Bourke's enemies. Bourke at once suspended him from the Executive Council on the ground that he had been disloyal, a step which forced matters to a climax. If the Colonial Office allowed this, then Bourke had won; if, on the other hand, they disapproved, the Governor's position was untenable, because either he or the executive officers would have to be supreme.

Unfortunately, Glenelg, a distinctly weak Minister who was soon to be ejected from the Cabinet under particularly ignominious conditions, did not know his own mind. Bourke had tendered his resignation, conditional upon the Ministry's support of his stand. Glenelg, while blaming Riddell and trusting that Bourke would not resign,

[13] Bourke-Glenelg, 1 March 1836. Reasons in 28 February 1836.

ordered Riddell's reinstatement in the Council. He found no proof that the Colonial Treasurer meant to thwart the administration and was certain that Riddell would perceive the error of his ways! Bourke had effectively disposed of both the mutineers—both the Colonial Secretary and the Colonial Treasurer—and Glenelg could reply only that neutrality in party politics was 'at once the duty and the privilege of their situation!' By deciding for neither side, he indefinitely protracted the struggle, and, fortunately for the colony, Bourke effaced himself and insisted on his resignation (30 January 1837), a step that vindicated his stand and brought home to the Colonial Office the real nature of the issues at stake.

It must not be understood that he was entirely in the right, or that he acted in the most tactful manner. On the contrary, he was more than a little specious in his despatches on M'Leay, Riddell, and the dispossessed magistrates. He often failed to reflect the intensity of public interest aroused by his acts; so much so, in fact, if the Secretary of State had not either the local papers or outside information, he would have been quite incapable of estimating the given situation from Bourke's despatches. Bourke understated the force of the opposition and often failed to place due emphasis on certain factors.

But, over and above this, he was fighting for the best interests of the colony. The 'official clique' had to be broken and Bourke had practically accomplished this, though he himself was swept down in the wreckage. M'Leay had resigned, Riddell no longer counted, and it was in a way fitting that Bourke too should go. It would be easier for a new Governor to reap the fruits of the struggle—Bourke had been too intimately a combatant to act as an impartial agent of reconstruction, once the victory of principle had been secured! He had done the storming work, it was for his successor to consolidate the ground won.

Rightly viewed, therefore, Bourke's resignation marked his crowning achievement. He had finished his work in New South Wales. He had secured for ever the principle of equality for all men, emancipist or emigrant, and had established the rule that all men, irrespective of their past, were to have an equal opportunity in community-life. The social struggle, which may quite conceivably have rent the colony for decades, was thus practically solved. From this, he had gone on to indicate the lines on which the colony could develop politically, and lastly, he had broken the claims of an executive minority. In a word, he had, by this triple task, prepared the way for the changed conditions of the squatting era. The victory was to the free people, emancipists as well as emigrants being included within that term—to the flockmaster and the merchant and the mechanic.

The old days were setting in a dusk of transformation—a change due in no small measure to Governor Bourke. He had worked in all directions. As will be seen later, it was he who first grasped the importance of the new squatting interests and legalized the march of the stockmen: it was under him that Port Phillip was satisfactorily settled, and communication set up with the infant colony of South Australia: it was he who made the convict-system orderly and established the system of selling colonial lands, thus laying the basis for free immigration; and, over all, it was his firm personality that co-ordinated the changing elements of New South Wales in this period of transition from convicts to freemen, from life in the narrow Counties to the age of the squatters! Modern conditions of freedom and democracy were emerging in his time, and he was convinced that the future lay with the freemen and the flocks, and that transportation and assignment had to go. In carrying out this conception, he helped the squatters, aided the immigrants, raised the Land Fund, encouraged representative government, built up the freedom of the press, attacked the stranglehold of the magistrates and raised the smaller settlers against them, and reduced minorities of all kinds to their proper places.

The colony was metamorphosed in those years, and Bourke knew this, as he set out on the long way home round Cape Horn. Naturally, he was not entirely pleased with the manner of his going, but the wound on his face must have given its peculiar twitch of satisfaction as he thought of the changes since he had landed in 1831, of the statistics of the year in which he was leaving, and of those stockmen who were even then in the New England ranges and down to the limit of Port Phillip. A Home Government, more sagacious than Lord Glenelg, offered him control of Jamaica, and even the Commandership of the Forces in India (1839), but he retired to his Irish seat, and for eighteen years, watched the growth of the colony whose destinies he had moulded. He had started the age of freemen and the age of squatting—and no work could have been greater!

2

THE WOOL TRADE

I The Decline of English Wool

ONE OF THE most disquieting features of the bad years after the
Napoleonic peace was the chronic decline of one of England's
staples—that wool-trade which had been a mainstay of the country's
industry since the guilds of the Middle Ages. Now, however, the
export-trade was cut away at the roots, and English wool could not
even hold its own in the home-markets. English sheep-farmers could
no longer face the competition of cheap foreign wools and it was
soon observed that a declining prosperity was accompanied by a
falling-off in quality. The farmers met decreasing prices by negligence
and a cheaper product, a policy that battened on itself and rapidly
set the seal on their ruin. The gorsy Downs and the bleaker Cheviot
regions suffered alike, for foreign competition recognized no pride of
place, no ingrained local traditions. Lincolns and Leicesters, South
Downs and English merinos all swept down. The one obvious fact
was that foreign wools—very serviceable and, according to the
whisper of not a few shrewd manufacturers, better adapted for the
new cloths than the English—could be bought for less than eighteenpence a pound, duty notwithstanding; and what had tradition to do
with the price of raw materials? The public demanded cheap cloths,
the manufacturers had to live, the new interests in the North were
clamorous for their rights; and, in all the hubbub, the sheep-farmer
was forced to the wall. Despaired of by others, he completed his own
ruin by trying to market an obviously inferior product. The circle of
his ruin was complete.[1]

The trouble had commenced directly after the peace, when prices
began to fall, because the artificial protection due to the Continental
War was now removed and the English growers had to face the competition of Spain and Silesia. But, despite ominous signs, the position
was not fundamentally changed until the years after 1819, when

---

[1] The full story is told in the evidence of the *Committee appointed to report
on the cause of the depression in wool-values, with special reference to the
probable increase of colonial production*, 8 July 1828.

prices and quality both began to decline. Matters went rapidly from bad to worse. The twenties deepened in despair, despite the advent of small quantities of colonial wool; and at last, after 1824, home-grown wool became absolutely unsaleable.

So obvious was the catastrophe that the House of Lords appointed a Select Committee (July 1828) to investigate the causes of the decline, with especial reference to the means of combating the cheap German wools. The report of this Committee was brusquely decisive. It was a tale of ruin brought on by the inherent defects of the system of home-production and by the opening of new sources of supply. Perhaps nowhere in the history of English industry is there a more complete—almost lugubriously complete—story of decline. Over 400 pages of evidence were collected, but exporters and manu-facturers, Sussex yeomen and gentlemen-farmers of the North all agreed on the essential points of the situation. The facts were too clear—a great English industry had fallen, had been pressed to the wall by the incidence of new economic facts.

The fall was too general to be explained away by local peculiarities. The best as well as the worst went. All of the British short-wools, in particular, were ousted from the market. Previously, the South Down sheep had been the pride of England, with their close, fine curled wool—theirs had been the pick of the short wool, and Surrey, Kent, and Sussex had set the standard. Arthur Young, in 1776, had seen them in their hey-day, and to him, their small speckled heads and their bellies as straight as their backs had been as distinctive a feature of the landscape as the rolling downs and the gorse-clad hillocks of the South. So paramount was their position, so un-questioned their supremacy, that the decline of such a stock ac-centuated the general rout. South Down wool fell from 2s. 6d. in 1815—its average price throughout the long wars—to 1s. 6d. in 1820, and less than ninepence in 1827. The year after the peace saw a fall of 25 per cent, but growers attributed it partly to the revaluation of everything in the painful reconstruction process, an analysis that seemed justified when prices held in 1817 and even rose in 1818. But the next clip saw a fall to eighteenpence, and neither good nor bad seasons could budge the buyers to give a groat more for six years. They remained immobile, and pointed only to the rapidly increasing stocks of Silesian wool at 1s. 4d. When at last they did make a move towards revaluing the best English shorts, it was to bid a shilling in 1825, and even explain away this as temporary weakness due to the desire to help a struggling English industry.

Wool had become practically worthless. It was mockery to offer a shilling a pound, and simply insane to expect English sheep to survive under the conditions of 1827, when the highest that could be obtained for superlative samples was a meagre ninepence, with ordinary South Down wools unsaleable at any price. And, if this were the case with the prime stocks, what chance of survival had the Lincolns and the Leicesters and the cross-breds? The case was too clear to need exposition. Henry King, of Chilmark in Wiltshire, was but typical in the tale he told the Committee. Eighteenpence, he admitted with the others, was the absolute minimum needed for survival, yet his average in the twelve years before 1824 had been 1s. 7¼d., and, at the time of speaking, he had three years' clips in his barns utterly unsaleable at any price. If he sold at the ruling price of eighteenpence, instead of the basic level of 1s. 6d., he would lose £2,437; and, unless some means of recovery were held out to him very soon, he had no alternative but bankruptcy and migration to the colonies!

Nor was this case in any wise peculiar. The taste for English wool had commenced to decline in earnest in 1819, when two factors combined. In the first rank was the fact that the Germans, who had been crossing their animals with Spanish merinos since the dawn of the century and pandering to the desire for extreme fineness and softness, could sell as much wool as could be absorbed in England for about a shilling a pound. In despair, the Peel Cabinet raised the duty on foreign wools from a penny to sixpence a pound in 1819, but the effect was scarcely noticeable. The Germans more than counteracted this by the fillip given to their home-production, especially in the field of cheap, coarse wools. They knew that the fine merino field was theirs for the taking, and so concentrated on dumping into England wool that would compete with the staple shorts of the Downs. The upshot was that the same German wool which had sold for 1s. 4d. when the duty had been a penny could be obtained for as little as 1s. 1d. when the duty had gone up to sixpence![2] No other commentary on the impossibility of competition was needed, though it seemed a gratuitous blow when the reconstructed Liverpool Cabinet, under Huskisson's desire to remove restrictions on trade, took off the duty in September 1824, and left the English industry utterly unaided in its fight with foreign competition. Huskisson was a whole-hearted Free Trader and much preferred an industry to disappear if it could not survive in the face of open competition; moreover, he would sacrifice any local producers of raw materials if the manufacturers could thereby obtain their supplies more cheaply,

[2] For failure of duties, see table in 1828 Committee, p. 362.

and would count the ultimate survival of the manufacturing industry as an additional triumph for the country and his principles!

This was the last blow. English wool-prices had been reeling for a decade; now, foreign supplies were admitted without restraint, and, to make matters still worse, the country plunged into 'the mad year of 1825', in the excesses of which declining concerns like the English wool-industry were the first to suffer. Prices, hitherto still at rates that allowed survival, dropped suddenly to a shilling and less, and never recovered.

At this stage, the wool-growers met the full effect of the second great factor that had been making for change in the previous few years. German competition of itself would have explained the crisis; but far more fundamental, from the point of view of the industry internally, was the change that had taken place in the demands of the manufacturers. The simple fact was that the Germans were giving, not only a cheaper, but a more satisfactory product. The farmers emphatically insisted that their wool retained its old quality, but the manufacturers quite dispassionately contradicted them—the mutton was larger, the farmer was going in for size, the wool was getting longer and stronger, and the old short-staple, particularly with the South Downs and the Cheviots, could no longer be obtained. The growers were crossing their breeds, as in Norfolk, to obtain a longer wool, thus, in effect, depriving their product of its essential qualities.

But this was somewhat a minor issue. Whether the growers were changing the characteristics and quality of their wool or not, there was a wider point. The demand at the moment was for newer cloths, and this demand the English wools were incapable of meeting. The cheap foreign wool—that from 6d. to 1s. 6d. a pound—had almost entirely thrown out the English short wools, principally Sussex, that had hitherto been used to manufacture second cloths; but now newer species were wanted. British fine wool was not to be compared with the new silky varieties that were coming out of Saxony, and British coarse wools were passed over in preference for foreign ones, even at a similar price, because the latter were cleaner. Moreover, the typical coarser wools of the local sheep found no market at all under the changed conditions. The South Downs, with their softness and elasticity, were hard hit, but it was simply a rout with the others. The Lincolns, the longest-legged and largest of all, were easily ousted—'living squares of wool' though they were; the long-woolled Leicesters, even as improved by Bakewell, fared no better; and with the white-faced Cheviots, the ruin was complete. There was absolutely no place for wool such as theirs, which was too thick for combing, and scarcely any for the majority of the coarse wools. The nature of the public demands and the conditions of wool offering from abroad made the manufacturers turn to the finer sorts. Coarse wool was too dear in comparison with fine, and they were putting into blankets such wool—that of Sussex and Norfolk, for instance—as they would not have dreamed of using a few years before.

The wool-staplers soon realized that the English goods offering were not well adapted to the existing taste, either in cloth or blankets, and so turned deaf ears to the offers and plaints of local farmers. They offered sixpence for the South Down wool that was worth at least eighteenpence, and did not care if their offers were refused, because the manufacturers could scarcely use supplies at any price. The British wool no longer had the qualities of the foreign, as more than one merchant bluffly told the investigating Committee, and the manufacturers insisted that it meant ruin for them if they adhered to the traditional British wools, even the better varieties. They could make cloth of English wool up to 1814, and compete; they could even hold on until 1824 if their methods were conservative and if they mixed English wool with the softer German varieties; but, after that year, no firm could hope to survive if it used any local wool. As the tale was clearly told by John Brooke, himself a Yorkshire broadcloth manufacturer, when asked why he had abandoned the home-grown wool:

In consequence of the deterioration of the quality of English wool, we found it not applicable to make the cloths of the same qualities we formerly did from English wools ... We had a very large connection for the purchase of English wool, and we kept to English wool, I should think, longer than any House in our neighbourhood, in consequence of having our connections different; but we found our neighbours were sending out better cloths than we were!

This summed up the matter. It was all very well to speak of traditional usages and national interests, but, unless a manufacturing house had a specially conservative *clientèle* who would pay for the English product irrespective of competing varieties, it could not hope to keep afloat. Moreover, in the general tightening-up of trade conditions after the bubble-year of 1825, when competition became more and more rigorous, such cases were very few. Several witnesses showed how different methods of doing business were emerging and how, in the ultimate struggle, only those concerns that were organized on the most strictly economic lines could hope to weather the crisis. The John Brookes, sturdy patriots as they were, were unable to hold out unless they joined the common herd and bought in the cheapest and most suitable market.

Hence, the position and prospects of English wool became meta-morphosed within a single generation. The average Englishman no longer wore clothes made of South Down and other short wools: no English wool could compete with the middling and cheapest foreign products: broadcloths, and even seconds, were now made from German wool; combing wools suffered less, but still considerably: and, in the fine-wool section, nothing could compete with the newly-improved Cliphausen flocks of Saxony. Sixpence a pound was non-chalantly offered for South Down wool by staplers who had their eyes on the newer products of Germany, and the lesser English breeds declined in proportion. Lincoln wool fell from a normal value of 1s. 2¼d. to 11½d. in 1827; English merino halved itself to 1s. 9d. and remained unsaleable for three years; while the Cheviot consignments from Scotland and the border-country were at 5½d. in 1827, and no buyers! Every clip intensified the weakness of the position, and the sheep-industry seemed doomed. The short-clips fought to the last, but even the South Downs went under, and sheep-growing became a ruinous luxury, for other than meat-purposes. Meanwhile, the staplers of Leeds and Manchester turned eagerly to Germany and, though much less confidently, to the new colonies of the South!

II   The Entry and Growth of Australian Wool

At the time when the English wools seemed completely to have succumbed to the German competition, a new note was heard; wool, at first dirty and scraggy, but later of much better quality, started coming in from the convict colonies of the Antipodes. Hitherto, all that the average Englishman knew of Australia was that 'Botany Bay' was a term of reproach, and that those far-away places where everything in Nature seemed awry considerably lessened the con-gestion of the county gaols in England. But now, these penal-dumps, looked upon only as sinks for the refuse criminality of England, were actually producing raw materials. It was a huge jest, and the men of the city gathered at Garraway's Coffee House in Cornhill to joke with each other about the new economic forces of the South and, not a little facetiously, to bid 10s. 4d. a pound for the first lone bale of convict-wool that John Macarthur had shipped on the Dart in 1807. A few far-seeing merchants pondered on the future, but most scoffed and eagerly sought to get a memento of this prodigy—Botany Bay wool.

This attitude continued for at least a decade, because the rot in English wool-production had not yet made itself sufficiently felt and because it was not until the twenties that the crisis, though nascent before that date, really emerged in its full intensity. Buyers still strolled along to Change Alley and sometimes made casual bids for the Australian lots, which usually consisted of single bales: some gravely, or even ponderously, commented on future Imperialism—stray voices in that Huskissonian age of Free Trade—but most let the inch of candle almost flicker out (it was still the immemorial system of auction 'by the candle') before they would offer a few pence. The sales lasted only an hour each day and were decidedly haphazard. Three-fourths of England's overseas wool came from Spain in 1800, the rest from Germany, and prices were well-known: and even after the war-era, when the places of Germany and Spain were reversed, the position of colonial wool remained unaltered. Australian wool forced a way into the English market by sheer persistence, and because very few people took it sufficiently seriously; it remained by force of merit.

As this would imply, the fight was steadily uphill, though little was done until the decline of English wool-growing and the imposition of a duty on German wool in 1819. Up till then, something like sixty or ninety thousand pounds of Australian wool had been coming in for six years, but progress after that date was rapid, almost tumultuous. The duties on colonial wool, thanks in part to Bigge's vigorous agitation, became almost nominal: freight-charges fell to threepence a pound after 1818, and remained constant at that low rate for years; and the quality of the Australian product constantly improved.

Conservative staplers still denounced Australian wool as 'low and coarse', but, on the other hand, Macarthur produced a wool quite as silky and as good for combing as that from the best Electoral flocks of Saxony. A manufacturer who had seen the samples Macarthur exhibited before a Select Committee of the Commons refused to believe the story of their origin but, once convinced, predicted that, if produced in sufficient quantity, such wool could be made into cloths of a texture hitherto deemed impossible and would effect nothing short of a revolution in the English woollen industry. This led to nothing at the time but, years later, Macarthur's stand was justified, when in 1822—in what was perhaps the pivotal point in the history of the Australian wool-trade—the Society of Arts voted him two gold medals for importing wool as good as the finest Saxon. The Duke of Sussex presented these medals at a large public meeting in London, and the whole event was sufficiently advertised to stamp the new import as an economic factor of note, and not simply a joke or a pitiful travesty of Old World industry.

This was the turning-point. Parliament responded by reducing the new duties on colonial wool and thus discriminating against the German imports which now had to pay six times as much: and manufacturers, looking round for raw materials to put into the new cloths which were so much in demand, began to take notice of the Australian product. The new cloths which were so soft and fine—the *Indianas* and *Merinos* in which a post-war generation wished to besport itself—required wool of peculiar softness of texture and a length of staple that the South Down varieties of England simply could not supply. Superior felting and combing qualities were demanded, and all of these the wool of New South Wales offered. It was longer, softer, silkier, and more resilient than any but the very best Saxon, and seemed ideal for the upper-grade cloths then in demand.

There was little doubt of this fact. Save for a few ultra-conservative dissentients, the witnesses before the 1828 Committee agreed as to the superiority of Australian wool. Stuart Donaldson, a merchant trading to Australia, had shipped colonial wool for four years and noted a distinct improvement every year: 'I have no hesitation', he concluded, 'in pronouncing that they are decidedly preferred to the apparently similar descriptions of German wool.' They could compete with the fine wools of Saxony and yet help the decaying British industry by mixing with the harder staple of English wool. More—went on enthusiastic merchants like Hughes—in fifteen years, Australia could make England entirely independent of Spain and Germany, even for the silkiest product of Cliphausen! He could land wool from Sydney or Hobart Town cheaper than from Vienna or Leipsic, and his fellows predicted a complete triumph of the soft wool of the South.[3]

The result was immediate. In 1821, Australia sent 175,400 pounds of wool away to England, and then, following the preferential reduction of duty from the commencement of 1823, an average of 400,000 pounds a year until the bumper-year of 1826, when the imports passed the million mark—1,106,300 pounds.[4] From this point, there was no looking-back. Up and up jumped the figures, until the two-million mark was reached in 1830, and next year, New South Wales and Van Diemen's Land, which between them had sent away only

[3] 1828 Committee, p. 41: Bonwick, *Romance of the Wool Trade* (1887), p. 194.
[4] For details, see Table in Appendix I.

175,000 pounds of wool ten years earlier, were exporting no less than a million and a quarter pounds each! Still the figures rose—to $4\frac{1}{4}$ millions in 1835, seven millions in 1837, and over ten in 1839, when Australia was beaten only by Germany in introducing wool to England.

Australian wool was now definitely established on the market: Spain had gone, America was declining in this field, English wool was still far from being a commercial proposition, and the field was cleared for the struggle between Germany and Australia for supremacy. Already, Australia had topped the market for quality and had ousted Germany from all save the specially fine lines: and now, the issue was joined for a fight to control the English market over its whole range in quality—and for its total in quantity!

III   *The Australian Fight With Foreign Wool*

It has been seen how Australian wools had established themselves on the English market during the twenties and how they had triumphed over the massed forces of indifference and misrepresentation. At first, they had been an experiment but, by 1830, they had become a national feature with which England was confronting German competition. They had successfully tried themselves, both as regards production in sufficient quantity and suitability for the newer manufacturing processes: now, it only remained for them to convert the recognition they had hardly gained into a supremacy over all others.

This resolved itself into a prolonged fight with South Germany— ambitious though such a project may sound for a struggling convict-settlement twelve thousand miles away, and practically hemmed into two small coastal settlements, with an unknown but supposedly inhospital interior. The odds seemed too great and were in no wise lessened by the metropolitan indifference which set in when Liverpool's dying Ministry set to work to repeal the protective Navigation Laws and expose the infant colonies to the full competition of Free Trade. Yet the Australian growers had to triumph or else be continually exposed to uncertainty—to the fear that they would not be able to dispose of their product at reasonable prices. The Saxon farmers quickly realized, therefore, that the special investigations of the 1828 Committee, supported as they were by the English manufacturers, meant open warfare. *The two million pounds of colonial wool shall become ten, and even twenty!* asserted the English; *Germany shall alter her flocks and change her methods to expel the*

Australians from every specific class of the English demand, as she had done the Spaniards, retorted the Saxons, as they proceeded to revolutionize their methods of production.

The position was fascinating. The romance, even from the German side, was quite as striking as in Australia, and, moreover, their wools were quite as new. Before the Napoleonic Wars, Germany had had few merinos. It was not until the French occupied Spain and exported the exclusive merino-flocks in large numbers that the northern countries could put their hands on the jealously-guarded Escurial flocks. This diffusion of merino-blood proved not the least of the Bonapartist benefits to Europe, however the Spaniards suffered in the process, for it completely transformed the methods of sheep-breeding over most of the Continent. The German States, for instance, rapidly studied the new breeds between 1805 and 1815, and began to compare and contrast the merino with ordinary wools and to concentrate on producing the fine-woolled merino flocks.

In the first ten years of peace, this desire for fineness became almost an obsession—fineness, and more fineness, were asked for, and, if softness could be produced in addition, as with the far-famed Electoral stock, so much the better. It was thus not to be wondered at that the typical German animal, especially in Silesia— the most important province, where these tendencies were carried to extremes—became a delicate production with an unbelievably fine fleece, but, for the rest, almost useless. Overbred for one particular, it was a physical weakling, deficient in wool, meat, and vigour.[5]

The advent of a million pounds of colonial wool to the English market and the praise bestowed on it by the expert witnesses before the Committee of 1828 combined with other set-backs to make the Silesians once more consider their position. Their spindly sheep seemed scarcely able to stand and were almost transparent; what extra fineness they had obtained had been at the expense of softness, elasticity, and strength. Moreover, the price of wool fell so rapidly that it no longer paid to concentrate on quality alone. Manufacturers were demanding a wool of average fineness and softness, like the best Botany Bay product—the famous J.M.A. brand of Camden—and the Germans had been gravitating away from this norm.

Their response to the challenge was as immediate as their recognition of past error and, from just before 1830, they began to change their methods and objectives. To compensate for the almost cataclys-

---

[5] For this story, see report of the American Commissioner in Silesia, 1845, in full, in T. Southey, *The Rise, Progress, and Present State of Colonial Wools* (2nd edition, 1851), p. 30, *et seq.*

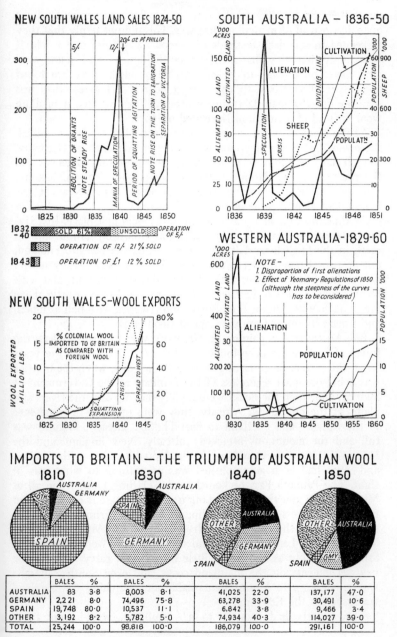

NEW SOUTH WALES LAND SALES 1824-50

5/-   12/-   20/- at Pt PHILLIP

ABOLITION OF GRANTS
NOTE STEADY RISE

MANIA OF SPECULATION

PERIOD OF SQUATTING AGITATION

NOTE RISE ON THE TURN TO EMIGRATION

SEPARATION OF VICTORIA

1832-40 SOLD 61%   UNSOLD OPERATION OF 5/-
OPERATION OF 12/- 21% SOLD
1843 OPERATION OF £1 12% SOLD

SOUTH AUSTRALIA – 1836-50

'000 ACRES   '000   '000

ALIENATED LAND   CULTIVATED LAND

ALIENATION

SPECULATION

CRISIS

SHEEP

CULTIVATION

DIVIDING LINE

POPULATION   SHEEP

POPULAT'N

NEW SOUTH WALES–WOOL EXPORTS

WOOL EXPORTED MILLION LBS.

% COLONIAL WOOL IMPORTED TO GT BRITAIN AS COMPARED WITH FOREIGN WOOL

CRISIS

SPREAD TO WEST

SQUATTING EXPANSION

WESTERN AUSTRALIA-1829-60

'000 ACRES

ALIENATED LAND   CULTIVATED LAND

NOTE –
1. Disproportion of first alienations
2. Effect of Yeomanry Regulations of 1850 (although the steepness of the curves has to be considered)

ALIENATION

POPULATION

CULTIVATION

POPULATION '000

IMPORTS TO BRITAIN — THE TRIUMPH OF AUSTRALIAN WOOL

1810   1830   1840   1850

AUSTRALIA GERMANY OTH
SPAIN

AUSTRALIA SPAIN GERMANY

AUSTRALIA OTHER GERMANY SPAIN

OTHER AUSTRALIA SPAIN GMY

	BALES	%	BALES	%	BALES	%	BALES	%
AUSTRALIA	83	3·8	8,003	8·1	41,025	22·0	137,177	47·0
GERMANY	2,221	8·0	74,496	75·8	63,278	33·9	30,491	10·6
SPAIN	19,748	80·0	10,537	11·1	6,842	3·8	9,466	3·4
OTHER	3,192	8·2	5,782	5·0	74,934	40·3	114,027	39·0
TOTAL	25,244	100·0	98,818	100·0	186,079	100·0	291,161	100·0

The position of Australian wool in the
thirties and forties

mic fall in prices, they tried to make the fleece larger and sought
quantity instead of meticulous fineness. This did not imply that they
descended to slap-dash methods or turned away from fine wool: it
was simply that they abated their scientific desire for ultra-fine wool
and gave preference to a marketable product that combined
quantity and vigour with the utmost degree of fineness that was
requisite for the manufacturing processes. They wanted a medium
wool, instead of a ridiculously refined product.

At the moment when the issue with Australian wools was joined,
these modified Saxon merinos were in great demand in Germany,
though more in Silesia than in Saxony, because mismanagement and
the pressure of population on the commons had displaced Saxony.
The scene of the most progressive experiments of twenty years before,
it now had yielded pride of place to Silesia.

At that time, Germany as a whole easily held first place. In 1834,
for instance, the year when Australia was almost on its four-million
mark in the English market, Germany sent 62,553 bales to England,
out of a total import of 136,277 bales. Australia was already second
on the list, but far down, with 16,279 bales to her credit, and with
Spain down to 14,000. Barbary and Turkey stood next, a little above
New South Wales alone; then Russia and America with half as much,
and a mere fragment from the Cape of Good Hope.

But Australia was gaining on Germany year by year, and all the
forces of Nature for once fought on her side. These were the years
when the system of 'squatting' was in its hey-day, when the interior
was being occupied regardless of the mandate of the Government at
Sydney, and when the flocks were rapidly moving over the rivers and
plains of the far inland. Already, they were up the Murrumbidgee
to the Murray and overland to Port Phillip: already, Monaro was
full and the mountains attacked: already, New England and the
Liverpool Ranges were meeting the flat-footed invaders in the north:
and what had been accomplished was as nothing to what was in
sight. The Pandora Pass beckoned to the Darling Downs and all of
Moreton Bay; and the *Major's Line* urged flockmasters on to the yet
unoccupied rivers of Port Phillip; and the Murrumbidgee rolled
turgidly on to the unmastered dry plains of the Murray-junction.
Van Diemen's Land was full, and the sheepmen were crossing the
Strait as quickly as the tubby little boats could carry them to the
new settlements on the mainland coast, and even South Australia
was moving up to Mount Remarkable and watching the overland
tracks across the Kooyong.

The exports had swollen to 3½ millions, wool-buyers fairly

besieged squatters on all the trunk-roads of the colony, and men talked of bales and ships for five millions this year, eight next, and ten the year after. *Put everything in four feet*, they cried; English capital was pouring in, the seasons were good, and stock and wool at very high figures. The whole of Australia was in a ferment of sheep-growing. Men spoke of sheep and dreamed of sheep: they lived in an atmosphere of sheep unbelievable to one unacquainted with the inexorable directness of colonial life and the unbounded optimism of expectations in a new land. They had the men, the sheep, the land, the ships, and now England was sending the capital in no niggardly quantities (witness the new Banks and Credit Companies!). A man could borrow on his own name—and so the fever quickened.

Meanwhile, in Germany, conditions had become worse. Saxony, having given to the world its improved merinos, had surrendered. Industrialization and the pressure of population had made sheep-growing a dwindling occupation, and what had already happened here threatened the whole of pastoral Germany. Even Silesia, the centre of resistance though it had been in the thirties, was feeling the rise of new forces. No pasture land was left, the commons had been divided, and the old right of depasturing stock on peasants' land existed no longer. No increase in numbers was possible in Silesia, reported an American commissioner who investigated the German position in 1845, the only scope for improvement was in quality. The farmers were turning to cattle, because it was ruinous under the new conditions to think of reserving an acre for every sheep, and the land could graze no more.

Every province told the same story. The German sheep-walks were diminishing in every year of the forties, and the producers thinking of grain-crops. Australia had the land, and, as for transport, it actually cost less for wool to go from Sydney to London than from the south of Germany, because the export-trade to Australia in the boom-period was so vast that many bottoms were faced with the prospect of returning home in ballast, unless they took cargo at abnormally low figures.

The issue was thus a foregone conclusion by 1840. Australian exports to England once more jumped up at an amazing rate—from four million pounds in 1835 to ten in 1839, thirteen in 1842, seventeen in 1844, twenty-four in 1845—and the supply still seemed without a visible end in sight! The only German answer—the only answer an old country could give, when it had an increasing population and a constant subdivision of the land—was a diminished output, both relatively and actually. In 1840, Australia countered

Germany's 63,278 bales by 41,025 (ten years earlier, she had produced scarcely a tenth of the German output!), whereas, in 1850, she poured in 137,177 bales to Germany's 30,491.[6]

The rout was complete. The victory was so crushing as almost to lead the observer to cry for mercy on an embarrassed old-world country; but the bounty of nature in a new world knows no such chivalry, and still the greasy, smelling bales of Australian wool poured out of the holds of the new rakish clippers, and still the squatters, now safely and permanently ensconced in their station-holdings, added to their flocks and turned to new lands, this time to the lower Darling, the Namoi, the lands north of Mount Remarkable, and even the Murchison in the far west of the continent. Germany perforce had given up the struggle, the final blow coming when the combing wools of the Antipodes began to compete on the German home-market. Already in 1845, firms near Meningen had to face the logic of facts and import wool in large quantities—the victim was not only beaten, but impishly mistreated!

[6] *South Australian Record*, 8 August 1840. For the demand see J. Adamson's letters in the *Riley Manuscripts*, Mitchell Library, Sydney, 25 November 1843, 2 December 1844.

3

THE ORIGIN OF SQUATTING

IT HAS BEEN SEEN how conditions both inside the colony and in the Old World combined to effect a vast expansion of settlement in Australia just when the convict-stage was ending. In England, especially after 1828, the demand for colonial wool continued unabated, and, once the eclipse of the home-flocks was taken for granted, English wool brokers even favoured the colonial product as against the German.

Concurrently with this demand for Australian products, attention had been focused on the Antipodes by the 'systematic colonizers' who, under Edward Gibbon Wakefield, were advocating a bridge between homeland and colonies—a connection by means of which the surplus labour and capital of the one could join and fructify the surplus land of the other. England had fully recovered by this time from the 'mania year' of 1825 and had much capital seeking a field of investment.

This surplus money was sent to New South Wales all through the thirties, the high return received by the first allotments swelling each successive stream. A foretaste of this influx of capital had already moved stock-prices up to absurd levels in the years after 1825, when prices were determined almost entirely by the frantic bidding of capitalists with too much money, and scarcely, if at all, by the intrinsic worth of the cattle and sheep offered. The new Banks and Trust Companies helped all this by making money too easily available and, since they could only discount bills, they directly profited by an increase in the advances to settlers and merchants. It was a merry movement of inflation that the migration of capital had engendered —and it must be borne in mind that the displacement of labour, or even of moneyed immigrants, foreseen by the Wakefield theory, had not kept pace with the movement of capital. Wakefield had emphasized a harmony: what happened in practice was that capital, and still more capital, was sent out, but, with the exception of the new colony of South Australia, it was unaccompanied by sufficient immigrants. The consequence was that practically anybody could obtain money from the banks on his personal note; and naturally the borrowers convinced themselves that they could pay the exorbitant rates of interest.

Thus far, the position was clear. Stock were plentiful after the long succession of good years and the keen demand, and sheep had been improved in stamina and quality by the new Saxon merinos. Money was available for any reputable person to buy this stock, even at the high prices then ruling, because men spoke of profits of 50 per cent and other absurd amounts in a single year. There was assigned convict-labour and a fair sprinkling of immigrants. In short, everything was in Sydney except the grazing grounds—and, in that connection, the position was so simple, so very obvious, that its very simplicity made people wonder why they had not seen the solution earlier.

It will be remembered that the Government believed in a policy of *concentration of settlement* and really thought that neither communal nor individual interests were furthered by any dispersion over the unknown wastes of the interior. The benefits of civilized life, effective protection, the amenability of the population (and especially a convict population) to the law, and the safeguarding of Government interests—all of these could be obtained only if settlement was in circumscribed areas. Macquarie, for instance, had been very chary in allowing settlement to cross the Blue Mountains; Darling had laid down the Counties with the specific aim of preventing the spread of occupation; and Bourke, though ready to consider any new situation as it arose, was inclined to follow his predecessor. His superiors at home—Stanley, Aberdeen, and Glenelg alike—were all keen upon the theory of concentration, especially now that land could only be obtained by purchase; and the Wakefield theory, which was based on this idea of preventing any premature dispersion, was at the height of its popularity. In answering the claim to settle Twofold Bay with Ulstermen, Aberdeen had clearly stated in December 1834, that

His Majesty's Government are not prepared to authorize a measure the consequence of which would be to spread over a still further extent of Territory a Population which it was the object of the late Land Regulations (Ripon's Sales Regulations of 1831) to concentrate.

And this policy Bourke approved, though he was in favour of the specific venture mentioned. When Batman's party from Van Diemen's Land occupied Port Phillip, for instance, he strongly protested.

But the problem had already entered a new phase. The stockmen had perceived the obvious weakness of the Government's position.

The very emphasis the Administration placed upon concentration showed how they feared dispersion, and the pioneer stock-holders, looking round and perceiving a fifth of the old Counties already alienated and the remainder largely bad or mountainous land, saw that nothing could prevent them from going beyond the boundaries. It was notorious that the Government could not afford adequate police protection even to the settled districts and that the redcoats at Sydney had to stay there to keep the convict-population in check. In other words, the lands beyond the Counties were lying idle for whosoever cared to drive stock across to them. The Government could not prevent such a movement, if it placed every man it had on the hundreds of miles of boundary; its disapproval could not stop the production of bales of wool; and its general attitude mattered as little as its early mandates of prohibition. A man with sheep or cattle could go anywhere. He asked nothing from the Government, his survival was on his own head, and, if the Government was demanding five or twelve shillings an acre for land within the official bounds of settlement, with millions of acres of dream-lands available outside, he had no other choice. Necessity and inclination pointed in the same direction, and outside the boundaries they trooped!

Such an outcome had been inevitable from the beginning—for the pioneer Australian squatter was the first saffron-clad convict to break from the Rosehill stockade and drive off some Government stock into the scraggy Cumberland bush. The crossing of the Blue Mountains and the increase of stock on the coastal lands pointed the lesson: and, when John Howe crossed the unknown territory between the Hawkesbury and the Hunter in 1819, and found grass on the lowlands 'equal to the meadows in England', the squatting process was already fully developed. Howe's followers drove stock to the new lands—to the Hunter River districts—and, in epitome, this was what happened all over Australia in the next thirty years. *New land* was for ever being reported, with all the exaggerations of the unknown, and stockmen as readily undertook the hazardous task of turning their backs on settlement and pointing their bullock-drays towards some hazy spot beyond the ranges,

> And rode for the Range's outward fall,
> Where the dingo's trail was the only track.
> Slow through the clay-pans, wet to the knee,
> With the cane-grass whistling overhead;
> Swift o'er the plains with never a tree;
> Up the cliffs by a torrent's bed.
>
>   Mary Hannay Foott, *New Country*

Oxley traversed the northern rivers, Alan Cunningham covered the New England coast in 1827, the Murrumbidgee loomed out of the unknown in the late twenties; and in each case, there was the same feverish rush, the same outward movement, the same turning away from the furthest outpost. Down each coast, along each inland river, went pioneers intolerant of a restrictive Government and seeking new pastures for their rapidly increasing flocks, either along explorers' tracks or cutting a way for themselves.

By 1830, some 15,000 head of cattle were feeding on the Murrumbidgee, and the Hunter River was already a well-settled district and no longer deemed a frontier zone; and, by the time of Major Mitchell's expedition across to Port Phillip five years later, the spaces in between were fairly well filled. Bourke, in 1835, for instance, found the country between St Vincent's and Twofold Bay filled with flocks and herds, and Mitchell had been in settled land up to Boree, west of Bathurst, and was pointing to excellent pasture on the Bogan, further out. Yet these were only typical instances. The agitations for townships at Twofold Bay and Port Phillip were thus not theoretical demands, but simply requests for the Government to take cognisance of something that had already been effected; it was not the foundation so much as the coping stone on the building already erected! In other words, as Bourke pointed out, the Government could only acquiesce in that which it could not prevent, for, even if it were resolved not to encourage such dispersion, it could not hinder it; nor, he added, would all the theories of concentration that had ever been postulated make such a course of repression available! The flocks were already there and the camp-fires were out further each night, and no other fact counted.

In this way, the various factors above-mentioned united in a movement that could not be held back. Pioneering spirits, capital, stock, labour and land were all available: the result was the occupation of the untracked interior. What was afterwards known as THE SQUATTING MOVEMENT was thus engendered, and was already enjoying a lusty life by 1835. The upshot was now only a matter of time— the most difficult steps had been taken and the issue practically decided.

But here we must pause and go back. It has been stated that, in the twenties, New South Wales was a colony organized along deceptively simple lines. Its population consisted of a vast majority of persons who were, or who had been, convicts: the remainder were a few settlers of good social position, either favoured immigrants or ex-officials: and the only extraneous feature was in the presence of a mere sprinkling of free immigrants, of much lower social and economic standing. For all practical purposes, the community was divided into convict-servants and a minority of landed proprietors who had received their holdings under the system of free grants then in vogue. Expirees of good behaviour could receive small blocks in the country immediately around Sydney, but most of the estates were relatively large and held by upper-class *seigneurs*—men of the type of Macarthur, Bowman, Riley, Wentworth, and the like. Something approaching a feudal system had been implanted, and any intruder of smaller rank, any yeoman-farmer for instance, was given short shrift. The early settlement of New South Wales was thus intensely aristocratic—the Macarthurs of Camden were the type of landed magnate.

The increase of the twenties merely aggravated this state of affairs. There were very few immigrants, and most of them preferred to stop in the town. It was very difficult for small men to get good land, when most of the accessible areas had been seized by favourites of the authorities; and, moreover, settlement was a costly business in this freehold stage. Convict-servants were usually the appendage of wealth and social position, just as much as the area of the grant was; while the stock, especially after the boom of 1825, ran up to absurd figures. It was no wonder, then, that New South Wales consisted of huge estates, of the type ridiculed by the popular news-sheets of the thirties.

But all of this changed with the growth of emigration from England, with the increase in the number of emancipists, and with the illicit move of the stockmen towards the bush. The lower classes, objecting to the feudalistic structure that had emerged, simply placed themselves on small holdings, sometimes legally by purchase or lease, but usually without any man's permission. Exactly the same argument that appealed to the larger stockholders applied on a smaller scale to these men. Land was there for the taking, and the Government could not remove everybody! The force of this was soon perceived and the entire colony was riddled by the settlement of small men on favoured spots—on places where they could farm, or raise stock, or steal other men's stock, or sell grog, or raise *cribs* as bush resting-places, or do a thousand and one things that sufficed to carry on their brutish existence.

With a population of 50,000 freemen and many hundreds loose on tickets-of-leave, and with the prices of land and stock beyond what any poor man could honestly pay, it was not very strange that thousands should live more or less predatory lives of this kind, especially as settlement progressed inland and effective surveillance became increasingly difficult. Labour in those days was curiously mobile, convicts were taking to the bush and could secure an existence now that pastoral establishments were dotted down in the interior; and, all in all, the dubious characters tended to leave the ill-farmed *purlieus* on the north shore of Sydney township and go inland. Gangs could loot the respectable establishments, or at the least, harry the stock; individuals could erect shanties to serve as grog-shops or resthouses for wandering labourers; and so-called settlers could cover their 'bushranging' and stealing activities with a mask of legitimate stock-raising. There were no strong graziers' combinations, the police were confined to the settled districts, and it was difficult to identify stolen sheep and cattle.

This unsavoury class became the chief menace to legitimate settlement in the early thirties and were regular camp-followers of any movement that had pastoral expansion as its goal. They harassed the stock-owners and conspired with their servants, they rendered property and at times even life uncertain, they haunted the bush-tracks like so many evil scarecrows. Scarcely a mail-coach got through from Yass or the Hunter without some tale of new pillaging. Everywhere, too, they erected sapling stockyards and, more or less openly, gathered stock—*clearskins*, or unbranded animals from the bush, unmarked calves from their mothers, and even branded or ear-clipped stock from neighbouring settlers. The bush was thick, its tracks little-known, and every region of timber or mountainous tangles became a looter's paradise. At times, they openly defied the larger settlers, relying on their stocks of execrable Indian rum to spread disaffection among the convict-servants, and forcing the masters, by mere pressure of numbers and distance from police and magistrates, to submit to their outrages. On other occasions, they pretended to be respectable settlers on a small scale, but their flocks increased at an enormous rate and without the aid of any outside capital! In all cases alike, the larger stockmen suffered and knew no redress, except superior strength.

Such vagabonds were known as *squatters*, and, in the middle thirties, the term was universally used as one of opprobrium. There is not the slightest doubt as to either the meaning attached to the term or the extent of its use. It was the direst insult to call a man 'a squatter'—even worse than challenging him with the taint of convictism, because not all the convicts were petty sneak-thieves. The looting by 'squatters' was the lowest form of villainy conceivable at that time in the colony: it was an idea opposed to that of respectability, or even of enterprising crime!

Nor did it have anything to do with the limits of location or the boundaries of the Nineteen Counties. Any man who lived a precarious existence by means of his neighbour's stock was a 'squatter', whether in the settled districts or on the furthest outpost of explored land. There were 'squatters' just outside Sydney itself, as well as on the Hunter and the Murrumbidgee. Indeed, practically all of the trouble that was ventilated before the Committee of 1835[1] was concerned with the settled land *within* the boundaries! A squatter was simply a person who illicitly occupied Crown land in the vicinity of alienated estates and plundered the flocks and herds. By implication, when the larger settlers moved part of their establishments to the outer lands and dispensed with the formality of freehold, the term was extended to the same class of dishonest persons; but, at the outset, it meant anyone who lived on the fringe of a big estate and acquired a living by dubious means.

This was the common significance of the word when the evil began to attract notice in 1835—when the entire colony was threatened by a plague of pests of ill-repute. The *Sydney Gazette*, for instance, in a long leader of 28 April 1835, summed the matter up very clearly and forcibly, in saying that,

The system of *squatting* has lately increased to an alarming extent; and cattle-stealing and every other crime that not only tends to demoralize the moral population, but to increase the general insecurity of property, continues to keep pace, in a remarkable manner, with an evil against which the Governor has hitherto strangely neglected to apply any radical or alleviating remedy.

Its turgid and involved sentences were the more convincing, because this paper usually supported the Government and, being in the hands of convict-editors, was not at all inclined to attack the lower classes.

In every part of the country, *squatters* without any reasonable means of maintaining themselves by honesty, have formed stations, and evidently pursue a predatory warfare against the flocks and herds in the vicinity.

Then it concludes, in a tone of unmitigated condemnation, 'we have seen and unavailingly deplored the evils of squatters'. Another paper spoke of 'squatters—*anglicé*, den of thieves!'; and practically every news-sheet, even in this age of cut-throat journalism, joined

[1] *Council Committee on Police and Gaol Establishments* (A. M'Leay, chairman), several reports, June-October 1835—the copious evidence is the primary source for this section.

in the cry. In a convict community, where safety depended on the maintenance of order among the felons and emancipists, such a movement, amounting as it did to a tacit insurrection, could not be lightly passed over.

So obvious was the menace and so rapidly was it increasing, that the Legislative Council appointed a Committee to report on the police and gaol establishments, with special reference to the increase of crime in the outer districts. Led by the Colonial Secretary, M'Leay, this body reported in the months between June and October of 1835, and gathered a strikingly unanimous body of evidence, which showed how the same evil had emerged in every part of the colony where grazing was on the increase. All the witnesses agreed in emphasizing the extent of the land-piracy, in deploring the absence of police-protection, and in terming the intruders 'squatters'—an important point since so many commentators have been needlessly confused on the origin of squatting and the first meaning of the term. A 'squatter' was a villain and a thief: he was the convict in whose hands the changing pastoral conditions were placing the stock of the colony as loot—the thief who found a better opening in the bush than the city. This point is fundamental, and the evidence of both the Police Committee and the Immigration Committee of the same year leaves no vestige of doubt about it. It was not that some shady members of the pioneers were called 'squatters' together with the respectable, far from it. A respectable grazier would have taken his musket or kangaroo-whip to anybody who dared term his class 'squatters', because that was a term of reproach signifying only criminals.

Settlers and officials of all degrees and all political opinions bore evidence on this point. Terence Aubrey Murray, for example, a son of a Lake George pioneer, and himself a magistrate and afterwards a knight, showed how even the comparatively older settlements of the south were terrorized by such men, who could almost be described as 'bushrangers with a base'. Speaking moderately, he reported that 'there are several parties of squatters in my neighbourhood'; that he had 'strong reason to suspect that these people are, in general, illicit sellers of spirits'; and that nothing could be done to check their open or covered depredations. They were either thieves themselves or 'fences' receiving stock stolen by servants, and sometimes even full-time raiders. 'The squatters are, in general, serious nuisances in the neighbourhood. We have no means of getting rid of them; and it is almost impossible to convict them of the crimes which they are in the habit of committing.'

Why this was so was made clear by the evidence of W. H. Dutton, a Yass magistrate. Even if evidence could be collected (a proceeding almost impossible in bush-country) and if witnesses could be collected to swear against the concerted perjury of the squatters, the whole assemblage had to travel from the Yass district to Monaro or Rose's station on the Murrumbidgee before the trial could take place—a distance of either 120 or 100 miles, with temptations of drink, bribery, and force the whole way. Moreover, the emancipist or convict who would alienate his class in a community as faction-ridden as the New South Wales of 1835 was flirting with death in an unpleasant form: it must ever be remembered that the great bulk of the population were present or past convicts and were opposed to the great landed proprietors by their every inclination. In addition, since the recent reforms, the juries were usually composed of ex-convicts with whom gentlemen would not sit and who could thus acquit their fellow-felons at their wish!

As Dutton pointed out, the position was unavoidable—a kind of reflex of the convict-structure of society, especially in the newly-settled outskirts where the law did not run.

I regret to add that there can be but little doubt of the fact of food and shelter being readily afforded to bushrangers, in many instances, in this district, by squatters; and the facility with which men becoming free can, as such, occupy Crown lands in the immediate vicinity of their former masters, or as ticket-of-leave holders, hiring themselves as labourers and stock-keepers already established, has become a source of great and increasing evil. These persons are almost invariably the instigators and promoters of crime—receivers of stolen property—illegal vendors of spirits, and harbourers of runaways, bushrangers, and vagrants. The congeniality of habits between master and man, the absence of all restraint, and the predatory life they lead while collecting stolen cattle, has a charm for them which even considerably higher wages in the service of respectable employers will not induce them to quit. They keep up a constant intercourse with our assigned servants and, knowing the weak points of each establishment, seize their opportunity and commit depredations, especially upon cattle, with impunity. I am convinced that all of the petty pilferings occurring on our properties might be traced, directly or indirectly, to the agency of the squatters.[2]

Thus, it is clear, the word 'squatter' was definitely employed to designate this class of small men who pestered the larger holders. The squatters were not small settlers as such, because some witnesses spoke in juxtaposition of 'a thick population of small settlers and numerous squatters', and of 'new settlers and squatters': what made

[2] 1835 Committee, June Report, p. 23 of evidence.

them squatters was the fact of being bush harpies. The term 'settler', on the other hand, was a mark of honesty. A man might have a large or a small holding, it might be freehold or occupied without any legal grant, but, so long as he was a 'settler', his honour was not impugned. The rural population was clearly divided into *settlers* (small or large, as the case might be) and *squatters*, and it would be quite erroneous to say that the former were land-owners and the latter only occupiers. That was not the difference at all. A squatter was a man of ill-fame, whether he had a small slab-shanty with a cellar of grog or a large establishment built up on a basis of 'lifted' or stolen stock.

The evidence went on to multiply itself. Captain Phillip King, a naval officer settled in Murray County near the southern limit of official occupation, expressed himself in unmeasured terms. Though a magistrate himself, he could do nothing against these malefactors and usually had to go fifty-five miles away to Goulburn, because the magistrate nearer to him at Lake George was, as a rule, inaccessible. The region in general was 'numerously inhabited by small proprietors and squatters, who are in general sly-grog sellers and connected with bushrangers'. Then he went on, with some asperity:

I cannot express myself too strongly on the subject of squatters. The mischief they do is almost incalculable. They harbour the settler's run-away convicts: they steal his cattle and sheep: they sell spirits *on the sly*: they entice shepherds from the care of their sheep: they shelter and feed bushrangers, and afford them information (and, to point his evidence, armed bands were even then 'holding up,' not only the isolated holdings, but even the townships of his district!).

Here again was the distinction between 'settlers' and 'squatters', and the good gentleman, though his ire destroyed his grammar, added:

I think that the interference of the Legislature is highly necessary to protect the landed and stock proprietors of the interior; for, under the present system, no honest man can contend against, and as long as they are permitted to occupy stations, so long will the interior be infested by bushrangers and bad characters, and the free and convict servants in a state of insubordination and drunkenness.

King obviously meant the squatters, and not the landed proprietors, as the butt of his condemnation; and he certainly had every right, as a southern land-owner, to complain of the existing state of uncertainty.

Captain King, an associate of Governors and the Macarthurs, was clearly a reactionary Tory; Sir John Jamison was a knightly person associated with the liberal reforming party of Wentworth, yet he, too, swelled the chorus of complaint. He wanted the strictest measures 'to prevent pauper free and freed men from squatting in such unlocated situations, to live by stealing stock and other dishonest means'. To accomplish this, reformer though he was, democrat though he professed himself, he urged the despatch of itinerant magistrates, with clerks, scourgers, and mounted police, all complete! Because how else, he argued, could intruders and criminals be kept from harrassing the widely-scattered estates, with anything from thirty to two hundred miles from the nearest magistrate?

Equally clear was Thomas Icely, a different type of settler. Still a young man, he had almost twenty years of colonial experience behind him and possessed that combination of common sense and energy that had made him a successful merchant, now a grazier. Speaking of the country south-west of Bathurst—that is, in the west, comparatively close to the centres of population and not an isolated post—he said:

In that part of the country I have mentioned, a very great number of squatters reside. These people are very serious nuisances to the respectable settlers and are the chief promoters of crime in their neighbourhood.

After confirming the evidence of every preceding witness that they were notorious sly-grog men and receivers, he sensibly argued that 'the very short periods in which they become possessed of large herds of cattle sufficiently prove that they are also cattle-stealers'. No issue could have been of greater gravity in the eyes of this man of affairs, because not only was property imperilled at the moment, not only was a perpetual uncertainty involved, but these depredations were building up a state of mind that could only be subversive of future peace. A community depraved by this idea of rapidly acquiring stock by illicit means was placing a premium on dishonesty: it was like offering the shops of Cheapside to the pick-pockets of St Giles and Wapping, and taking away the threat of gaol!

Other witnesses followed. Andrew Gibson, a Southern magistrate and obviously a simple, straightforward pioneer, spoke of 'the daily increasing number of squatters', and said that 'almost all the people who obtain their freedom in the district locate themselves in it as squatters', though, penniless as they are, their services can never be obtained by the neighbouring graziers! The chain of evidence was complete—representative land-owners of all political beliefs told of terrorism and annoyances in every district. In the Hunter River to the north (where Supreme Court trials were even then pending), in the Bathurst lands to the west, and to the furthest limit of Murray country in the south, was the same story. It is true that all of the witnesses were interested land-owners, and certain that not all of the small men grouped under the common opprobrium of *squatterdom* were villains; but, as against this, it seemed patent that to fling convicts into freedom and leave them to wander through a bush which was even then being occupied by graziers who were beyond police protection was a fatal course of procedure. Under these conditions, the squatting system, in the form in which it was then known, was inevitable. Such a cancerous growth had to accompany the extension of settlement in a convict-colony.

The Committee ultimately issued a very disjointed report in several parts and concealed its findings so effectively that successive historians have found great difficulty in even discovering its conclusions. Run to earth, however, its reference to the squatting system in its early days is full of historical interest and best sums up the position and people included within that term in 1835. After regretting that there were only 111 mounted police for patrolling half a continent, and showing that no fewer than 220 bushrangers and runaways had been apprehended in the preceding five months, the *Report* stated:

And finally, your Committee would direct your attention to the fact that the interior of the Colony is infested by gangs of cattle-stealers and other disorderly persons whose depredations are carried on to an alarming extent. These groups consist of freed men who have served short sentences, or those of long sentence holding Tickets-of-Leave, who combine with the assigned servants to plunder the herds of their masters. The nefarious practices of these men are greatly facilitated by the system of taking unauthorized possession of Crown Land, or *Squatting*, which now prevails. It appears that many convicts who become free by servitude, or who hold the indulgence of Tickets-of-Leave, take possession of Crown Lands in remote districts, and thus, screened from general observation, erect huts for their temporary purposes and become what is generally termed *Squatters*. These people move from place to place, as suits their convenience, and conceal their practices whilst they raise a property by committing depredations on the neighbouring flocks and herds; or by selling spirits and providing other inducements for thieving, gaming, and every species of debauchery, seduce the servants of established settlers to assist in their lawless proceedings. Many of these men are known to possess large herds of cattle obtained in a very short time, by a series of schemes for stealing them, which cannot be detected or prevented, so long as they are permitted to move from one part of the country to another and take uncontrolled possession of remote and unfrequented tracts of grazing ground.[3]

[3] Final report, 9 October 1835, p. 44. Compare *Immigration Committee*, 1835, evidence, p. 73.

That leaves no doubt as to the status of the class who were first called *squatters*. A squatter was a person who sat down and raided the properties of respectable settlers. He may even have been a drink-seller with no stock at all; the distinguishing features of his *genus* were dishonesty and locating himself on ground to which he had no title. The latter alone was not sufficient to distinguish him from many large owners who did the same in respect of Crown Land, and yet, being respectable, were not 'squatters'. The possession of stock, it must again be asserted, was at that time only an incidental characteristic. A squatter was not necessarily a stock-owner (though the nature of his situation compelled him to have either stock or rum), and not merely an unauthorized occupant; he was a dishonest man distinguished from his slum-companions in the towns by 'squatting' on lands to which he had no claim. But a rogue alone, and not every man who 'squatted' on Crown land, was a squatter![4]

It was not until about 1835 that this movement had become troublesome in New South Wales and that Government action to check it was being considered. But already the issue was an old one in Van Diemen's Land. There, with the available plains circumscribed in area, and with ideal hiding places in the ranges coming down almost to the sea, even an honest population could not have failed to notice how the configuration of the country was a direct incentive to stock-lifting: and, of course, the outcome was obvious where the worst of the felons of Britain were gathered. Every settled district in the island was at the mercy of organized bushrangers in the twenties, and these gangs of armed men who openly defied the Government and who plundered the countryside at will, from bases in the plains, were called *Squatters* and their holdings *Runs*—even in the mid-twenties.

The terms were so accepted that they were used in Government proclamations, without any explanations attached. In one of Arthur's proclamations of 3 June 1828, for instance, they found their first official use in Australia. The *Order* in question was to limit un-authorized occupation,

which has been the means of keeping up a system of depredation upon the Flocks of respectable Settlers. The practice of *squatting*, as it is denominated in the Colony, has been followed for the most part by freed Convicts possessing Sheep, probably acquired by the most excep-tionable means; and the huts of these people (some ostensibly pur-suing the occupation of Sawyers or Splitters) have been the constant

---

[4] In this sense, see T. H. Braim, *History of New South Wales* (1846), I, p. 235; W. Pridden, *Australia: Its History and Present Condition* (1843), p. 334.

resort of runaway Convicts and others whose characters are of the most vicious stamp, and the area of their *Sheep Runs* has formed a most convenient depot for stolen Sheep.

Four months before, the Lieutenant-Governor had issued an *Order*, defining the evil (but without using the term *Squatters*), warning intruders off Crown Lands and adopting the queer procedure of leasing land to settlers if they undertook to keep off all other persons.[5]

Where this word, *squatter*, came from is not clear. The *Order* and the accompanying despatch make it clear that it first came to Australia through Van Diemen's Land, for it was not until a couple of years later, when the Australian Agricultural Company found intruders on its lands, that it crept into Government correspondence in New South Wales proper. But it did not originate in Australia, or even America, as is commonly supposed. It is an old English word, of medieval origin as far as its stem goes, and was used, especially in Wales and Scotland, to refer to persons who camped on commons or private lands where they had no right. The Sussex gypsies, especially if they settled in one locality for a time, came under the designation of 'squatters'; so too did the dispossessed crofters of the Highlands if they built cottages on vacant lands, and the shepherds in the wilder Welsh hills who merely "sat down' where they happened to find themselves and erected more or less permanent huts.

Its more common use, however, was in America, where the word, though retaining its original significance, obtained a far wider application. Any person who pushed out beyond the few coastal settlements and penetrated to the middle rivers and beyond was a backwoodsman; if he settled in one spot—if he 'squatted down' where he was—he was called a 'squatter'. Later, any man who chose an unoccupied piece of Government land and settled down to build a homestead for himself on his section or half-section was a squatter; and, as the big stockmen pushed west, the term came to be applied in contempt to the small farmer and more particularly to persons who settled either within or on the boundaries of the big ranches, either to build up a home or to harass the stock-owner.

When the squatting problem arose in Australia, however, the American type of squatter was simply a backwoodsman—one who had pushed out beyond the recognized boundaries of settlement and was taking his fate into his own hands. As a Mississippi official wrote

[5] MS. despatch, No. 39/28, Hobart: *Hobart Town Gazette*, 15 March 1828.

in 1800: 'I wish also to be instructed towards these people *squatting* or establishing themselves upon the public lands.' Earlier still, in 1788, Madison had spoken of 'Squatters upon the people's lands', and, from the beginning of the new century, the word was accepted in popular parlance. Its significance was entirely in the act of 'squatting'—in the occupation of unclaimed land. It implied no moral attributes: a squatter was not necessarily good or bad, he was simply an unauthorized occupant. That is made quite clear by the examples collected for the *New England Dictionary*. A citation of 1832 referred to 'that prescriptive tenure which we quaintly call *squatting*'; while Marryat, seven years later, specifically defined squatting as 'taking possession of land belonging to Government and cultivating it'.

But the *Dictionary* has missed instances much further back. Between 1800 and 1820, settlers were moving, despite the Government, into the public lands on both sides of the Ohio and west of the Mississippi. Kentucky and Tennessee were riddled with unauthorized occupants, and the Reserve-lands were filled with residents in every State. The mass of the pioneers engaged in the Western movement knew nothing of land-laws and did not care if they were affected or not—they simply 'squatted'! And this designation was theirs from the time of the first days of independence. Madison, as has been seen, used it; Washington, in 1784, pointed to the action of squatters on the Indian side of the Ohio, the then West!; and the frontiersmen of Virginia and Kentucky who crossed the river and settled by virtue of their 'tomahawk right' were freely termed squatters. The word itself appeared in the *Congressional Debates* in 1806, when 'squatters' in Indiana were referred to. This had been an urgent matter as early as the very first Congress, and there was a considerable feeling that the squatters should have some kind of pre-emptive right. In spite of the Indian forays, whole provinces were opened in what the Government called 'the closed West', and strict laws of 1807 against unauthorized squatting availed little. The President had been given permission to use military force against such squatters in Louisiana in 1804, but soon the tide turned, and by 1820, the Government had so far recognized the system of squatting as to grant a measure of pre-emption to every State and territory except Indiana. By this time, the squatters had developed from trespassers to recognized pioneers, and there was even agitation for a general pre-emptive right to meet the case of every man who had pushed ahead of the legal boundary. The 'squatter' was thus a pioneer who had settled on Crown land without permission—and this meaning had been sanctioned by forty years of usage when the problem arose in an embryonic form in Australia.[6]

It is probable that it first came to Australia with this meaning; but, however this may be, the composition of the colonial population made the first 'squatters' almost entirely rascally convicts. Such men gave to the term a meaning that was primarily concerned with moral values and only secondarily with the act of unauthorized occupation. This was an accidental local interpretation, but it gave the word quite a different connotation from the American usage. The first squatters in America were unauthorized occupants, the first Australian ones men of bad repute who lived in the bush. Then, with the progress of settlement, the American 'squatter' came to be a small settler, either good or bad, in juxtaposition with the larger ranchers, but it was not used in this sense in Australia. Nor, conversely, was it ever used in America, as it afterwards was in Australia, to denote the large and respectable stockmen who utilized vacant Crown Lands, and later still the capitalists who even had their own lands in fee-simple. Squatting was not connected in America with criminals, as it was at first in Australia, or, later, primarily with the act of cattle or sheep-raising on a large scale. Always in America, it was concerned with unauthorized occupation on a small scale. Its interpretation there was, so to speak, on the basis of the lands occupied; whereas, in Australia, it had first a moral signification, and later a vocational one.

In the Australia of 1835, however, there was no doubt as to what constituted a squatter. The Police and Immigration Committees had expressed themselves quite clearly on this point, and the newspapers were following them. The system of squatting, said the *Sydney Gazette* in April 1835, was increasing alarmingly, and meant that 'the seeds of vice, ignorance, and reckless roving will be communicated from father to son'; it referred to them elsewhere as 'dens of thieves'. James Macarthur, in a book that enjoyed a large circulation in England in 1837, referred to 'persons denominated *squatters*, mostly convicts holding tickets-of-leave, or having become free by servitude' and who constituted 'the vortex of crime and depravity' in the colony: and Wentworth and his reformers were holding up the squatters as examples of the results of a bad land-policy. A squatter was a villain, a squatter was a thief; it was almost a refrain, and no respectable man could do otherwise than try to extirpate them.

[6] Payson Treat, *The National Land System*, 1788-1820, references in index to 'squatters'.

But, at this moment, a rapid change occurred. From 1836 onwards, though the first connotation lingered, the word 'squatter' was coming to include persons of respectability as well as bush-looters. Once the flocks began to cross the official boundaries, once persons of all social status began to dabble in 'anything on four legs', the position was changed. Observers looked around and saw men of all stations in life pushing off to the interior with sheep. Army officers, the young sprigs of the Macarthur and Riley trees, immigrants of means, ex-officials all joined in the movement: all sought unoccupied lands within the Nineteen Counties or crossed the boundary and settled on particularly inviting locations outside. Stockmen large and small, honest and villainous, were breaking through the recognized limits of settlement in all directions. They were not concerned with buying land or stopping within the surveyed Counties: all the interior was their hunting-ground, and they settled and erected their huts and sheep-folds wheresoever they listed.

Such a movement was too universal to be lightly passed over. At first, the old nomenclature was extended to the new lands beyond the boundaries: the respectable large holders were 'settlers' and the undesirables 'squatters', but, clearly, this would no longer serve. From the earliest days of the colony, a 'settler' had always been a freeholder; and the term could not with relevancy be extended to the unauthorized graziers beyond the boundaries, however respectable they might be. The fact could not be gainsaid that they were poachers on Crown Lands—unauthorized persons who just 'squatted down' in localities they desired. In a word, they were *squatters*, and, with a somewhat startling rapidity, the word, from symbolizing the dregs of the populace, came to denote the respectable and enterprising settlers who had extended their activities from the freehold lands to the wider fields beyond, and sent their stock out into the Government 'bush'. 'The principal settlers are also the principal squatters,' wrote Judge Therry, Bourke's right-hand man, 'settlers as to their own lands, squatters as to the Crown Lands they occupy!'

A squatter now was a stockman who settled on Crown Lands without any of that land passing into his ownership. The term had less to do with the moral attributes of a given class of persons, until soon it came to mean nothing more than a stockman beyond the boundaries—a stockman who, since the Government forbade the sale of any land outside the settled Counties, was simply occupying Crown land on his own initiative. This more reputable meaning grew apace after 1836, when the Government first placed the system of occupation on some kind of legal basis, and, within a few years, the original meaning was entirely lost, except as an invective in the hands of the squatters' enemies.

No little credit for clearing up this situation must go to the Governor, Sir Richard Bourke.[7] He perceived almost from the first how invidious it was to discriminate between the poor and the rich settlers who dumped down their stock on Crown Lands—the offence, he maintained, was precisely similar in both cases, and the social or economic status of the perpetrator had little, if anything, to do with the matter. Referring to the older class of 'squatters', so detested by the wealthier settlers, he reported in December 1835 that all men were tarred with the same brush. 'It must be confessed that they are only following in the steps of the most influential and unexceptionable colonists, whose sheep and cattle stations are everywhere to be found side by side with the obnoxious squatter, and held by no better title!'

Indeed, Bourke's main trouble in this matter was to prevent the richer squatters raising the bogey of the poor criminal outcasts as a cloak to cover their own depredations on Crown property. They were directing attention to the smaller stock-stealers on the fringes of their own properties to conceal the fact that they themselves were settling in precisely the same manner on large areas, especially now that the boundaries had been crossed. Hence, the almost too perfect concurrence of evidence before the Police and Gaols Committee of 1835, and the too solicitous attitude of the Council, practically every member of which was himself an offender! As a necessary appendix to the attitude of the wealthier settlers and the Police evidence, must be added Bourke's own public statement towards the close of 1835, a statement given full publicity in the *Sydney Monitor*:

My chief difficulty is a fear, I cannot but entertain, lest even those wealthier Settlers, who are most loud in their complaints of the Squatter, should prefer their present unauthorized Title to a lawful one acquired even at the slightest Expense.[8]

Squatting was a different question now that the problem of regulation was being raised, and now that it was impossible for the richer settlers to enlist the aid of the Government to eject their lesser *confrères* while they themselves continued their marauding tactics on a large scale. With rich squatters already across the Murray and be-

[7] For his views, see collection of despatches given by Gipps to the Council, 30 May 1844, in *Votes and Proceedings*, 1844, vol. I.

[8] *Monitor*, 21 November 1835, three columns, an important address. See Bourke-Glenelg, 18 December 1835.

yond New England, with stations far beyond Gundagai on the Murrumbidgee and into the furthest recesses of the Australian Alps at the back of Monaro, it was absurd to stigmatize squatters as a class of convicts.

Gipps was still more emphatic on this point. 'I have not discovered from the Returns of the Magistrates which I called for, that more than from twenty to thirty ticket-of-leave holders occupy Crown Lands throughout the whole Colony, and of these, a great proportion are reported to be particularly industrious and honest.' Of course, this referred only to the settled lands under the surveillance of magistrates, but it was here that the convicts were supposed to be so strong! As for the squatters further out, the Governor was equally explicit. In December 1840—and this statement was true in any of the previous four years—he stated in a carefully prepared memorandum on the land-question that

a very large proportion of the land which is to form the new district of Port Phillip is already in the licensed occupation of the Squatters of New South Wales, a class of persons whom it would be wrong to confound with those who bear the same name in America, and who are generally persons of mean repute and of small means, who have taken unauthorized possession of patches of land. Among the Squatters of New South Wales are the wealthiest of the land, occupying, with the permission of the Government (since 1836), thousands and tens of thousands of acres. Young men of good families and connections in England, officers of the army and navy, graduates of Oxford and Cambridge, are also in no small number amongst them.

By that time, the 'squatter' was clearly the progressive stock-owner beyond the boundaries. As early as June 1835, the *Sydney Gazette* had definitely referred to 'gentleman squatters (that is, the large settlers who have stations far in the interior for the maintenance of their superabundant flocks and herds)'; and, from that moment, the term 'squatter' usually meant an inland grazier. The older grantees were compelled, by the very poverty of their coastal estates, to send stock inland, where the rich pastures easily lured them on; and every new settler, especially when the middle thirties saw a considerable influx of respectable immigrants and capital, naturally bought stock and pushed off into the bush to 'squat'. At first facetiously, they would refer to themselves in Sydney as 'squatters', but the term was so applicable that it soon stuck. The change was hastened by the first Act of 1836, which allowed any respectable man to occupy Crown Lands without placing himself outside the law.

The result was that, whatever an occupant may have been before, he became a squatter after that date—a member of a class including practically every man of means in the colony, and composed of persons who were almost at once bound together in a militant group fighting for what it deemed its rights. A squatter may have been a sheep-stealing outcast before 1835, it may have been a joking term of self-deprecation in 1835 and 1836; but after that year he was a legally recognized occupant of land in the interior—land which he did not own, but over which the Government had yielded him permissive rights of occupancy.

When everybody joined in the movement, when the highest of the land *went in four legs* (that is, bought sheep), any nomenclature, however despised its former application, would have been cleansed. Had it been appropriate, the pioneer stockmen might have been called *canaries* or *lifers*, or any other convict-designation. Whereas, on the other hand, 'squatter' had a very real connection with the act involved, and perhaps had been applied to a section of the convicts only for purposes of propaganda.

And what did it matter when the whole community was stock-mad, and all were singing of the Major's new country to the south, and all either going squatting or envying those who were in a position to 'push out'? As their chants ran : 'It was the time to light up your *duddeen* and get out the bullock-whips, muster the sheep and watch the lambs, out with the dogs and lumber up the dray, and heigh-ho for the South Countree! We are all Squatters—Squatters bad and bold ! Down with the Government, and up with the wool, let squatters roam, and the drays creak on. Heigh for the new countree !'

So the drays went south, and still the recruits poured in to join that exuberant class of overlanders—the 'squatters'. Could the transition be clearer? A squatter had been a convict marauder; he had changed into an unauthorized occupant, irrespective of class; now, he was a licensed man beyond the boundaries; and the day was already dawning when he was likely to be a conservative, opposed to agriculture and to the townsmen. The term had already gone far on its chameleon existence.[9]

[9] A good account of the change is in T. McCombie's *Australian Sketches* (1861), p. 128.

4

THE FIRST REGULATION OF SQUATTING

THE QUESTION of regulating the unauthorized occupants of Crown Lands first arose in an acute form in 1835, when the stockmen were about to enter the new lands of Port Phillip and New England. With the flocks already three hundred miles from Sydney in two directions, it seemed useless to deny the existence or the strength of the new movement; and the only question was how the Government could control and regulate that which it could not prevent. The day of emphasizing the Nineteen Counties was past, they were as archaic in such a rapidly moving colony as were the English theories of concentration of settlement. The movement of the flocks had put an end to all that; and the flocks that were then on the Murray and the Namoi would soon be to the South Australian boundary and the Burnett. This was a convulsive movement that brooked no delay: all that remained for the Government was to choose between aiding the onward sweep or virtually abdicating its authority over most of the land.

The main difficulty was the theory of the day which was based on the assumption that dispersion of settlement meant the ruin of any colony. By 1835, the Wakefieldians had not only won over Downing Street but had actually planned the new colony of South Australia; and they were not likely to stand aside and see in adjacent territory the rise of a movement that was diametrically opposed to everything they stood for, and which would probably drag down their own projected colony. So they first denied the force of the squatting movement and then ruthlessly opposed it.

They were too well organized in that day of indistinct colonial views not to triumph. Wakefield, Torrens, and Rintoul led a strong movement, through the columns of the *Spectator* and the *Colonial Gazette*, while, within the Commons, Molesworth and Buller won over or intimidated each Secretary of State, particularly when they were theorists of the Stanley type, nonentities like Spring Rice and Aberdeen, or weaklings like Glenelg. The peak of their agitation had been reached in the important *Committee on the Disposal of Crown Lands* (1836), which was practically an exposition of Wakefieldian doctrines. It mattered little what practical views were raised against its members: secure in the ignorance of their rounded periods, they theorized—and conquered! The *Quarterly* might thunder and the *Westminster* be lightly dubious, and M'Culloch muster the older economists against such 'a tissue of delusions and contradictions'; but against these, the reformers adduced the *Edinburgh* and the *Spectator*, and evoked Merivale and Mill to speak for the economists. Thus, they maintained their somewhat tortuous path towards the realization of their ideas, or, as it more frequently turned out, towards the hindrance of men on the spot, like Bourke and Gipps.

From the birth of their body, the *National Colonization Society*, in 1830, they had taken a firm stand against what they called the dispersion of settlement, quoting the existing colonies of New South Wales and Swan River as proofs of their contention. In short, they wanted land to be sold instead of granted; the proceeds to go to an emigration-fund to bring in labour; and settlement confined to those regions within which an equilibrium could be maintained between labour, capital, and land—the result being a perfectly balanced society. Labourers were not to be enfranchized too soon, settlers were not to spread over the face of the land and encourage ruder habits of life, and colonial land was to be the bridge between the distress of the old country and the needs of the new. One of their basic assumptions was that a too rapid dispersion of settlement— just such a movement of the flocks and herds as has already been described—was fundamentally undesirable. Dispersion, as the *Westminster Review* said, would 'convert the nation, in short, into a horde of wandering Tartars, living upon milk and flesh, and getting drunk on fermented mare's milk', and would mean a lower type of civilization. In the first statement of his principles in the *Letter from Sydney* (1829), Wakefield aggressively asserted that 'Concentration would produce what never did, and never can, exist without it— CIVILIZATION!'; and the reformers continued on this note throughout.

'Concentration of settlement' was to Wakefield the greatest result of his scheme, and, however much he juggled by defining such concentration as 'a more equable diffusion', such a term in the eyes of the Colonial Office and the local administrators meant absolute geographical limitation. Whatever he may have meant, concentration in practice meant laying 'an iron band' round the Nineteen Counties and forbidding settlement outside. Secretary after secretary insisted on this point, Glenelg in particular stating that the Sales Regulations of Ripon in 1831 had been framed almost entirely with this end in view. Goderich started this emphasis, Aberdeen made a fetish of it, and it lost nothing under Glenelg.

The upshot was that the colonial Governors in the thirties could do anything, as long as they did not allow settlement to creep onwards to new districts! Confronted with the squatting problem, the Colonial Office adduced the eradication of similar menaces in Wales and Scotland, and compared squatting with poaching on the Royal Estates at Windsor! Their oracle Wakefield replied as late as 1836 that 'it seems to me to be just as possible to prevent squatting in a colony as it is to prevent it on the extensive districts of Crown Land in Wales'. New South Wales differed not one whit from old Wales in this regard; and mandate after mandate issued from the Colonial Office ordering Bourke to stamp out the unauthorized settlements that were springing up in places like Portland and Twofold Bay. It could be done, it had to be done, and it was better for the individuals concerned that it should be done—so ran the fiat: and, as for its possibility, had not Wakefield said that 'it is impossible to use waste land without the active assistance of Government'?

In Sydney, Bourke was thus in a quandary. His orders from home left no possibility of doubt. The Colonial Office might differ from Wakefield in many ways, but there was a striking unanimity of opinion on this question of concentrating settlement. Bourke was categorically ordered to assert his power and eradicate the unauthorized settlements of these land-freebooters: otherwise, he would be bringing his Government into disrepute and flouting his superiors at home. But he had few soldiers, and the squatters were spread over a bush territory of perhaps 120,000 square miles, and practically every man in the Territory had invested in sheep and sent them inland to graze on Government Territory. The Bishop of Australia protested that he was the only man of note who had no stock, other than a domestic cow; and, accordingly, the Bishop's cow became the butt of the colony.

Bourke was thus between two fires—the despatches ordering concentration at all costs, and the colonists who spurned theories and dispersed themselves over thousands of square miles. He could neither deny his orders nor stand against such an irresistible force. He therefore resolved to face the facts, and decide his policy in the light of those facts, even should his own future prospects be ruined in the decision. He neither dallied nor falsified the situation, but frankly considered every pertinent factor. A lesser man would have postponed the solution or misconstrued such facts as did not come within his official purview, whereas Bourke went to great trouble to secure all relevant information and to invoke the aid of the leading colonists in settling the problem. Then he faced the logic of the facts he had gathered. 'The question, I would beg leave to submit, is simply this: How may this Government turn to the best advantage a state of things which it cannot wholly interdict?', he repeated, and proceeded to take up a midway stand, neither denying nor unduly surrendering to the squatting movement, and favouring neither the large landowners nor the small settlers.[1]

He commenced by stating his views on the theory of concentration. Taking advantage of applications to recognize settlements at Port Phillip and Twofold Bay, he showed how the theory evolved in England from *a priori* considerations could not possibly fit in with the natural conditions as he found them.

Admitting, as every reasonable person must, that a certain degree of concentration is necessary for the advancement of wealth and civilization, and that it enables Government to become at once efficient and economical, I cannot but avoid perceiving the peculiarities which in this Colony render it impolitic, and even impossible, to restrain dispersion within limits that would be expedient elsewhere.

Wool is, and must remain, the colony's chief wealth, he argued; and any measure that tends to restrict wool-production is a direct blow at the colony's prosperity. Even the existing flocks could not feed within the official Counties, quite apart from the large annual increase: so that, if the flocks were not allowed to range in the interior, artificial food must be imported, and that would obviously be sacrificing facts to a shibboleth—'a perverse rejection of the bounty of Providence'. The flocks had to spread over the interior if the land were to prosper; moreover, they *would* so spread whatever the Government had to say. 'It is not to be disguised that the Government is unable to prevent it,' Bourke reported in October 1835, for he already saw that not all the redcoats in England could patrol the thousands of miles of bush-front. The best thing, the most economical thing, and the *only* thing the Government could do was to protect and control the country occupied by the stockmen: and Bourke, looking far ahead, wrote of selling land in advantageous spots, however distant from other locations it might be, and then, by linking up with towns and means of communication, 'gradually to extend the power of order and social union to the most distant parts of the wilderness'. The old boundary of the Nineteen Counties

[1] Bourke-Glenelg, 10 October 1835.

had no significance in Bourke's new scheme of things: the limit was to be no Government-line, but one determined solely by economic pressure, and settlers were to be allowed to go anywhere within that limit, whether to the remotest parts of Port Phillip or Moreton Bay, and, as far as possible, to be protected by the forces of the State. At a step, Bourke had placed the official theory of concentration far behind him, and himself half a century ahead of his time.

His immediate problem, however, was not so wide. He had to frame a practical line of action that would apply to the conditions at that moment—to regulate squatting, and yet refuse to every pastoral wanderer undue civil or military protection. To this problem, his attention had been directed since the beginning of his period of rule. The growing spread of the flocks and the herds had been with him for some years. In July 1834, for instance, he had written home that squatters 'are to be found in great numbers in Monaro Plains to the westward of Twofold Bay, and some are said to roam as far to the southward as Cape Howe', while others 'are numerous to the south-west along the banks of the Murrumbidgee, and to the North, they have crossed the Mountain Range into Liverpool Plains'. Somewhat plaintively, he looked at the maps of the Surveyor-General, and noting the limits of official location so symmetrically drawn on them, wrote that 'in every direction, the desire of procuring good pastures for sheep has led the Colonists far beyond the limits of location'.[2] He had even to offer a further stimulus to this outward sweep by sending out Major Mitchell first to the north, and then to the plains of promise far south of Lake George. Rumours of settlements still further out were constantly cropping up: now it was islanders intent on crossing to the mainland, now Verner who wanted to plant a new County Armagh at Twofold Bay, now stockmen who were far out and beyond the lands of the Australian Agricultural Company. Yet, with all of this evidence before him, and with pioneers almost to the nebulous *Lake Omeo* in the southern mountains and above the Namoi on the north, the larger colonists were trying to tell him that these men of the outside were rascally escapees —ne'er-do-well convicts who had to be discouraged! Perhaps a million sheep were beyond the boundaries: certainly, the life of the colony was in the movement, and something had to be done, unless the Governor's worst fears were to be realized, and some title to the land created in the occupier.

Bourke had ample precedents in front of him, because, fundamentally, the issue was no new one. It had existed ever since the

[2] Bourke-Stanley, 4 July 1834.

coastal-pastures were cramped and since Macquarie had tried to prevent the long-horned cattle being driven across the mountains. Once the woollen industry had been implanted, and once the old idea of farming on freehold estates had been discarded, the colonists were soon demanding rights of pasturage. 'Three acres for a sheep!', they cried, and simply let their sheep roam on the Crown Lands. This earlier flowing-over, it is true, was in the Counties, where land could be alienated; but basically, it was the squatting problem on a small scale. To deal with it, the Governors of the twenties had allowed a new limited tenure to spring up—a man received what was called 'a ticket-of-occupation', which allowed him to take his flocks wherever he would but gave him no legal rights over the land he occupied. The Colonial Secretary would give an authorization to a respectable settler in this form:

I am commanded by His Excellency Sir Thomas Brisbane to convey to you his sanction for your occupation of all the land hereinafter described for the use of your flocks and herds as a grazing-run, until such times as Government may choose to revoke this indulgence and resume possession to itself.

Such orders were very simple and vague, but, in effect, converted the holders into legalized squatters. It was not long before they led to trouble. In a land with a backward survey and boundaries notoriously uncertain, such a general authorization led to frictions innumerable: and the main effect of the system, along with the totally unauthorized occupation that accompanied it, was that much of the best land was occupied and nobody chose to waste money in purchasing it. The local Land Board—those Bent Street officials who were so important in the twenties—therefore hastened to urge the Governor to revoke the Tickets, with the result that a Notice of August 1826 announced their termination with that year.[3]

The squatting question had thus emerged in a nutshell. Such occupants had clearly extended the limits of settlement, and to this extent there had been progress. But they had introduced a less onerous form of tenure and thus retarded the development of the inner regions—the alternative they provided was much easier than paying quit-rents or purchase-money closer in. Moreover, there was the problem of the improvements. Such occupiers in the outer lands wrested timber-tracts from the bush, cleared the land, erected huts and stockyards, and thus performed regular pioneer-services. What

---

[3] Bathurst-Brisbane, 20 July 1824; Darling-Bathurst, 22 July 1826, 24 February 1827; T. Callaghan, *Acts and Ordinances of the Governor and Council of New South Wales*, I. 361-4.

was to become of these, asked the local Government in 1825? In this problem—later known as *compensation for improvements*—fairness, even at this early stage, demanded some consideration for the claims of the bushmen. Darling referred to the Colonial Office, and they turned to their unofficial adviser, James Stephen, who had not yet become the Permanent Under-Secretary. All that he could do was to urge equity and the consideration of each case as it arose—'the reasonable pretentions' of each tenant might then be reconciled with Royal rights. Though a fair enough compromise, this was too vague to suffice when the issue rose on a larger scale; and the Government temporarily solved the problem by shelving it.[4]

But, objections notwithstanding, some such system had to go on, and all that the Government could do was to make it regular and orderly. From the beginning of 1827, therefore, Darling placed it on a mathematical basis. Instead of any Ticket-holder being allowed vague rights for no payment at all, he had hereafter to pay an annual rental of £1 per 100 acres, with a liability to remove his stock and establishment on six months' notice. Bathurst, the Secretary of State, had been most insistent on some such regulation and on a clear statement that the Government was in no wise committed by anything the occupier might do: and it was on this understanding that the new grazing-rights were given. To make the matter still clearer, a local Act of Council (10 G. IV, No. 6) in 1829 gave the Government still more effective rights to resume such lands, provided for summary eviction if needed, prevented any transfer of the rights of occupation, and distinctly stated that no compensation would be given for improvements under any circumstances.

This was the position of the law when Bourke faced the problem. People who were really squatters could obtain grazing-rights within the boundaries (outside was still 'not known' to the official mind!), on the understanding that they had no claims on either land or improvements, and could be removed on short notice. They were practically squatters paying rental, but denied security of tenure or compensation for improvements. The squatting problem, then, was no new one—it was simply an extension outside the boundaries of the same difficulty that had occurred, on a smaller scale, within the recognized limits of settlement.

The problem of pasturage had been always there: it was simply its *locale* that had changed in the changing conditions—and even this extension had for long been foreseen. Oxley, the Surveyor-General in January 1826, had commented that 'Individuals are not

[4] Correspondence in *Hist. Records of Aust.*, ser. IV, vol. I, p. 616.

restrained from settling unauthorizedly beyond what may be termed
the settled limits of the Country', and, two years later, had complained in an official report that 'good land is now selected wherever
it can be found; and it is so scarce that, even with the present small
population, various selections have *already* been made beyond the
prescribed limits'.[5] With settlers down the line of the Murrumbidgee,
this was speaking with official reserve, to say the least: but the point
was that the Government had already realized how its official
definition of settlement was giving way and how grave a problem
was emerging beyond the boundaries. When Bourke came, the
boundaries were thus no longer creaking, they had been roughly
thrust aside in all directions, and the flood had broken through
everywhere.

But what could the Governor do? He could look on the squatters
as convicts to be repressed, but that seemed beside the point when
the Murray and the Namoi had been reached and men of all social
classes were following the bullock-carts out. Or he could continue
and extend the existing system of rentals, but this meant disobeying
his instructions and facing infinite difficulties in an unsurveyed and
unknown country. Or he could recur to the older notion of general
Tickets-of-Occupation, allowing the holders to range where they
pleased; but that meant the revival of a system that had been
officially condemned and, moreover, reduced supervision and restraint
to a minimum. Or he could think of various schemes of a *per capita*
taxation of stock; but that did not settle the difficulties of controlling
the areas occupied, and, in itself, presented difficulties of collection.
Or finally, as the King's representative, he could draw attention to
the breach of law squatting entailed. He could threaten offenders with
dire punishments for going beyond the boundaries, and then, having
done his duty and reported to the Colonial Office, he could let
matters take their course. A less conscientious man would have been
strongly drawn to the last alternative, but Bourke had the interests
of the colony too much at heart and loved a problem too dearly to
pass one over unsolved.

Setting to work to collect evidence, he was soon satisfied that the
movement included men of all ranks and positions, and that its
development was essential to the colony's welfare. It was equally
obvious that property-rights were being built upon a large scale,
and that, if the Government did not soon undertake an effective
control, it would be too late to do so by any means short of military

[5] In 3rd *Report of Commission of Colonial Inquiry on Receipts and Expenditure*, 1831.

coercion. Again, it was evident that, both in themselves and as a blind used by the larger settlers, the 'squatters' of evil repute—the convict land-raiders—were the most immediate evil. And lastly, a man of the world of Bourke's type could not but perceive that the worthy members of Council and the richer settlers of the *pure merino* class were attempting to secure the new prize for themselves and to enlist Government-aid in checking the smaller settlers.

With all of these tangled influences, it was no small problem for Bourke, especially with his superiors at home dinning into his ears that he had to prevent any form of dispersion and to restrict settlement in New South Wales so that the ideal colonizers at St Vincent's Gulf could keep their lands at an artificially high price. To make matters more difficult for himself, too, Bourke persisted in looking on Australia as a society of the future. Always a Celt, he dreamed of the ages to come, and the idealistic dreamer in him conflicted with the part that was practical soldier, and saw the present with a too prescient, almost a too conscientious, eye.

Events were rushing towards a conclusion all through 1835. The *Police and Gaols Committee* had produced ample, if not disinterested, evidence of the way in which settlement had outstripped Government provision for it, and how control was very largely falling into the hands of the camp-followers of the bush. Menaces in some districts, obstacles in all, their repression was an obvious one, as the papers admitted in supporting the *ex parte* evidence of the Committee. 'At present,' wrote the *Sydney Gazette* of 14 July, 'there is no authority in the hands of a local magistrate or Bench to eject any squatter from Government ground. He can despise the power of justice and continue with impunity to browse his flocks and herds upon the very boundary-lines of a resident who has probably laid out a large capital, thus to have it by driblets drained away through the covert craft and villainy of his own stockmen and the rascally vicinity of receiving squatters.'

This phase of the situation was just then pointed by various cases of sheep-stealing in the Supreme Court. Early in 1836, for instance, William Warby, quite a rich man, was sentenced before a crowded Court to fourteen years' transportation for receiving stock stolen from Henry O'Brien of Yass, one of the most respected of the Murrumbidgee pioneers.[6] Such cases, together with the Committee's evidence, led to a petition making the rounds of the colony (March 1836), praying the Legislature to pass an Act 'for the prevention of *Squatting*, through which so much crime was daily occurring, inas-

[6] *Australian,* 19 February 1836.

much as squatting was but another term for sly-grog selling, receiving
stolen property, and harbouring bushrangers and assigned servants'.
Throughout the colony, and especially in the richer Hunter River,
various Associations—local vigilance societies—were formed for the
hunting of stock-raiders, and there was a universal agreement to
prevent convicts from 'squatting'. This latter was mainly supported,
it must be added, by the followers of James Macarthur and the new
Tory Association who wanted to refuse the full rights of citizenship
to emancipists. Still, the evil was very real.

In opening the 1836 session of Council, Bourke explicitly stated
that the colonists' memorial was the direct reason for the Bill he
proposed—*a Bill to restrain the unauthorized occupation of Crown
Lands*. He had experienced great difficulty, however, in arriving at
some basis of control. The need of intervention was obvious, and the
necessity of stamping out the convict-squatters no less so: but what
troubled him was how to effect this end, and yet neither hamper
decent small settlers nor offer an unfair patronage to the capitalistic
land-owners, the *pure merinos*. The disjointed report of the Police
Committee certainly could not have helped him very much, beyond
multiplying evidence as to the desirability of control—a fact sufficiently obvious in itself! Most witnesses, like Dutton, had simply
urged 'the interference of the Legislature' in general terms, but that
was not very constructive when it came to specific measures. The
general concurrence of opinion (possibly because most of the witnesses were themselves on the Commission of the Peace) was that
surveillance would come most effectively from the various Benches,
but Bourke probably remembered the adage about big fish eating
up little ones in the same pond, and was not very attracted towards
any such measure of decentralization and local control.

The first feasible plan had come from Sir John Jamison, himself a
stockman and magistrate from Penrith, a liberal in politics and a
pioneer in the newer lands. After voicing the general opinion that all
convicts and ticket-of-leave men should be prevented from squatting,
he argued that, in view of the droughts and the cramped lands inside,
the enterprise of graziers should be allowed anywhere, either within
or without the boundaries. 'Indeed,' he continued, 'it might be
beneficial to establish a system of Licence to occupy tracts of land
either within or without the prescribed limits, in order to prevent
pauper free or freed men from squatting in such unlocated situations,
to live by stealing live stock and other dishonest means.'[7] To enforce

[7] *Sydney Gazette*, 16 July 1835.

the law, itinerant Justices and mounted police could go on circuits and thus maintain control beyond the regions where towns and benches of magistrates were to be found. Captain Phillip King followed in the same strain, but wished to make every applicant prove character and means before a local Bench. Rankin of Goulburn also wanted such a licence, either from the Government or the neighbouring magistrates, but the Committee made no recommendations in its final report, beyond urging an Act of Council to control the squatters, to vest summary jurisdiction in the police, and to keep any ticket-of-leave men from even renting or occupying land.

From this jumble of facts and opinions, Bourke could see that a licence was desirable, though the Committee's evidence was itself the best argument why control should not be given to the local Benches. But the less reputable squatters had to be discouraged in some way or other, and it was absurd to think of control by the Courts which were so far away. In the Bill, therefore, Bourke proposed to issue Government licences to squatters and to give more power to the magistrates to remove suspected persons in their districts. The Bill was not to prevent occupation, he argued, but to aid it—not to remove all graziers, but simply the disreputable ones hitherto known as 'squatters'. 'It is not intended by means of its provisions,' he wrote in the *Minute* that accompanied his first draft, 'or by any other course of law, to interdict the use of the vacant Crown Lands to persons of good repute.' It was, in the phraseology of the time, 'a law against Squatting, which has been called for almost universally',[8] but equally a law to recognize and encourage legitimate grazing. It was to kill squatting in its first sense, but to implant it in a new. It allowed licences to all, without distinction, save to persons of notoriously bad character—the emphasis was on the right, not the disqualification.

Any reputable person was to be allowed to take out a licence which, for the payment of £10 a year, authorized him to graze stock over as much land as he pleased. This was the main gain of the Bill—that the whole interior, limits or no limits, was to be opened to the stockholders by Government sanction. Henceforth, they were no outcasts, no roamers on Crown lands in defiance of their Government, but duly authorized occupants. The old limitation of the 'boundaries of location' had received its deathblow. It mattered little for the moment whether settlers could buy land or not in the far interior: all that they wanted was a legal right of occupation, because the other rights

[8] *Australian*, 7 June 1836: *Bourke's Minute* of 1 July 1836.

would flow from that in due time. They wanted a recognition of the pastoral movement—the sanction of the law; and this the licence-system gave them.

The difficulty at the time was almost entirely due to the undesir-ables, because, as has been seen, the public in general held an alto-gether distorted view as to the place of these escapees in the squatting movement. Instead of being viewed as so many carrion-thieves, they were magnified in public esteem until they constituted the squatting movement—they *were* the squatters, and it was their removal that the Act was supposed to effect. Bourke himself was hard pressed to keep a sane head on the matter and, by dint of the continued oppo-sition, had to go too far in the opposite direction—of calling up the poorer settlers against the wealthy. The established landowners wanted to keep the graziers in a closed ring, with themselves, in their magisterial capacity, determining the qualifications of new aspirants. Theirs was to be the power of giving or withholding the right of run-ning stock on Crown lands, their fiat the final word. But Bourke, knowing too well the absurd class-consciousness of the exclusives of New South Wales (for was it not hastening his own downfall?) stood out and refused to favour any class unduly, least of all the land-owners. He therefore insisted on Government control. The opposition paper, the *Australian,* helped him in this fight against 'the aristocracy of the woolpack' and showed how the larger settlers, safe in the base of their freehold estates, wished to kill the small men. 'While squat-ting is tacitly permitted to one class of free men, it must be so to all, and we should lament the introduction of any measure to interfere with any of them,' excepting, of course, the convicts. The *Australian,* the *Colonist,* and the *Sydney Gazette,* discordant unity though they made, were all at one on this point, so that the Governor had the masses behind him in allowing all freemen to have licences.

In retaliation, the Council—a nominee body without elected repre-sentatives—tried to introduce amendments to penalize the poorer settlers, 'alterations in favour of the rich', as Bourke called them. They wanted power for any landowner to set the law in operation against intruders—a step that would have meant, under the existing conditions, 'the oppressive enforcement of the law against the poor'. To prevent this (and, it is important to note, solely as an after-thought), Bourke proposed the appointment of Government officials called Commissioners of Crown Lands, each of whom would have charge of Government interests within a given district and who would alone have power to take measures against undesirable squatters. These officials afterwards became the leading feature of the whole scheme, but their inception came about in this quite haphazard manner—as a move of the Governor against the landholders he hated.

The Act went no further than this. It was aimed at the legalization of occupation—and this it accomplished. Its machinery was quite embryonic. Nobody expected much of the Commissioners; in fact, their precise duties were not even defined, save that they were to remove intruders. The licence-fee was irrespective of place or area, and was scarcely expected to pay the expenses of the new Commissioners. One such officer was to go to each district—and there the Act stopped!

But it was a start. It placed the squatting system on a new basis and envisaged a spread of occupation over the whole colony by legal means. 'I have no desire', reported Bourke to Glenelg in September 1836, 'to disturb any honest occupier without the limits of location, nor to remove any within those limits, unless to make room for a purchaser within the limits.' It was to encourage respectable occupation, not to check it; and it was effective for the time being. The Government had re-asserted itself, occupation was legalized, the monopolists were checked, the undesirables were tied hand and foot, and the whole interior placed at the legal disposal of the stockmen— and what more could have been achieved at this early stage?

The exclusives and their organ, the *Monitor*, might taunt the Governor with democratic, and even convict, sympathies, but Bourke knew that the menace they presented was quite as real as that of the original convict-*squatters*. He had effectively dispelled both and, in addition, had enlarged the Government's horizon from the coast settlement to the remotest spinifex lands of the interior. He had envisaged a future development for the whole land, while sacrificing neither private nor public interests. The terms of the short Act of 1836 made up Bourke's claim to deserve well of his country— it was the seal of his statemanship, however much he may have felt thwarted on his departure.

But the battle did not end in the Council Chamber. Bourke had triumphed there, but, under the old colonial system, still had to face the opposition of Downing Street. The Act was passed in Sydney in July 1836—when the storm against dispersion was reaching its height in London. Stanley, Aberdeen, and lastly Glenelg (in Melbourne's new Ministry) were all inveighing against dispersion, especially now that emigrants were being poured into the wastes of Kangaroo Island and the marsh of Holdfast Bay to build up the model colony of South Australia—the very embodiment of the prin-

ciples of social concentration! Yet, in that very month, a local
Governor in an adjacent colony had the audacity to pass an Act that
would not only allow, but positively give Government aid to stockmen who could push across to the very boundary of South Australia
—and occupy land, for which the South Australians were paying £1
an acre, in thousands of acres for a mere £10! The South Australian
Commissioners had already complained about the squatters of New
South Wales, and, in particular, of the illegal settlement at Port
Phillip; now, the Governor had placed the approval of the law on
all this!

The Wakefieldians hovered in wrath at the doors of Downing
Street, and Glenelg, harassed and uncertain Minister with no
opinions of his own and mortally afraid of the press and his colleagues, could do nothing but refer them to Stephen, the Under-
Secretary. The latter, having had a long experience with this matter
(it was he who had been consulted on a similar question as far back
as Brisbane's time!) was wise enough not to deny the position of the
squatters, and, while still disapproving, tended to point to the logic
of the facts. Glenelg, passively acquiescing in everything Stanley
and Aberdeen had left, had accepted the theory of concentration as
a matter of course, and bullied the colonial Governors into worship-
ping it as their official deity; but fortunately, 'Mr Over-Secretary
Stephen' had more power at the Colonial Office than its nominal
head, and his views were reasonably sagacious.

In replying to the South Australian Commissioners, he pointed
out that the situation was governed by circumstances rather than by
any wish of the Executive, and that the most cherished theory had
to give way in the light of facts. He might be convinced of the
equity of a high price for land and of the desirability of concentration, but, if the situation made both of these impossible from an
administrative point of view, then they had to go. Explaining himself in a formal statement of policy which Glenelg accepted (though
it was quite opposed to the bewildered Secretary's previous statements!), Stephen wrote,[9]

In the remoter part of the vast region comprised within the range of
the Australian colonies, the power of the Law is unavoidably feeble
when compared with the predominant inclinations of any large body of
the people. In such a Country, unless supported by a Force either of
Police or Soldiery irresistible and overwhelming, unpopular Regulations
must become little more than a dead letter. Thus, in New South Wales,
the *Squatters* (to employ the significant Local Term), find in the high

[9] Stephen—Colonization Commissioners, 27 October 1836.

upset price of land some of the advantages which a smuggler in other countries derives from a high rate of duty. Their proceedings, instead of being condemned and opposed, are countenanced and supported by the Society to which they belong. Consequently, an exclusive Territory at a distance from the seat of Government has been occupied by unauthorized settlers of all classes—by the wealthy not less than by the poor, and, in this systematic violation of the Law, each class finds support and encouragement in the example and common interest of its various members. With the most earnest desire to repress the growing evil, the local Authorities have experienced the impossibility of making an effectual resistance to the general will. The case of Port Phillip is but an example and illustration of the prevailing triumph of popular feelings over Positive Law.

This long excerpt is doubly interesting, as containing not only the carefully-considered views of the permanent head of the Colonial Office on the leading Australian issue of the time, but a statement of policy which stands out clearly against first the undue repressiveness and then the untoward liberalism of the next decade. Stephen had attained a middle position, in which his own liberal tendencies had not yet been throttled by the exigencies of his office, and yet one in which the difficulties of the situation were fully perceived.

In these views Glenelg acquiesced, but this shuttlecock of the Ministry who had no opinions on anything would have accepted any document. He was the Minister of whom Sydney Smith had said that he would still feel that Britain had colonies if Glenelg went —the Minister who adopted everything put in front of him. Now a Wakefieldian, now reacting to Stephen or the bureaucratic clerks of his office, he was at all times undecided, remembering only the last thing said to him. The poor man had everybody against him, from Lord John's rudeness to the blunt hostility of the King himself, so what could he do, when he wanted to please everybody and desired so much to remain a Minister? So that, when these Australians turned up—these squatters whom one despatch explained as runaway convicts and the next as the intelligent young men of the colony—he simply wrote what everybody told him! One of his despatches would breathe the spirit of Wakefieldian concentration, another speak of compromise; but the significant point was that, when Bourke's first *Squatting Act* was received, Glenelg was too troubled by party intrigues to bother about it, and simply sent a statement of Stephen's views.

This in turn meant that the breach of the concentration-theory passed uncensored, and Bourke's *Act*, probably because no one understood it, and certainly because Stephen had had a long experience of the problem, was approved. The weakness of the Minister, the hold of Stephen, and the lack of interest combined to give Bourke the scope he desired. Downing Street had no clear executive policy in those years, however much South Australian views were sponsored; and so we have the contradiction between the despatches on the first settlement of Port Phillip and those approving the general squatting occupation. Though usually interfering in the smallest details, the Colonial Office allowed this huge question to pass almost unnoticed— or, in other words, placed the onus of dealing with the matter on the colonial authorities, who would pay with their posts if trouble cropped up at a later date.

Meanwhile, the first Squatting Act was being administered in the colony. Bourke appointed his Commissioners from the commencement of 1837, but their powers were too vague and inadequate from the outset. They could do nothing beyond insisting that every occupant had a licence, but even this was almost impossible in a country ranging from New England to Portland Bay. Even if they found trespassers, such persons simply moved on or defied the Government official who had no means of enforcing his power perhaps hundreds of miles from the nearest civil centre. The Act had provided penalties of £10, £20 and £50 for infringing its rules, but the imposition of such a drastic fine implied trial before magistrates, and where were the nearest magistrates, say, to the Ovens or the Namoi? Glenelg, in acknowledging the Act, had so misconstrued its general bearing that he thought it was primarily a preventive of squatting and entertained doubts 'whether the penalties are sufficiently high to check the temptation to the unlicensed occupation of Land by the wealthier class of Settlers'; what became obvious, to the contrary, was that even the stipulated penalties could not be enforced. The bush was wide, and the Commissioner, even assuming that he could cover sufficient ground to find unlicensed men, was miles away from his base and could be ignored with safety.

Matters stood thus when Governor Bourke left the colony. The machinery of the Act was in motion, but simply rotated uselessly; and the only effective restraint was in the desire of respectable settlers to receive legal approval of their acts. Those who wished to evade the measure could still do so with impunity. The Act had served to legalize squatting, but had proved unable to eradicate abuses. After being in operation for two years, argued the *Sydney Gazette*, 'it has to all intents and purposes been a dead letter', owing to 'the culpable negligence of the Governor in the non-enforcement of the penalties' and the inactivity of 'those useless drones called

Commissioners'.[10] There was a fair amount of truth in this, but it must equally be admitted that the Governor was powerless in the matter and that the Commissioners had no punitive sanction for their acts. The fault was not so much in the execution as in the short-comings of the measure itself: it had sanctioned occupation but pro-vided no means of controlling it.

When Sir George Gipps succeeded Bourke, therefore, he lost no time in reconsidering the problem, for it was obvious that he had either to consent to a purely nominal function on the part of the Government or pass a new Act going much further than the old one. Naturally, he chose the latter alternative and at once put an Act through the Council. Strangely enough—and although he had so far gone no further than the previous Act—he found himself opposed by two of the three Supreme Court judges. Nine days after the passage of the Bill, Justices Burton and Willis protested that it was repugnant to the laws of England—a most amazing stand, utterly unexpected by the Governor, who thought that he had the right to expect the support of his main legal officers, especially on such a matter of policy. In a confidential despatch of the same day (2 October 1838) he explained the opposition as due to quite personal idiosyncrasies. Burton, a Puisne Judge since 1832, was the person so solicitous of the colony's morals and the author of the famous attack on the growth of crime. He suffered from sincerely and conscien-tiously-held opinions in a colony where both of those features were at a discount, and was sufficiently human to like his own voice. He prefaced his legal work, for instance, by long sermons on govern-mental matters and bitter attacks on the social system in general. As Gipps reported,[11]

Mr. Justice Burton is a person whose character, both public and private, stands too high to allow for a moment the supposition of his having acted with any view to embarrass the Government or from any but the purest motives; he is, however, known to have long entertained some peculiar notions respecting the rights of the Crown to dispose of lands in the Colonies; and it is perhaps not unreasonable to suppose that he looked for an occasion to bring them forward.

Burton declared that the £10 licence-fee was a tax on the people and that any alienation, even of limited rights, had to obtain the consent of Parliament. Willis, who was simply a chorus in the matter, was the judge whose eccentricities later caused him to be

[10] *Sydney Gazette*, 25 November 1837.
[11] Gipps-Glenelg, 7 November 1838.

removed from the Port Phillip Bench, but his support sufficed to place the majority of legal opinion against the Governor.

The Judges' remonstrance had been received on the eve of the last day of the session, and Gipps had to keep members together for several days after this, because the law provided that such a remonstrance had to go to the Council. Though they, of course, knew the reason, which became quite a matter of notoriety in the colony, they were none the less annoyed, because this was the time when their overseers needed their supervision during the shearing-season. In his turn, Gipps secured the contrary opinion of the Attorney-General and the Solicitor-General, and induced the judges to substitute a different and modified remonstrance. Burton, having gone too far, unequivocally withdrew his opinion and agreed to look upon the licence-fee as a Territorial revenue and not a tax; while Willis withdrew, but, with that uncompromising lack of tact that was to end in his disgrace, retained his opinions, and told the Governor so !

But Gipps now had his revenge. The law provided that any such remonstrance had to be submitted within a fortnight; this period had more than elapsed, so the Governor solved the difficulty by throttling it, and refused to accept the new remonstrance—a somewhat dubious but excusable subterfuge. The wider question, however, still remained and, though the irate Councillors could now go to their sheep-stations and though the Governor had outwitted his opponents, the incident had tied the Executive's hands. In due course of time, Gipps received the complete support of the Colonial Office on the question, and he was supported throughout by the Chief Justice in the colony; but, none the less, the recalcitrant judges had postponed a settlement of the squatting question for at least a year and prevented any enforcement of the penalties against unauthorized squatting, because their opinion would have prevailed against the solitary Chief Justice in the Supreme Court. Lord Normanby, and later, the law officers of the Crown upheld Gipps, but their despatches did not leave England until the middle of 1839, whereas, during every month of the feverish period that had elapsed in the colony in the interim, numerous questions were complicated by the state of doubt that prevailed. The Judges' opposition was a singularly illtimed expression of personal views, and a tacit, if not actual, breach of trust, because they cannot be acquitted of a desire to embarrass the Government.

It was not until February 1839, therefore, that Gipps could convene an extraordinary session of the Council to adopt measures for the tranquillity of the new squatting districts and the enforcement of Government supervision in them. By this time, all of central Port Phillip had been occupied; squatters ranged over the mother-colony from Tenterfield almost to the Lachlan-Murrumbidgee junction; and the outside men were thinking of Moreton Bay and the land over the South Australian border. In the latter stages of this rush—when the herders were crossing to Port Phillip and New England—the attention of the colony had been directed to the rule of terror that was possible in these new districts. Scarcely a mail arrived, scarcely a party got through without news of native-outrages in both of these directions; and, on the reverse side, rumours of atrocities by squatting parties trickled in with a disturbing frequency.

The Commissioners were practically powerless to prevent such massacres, or even to report on them, and there was a strong feeling in the colony that the settlers were not receiving the protection they were paying for. Men spoke of the massacre of Faithfull's overlanding party on the Ovens, and of the ravages on practically every outstation north of the Namoi. They attacked this new Governor, who seemed so filled with the humanitarian ideals of Exeter Hall that he believed every squatter cruelty incarnate and every native an outraged idealist living in primitive tranquillity. This feeling reached its climax with the famous *Myall Creek* trials. A party of shepherds had undoubtedly perpetrated a loathsome crime in this case and massacred almost thirty unoffending natives; but the colony fairly quivered when seven of them were found guilty, and Gipps insisted on hanging them. Hitherto, squatters and shepherds had shot natives as they would wild ducks, if they were not afraid to do so; but now, with the law invoked to enforce the utmost penalties, nobody quite knew where he stood. Gipps even ordered enquiries into the case of Major Nunn, one of his own police-officials, who was charged with undue cruelty in quelling native unrest; and it seemed that the natives were always in the right where the Governor was concerned. There was some degree of truth in this, but it must be admitted that Gipps desired both to protect the settlers and to safeguard the natives when he called the special session of Council in 1839.

Briefly, he proposed to end the mutual aggressions by setting up visible signs of Government authority beyond the boundaries and by clothing the Commissioners with real powers. Each of them was now to be a real arbiter of affairs within his district and was to have a force of mounted police to support him. In the forefront of Gipps's mind was the desire to put an end to the fighting between squatters and natives, but he was not sorry to have an opportunity of strengthening the Crown's authority, especially after the action of the Judges a few months previously.

He therefore wanted to place the Commissioners in directly administrative posts. They were to decide everything in connection with pastoral occupation and especially to adjudicate in questions of encroaching boundaries. They were to weed out undesirables, to collect the Government's taxes, and to decide the extent of each man's activities. Under the conditions then prevailing, they were to hold the pastoral future of each squatter entirely within their hands; they could make or break. They decided what constituted occupancy, what land a man could have, the number of stock he could graze, the amounts he should pay—in short, everything connected with grazing.

Before the measure was submitted to the Council, the Governor published his draft—or rather the draft prepared by Judge Burton—in order that there should be general discussion and criticism. In its original form, it provided for the vesting of very drastic powers in the Commissioner—such as cancelling any man's licence on the spot, calling on the surrounding settlers to fall in and serve him, destroying stock at will, and levying various charges on the countryside. The emphasis was all on the Government official, little on the rights of the settler. But Gipps was not long in getting the criticism he asked for. First the papers, and then a representative Committee of Council[12] submitted query after query, mostly directed against the aggregation of powers in the Commissioners.

The *Sydney Herald* (18 February 1839), to take a typical instance, objected most strongly. It fully realized the necessity of obtaining Government licences and admitted that settlers should pay some form of rental; it was quite prepared, in short, to accept any system that would end the evils of unlicensed squatting. But there it stopped. The proposed measure was too strong, its principle was too arbitrary, it conferred too much patronage on the Governor, and it raised up a race of demi-gods on the frontier—Commissioners who alone could distrain and sell stock, who could act as judge, jury, and sheriff in one, and ruin a man without any preliminary trial! Moreover, was it part of a free man's creed to be under a system whereby Commissioners could call for help at any time, could levy a sort of *posse comitatus* among the surrounding stockmen, and compel any man, rich or poor, to serve under them as privates of the line, and all for

[12] *Committee on Lands Bill,* in *Votes and Proceedings,* 1839, vol. I (43 pages of report).

five shillings a day? The paper thought not; and the Committee agreed with it.

This Committee consisted of both official and unofficial members—Jamison and Blaxland rubbed shoulders with Macarthur and Jones, while the Auditor-General and the Collector of Customs were there to look after Government interests. All of the witnesses and the members themselves agreed that border-police were urgently needed, for the reports of outrage were quite authentic, and the menace of native-aggression was ever-present in the outer regions. Glennie, for instance, the first man on the Gwydir, reported fifteen murders of shepherds in the preceding two and a half years, and the massacre of whole herds of cattle and flocks of sheep simply for the fat in each animal. Faithfull, from the opposite extreme of settlement, told how the blacks had murdered eight of his men at one time and kidnapped one of his brother's shepherds; and Routledge related how his shepherd was murdered, how his sheep were speared in tens and twenties, and how the blacks were again mustering in hundreds on the road to Port Phillip and would not disperse. To clinch the point was the evidence of a clergyman, the Reverend David Mackenzie, who, though he had fifty natives working about him, felt that their known treachery prevented him trusting them and compelled him to warn his servants always to be on their guard. He told, too, how a squatter on the Big River had 500 sheep wantonly slaughtered, and another his cattle slain, simply for the kidneys, and despite the abundance of native food all around. The Committee was therefore in no doubt as to the need for protection, though armed forces were urgently needed only in the two newer zones—the Liverpool Plains to the north, and the road from the Hume (the Murray) to the sea in the south. This particular menace was felt mainly in the outskirts, but a Border Police everywhere would serve to keep order and safeguard property.

But decided objections were made to the Bill as proposed by the Governor. Many squatters objected to the cost of the protection—even safety could be too dearly bought in their eyes—and some would have been content with 'mutual protection societies' or vigilance committees in each district, the Government's part being limited to the provision of a gaol. The more far-sighted of them, to the contrary, easily perceived the advantages of the new Force and started to consider how the plan would best work. There was considerable difference of opinion as to how the necessary money should be raised. Some wanted a rental on the land, others an assessment on stock; but the Committee adopted the latter, because it was more equitable and because they could keep control of money so raised, whereas a land-rental would be Territorial or Crown Revenue, and thus beyond their powers.

Much more agreement was felt on the next point—the power of the Commissioners. Every witness was in accord on this—that the Commissioners were to have too great and too arbitrary a part in the life of the border-regions. They followed Terence Murray, afterwards Speaker and President of the Houses, in his coldly-precise evidence, which analysed the whole field and methodically covered every clause. He objected to any single man withdrawing a licence, he wanted the prior consent of a Bench before any person should be allowed to squat, he strenuously opposed the Commissioner's right to call on the attendance of settlers armed and mounted, he refused to give rations to the police, he denied any man's right to shoot his cattle should he be in arrears, and he thought the assessment-rate too high. The general testimony followed closely on these lines, most witnesses approving the general principle of the Bill but counselling amendment in the directions indicated. The practical men from the outskirts showed how the Commissioners' power to decide the boundaries of a run and to punish for any fault he thought fit might be extremely vexatious under pioneering conditions; and it was more than once suggested that both Commissioner and squatter should present their cases before some outside umpire, as each was the advocate of a special point of view. But the emphasis was on securing prompt and decisive action, and the power remained vested in the Commissioner, redolent of future trouble though this decision was.

With changes along these directions, the Bill passed, leaving an almost unlimited power to each Commissioner.[13] He could not levy forces or do as much as Gipps had at first proposed, but he was still the arbiter of pastoral destinies; he and his men gaily trotted through the scheme of the squatters' existence and left it in ribbons or intact, as they pleased. The Commissioners remained, their armed troopers remained, and the assessment remained, when the Bill was passed.

In Council, there was little comment. Not even a quorum could be mustered for the second reading; the measure was pushed through because some action had to be taken when the squatters had jumped forward three hundred miles in a year at Port Phillip, and were even then concentrating on the lands beyond the Namoi. The Lake Colac and the Tenterfield countries were then in everybody's view; and the errors of the past had shown that a supervision, even too strict a supervision, was preferable to mere freebooting independence.

[13] *Sydney Herald*, 15 March 1839.

This—the only business of the extraordinary session—was over by the end of March 1839, Gipps seizing the last reading as an opportunity to make a long speech on the intention of the Act. Doubts still remained in many quarters, and he wished to dispel them. The Bill was avowedly introduced, he said, to prevent conflicts between aborigines and settlers, yet no mention of them was made in its clauses. That was because the existing laws were quite strong enough, if there was machinery to enforce them. The newly-created Police could do this. 'As to evils of dispersion,' he concluded, 'I fear it is now too late to talk of them, for we have beyond the boundaries nearly two millions of sheep and several hundred thousands of cattle, which all the powers of Government could not bring back within the settled limits of the colony.'

The Act was soon put into operation. On 21 May 1839, the Governor proclaimed nine districts—Port Macquarie, New England, and Liverpool Plains to the north; Lachlan to the west; and Murrumbidgee, Monaro, and the vast new Port Phillip to the south. The previous division had been very vague as to these southern lands: but the new one distinctly set up three new regions, each of which, like the others, had a Commissioner and an establishment of mounted prisoner-police.

This achievement marked a definite period in the history of squatting. Bourke had legalized the system in 1836; now, Gipps made Government regulation effective, and erected the necessary machinery to evolve order from chaos and make every squatter subservient to the rules and penalties laid down by the Executive.

The districts so supervised stretched from the edge of the Darling Downs to the new land being taken up between Lake Colac and the Portland Bay region; and hereafter, each successive stage of the squatting movement was definitely watched and controlled. In February 1839, when Gipps was passing his Act, there were 4,380 persons beyond the boundaries (a third of them bond); or at least, the Government had been able to enumerate this number—how many more there were remained a matter of conjecture. They grazed 233,000 cattle and 982,000 sheep, though Gipps believed that the figure was nearer two millions; and their recognized stations ran from Moreton Bay almost out to Fort Bourke on the Darling and up to the Lachlan-Murrumbidgee junction; then south to the fringe of the Port Phillip mallee and up to the outpost at Portland. By June 1840, when the Act was fairly in operation and something like a regular Census could be taken, there were 673 stations, with a population of 6,664 (now almost half bond), running 352,000 cattle and 1,204,000 sheep

—truly, as Gipps said, most important interests! As a result of the expansion, the average exports of wool had risen from 2¼ million pounds to almost 6 millions—from 36·9 pounds per head of population to 58·6!

The squatters, further, had consolidated their position and had gone far from the mere permissive occupancy first vouchsafed them by Bourke three years before. Gipps might insist that 'the temporary occupation of the land under the licence is expressly declared to give no permanent right over it whatsoever'—no more, in fact, than the right of commonage in England or the timber-licences of Canada; but practice had far outstripped this. The Supreme Court had recently held that a squatter's occupancy was good against all-comers except the Crown, and a judgment still later, Scott v. Dight, had even given a plaintiff £200 for intrusion, though his only claim was on a Crown Licence. Runs were bought and sold, permanent dwellings erected, and everything carried on as if the land were freehold!

The centre of the colony had moved outwards—out to the new lands of the north and the south: from there, its wealth came; there was invested its capital, and there, too, was to be found emerging the foremost political issue. A completely new class had been added to the population, and their privileges, starting from the barest legal rights, were already far too well implanted in 1840 to be seriously questioned. The next step was to be their claim to some permanent title in the Crown Lands they had built up to be their own and their heirs': and it was this claim that was in the forefront of Australian politics for decades.

Bourke had planted the seed, Gipps aided the sapling, and now, it was so imbedded in the very life-soil of the colony that no outside agency seemed sufficiently strong to control its growth, while it was simply chimerical to try to eradicate it or make it occupy a pre-ordained place. A million and a quarter, or perhaps two million, sheep spread over half a continent afforded a considerable problem, especially when guarded by pioneers who had wrested their belongings from all manner of natural difficulties. By 1840, they were resting, strong and expectant, secure in the vast advances they had achieved in the previous four or five years; and now, organized in a body as never before, they were ready for the next struggle with the Government—not for recognition (they had achieved that in 1836 and 1839!), but for supremacy and practically freehold rights in their squatting-runs.

5

THE EARLY POLICY OF SIR GEORGE GIPPS

WHEN, one fine morning towards the close of February 1836, the *Upton Castle* ended its long passage of 131 days by grazing past Pinchgut Island in Sydney Harbour, a wiry grizzled officer of somewhat dour expression stood on deck, and, as was his wont, rested with chin-muscles tautened and jaw pressed down, his rather irregular deep-set eyes gleaming first this way over to the bush of Mosman, then yonder to the opening of Lane Cove, and beyond to the rocks of the north shore. Sir George Gipps, ex-Major of His Majesty's Engineers, had arrived to assume the Captain-Generalship of Australasia, and more immediately, the Governor-Generalship of New South Wales.

While the dinghy bearing the senior officers was pulling out, he looked round him, over the curved quay, past the hillocks of the town, and up to the cliff-streets behind him, which the captain pointed out as the region of ill-fame. A quiet township of what appeared to be innumerable rocky headlands projected itself round the harbour, the many windmills adding variety and not a little grotesqueness, to the horizon-line. It was not a very attractive panorama, and one of a deadly dullness, despite the bunting on the small craft and the noisy hooting of anticipatory sirens: the squat grey buildings on the wharf, convict-work a mile off, stamped the township with an unmistakable seal of felonry; and the observer felt that here congregated the refuse of an Empire, and that the varied harbour and the green headlands were beautiful mockeries thrown in by Nature to point the contrast and emphasize the gloom.

In London, Gipps had been told that the colony was unprecedentedly prosperous—that free immigration had set in, that convict-assignment would soon be ended, that trade amounted to almost $2\frac{1}{4}$ millions a year, that two new colonies had been founded and a third was germinating, that the sheepmen had spread over half a continent, that the community was quiet and its finances flourishing; in short, that everything was succeeding beyond the dreams of the Colonial Office and that, soon, colonists could afford to pay much more for squatting rights, much more for land, and much more for convict-labour, which would henceforth be sold! It seemed as if the new Governor would be hard-pressed to spend the money that was to pour into the Government coffers: he departed towards a future aureoled with visions of taxes and still more taxes—taxes which would not keep pace with the galloping prosperity of the colony, taxes which would be flung aside by flourishing merchants and stockmen as bagatelles, taxes which would enable him to give full scope to his creative desires and erect a model community of the South!

Now Gipps felt himself abruptly brought up against the facts, symbolized by this slumbering little township, with its straggling streets and ditch winding through its midst. He found a society at war with itself, a little community of 98,000 persons divided into rival cliques. Minor officials fought major officials; merchants resented the pretensions of all officials; squatters despised the townsmen; the exclusive free proprietors ignored the lessees; freemen fought emanci-pists; emancipists wished to widen the gap between their past and their present by oppressing convicts; and the convicts resented all free or freed men. Such strife had ruined both of Gipps's predecessors, it had wrought an insidious influence since the very foundation of the colony, and now, not even the vigorous force of the squatting expansion could eradicate its hold. Almost on his landing-day, Gipps was forcibly brought up against the mutual detestation of the Bishop, the Commandant, and the Surveyor-General; and certainly, he felt at once the problem of how to treat the convicts and the emancipists.

Sydney soon revealed itself as a miserable little growth of putrefy-ing ulcers—a mess of social infection. The energetic conquest of the interior seemed far away, and the new Governor must have prayed for a whiff of action, for the smell of the herds that were accomplish-ing something, and for a throat-catch from the dust of the advancing army of sheep. His place was with the pioneers, but he was gripped already by the dank arms of Sydney—a place of convicts and prosti-tutes, clerks and grumbling labourers. Tied down to this, Gipps could but dream of the bush and the mountains, and the inland torrents and all the charm of beckoning country transformed by the appeal of the unknown. This was no work for a soldier—for a con-structive soldier like an engineer: a man of action, here, felt him-self tied to a desk; and what a desk! A bureau cluttered with com-plaints of the immorality of the manager in charge of the convict-factory, whinings for precedence and allowances, and the protests of an impotent Legislature! All complaints, all sterility!

Most of the population, despite the pastoral movement, was still concentrated in Sydney and the surrounding County of Cumberland. This was the haven desired by the convict and the freedman, the refuge of the free emigrant against the terrors of the bush. As yet, less than four thousand persons were beyond the boundaries, and the region within, save for the Yass, Bathurst, and Hunter centres, was sparsely peopled. The colony was clearly ill-balanced: even high wages could scarcely induce shepherds to go into the interior, and, in most cases, the owners themselves had to do rouseabout's work. Already, the problem was posed—unemployment in Sydney and stock rotting for want of shepherds outside, with seemingly no way of connecting the two. Those who had quit the city were content to rest in the congenial dissoluteness of the cedar-getters, some reached the large estates round the Hunter and Lake George, but only a few trickled beyond. Hence the disproportion between the amount of servant-labour and the vast output of wool in the interior.

Yet, when Gipps landed, he found the stock rolling on, in the same implacable way that had so impressed Bourke with a feeling of fatalism. In the west, they had, for some reason or other, avoided the land directly beyond the Namoi and had concentrated on the other side of the Gwydir—at the moment, they were filling up the gaps between Armidale and Tenterfield, and were resting, poised, their eyes on the Downs beyond Cunningham's Pass. They were on the fringe of what was afterwards Queensland.

At the other end of the colony, it was the Lachlan and the Lower Murrumbidgee that men were speaking of—the *New Country* beyond Dubbo, beyond Gundagai. Further south still, in the land stressed most of all, the flocks had come up from Port Phillip and joined with those overlanding by 'the Major's Line' from the Sydney-side. This combined movement was now going from the northern rivers to the west—out beyond Colac and up to Ballarat. Probably a line between these two places represented the approximate level of occupation at the moment Gipps landed, save for the Henty offshoots over near the South Australian border. Melbourne was a flourishing township —a lusty infant feeding on beef-steaks, it was said. Land had been sold the previous year, and already boom-conditions were emerging.

Gipps thus found the squatters on the move all along the eastern half of the Continent and an infant colony, as puling as it was lusty, set up by them at Port Phillip. All told, they had over a million sheep, and, especially in the north, 300,000 cattle, and contributed more than half of the colony's exports. Beyond these products, there was little trade. The once-flourishing whale-oil was fast declining, the New Zealand trade was distinctly uncertain, and there were no manufactures. Indeed, trade was so restricted by Old-World treaties that very few foreign vessels were allowed to enter the harbour at all. Usually only wool went to England to be sold, and imported products came from England, with a hurried appeal to the East and to South America in times of drought (for, strange to say, the colony did not produce nearly enough wheat for the needs of its 98,000 people !).

Gipps thus found himself the lord of this small community, most of them in a few settled districts, and the rest scattered over a territory some 800 by 200 miles, largely unknown except to the pioneers themselves. Or, from another point of view, there were 42,000 convicts to 56,000 freemen, a great proportion of whom had once been under the hold of the law. Each class—squatters and 'settlers', merchants and convicts—presented special problems, economic and social; and practically none of the major issues connected with the administration had been settled. The constitutional problem had been in embryo (Gipps at the moment he landed had confidential advices on this matter in his pocket !); the economic future of a colony built on wool had not been decided; the general principles of Governmental finance (at present built on a Land Fund) were not enunciated; the future of the convicts was just being discussed (though the place of emancipists was more or less won); and the position of free immigration was distinctly a matter of controversy.

At the moment Gipps could see only the two factors—wool and social quarrels. The rest of the problems were unfolding in the distance, and it was clear to him that none of them could be considered from any social point of view. New South Wales had not yet gone from the stage of class-interests to a community-viewpoint—its development in so far had been greatly retarded. Apart from the Governor, nobody could see anything but sheep. All questions came back to them. It was all the song of the sheep—money for the sheep, land for the sheep, labour for the sheep, roads for the sheep, merchants for the sheep, ships for the sheep—one long ruminant refrain !

The new Governor had to attack his problems practically from the beginning. Under his predecessor, land-sales had started, an emmigration-fund had been formed, a place had been made for all ex-convicts, a free emigrant-class was built up, and the squatters were placed on a legal footing. Gipps had to develop along each of these directions and, in addition, solve the financial and constitutional issues, and, throughout, adjust everything to the changing conditions. It has been said that Bourke left the colony at the crossways, with the outcome of the main issues still in doubt; but it was his successor who had to decide each of them and pilot the colony over the necessarily painful period of reconstruction—a reconstruction which was to include crisis and to border on ruin !

To effect this transformation, Gipps had the ever-present restraints of the Colonial Office and the legacy of social turmoil bequeathed him by Darling and Bourke, especially the disloyalty of the public officials who had ruined both of his predecessors. He had an Executive Council, consisting of the senior military officer, the Bishop of Australia, the Colonial Secretary and the Colonial Treasurer; but Sir Maurice O'Connell, Broughton, Deas Thomson and Riddell could scarcely have been described as the most helpful combination possible.

There was, too, the wider Legislative Council, consisting partly of officials, partly of nominee non-officials; but this was a very inadequate body—a body of old men out of touch with affairs and redeemed from complete ineptness only by the energetic protests of John Blaxland. Since 1835, however, aided by the newly-formed *Patriotic Association*—the instrument of Wentworth—the Council had protested on several occasions against the actions of the Government. But everybody recognized that the old Council was just lumbering on, awaiting its final extinction. Gipps knew that the new Act was being considered in England; indeed, it was one of the questions to which he had been requested to direct special attention : and the whole colony was impatiently awaiting a new and more representative body. As soon as he came, Gipps flung open their deliberations to the public, in order to connect them more directly with the interests they were supposed to represent; but the fact could not be concealed that, however much power might be allowed them from time to time, they were only an advisory body.

Gipps, therefore, had only to secure the support of his Executive Council and be sufficiently tactful with the legislative body to be virtually unchecked. He was tied down only by the dictates of prudence and the need of preventing any trouble grave enough to reach the ears of the Colonial Office : beyond that, he had a free hand. His actual Commission was not as wide as his predecessor's. He could not, for instance, levy armed forces or proclaim martial law, he could not exercise sovereign naval powers or try naval men, and his jurisdiction had been reduced by the separate foundation of South Australia; but, for purposes of practical administration, he was still in the position of the old Governors. The press might keep up their eternal excesses of attack and innuendo, and the reform bodies pursue their noisy way, inside and outside the Council; but the

Governor knew that the Colonial Office derided the press of a convict-colony and turned a deaf ear to reform (for was not he the only man in the colony who knew of Under-Secretary's Howick's real plans?), and that, so long as he did not offend against any of Downing Street's cherished theories and did not arouse the attention of the Commons, he could act as he pleased. Altogether, he was very satisfied with the plenitude of his power—so much so that he was inclined from the outset to under-estimate the forces of opposition. They were not mentioned in any constitutional Act, and he had his own estimate of their hold at the Colonial Office; so that it was not difficult to fall into the error of discounting them overmuch.

For the moment, however, none of these matters troubled Gipps. He was the leader who was going to govern, the reformer who would force the vagueness of colonial life into sharply etched reality. His previous executive record had been strikingly good—as might have been pre-supposed when a mere Major of Engineers, without wealth or high connections, could become Captain-General of Australasia, in succession to a long line of naval and military officers, all of high field-rank. Both of his immediate forerunners had been Lieutenant-Generals, Gipps was simply a hard-bitten Peninsula veteran, with the lowest field-rank. All that was known of him was that he had served from 1809 until the end of the Peninsula campaigns, was wounded at Badajos, and distinguished himself at the Pass of Biar. Routine duties filled the years after that, until he had acted as Secretary to the Commission enquiring into the causes of Canadian discontent in 1835. While this Commission's report was conciliatory to the point of effacement and did little to clear away the causes of dispute, it at least drew attention to the incisive views and forcible character of Gipps. He was the only man who seemed to know what he believed in : he had a doctrine—local government by means of 'district councils'—and anything clear-cut stood out in the welter of ineptnesses that was driving Canada towards the Papineau outburst. Therefore, when, two years later, Glenelg wanted a firm Governor to pilot New South Wales over its transitional period and to clear up the class-quarrels that had overawed Bourke, he turned to this vigorous Canadian Commissioner—a soldier with a long record, a student of colonial problems, a theorist with ideas, a man with a distinctly aggressive force, and withal still in the vigorous prime of thirty-seven years.

Indeed, the very qualities which were to rile the colonists were the grounds for Gipps's appointment—his almost irascible firmness and his steadfast advocacy of certain theories and a clearly defined attitude. There were no halftones about Sir George Gipps: where decision was wanted, where a firm hand was needed, there his qualifications shone, although, by a necessary implication, such useful qualities in a time of crisis and stress could become intensely irritating in more normal periods. Gipps, so far as his record showed before he came to Australia, was a man for an emergency, but scarcely for quiet consolidation. He had to have opponents, had to carry through a fighting policy in the face of steady antagonism—in short, he could transform lost causes to victory but hated ordinary garrison-conditions. He was the man of the Pass of Biar, the man who grasped one clear point in the Canadian struggle and stuck to it. It would be premature and unfair to criticize Gipps in the light of the later developments of his rule, but, confining one's self to his characteristics as known when he arrived, it may be said that he was forceful to the point of relentless obstinacy, keen-minded almost to an intolerance of those who knew less than himself, and so implacable in his moral standards that he tended to go out of his way to attack specific interests that sought unfair advantages.

There were the two sides of him—he was an inflexible incorruptible and the veriest paladin for his impartial cause, but against this, said Lang, quoting Horace, he was *impiger, iracundus, inexorabilis, acer.* Rude, arbitrary, sarcastic, intolerant, he was as hard upon himself as on his enemies, and lived a life of continual introspective turmoil. He was so anxious to be scrupulously fair that he stood out against all sections and would as willingly fight the Secretary of State, Whig or Tory, as any land-grabber in the colony. He made a fetish of abstract justice and was too conscientious, too troubled by any issue, to make the best administrator. Best described as a military Puritan, Gipps was condemned to a life of fighting on issues which racked him, because he had to combine a show of outward certainty with constant inner questionings, and because he had to take into account the class-conscious selfishness of his opponents while he wished to keep the argument on the plane of abstract justice. He was moral to the point of obtuseness—hence much of his trouble! But, when he landed, New South Wales knew him only as a man of force, with a long practical experience and devotedly attached to certain theories of colonial government. Rumours from Canada and his recent rapid advancement had focused attention on him, and the colony waited to see how he would respond to local conditions—and whose man he would be!

He found the colony much quieter than he had expected; 'the present state of the colony is one of remarkable tranquility,' he reported confidentially after two months' residence, but he was astute enough to add that it was probably because all sections were trying to win him over. The emphasis at that time was almost entirely on the subject of immigration. The end of assignment was in sight, and, with the rapid advance of the squatters over the interior, the scarcity of labour was becoming more acute every day. If assignment of convicts were to cease at such an inopportune time, a crisis would result, because labour was already difficult to obtain in Sydney, while all kinds of bonuses and premiums were not sufficient to drag men beyond the boundaries. The demand was increasing just when the existing supply was diminishing. Gipps at once perceived how illogical the situation was. 'That the sudden withdrawal of assigned servants would be fatal to the prosperity seems to be the impression of nearly everyone; and I must confess that I cannot help, in great measure, partaking in this opinion, although there is not, as I believe Your Lordship is aware, any bias in my mind in favour of forced labour.'[1] Capital was coming in to buttress the new squatting movement, yet every new draft increased the demand for labour. As against this, the convicts were going, the free immigrants were insufficient in numbers and unsuited for bush-life, and there were grave social and economic objections to the introduction of hill-coolies or Cantonese. Gipps, at this early stage, clearly stood for convict-labour. To him, English capital and Government-labour seemed the necessary concomitants of the pastoral expansion, and grave consequences would follow the continued introduction of the former without a corresponding addition to the labour-supply.

Equally disturbing to him was the financial position he found. He had been led to expect a quite exceptional situation, for Colonial-Office men had impressed him with the extent of the new Land Fund. Colonists were buying land, and were so prosperous that they could pay anything: the Colonial Office envisaged a future gold-lined with the yields of the Land Fund, and persuaded Gipps that he would find well-filled coffers. As a matter of fact, Bourke had previously pointed out that the colony could not balance its budget without assistance from the Home Government or the Land Fund, but the Colonial Office of Glenelg's time ignored this and was proceeding to raise the price of land from 5s. to 12s., thus diverting money from an already pressed colony by further taxation. What they meant was that there was for the moment a Land-revenue where there had been none a few years previously, and a striking temporary surplus of money in the colony due to the recent English importations. But the first was

[1] Gipps-Glenelg, 1 May 1838.

incidental to the establishment of land-sales, and the second only a passing aid to the new squatting interest; and it was foolish to regard them as permanent or to connect them with the ordinary internal budget.

Gipps soon let light on to this situation and directed a little coherent economic thinking to the vaguenesses of the official standpoint. He departed at the outset from presenting an unduly roseate view of affairs and wrote to Glenelg, who was now harassed on all sides by the turbulence of the colonies and the contempt of his fellow-Ministers, in a strain to which any Secretary must have been unaccustomed. 'The simple truth, my Lord, is that the reputation of being very rich has occasioned demands upon the Government, which, unless they are resisted, will infallibly bring us to bankruptcy.'

When he assumed the Government, it was spending £10,000 a month beyond its income—no small figure for a community of 56,000 freemen; and the Home Government was trying to make the local administration take over a further £90,000 a year for police and gaol expenses, and the like. In addition, new charges of all kinds were rising—protection of the aborigines (hitherto neglected), roads and communications, controlling the newly opened districts, and the thousand and one charges caused by the quadrupling of the colony's area within a few years. *To new taxes or to bankruptcy we must come*, ran the chorus of the Governor's refrain, and he went on to add that the seeming excess of capital was a point of weakness rather than of strength, because it misrepresented the real situation and encouraged gambling and boom conditions. Really, he argued in effect, the ordinary revenue was ominously shrinking, there was a severe drought, the stock were scourged with the new disease of catarrh, and all manner of fresh charges were cropping up. The position was fundamentally unsound, he reported to superiors who could think only of the land-boom and the excess of capital. It was embarrassing to find the actual position so different from what he expected, and he was compelled to postpone his more general plans and settle down to the cramping business of financial reconstruction. Land questions did not trouble him in 1838—they were simply a nuisance, and, anyhow, the colonists were not proving too bashful in using the Crown's domains! and immigration, troublesome as it was, could be postponed, particularly with South Australia absorbing English attention. All that Gipps could do at the time was to plunge into the fight for financial stability, with an occasional sortie into his other field of interest, that of native welfare.

No sooner had he started, however, than he found the Council arrayed against him. Supine and effete as they usually were, the members at once responded when their pockets were threatened. Gipps was inclined to override the Council, because he knew it was changing its form and because he thought it more or less a gesture to the larger settlers. He had opened its deliberations to the public soon after he came, so that the community might be more linked with the Government and might be more reconciled to the repeated post-ponements of the new Constitution Act. Gipps knew that any change in that direction would not come for a long time, because he knew Lord Howick's attitude and had even communicated the official viewpoint in confidence to a few of the leading colonists. Howick was inclined to think that the rivalry of the 'emigrants' and the 'emancipists' was too strong to justify any extension of represen-tative government. Naturally, such a Conservative measure would have satisfied nobody except Bishop Broughton, the Governor's most loyal henchman—even Gipps himself thought it too reactionary. As things stood thus, Gipps was willing to throw whatever sops he could to the colonists, and perhaps he was not beyond hoping that the greater publicity he was giving the Council would empha-size the obstructionist attitude it adopted towards him from the first.

The members had objected to any schemes of reform that would have increased their own burdens, and had reached the stage when they were unduly insistent on their own claims. In particular, they had two standing grievances. They held that, by the so-called *Com-pact* of 1834, Spring-Rice, the Secretary of State at the moment, had given them the right to appropriate land-revenue, and that Governor Bourke had recognized this. Bourke certainly had made injudicious statements in 1835 and had mentioned 'the income of the Crown Lands now placed by His Majesty under the control of the Council'; but the position was open to little legal doubt. Gipps was correct in asserting that the Crown had not unreservedly and perpetually abrogated its rights, and that such appropriation had not entered the head of the Colonial Secretary.

His strict attitude on this major claim automatically cut the ground away from the Council's more specific claim—that the Crown had no right to charge the ordinary revenue with the expenses of police and gaols—charges incurred by looking after English criminals. The unofficial members unanimously voted against the Governor on this matter, and his casting vote would have been necessary even in his first year, had he not promised to intercede with the Colonial Office. This he did, because his accounts could not meet the the new charge and still balance; but the struggle was far from over. Every act of Gipps's was against the ever-present grievance of police-and-gaols! It cropped up on every occasion, intensified every grievance, and coloured every official act with a tinge of pre-conceived villainy, according to the colonists.

Nor was the feeling abated by the continued postponement of the new constitution. Year by year passed, the new Governor's opinions became known in London; and still nothing happened. The land-system might be changed with annoying frequency, but the constitutional grievance was simply placed in one of the capacious drawers of the Colonial Office. Late in 1840, the long lethargy seemed ended when news of a Bill came,[2] with a fairly satisfactory franchise; but its failure restored colonial discontent. This gave way to waxing indignation when the Commons went on to reject Grote's motion to give New South Wales compensation for the expenditure on gaols: Parliament, it would appear, not only forbade advance but wanted to make the old shackles tighter and tighter. As a result of all this, Gipps was predestined to face a Council in opposition—an attitude confirmed by his own contempt of their status and his views on squatting and land-matters.

While the Council was thus regularly sounding its cacophony of discontent, the Governor was plagued by the question of land-prices. The Colonial Office at this time seemed interested only in a revenue from lands, and every new Secretary wished to arrive at a fresh system by what can only be described as a trial-and-error process. Each new official seemed to take the blocks allowed in this game, fling down each of them, and then, after convulsing colonial affairs with each move, end very much where he had begun. This was particularly so with Glenelg's two successors—Lord John Russell and Earl Stanley, both of them *doctrinaires* to a degree and both of very interfering dispositions. Glenelg had sought to mask his tragic inefficiency by letting things drift. On the most troublesome issues, this made him almost an ideal Secretary of State! But his successors wanted to be stern, strong men of destiny, and found their level in the jig-saw puzzle of colonial lands. There, they were quite safe: only Governors could protest, for the colonists were inarticulate, and Governors could easily be overridden or recalled!

The problem, as the Secretaries of State saw it, was simple. The colonies wanted labour: recent importations had given them capital, indeed, too much capital: and previous land-sales had proved very successful: why not, therefore, sell some of the remaining land for some of the remaining capital and use the proceeds to bring in

[2] Printed in the *Australian*, 12 November 1840.

emigrants? Why—they went on, carried away by the simplicity of their scheme—if the colonists are so prosperous, why not simply raise land-prices and swell Government-funds, whether emigrants are introduced or not? There is no end to arguments on this line.

In pursuance of such artificially simple ideas, change followed change in rapid succession. Just before he left the Colonial Office— indeed, less than six months before Gipps had arrived in Sydney— Glenelg took the initial step.[3] He raised the price of land from 5s. to 12s. an acre, declaring that the earlier price had been purely experimental and that the time had arrived for a change. He wanted to remedy the labour-shortage by providing an adequate emigration- fund, and incidentally, acting under Wakefieldian influence, to check the undue dispersion of settlers and reinforce the Squatting Act, which he viewed as a deterrent measure. To carry out these projects, he looked forward to a still larger increase, because past experience (in other words, the squatting movement) had shown the earlier checks to be insufficient. He was still suffering from that myopia which saw only the landed proprietors as settlers and which viewed all squatters as unwanted excrescences. He was very clear on this point, as if he wished to leave no doubt as to the extent of his mis- apprehensions. He even expected a further rise. If there is still a labour-shortage, ran his despatch, or if the colonists still rush beyond the settled lands, then the Governor has authority—nay, is ordered— to raise the price immediately, without awaiting instructions from home. At all costs, he must keep the population within the official bounds: Australia meant, not the pastured-lands then being won, but the alienated lands, beyond which were merely trespassers.

The colonists, already incensed by the heavy Police-charges foisted on them, and pre-occupied by the squatting expansion, were in no mood to brook such an antiquated point of view, and were most irate when news of the change leaked out in the columns of an opposition paper, the *Australian*, in the first days of 1839.[4] This was the last blow from 'the mean, jobbing Whig Ministry', and, accord- ing to the paper, 'it is clear as the sun at noonday that they have been influenced by corrupt motives—that the minimum price of land in this Colony has been raised for the express purpose of benefiting the swindling South Australian Company—a company founded on crude theory and experiment not yet tested'. The publication of the entire correspondence between Bourke, Glenelg, and the Company certainly proved the direct connection between the new colony and the rise in price, but it was not this so much as the ill-timing of the

[3] Glenelg-Gipps, 9 August 1838.   [4] *Australian*, 10 January 1839.

measure that provoked discontent. In a moment of drought and with every sinew being strained for the conquest of the interior, the Colonial Office could see nothing more desirable than adhering to an untried theory and imposing additional burdens on the country. The 12s. was not too large in itself, nor was the grievance sufficient to account for the outcry: it was simply that the colony's nerves seemed tautened, and the Crown authorities at home appeared unsympathetic to their pioneering struggle. It was not the measure itself, but the conflict of forces behind it. Hence, for instance, the almost hysterical language of even respectable news-sheets! The *Sydney Herald*,[5] not usually an alarmist paper, announced the measure by speaking of the Home Government as 'an intolerable incumbrance', by hinting at great changes that arise from small beginnings, and by urging a boycott of all British goods as a move 'to prepare for shaking off its rule at the very earliest possible opportunity' and to give a preference 'to those commodities produced by countries that may be useful to us as allies in time of need!' Such an emotional strain was evident in all of the papers of the day—even in this early stage before the concerted opposition to the personality of the Governor had gathered force!

Normanby, the next Secretary of State, went a stage further by unequivocally insisting on Crown rights over all lands, and over all funds derived from lands, thus at one stroke irritating both the general colonists and the Council. If anybody in the colony, judge or settler, went on Normanby, questioned such an absolute right, he would pass a declaratory Act.[6]

In the same year, Normanby gave place to Lord John Russell, who, in his usual abrupt, business-like manner, introduced a completely new system. He unhesitatingly laid down such-and-such a theory, and said it had to be administered, natural obstacles or no natural obstacles! Settlement was progressing so rapidly that something had to be done, he roared in effect, and he had done it.

He had merely declared himself dissatisfied with the existing system and introduced its opposite! Knowing the comparative success of the auction-system, especially in swelling the Land Fund, and knowing the resolute opposition of Sir George Gipps to any change, he had nevertheless set up a Board of arm-chair theorists, the Colonial Land and Emigration Commissioners (1840). They had never seen a colony, and so would not be biased or bound down by petty localisms, he argued. That they would know nothing of any of them, or that the vision from a Park Street window did not extend to

[5] *Sydney Herald*, 30 January 1839.   [6] Normanby-Gipps, 17 May 1839.

the frontier-lands, did not occur to him. They were Wakefieldians, and believed in a fixed and immutable price: so Wakefield and a fixed price it was!

Two factors really entered the official arguments. South Australia had proved that colonial lands could sell for £1 an acre, even in completely unimproved districts: where, then, was the logic in selling land in an older and more settled colony for less? In addition, the old colony now had good lands to offer in plenty. Van Diemen's Land, it was clear, was worked out, so much so that the best of the remaining lands were worth only a few shillings an acre; and the settled Counties of New South Wales were in much the same plight. But attention was focusing more and more on this new province of Port Phillip, which had more and better lands to offer. There, where the choice was wider, the Crown could increase its revenue the most easily. Lord John Russell therefore split New South Wales into various sections—the region from the south coast to the Murrumbidgee, in which land was to be sold at the fixed price ruling over the border in South Australia (£1 an acre), and the Middle District, the old colony, where the previous system of auction, with a 12s minimum, was to be retained.[7]

This was in May 1840, just in the midst of Gipps's difficulties. It was inevitable that a new change of land-policy, again in an upward direction, would renew discontent; but the Governor's trouble was that it forced him into conflict with everybody. He had to oppose both the Council and the colonists on the one hand, and the Secretary of State, with the cherished Land and Emigration Commissioners, on the other. Gipps, despite himself, found himself in a state of chronic opposition, for he endeavoured to plough a furrow through the morass of changing institutions and public opinion by rigidly keeping to what he considered the most equitable course. He was neither Whig nor Tory, neither pro-colonial nor pro-Government: he was caught between the fires and was every man's enemy—and he even wondered if he were true to his own conception of what was right. He went to great pains in these years to enunciate his own views on the land-problem beyond any possibility of misapprehension. To this matter, he devoted the bulk of his time and studies, for the well-being of Australia came down, at that time of pioneering, to a reasonable land-policy, one which both safeguarded the expectations of later generations and yet offered a scope to such men as the squatters of that period. Gipps's analyses of the many facets and implications of

[7] Lord John Russell-Gipps, 31 May 1840: Colonial Land and Emigration Commissioners-Lord John Russell, 15 April 1840.

this problem would fill a volume; and it is a striking commentary on his open mind to know that, while keeping the same basic principles throughout, he frequently changed his interpretations and in every case adapted his conclusions to the conditions prevailing.

Behind him were the theorists who controlled Downing Street, who all clamoured for higher and yet higher prices. In front of him, stood the solid array of colonial interests, demanding a reduction of prices, and giving point to their arguments by emphasizing the distress that unfortunately coincided with the changes of policy. Of the witnesses before the Committee of Council in 1841,[8] for instance, every one—bankers and merchants, land-owners and officials— opposed the rise as inordinate and detrimental to capital and prosperity, and this was but typical of outside opinion. Since 1839, there had been all manner of crises, due to drought, over-capitalization, general boom-conditions, and a score of other reasons, but the popular voice, seeing that they coincided with the rise in prices, argued that here was cause and effect, and that the collapse was due to the deliberately malevolent disposition of Downing Street. The coincidence in point of time, to them, could not be explained away; and perhaps they were partly right, because the change moulded public opinion in this direction, and the maintenance of the previously existing state of affairs had depended on the existence of a certain point of view. However this may be, Gipps felt the full blast of public disapproval, especially because he made no attempt to conceal his opinions, or even clothe them with sweet words.

In reality, he had been fighting the best cause of the colonists, and, in what he conceived to be their best interests, had flatly contradicted Secretary after Secretary and had protested in tones that presaged ill for his future, should his official opponents find any breach in his armour. Before he left England, he had informed the Secretary of State, Glenelg, of his moderate opinions, both as regards colonial land and labour, and the connection between them; and events in the colony had not been such as to convert him to any other theory.

On hearing of Lord John Russell's proposals in 1840, for instance, he wrote his famous *Memorandum on the disposal of lands in Australia*, definitely attacking the Wakefield System and taking a stand quite different from that of the Colonial Office. He started from the hypothesis that Australia was a pastoral, not an agricultural country, because not one-hundredth of the land sold was cropped, and because Australia did not produce nearly enough grain even for the

[8] *Committee on Debenture Bill, 1841—Votes and Proceedings*, p. 457.

small population at that date. That being so, the Wakefieldian theory of concentration had to go, because of what use was it to make people cultivate, or even occupy, lands in the order of their natural advantages, if pastoral land was esteemed far more highly than good agricultural? Moreover, under Australian conditions, to prevent dispersion would have been absurd and impossible. As well try to restrain the nomads of the desert within a line on the sand, went on Gipps in his well-known simile, as keep the Australian squatters within the settled lands! By the nature of things, settlers must spread over the face of the country, and not a hundred thousand soldiers, not all the armed forces of the Empire, could prevent this!

This did not mean to imply, however, that Gipps favoured a reduced price or other undue inducements to the squatters.[9] He opposed what he called *the South Australian principle*, but not because of the price it laid on Crown lands. To the contrary, he would have exacted a still higher rate. 'I am in favour of selling at a high price or of not selling at all!,' he said time and again, and found no patience with those who held that 12s. was too much to pay for an acre of land. What annoyed him was the idea of concentration and the determination of a fixed price by certain *a priori* arguments having this concentration as an end. He saw no reason why the Government should not get what the land was worth, and that was best determined by public competition at auction. This was especially the case in a country of such variations as Australia, where the most distant piece of land on the map might be worth as much as a city-block, and where the dry rocky plains were far better for sheep than the greenest meadow-lands. Australia was a country of 'eyes'—eyes which auction alone could pick out. Therefore, he concluded,

I have never been a blind follower of what is called the *Theory of Systematic Colonization*, or the *South Australian System*: and, though I fully admit many of the principles on which that theory is founded, I have ever regarded as visionary the attempt to carry out the principles of the theory in all colonies, notwithstanding the differences which they present to the most superficial observer. I have particularly, in respect to New South Wales, objected (and objected successfully!) to the abolition of sales by auction; and still more strongly have I endeavoured to show how inapplicable to New South Wales, or indeed to any pastoral country, is what is called the theory of concentration, or the anti-dispersion principle.

Thus ran Gipps's *Credo* in its final form of 1844: and it was for these

[9] Gipps-Russell, 19 December 1840. See collected correspondence in *Votes and Proceedings*, 1844, vol. I (given to Council, 30 May 1844), or 1842, p. 16.

principles that he fought the Colonial Office on the matter of a fixed price, and the serried ranks of the colonists, from the Surveyor-General downwards, on the matter of the raised minimum. From the first, he stood for auction at a high upset price, and for any degree of dispersion that might result from this.

His strongest fight was against Lord John Russell's change of 1840, setting up a fixed price in Port Phillip. With an almost malicious glee, he asserted that the Crown would lose a million pounds on town-lands alone, and, at the time of the first sale at Portland Bay, blandly added a note that, had the sale taken place on the South Australian principle, the sum realized would have been £337, instead of the £17,245 obtained at auction. He wanted the plan he previously had at Port Phillip. He would pass over, he said (though he set out at length the things he was going to pass over so magnanimously!) the South Australians' lofty vaunting of themselves, and their unredeemed pledge of appropriating not one penny of land-revenue for the purposes of civil government; and he would not be so obvious as to ruminate on their sacrifice of all lands near the city for £1 an acre. Writing with forbearance; he would discard all of these arguments and concentrate on the benefits of the Port Phillip system, mentioning in passing that already (February 1841) he had received twice as much for the Melbourne land as for the Adelaide and yet had half a million acres of unsold land within five miles of the town, whereas Adelaide had none! In Port Phillip, he sold the land at auction, with the survey continuously moving forward, and the land put up to auction as the Government willed—not, as under the old system, on anyone's demand anywhere within the Settled Counties. The new system was far more fruitful, far more controlled, and gave the settler the benefit of public works in his earliest days.

About the minimum price, he had little to say. Despite the revilings of the press and the groaning of the settlers in 1839, the rise had been accompanied by a rapid increase in the auction-values of land and by a far greater return for the Government. Speculation, it was admitted, had been encouraged, but this had no connection with the upset-price or the system of auction. The one obvious fact was that the Land Fund had swollen to £153,000 in 1839 and to over £316,000 in 1840: and, for this reason, Gipps was unperturbed by the proposal to raise the price, even to £1. All that he wanted was to stop wasting the nation's patrimony by a fixed price, which did not reflect the value of the land, which forbade variations *above* the minimum, and which played into the hands of 'land-sharks'.

So trenchant were his facts (and, it should be added, so biting his

irony!) that Lord John Russell had to give way. He quoted the
Crown Lands and Emigration Commissioners, and they quoted the
Governors of Van Diemen's Land and Western Australia and
Canada; but Gipps still thundered. One of Lord John's last acts, a few
days before he gave way to Lord Stanley (September 1841), was to
revoke the idea of a fixed price for Port Phillip—a change in con-
formity, too, with the recent report of the Commons' *Committee on
South Australia*. Auction was to be restored to all sections of New
South Wales: and Stanley added his voice a few weeks later by
stipulating that the minimum price should be £1.[10]

Gipps had thus triumphed all along the line and overridden the
Secretary of State on one hand and the colonists on the other. The
Commissioners of Park Street had been dealt a severe blow, and their
apostolic stand for colonial infallibility somewhat weakened; and
Gipps had ridden roughshod over everybody, over too many sets of
people, as he was to find, for his own future comfort. He was vic-
torious, and his arguments were correct: but the resentment remained. Victor or vanquished, he had arrayed forces against him,
and they were to maintain their array long after the fight was over.

The matter was finalized by Stanley's first instructions of October
1841, forecasting a general Act of Parliament to deal with all Australian lands. There was a clear tendency towards uniformity
throughout the whole continent, and Stanley, in this first despatch,
left no doubt that he wanted a higher price. He was invoking the
aid of the British Parliament to secure one Australian system—of
sale by auction at a minimum price of £1—in a word, he was to give
Gipps's arguments a Parliamentary apotheosis. But the colonial discontent lingered and gathered force to recoil on Gipps's head. Committee after Committee reported against the minimum price, and
the colonists, as before, attributed the grave crisis of the early forties
to the land-system; but Gipps by now was immersed in wider problems. He had settled the system of disposing of land and had
imposed his views on, first the Colonial Office, and now Parliament:
and, having done this, tended to look upon his colonial opponents
as mutineers who were still protesting after the event. He himself
had gone forward—to newer fields—but this time, to a disaster.

The land-question had absorbed his attention in the years between
1838 and 1841; but, towards the latter part of that period, immigration had forced itself into the first place, and in its track followed
the great crisis. The first faintly ominous hints of trouble had come

[10] Except that it could be 12s. in the old Middle District. Despatches of Lord
J. Russell, 21 August 1841, and Stanley, 18 October 1841.

in Gipps's earliest days, when he found the State finances in an unstable condition, though, owing to the general feeling of buoyancy,
something like boom-conditions were being experienced. Stock was
bringing unheard-of prices, and English capital was available on
remarkably easy terms. Everything was surging forward, and Gipps,
when he voiced a note of warning, found himself viewed as a
pessimist, utterly opposed by the community in general. It was all a
tale of borrowing money, buying stock at inflated prices, and then,
in the words of the current refrain, packing up one's bullock-dray
and going to the West! Land there was in plenty, capital for the
signing of one's name—and what more was to be wanted?

At a much later date, Gipps was to write about human action in
general, 'When vast numbers of persons agree in any opinion (however erroneous), the mere concurrence of opinion will (for a time at
least) produce an effect nearly as great as if the opinion were
well-founded.' And so it was in 1839. Everybody believed that
conditions really were what they appeared to be on the surface: the
profits derived from the general boom in Port Phillip, for instance,
were very real, and it appeared as if the doubters were the only
persons who suffered, and they only because they lacked initiative!

So events went on, capering gaily in a *valse caprice* of speculation,
until the severe drought made men pause. The colony was suddenly
stricken with the worst dryness since 1828-9, the newly occupied
country frizzled up, and the Murrumbidgee stopped running in its
bed. The squatting occupation stopped, and the treacherous interior
proved itself a land of parched plain and dry water-courses, with
even the salt-grass and the grey mulga gone. The stock could not
live, they could not be taken far enough away; and the overland
routes became clearly marked by the gleaming bones of dead
animals. Stockmen learned, then, with a sufficient emphasis, that the
drier plains were far more certain than the thickly-grassed meadow
lands—that rock-country with edible shrubs was a more perennial
certainty than denuded fields where everything went with the
thick, dank grass; but it was too late for them. The years before had
witnessed the *Hegira of the sheepmen*; this season saw the answer
of a malevolent Nature—and the answer was final for many of
them.

To point the moral, the colony faced a severe food-shortage. Gipps
had relaxed the corn-duties in January 1839, when the crops had
failed; but no supplies seemed available from Van Diemen's Land or
South America, and, to make matters worse, the maize-crop in its
turn shrivelled up. Gipps at once reduced the convicts' rations, but

that was not enough. Hundreds of miles, even in the located districts, were without a blade of grass or a drop of water, while, beyond the boundaries, the scene beggared description. It seemed as if a terriffic stench—the smell of dying stock—were rolling in as the answer of the newly violated interior; and the colonists had no defence. Wheat was now 20s. a bushel, maize six times its normal value, and butter and vegetables practically unprocurable. Yet the convicts had to be fed, and the newly arriving immigrants cared for, although there seemed no alternative supplies in an isolated colony which had emphasized its wool-staple to an almost total neglect of farming products.

Gipps, in desperation, entered into agreements with commercial houses to import 100,000 bushels of rice from India, guaranteeing them a certain minimum return. But this outside aid did not arrive until the last days of July, when distress had verged on starvation in the remote parts of the colony, and when people in Sydney had been obliged to go without food for a few days. What would have happened had the barques not arrived from India that week is hard to say, because the crisis was more serious even than in those early days when the entire community lingered on the sea-front eagerly scanning the horizon for the solitary convoy of food. Flour had risen to ninepence a pound, the quarter-loaf to 2s. 8d., and ordinary people could not pay those prices! The expected shipments of wheat from India did not arrive, and none could be expected until the colonial harvest late in 1840. By May of the new year, therefore, conditions were again so bad that Gipps had to support the populace afresh. The only way the poor could get food to eat was by the Government supplies distributed through the local Benevolent Society, because the price, in money-terms, had become absurd.[11]

It will at once be asked why supplies were not shipped from other countries, but the answer is not difficult. Van Diemen's Land, hitherto an alternative granary of the mainland, was itself in difficulties; India had proved a broken reed; and South America presented obstacles, because of the lack of shipping and the quarrel Gipps had been having with those countries over the Navigation Acts. Under these conditions, it was not until the close of 1840 that American wheat really commenced to come. Once it started, however, it poured in, so that there was grain a-plenty in the colony by the end of September, and, a month later, it was a drug in the market at dumped prices. Within twenty months, wheat had fluctuated be-

[11] Gipps's despatches, 8 April 1839; 9 September 1839; 30 November 1840.

tween its normal value of 7s. 6d. and 25s., and now could not be sold at 5s. 6d.

Gipps knew, however, that the relief was only temporary, and that the colony would for ever be faced by the same evil, until due importance was attributed to farming: though, an inveterate free-trader, he did not sufficiently see the importance of being self-sufficient in this regard and was more inclined to look to the cheaper South American and Indian markets than to home supplies. Instead of looking into the future, he kept his eyes fixed on the flocks. He thought he could solve the problem by storing foreign wheat when it was superabundant and selling it, at prices fixed by the Government, when a drought came. That this implied an undue extension of Government activities and a chronic interference with the normal economic life of the colony did not occur to him; nor did he see that he would be thus acting as a direct deterrent against the cultivation of crops within Australia. To the contrary, when wheat was selling for three-quarters of its normal value, he bought large quantities (which, he argued, would, in the normal course of trade, be either exported again or distilled), and kept it in the colony by storing it in the huge bottle-shaped excavations he had made in 1839 in the solid sandstone rock of Cockatoo Island. There, hermetically sealed in these rock silos, it would retain its freshness and afford a constant guarantee against starvation. He claimed that this was both taking advantage of the low prices then ruling and safeguarding the future: but his promising experiment suddenly ended when his enthusiastic despatches met the coldest of welcomes from Lord Stanley and he was ordered to sell the supplies at once and confine himself to the legitimate functions of Government.

By this time, the drought, in the normal course of affairs, had abated, though its consequences were just being realized. The money that had seemed so easy to raise now presented quite a different complexion. Interest had to be met, but there had been little wool and, when the lenders attempted to realize on their securities—to collect the sheep bought with the money they had advanced—they found too often that the drought had carried with it their capital, leaving behind a few heaps of putrescent bone. The squatter was forced to the wall, the capitalist lost his money—and the community in general found itself coming to a new scheme of values. But all of this happened slowly: the first drought-year was explained away as something freakish, the second saw an extension of facilities because nothing was to be gained by a premature distraint, and, before the matter of renewal cropped up once more, the end of 1840 had come—and, with it, radical changes.

Beyond the drought, 1839 had been a year of little interest. Attention focused on Port Phillip, where the west was being occupied; and the entire community seemed irresponsible in the grip of 'the champagne-bubble'—that fever of speculation which had led men's minds astray and forced them to pay ridiculous prices for stock and city-allotments. The drought in the Middle Colony was somewhat obscured by this tumultuous boom which, indeed, served to continue for another year that spirit of delusive prosperity which Gipps had found on his arrival.

Observers still thought that large-scale immigration would right matters and that the former rate of progress could be maintained if sufficient labourers could be found for the flocks that had moved into the interior. While the South, therefore, was speculating in land-values, the older colony was concentrating on schemes to quicken the flow of immigration. In 1839, for example, a Council Committee, presided over by Bishop Broughton, had reported in favour of a renewed Government-effort, but the year actually saw a decline in the number of arrivals.

Otherwise the session was very quiet; the only interest lay in the drought and the raised price of land. Gipps, it is true, presented an important *Minute on Education*, revealing still another problem arising from the occupation of the interior, but nothing came of it. The question of a gas-supply aroused passing attention, the colonial distillery slightly more, and a very long report of a Police Committee covered old ground; but nothing was really outstanding in public interest. Certain important movements were slowly emerging—the decentralization of justice and the abolition of imprisonment for debt, for instance—though their significance was scarcely seen. It might have been thought that the end of transportation, when announced in this year, would have attracted notice, but it had been heralded for so long that nobody was interested in the actuality.

The new year (1840) was practically as bad. Outside of the legal changes, the record of Council is unusually dull reading. Broughton's Committee again made a scrappy report, Maconochie started a new convict-experiment at Norfolk Island, Wentworth tried to snatch all of the South Island of New Zealand; but, in the main, the year was dull and unimportant. No crisis relieved its tedium, no energy disturbed its lifeless sterility: Its roster of weary months simply slipped by, with a few distant reverberations of Lord John Russell's thunderings in London. Little new land was occupied. In Port

Phillip, only a few gaps in the previous line were filled, except for the Hopkins mouth and Macmillan's penetration of the Monaro; while squatting settlement even receded in the Middle District, driven back by the threat of drought. Further north, the outer fringe, which seemed to have been fixed round Tenterfield for some years, was brusquely pushed forward by Patrick Leslie, who crossed the frontier of modern Queensland.

But the record was a feeble one as compared with previous years. Consolidation in the south and defence in the centre were the orders of the day, and the outside men began to wonder a little about the future. In New South Wales proper, they already felt the pinch, though the land-bubble was still misleading Port Phillip. The panic there was slower in coming because the colony was not so developed; and, indeed, the year passed, even in the older colony, in an apparently prosperous manner.

On the surface, all seemed well. The boom in the south had doubled the land-sales, and the ordinary revenue seemed on the increase as well; but, for all that, convulsive movements were taking place under the surface dullness. Signs of financial distress were becoming evident and the ordinary Government expenditure was still increasing tremendously, as it had in the previous five years. The ordinary revenue (that is, all except land) was not equal to this, and the Council wanted to fall back on the land revenue instead of levying new taxes. It only needed some striking business-failure, some tightening of credit-facilities, or a new drought to precipitate disaster; and this was brought home to everybody before the year was out.

Lord John Russell, at home, was the first to take alarm, because it appeared as if the Governor, despite his protests of two years before, had also been carried away by the outward signs of prosperity and by the ease with which the colony recovered, or seemed to recover, from the drought.[12] In reality, this recovery was in itself a sign of the times, the strongest possible indication that the colonists were not facing the facts of the situation and were sleeping in an illusory security. Any natural phenomenon of that magnitude must have caused distress and a painful period of reconstruction in a normally constituted economic community: the absence of such travail indicated an abnormality.

The Secretary of State, who seemed in a particularly querulous mood all of this year (perhaps because the life of the Whig Ministry was ebbing fast!), was seeking opportunity to chide the Governor

[12] Lord John Russell-Gipps, 28 June 1840.

who had triumphed in the land-dispute. Lord John had set up the Colonial Land and Emigration Commissioners in London and was attempting to centralize colonial administration and introduce a uniform policy. As a foretaste, he had introduced a fixed-price in Port Phillip and was ready to question any new move of the Governor's. The colonists grumbled at having to meet the Police and Gaol Expenses, now amounting to £104,000 a year; he gave short shrift to that complaint. They pointed out that the total revenue, apart from the separate Land Fund, was only £202,000 (1838). Lord John replied by criticizing their extravagance. The financial embarrassments, he said in as many words, were not due to police-expenditure but solely to the general increase in spending. The colony was blinded by its own prosperity, Governor no less than populace, he hinted, because why otherwise had the four main departments more than doubled their expenditure in four years? And why did the colonists always assert that the Land Fund should go for general expenditure? And why didn't they raise new taxes, instead of relying mainly on taxing spirits and tobacco? And why had they recently proposed a loan of a million pounds? They were altogether beside themselves, thundered Lord John, hinting that they should confine themselves to hard work rather than grievances, and should arrange for immigration rather than bemoan the lack of it. He was not at all sympathetic with their complaints and openly scorned their short-sighted complacency. But neither Governor nor colonists were in a mood for blustering reproof, and Lord John's hints, arguments, and advice all passed unheeded.

As soon as 1841 dawned, the change burst like a thunderclap in a surcharged sky. Gipps opened the year by advising the Colonial Office quietly, and as if it were an everyday matter, that the total amount of outstanding bounty-orders was practically *a million pounds sterling*—£979,562 for 71,315 persons. All through the previous years, the emphasis had been on immigration. The squatters could not obtain enough labour, whatever prices they were willing to pay, and each shepherd had to mind ridiculously swollen flocks. Broughton's Committee, now almost a standing body, was dinning its prosaic refrain every year, and the Council records were practically long collections of immigration-documents. Gipps, therefore, had argued that it was impossible to give too much aid to emigrants and had offered unrestricted permission to anyone to import them, a bounty of so much being given for every person. He had thought that the new revenue from Port Phillip could pay for hundreds of thousands, but, when it was too late, he was informed that a revenue thus derived from one district could not be diverted to meet the requirements of another—that, in a word, the Melbourne land-revenue could not pay for the emigrants he was landing in Sydney! The situation was unbelievable. Gipps was faced by the prospect of receiving 70,000 emigrants for whom he had no money, while the Colonial Office, without being advised or consulted, was saddled with a bill of a million pounds.

The trouble was that Gipps had been led astray by the perennial complaints about a shortage of labour. He could not envisage conditions under which labour would be super-abundant, and so was led to neglect certain factors. He had so miscalculated that, only a few months before—in September 1840—he had asked the Colonial Office to supplement the bounty-system and resort to Government-emigration, if the total supply did not exceed 10,000 a year. That is, he expected too few immigrants whereas, in reality, they flooded in, took out orders to the extent of a million pounds, and forced the Governor to ask Lord John Russell to restrict the number leaving the United Kingdom. Gipps was regulating the supply by the demand—indeed, by a demand that he should have seen was largely fictitious—and neglecting the basic principle that immigration had to be restricted by the ability to pay for it.

To intensify matters, he had to open another painful subject in the same month! The signs of commercial crisis were so obvious that he could not longer pass over them but had to report that his huge debt of a million pounds coincided with a stringency in every sphere of commerce. The colony had drifted into a state of crisis: his new blow threatened to kill it! The crisis had set in about October and soon destroyed the normal economic life of the land. It started with the Land Fund. As the months went by, it was seen that sales were only a quarter of those of 1840—and this was typical of the general shrinkage.

From a system, indeed, of nearly unbounded credit, the transition has been sudden to an almost total denial of it; and consequently persons, who can no longer get accommodation at the Banks, are obliged to dispose of such property as they may be possessed of at very depreciated prices.

The prick was being felt and money was as ridiculously scarce as it had hitherto been plentiful, even for the most legitimate enterprises. Panic was setting in and a monetary crisis followed close on the commercial. A considerable part of the previous boom was now seen to be the work of speculators, especially in station-properties and land-values; and securities, at that time thought adequate, were found to have little permanent or intrinsic value.

A disease of faith had given place to one of despair, though conditions had called for neither. It was a new form of boom—salutary at the expense of throttling life, reforming by a process of obliteration. The earlier boom had at least been accompanied by growth and development; but the despair could mean only a decline. It was not healthy, but only suicidal, to deny every advance of the previous ten years and to ascribe every pastoral venture to illicit speculation. The avowed evils could not be redressed by shutting out all activity and denying the healthy progress along with the speculation. That the previous stimulation had been largely artificial was quite clear, but this new attitude was completely negative. The community, stricken with morbidness, was entirely unreasoning in its acceptance of the passing check as a final disaster. Without recognizing this unhealthy exaggeration of the symptoms, the observer cannot pretend to understand the absolute despondence of the colony in 1841, or its acceptance of the finality of the blow dealt it. The trouble was as much psychological as financial: the community was for the moment exhausted by the efforts of the period of expansion. Hence the unjustified phantasm of gloom that was deliberately conjured up. It was the emotional excoriation of desperately tried souls—a bill for pass excesses, both temperamental and economic!

Of course, there were the more obvious evils—the colony had been spending too much; it had been wasting huge sums in land-speculation, especially at Port Phillip; stock-prices had been absurd; loans had been made on the slightest security; profits had been calculated on too generous a scale; Banks and Government had based their plans on a transient and exaggerated degree of prosperity; and—the basis of everything—money had been coming in from England to upset the general economic equilibrium of the colony. When this stopped, a general deflation was necessary—a calculation according to a far more stringent set of basic values. All of these weaknesses had been accentuated by the long drought and the setback of the squatting movement—by the end of assignment and the shortage of labour—by the fall of wool-prices and the close of land-sales: and the day of reckoning was at hand.

Gipps thus had no other alternative. He had to announce his twin bombshells, and the several grave reports he made during the year reinforced his earlier description. The bounty-orders remained, the Land Fund that was to meet them dwindled, and the wider crisis gained in intensity.

The answer of the Colonial Office was what might have been expected, and, on the whole, justified by the circumstances. Lord John

Russell, the Whig *doctrinaire*, was still at the helm when the news reached England, and, never an admirer of Sir George Gipps, he was only too ready to seize this cause of reproof. Nor can it be said that he suffered from any undue restraint! He sent out a stinging castigation in July 1841, going over the points of censure again and again, lest the Governor should miss them on the first reading. Lord John always had a sledge-hammer hand: joined to a biting reiteration, its cumulative effect was quite unmistakable. He treated Gipps like a little schoolboy.

Asking at the outset whether Gipps's Government may not have been in some sense responsible for the evils, Russell pre-judged his case by asserting that 'there is but too much cause' for such a supposition. That being so, Gipps had to consider himself gravely censured. As far as bounties were concerned, he said,

I must disclaim any responsibility for this proceeding and any obligation to ratify your engagements to the enormous extent to which you have entered into them. If you will refer to my former despatches on the subject of the Land Fund, you will see that not only have I never imparted to you an authority for such an outlay as this, but that, to the extent to which you have now engaged in it, you have acted in entire disregard of those instructions.

So far, this was an unrestrained condemnation. But, drastic though it was, it was mild as compared with what was to follow. Such a procedure, went on the Secretary of State, gathering momentum as he progressed, was unfair and ruinous to everybody. It perhaps meant ruin to the individual emigrants who had sold up on the promise of the Colonial Government. Why, he added gravely, they may even have got married!

Leaving the private aspects at this climax, the despatch went on to the governmental aspect and openly charged Gipps with aggravating, if not indeed causing, the existing commercial crisis.

As to the colony, it appears that at the moment of commercial embarrassment to which you have referred, there were afloat in the market Bounty-orders amounting to nearly a million sterling, the whole of which it is but too probable the Colonial Treasury may be called upon to redeem. It is difficult to measure the effect which such an operation must have had in stimulating that reckless spirit of commercial enterprise to which you ascribe the disasters of the colony. But it is clear that the effect must have been very considerable.

That being so, and the evil now done, Lord John has no other course than to attempt to limit the flow of migrants from his end and to lay on Gipps 'the most distinct and peremptory instruction' not to issue any bounty-orders beyond the net amount of land-revenue applicable to them in the ensuing financial year. He concluded his despatch by the most unequivocal hit of all, using language of a kind rarely met with even in Whig despatches:

I have not written this despatch without very sincere regret. I am deeply sensible of your claims to the respect and confidence of Her Majesty's Government, and of the difficulties in which you are placed by the pressure of local interests upon you. But it is my duty to record my disapprobation of an unauthorized proceeding which may affect the Revenue of this Country, and which, by unduly stimulating speculation, may be highly injurious even to those local interests which it was designed to promote. I shall endeavour, however, to the best of my power, to counteract the mischievous effects of your improvidence, for which you alone are responsible!

Next month, the Melbourne Ministry resigned, and Lord Stanley became the Colonial Secretary of Peel's exceptionally strong Cabinet. Affairs at home were particularly grave at that moment. There were wars abroad, distress among the poor, mounting unemployment, commercial crisis, and a grave deficit. Peel likened himself to a Chancellor sitting on an empty chest, fishing in a pool of bottomless deficiency: and his reception of an unwanted colonial bill of a million pounds may be imagined. Stanley, his colonial henchman, was young, over-brilliant, and dogmatic, with a reputation for cleverness to maintain and a freedom from the rebounds of indiscretion. The repercussion of this union on the unfortunate Gipps is best left to the imagination. Stanley at once went out of his way (14 October 1841) to affirm his precedessor's censure and, if anything, to use even less restrained language. The condemnation of the Whig may have been slightly relieved by its brusque *gaucherie*: the Tory's now had the cutting incisiveness of etching-acid. This very young scion of the Derbies wrote:

I am compelled to adopt to the full extent the language of censure which Lord John Russell felt himself under the necessity of using, and to take steps which may appear to weaken your personal authority in the Colony over which you preside. But the dangers to the welfare of that Colony, arising out of the improvident Course which you have allowed yourself to pursue, in disregard of positive instructions, are so serious and so imminent as to supersede all other considerations and to compel me to resort, as I am assured my Predecessor would have resorted, to the most decided measures to arrest or mitigate the impending evils.

These censures reached Gipps after a troublesome year. The commercial crisis and his own fiasco regarding immigration were with his every waking hour; and he felt that he could not count on the support of the Whigs at home, especially when his wheat-buying policy had been brusquely reversed. Assignment had ended on 1 July, and that had naturally meant a vast amount of reorganization, both in withdrawing the convicts from private landowners and in arranging for their future disposition. Immigration to fill the gap had been so inordinately stressed that there were not enough ships to go around, though the emigrants still came in such numbers that they could not readily be absorbed, and wages rapidly fell—a striking proof of how the previous agitation had been manoeuvred by interested sections !

In June, the crisis had necessitated a short session of Council, and again in November. Debenture-schemes and loan-proposals had been launched, and a widely-signed petition circulated to advocate the introduction of hill-coolies from the United Provinces; but Gipps had no money and wages were falling ! The session passed very easily under these circumstances; the old dogmatism, both of Governor and Council, had gone, and both sides were now prepared rather to watch the course of events.

Matters were changing so rapidly that it seemed folly to advocate particular policies: all that could be done was to try to keep abreast of each new phase of the crisis. Every concrete proposal was thus pushed into the background. The plan to raise debentures on the ordinary revenue could not be accepted, while the loan-project was still more unpopular out of doors. Gipps, too, seemed to have lost that peculiar distinctness which had hitherto characterized his views. Towards the middle of the year, he had become alarmed at the changes, and, losing faith in his general policy, was frankly nonplussed by the growth of expenditure and the position regarding the outstanding bounty-orders. His revenue in all branches was declining, his expenditure increasing—and the deficit seemed permanent.

The gloom deepened as the year went on, reaching its nadir about September.[13] In that month, Gipps reported the money-shortage more acute than ever; and a new factor to cause disquietude was the arrival of the agents of two great loan-companies, to whom the settlers were recklessly mortgaging their estates. The only bright spot was in the complete absence of faction in the Council; the crisis was too real to allow of sectional attitudes and, for once, the Governor found himself supported by the Council. 'The country was never more

[13] Gipps-Lord John Russell, 9 September 1841; 17 July 1841.

free from party-spirit,' he wrote in December, 'or from any desire
to oppose or thwart the Government'; and he hoped much from the
crop-prospects and the revival of wool-prices in England. But he could
not conceal the gravity of the situation. Immigrants were coming in
far too rapidly—by December the June agitation for coolies seemed
ages away!—and Gipps was forced to refuse the payment of those
bounty-orders that had been conditional and thus left a loophole for
evasion. He had no funds, now that the land-sales were ceasing, and he
knew that Lord John Russell was decidedly against a loan. By October,
he was too well aware that he had spent five times the land-revenue
on immigration—with two more months to run! Therefore, very
warily and somewhat late in the day, he requested the Colonial Office
to limit emigration in 1842, and threw out tentative proposals for a
loan.

Before the gloomy December went out, however, Gipps received
another surprise. Nine days after he had sent an optimistic despatch
—one which sent a somewhat watery gleam of light over the situation by neglecting nine-tenths of it and by emphasizing the few
hopeful tendencies—the *William Jardine* brought him Lord John
Russell's censure on his bounty-orders. That was the day before
Christmas Eve, and it must have been a cheerless Christmas at
Government House in 1841, especially because the Governor had
learnt a week earlier of the defalcation of Manning, the Registrar of
the Supreme Court. The censure itself was a staggering blow to a
martinet like Gipps who took his work so seriously and who had
only done what he thought was right. Then, to be chastised like a
careless schoolboy—and worst of all, to have the local opposition get
hold of a supposedly confidential despatch and flay the pride of a
man as inordinately proud as he was—was unthinkable!

The reception of this despatch marked the lowest point of Gipps's
career, the more so because his own miscalculations had been mainly
responsible for the collapse. He was condemned in the crudest terms
at home; his policy was looked at askance by the Colonial Land and
Emigration Commissioners for his heresy against the South Australian principles; the colony was drifting deeper and deeper towards
a morass of commercial ruin; the seemingly-endless drought had
given way to only a fair crop; and the opposition and newspapers,
despite the greater harmony of the past session, were ready to unite
against him in a paean of hatred. First, the Colonial Office, with all
the attendant public laughing, had made him sell the thousands of
bushels of grain he had laid into his rock-granaries against the
drought; now, after having made him the laughing-stock of the

ribald crowds at the auction-rooms, came this condemnation—already, by some means or other, public property! Nobody would, as the street aborigines said, 'gib it tickpence' for the Governor's prestige, and the Wentworth faction, still smarting under their rebuff of the year before, held high revelry. Parodies were sung about '*My power is over the border*' and new verses added to the lewd songs of the stockmen; and, the while, the over-serious Governor moaned at Government House, his conceit pricked, his earnest desire to sacrifice himself for the colony weakening. '*The Patriot*', he liked to see himself—he was suffering a patriot's reward!

He closed the year explaining away his own improvidence and exaggerated expectations—blaming the Colonial Office for giving no hint of disapproving of the loan-project that had been discussed since 1838; blaming the Banks for excessive credits and for acting without due caution; blaming the colonists for misrepresenting the situation; and, in fact, inveighing against everybody. Even assuming the worst, he argued, the situation was not irremediable. Most of the bounty-holders could be deterred from migrating; and what was the use of the Agent-General and the Board of Commissioners in London if they could not watch over the flow of emigration, and to some extent control it? It was not a wise attitude for one in his circumstances to adopt, but this was one of those adverse occasions when Gipps's worst characteristics were as obvious as his best, and his statements must be discounted by remembering the blow to his prestige.

The next year was throughout an epilogue of the drama that had unfolded itself in 1841—an uneventful, lifeless quietness, serving only to point the evils that had emerged in the earlier stage. Its blank drabness was the perfect foil, its lack of interest the most dramatic way of emphasizing what had gone before.

Nothing at all happened. Gipps was still smarting under his rebuke, and the check was so complete that no extra stimulus was needed from the Council. Politics were therefore very quiet, the members doubtless having sufficient private matters to absorb their attention. The squatting crisis, it is true, was emerging, and the first concrete case at issue was in 1842; but everybody realized that the time had not yet come to join forces. James Macarthur moved for a *Squatting Commission*, but the motion was withdrawn. The only important matter in the short session was the incorporation of Melbourne and Sydney, though this caused an altogether disproportionate amount of bother and agitation. It was, as far as it had any character at all, a session of documents. Merewether, the Colonial Agent, presented a report on emigration, the Bishop's Committee added one more to its line of detailed reports, and the Governor laid before the Council all the documents regarding the price of land and the division of the territory—a dull list and duller reading! The Council, all in all, seemed curiously impotent in this short session. It was a spectator rather than an active agency: the centre of events was elsewhere.

Gipps, in opening the Council in May 1842, made a very good speech, really analysing the problems of the moment and quite devoid of the customary platitudes. The finances were very involved, he said, and the future dark. The ordinary revenue in 1841 (unimportant because it did not include land-sales) had been the greatest yet, but the land-revenue, which was really the key to the colony's prosperity, had dwindled from £316,000 to £90,000, and was far from meeting the claims on it. The Governor, therefore, had recourse to £65,000 of debentures, but the gap still grew steadily. Despite the censure of the two Secretaries of State and despite the condemnation in a Commons debate, Gipps had to keep on paying for bounties. In March 1840 he had ill-advisedly increased the bounty-rates, the result being that, in less than eighteen months, he found himself confronted by an actual bill of £468,000—and this apart from the outstanding ones above-mentioned! At this prospect, England, herself undergoing a period of distress, was alarmed—'perhaps not unnaturally', magnanimously added Gipps—and lessened the flow of emigration. Beyond this, Gipps had little to say: he appeared to want a *laissez-faire* policy, urging the colonists to wait and see how events would shape themselves. He could do nothing beyond hope for the best; and, as for them, at least their labour-difficulty was partly solved and they could continue their squatting movement.

This was sound enough as far as it went; but in reality the colony was suffering from the inanition of prostration. From the commencement of 1842 to August 1843 was probably the quietest period in its history: there was no agitation and little life—the shade of the crisis was over everything. Clearly, one phase was ending and another beginning. In September 1842, a new Land Act was sent out—Stanley's measure to give uniformity and stability to all Australian land-laws and to ensure a fixed statutory appropriation of the land-revenue.[14] Hereafter, all land was to be auctioned, at a price never less than £1 an acre; and, of the proceeds, at least half were to go for immigration, 15 per cent for aborigines, a little for roads, and the remainder to the general accounts of the colony concerned. The old

[14] Stanley-Gipps, 15 September 1842.

differences and the ceaseless mutability were to go, and the land-system was to be simple and uniform.

In the same month, the long-promised Constitution Act had been sent, arranging for a representative Council with enlarged powers. The colonists were at last to have a Council proportionate to their real importance—one which, even if limited in its powers, would really represent them and would be a real check on the Governor. At the same time, Lord Stanley clearly deprecated the excessive degree of governmental activities in the colony—'So long as the Government is regarded as a kind of universal Agent, it must be a Government of a very costly nature.'[15] He urged a contraction of central activities and a considerable extension of municipal institutions—the famous District Councils of which Gipps was so fond. Though a Tory, he was in favour of a reasonable amount of decentralization and thus, by implication, an extension of the Governor's supervisory duties and a decrease of his actual administration. The incorporation of the two towns had been a start, the Constitution Act a great realization, and now, much could be expected from the District Councils.

When the new Council met in August 1843 therefore, it was in a world of changing values. The colony, from being a penal receptacle, had become free: convict labourers had given place to free migrants: the form of legislature had changed: the system of disposing of Crown lands was altered: immigration, so much in demand a few years before, had become so rapid as to constitute an evil and had been stopped: capital, once flowing in too rapidly, was being drained away, much specie being exported; land-revenue had fluctuated between £300,000 and £15,000, and now stood practically at nil—everything was changing! New classes were merging; labour was becoming arrayed against capital; the first workmen's organizations, now that free immigration was so pronounced, were being definitely built up; and problems of a new nature were making themselves felt in the industrial world. The old simplicity of the thirties—convicts, officials, and landowners—was being thrust aside, and in its place came the newer complexity.

The colony remained depressed, it is true, but for all that, evolutionary forces were rapidly working. Gipps thus found himself confronted by a new set of issues: land, squatting, financial, labour, immigration, constitutional. All of them had assumed new proportions and characteristics, and it seemed a long throw to the old convict-days, and even to the earlier stage when Gipps had been

[15] Stanley-Gipps, 15 December 1842.

such a martinet. The Governor alone remained steadfast in a changing world—though he too had a new position, especially after Stanley administered a third reproof in February 1843, and called for 'an implicit and punctual obedience'! After the quietness of 1842-3, the Governor faced quite a new alignment of forces, quite a new set of issues, and it would have been difficult to imagine a more complete change from the old fights of 1840-1. The focusing of so many alterations in such a short period of time transformed the face of Australia, and Gipps had to muster his strength for the new struggle—a stronger and a greater one than he had ever fought before, this time to conserve the land of the continent for posterity. And this fight that was to decide the new stage in Australia's history was joined when the people's representatives first came together in the August of 1843.

6

THE SQUATTERS' TRACKS

PERHAPS THE MOST fascinating story of Australia is the way in which the stockmen, absolutely unaided by the Government, and often in defiance of it, pushed out into newer and ever newer country and gradually spread over the face of the continent. The lure of 'better country further out' was too much for the most settled of mortals, and it required only a blackfellow's incoherent signs, a vague indication of an early explorer, garbled pothouse whisperings, and often nothing more concise than an adventurous urge to make men saddle their horses, yoke up their bullocks, and simply—set out! They might have some definite objective—perhaps a tree cut by an explorer or a river placed tentatively on a hearsay map—but, more often, they took fate in their own hands and led their flocks on to find the valley of their dreams, to see what was behind the purplish hills which were always on the horizon, or to find where the gauntly stretching plains ran out. The lust of the unknown was on them: the envy of their fellows and the determination to themselves win through in the competition spurred them on; and, apart from the appeal of it all, the annual increase of the flocks provided an adequate economic motive. The sheep needed food; and the pastures had to be wrested from an unknown continent and sorted from the inter-vening gullies and spurs and plains and rivers. It was all a huge lottery, with dogged pluck and character determining survival—helped not a little, it must be added, by trained bushmanship and 'a stock-sense'.

All the horrors of penetrating unknown country and depending only on their own initiative did not deter them. The weaklings stayed in Sydney, trading or loafing; the bush was hard, a man paid for errors of judgment with his life, and only the picked characters could come to success. The man and his dray and his dogs and his sheep went in where the tracks ended; he came out next season with his bales of wool, or his bones bleached on some inner run and his dogs ruled a pack of atavistic canines in the bushlands. There was no half-way: a squatter wrested everything for himself, with all the forces of Nature loaded against him; he had to fight and to hold, and for him, the rest of the world did not exist.

So they went in, cracking their rawhide whips in farewell to the last settled station, giving a last look to their waterkegs and their Negrohead twist, and ever facing outwards. A slow eddying of dust-spirals marked their winding way to the horizon, and perhaps a blue-grey curl of smoke showed a last camping-place on a far ridge; and then they had gone, their stock and themselves depending on their skill, their tenacity, and—here came the trouble!—on Nature's vagaries. No Government marked their tracks, no record their efforts. The bullock-dray groaned its protesting way onwards, over gully and rise, river-bed and rock outcrops. '*Another dray went in a few days ago*', the gossip would run in the frontier shanties: and that was all.

But the individual squatters had little time for thoughts of this kind. They were simple stockmen, facing the circumstances their job demanded; and introspective heroics were very foreign to their nature. To die of thirst on a stony plain, to end crippled and delirious in a mountain-gully was part of the risk; but it was all in the price paid for wool and hides, and they risked it as if it could not have been otherwise. There was a strange fatalism in the spirit with which they approached the bush-tracks—a fatalism not of ignorance but of acquiescence in the price demanded. Thus, from the first, they radiated out from the settlements, and there was no looking-back until the limit of penetration had been reached, until the furthest interior had been occupied or passed over.

Settlement had progressed very slowly until the colony outgrew the notion of 'the settled counties' and forgot that the boundaries of occupation were artificial limits laid down by Government. Before the great stock-boom of 1826-7, it may safely be said that the adminis-tration restricted every migratory instinct of the settlers and frowned at the idea of a natural spread of occupation. Such a move was anathema to the paternal autocrats of the early stage; to them, the settler was a kind of convict whose every action was to be laid down for him. With these ideas before them, it is not strange that the colonists were for long discouraged and allowed themselves to be dumped down only in the districts the Government consented to open.

I   *The Occupation of the Counties*

The Hawkesbury thus seemed to them the outermost limit—the last link with the coastal plain, and the point where Nature and the mountains appeared to set a natural pause on their activities. After twenty years of occupation, then, the colony was confined to a narrow strip between the circle of the Hawkesbury and the sea. Townships like Richmond, Windsor, and Parramatta were dotted on the uneven land that intervened, and only the venturesome spirits crossed into the Cowpasture beyond, where the wild cattle roamed. The coal-cliff at the Nepean mouth was frequented by a few cedar-cutters; Macarthur and Davidson, arguing from the analogy of the wild cattle, had set up sheepwalks at Camden, over towards the Wollondilly; and a few grants had been made in Cook County, on the outer bank of the Hawkesbury; but that was all. In 1807, the colony, to all intents and purposes, meant the narrow circle from the river to the sea. Up north, doubly-convicted criminals were sent to Port Stephens and Newcastle—and this seemed the limit of outer exile, the ultimate punishment.[1]

Matters stood thus when Macquarie came in 1809—and even ten years later, as far as the coastal settlement was concerned. The county of Cumberland—the region described above—remained the bound of settlements; it was occupied a little more intensively; the rich alluvial flats of the outer river had been filled in; but the colony was still in the coastal stage. Yet a new note was making itself heard. The first pressure of the flocks was sounding the warning that was never afterwards to be absent from Australia's problems. There were only 35,388 sheep and 12,442 cattle when Macquarie came; but eleven years later, when he left, the numbers had swollen to 290,000 and 103,000 respectively, and, since one sheep needed an average of three acres, this was a far different proposition, especially with most of Cumberland poor-quality land. The Governor, faced by this prospect, threw open the land between the Hawkesbury and the frowning scarp of the Blue Mountains, but this was of no avail, and it was borne on all that the mountains had to be crossed, or the colony perish. The settled farms were miserably bad, settlers reckoning on at least a third of each grant as worthless; and the prospect was daily becoming worse. The peaks closed in on three sides, and explorers had been thrust back from all directions. The distant ranges seemed so tranquilly blue, as if to emphasize the death of attrition they were forcing on the colony; but those who had been repelled by their precipitous maze knew their menace.

At last, in May 1813, three youths, Blaxland, Lawson, and the student Wentworth, starting from a Nepean farm, broke through the ramparts. Past the heathy flats and over the foothills, through the

---

[1] For this extension, see author's *History of Australian Land Settlement* (1924), ch. III. The range is shown in Macquarie's MS. *Tour of Inspection, 1810* (Mitchell Library, Sydney).

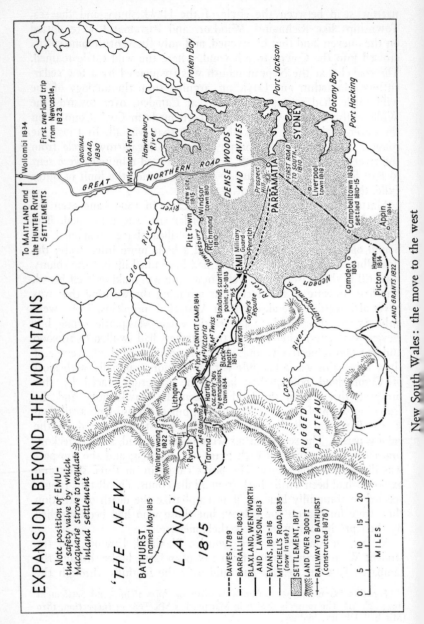

New South Wales: the move to the west

starkness of the gorges ('like the remains of some dreadful earth-
quake', wrote the student), they pushed to a point where they finally
looked down on the west—and in a moment, extended the colony's
outlook from the mountains to the farthest hazy horizon where the
plains stretched out in the sepia mist. It was a new land, 'intersected
by rills in every direction'—an ideal grazing ground. To Blaxland
the settler, in particular, it promised pasture far superior to the rocky
meagreness of the coastal zone, far more extensive than the river-
flats, and the more attractive because it was only the harbinger to
countless inland plains. 'A *land of fatness all untrod*'—'*an Outlet
for the Increase and Redundancy of population for a Century to
come*'—thus the colonists raved of it. The way was free for the inland
march, and the feelings the explorers experienced looking down that
day on the scantily-timbered plains of Bathurst were re-echoed in the
hearts of outgoing stockmen for a century to come, until the sandy
reaches of the Macdonnell Ranges and the far North-West were
reached. The first squatting spirit thus dramatically jumped into
existence, set in the fantastically unreal background of the Blue
Mountain Gorges, and impressive beyond the daydreams of imagination. Sheep and cattle were mustered, the rocky ridges of the old
settlement were left,

> And straightway from the barren coast
> There came a westward-marching host,
> That aye and ever onward prest
> With eager eyes to the West
> Along the pathways of the sun.
>
> Paterson

The sun-motes lured them, the intoxicating smell of dust stirred by
moving feet was in their nostrils, sweetly pungent—and the flocks
moved on. The drama of Australia was being unfolded—the mountains were unbarred, and the inland called.

From this moment, there was no looking back. Macquarie, though
very wisely regulating the first settlement, was far too broad-minded
to reject the proffered gifts.[2] He at once built a road along Blaxland's
line of march, set up a halfway post at Cox's River, and laid out
Bathurst, in the midst of the new plains. '*West-more-land*', he pun-
ningly called the new regions, and ran his trunk road of 130 miles
through their midst, undeterred by the chaos of precipices and
gorges. The large stockowners scarcely waited for his formal permission to cross, but pushed up past the provision-depot near Mount

[2] Macquarie's MS. Diary, 2 February 1818, or Despatches, 28 April 1814,
24 June 1815, 18 March 1816, 16 May 1818.

Blaxland and over the last ridges down to the plains, where their herds prospered so amazingly that the first cattle for sale came out from the inland in October 1815. The natives were difficult to repel, and the little detachment of the 46th at the river seemed insignificant, but, however much the depots were plundered, the stock remained. Small agriculturalists followed three years later (1818). Bathurst became a town, and the conquest of the nearer West was obviously a *fait accompli*. That meant, especially after Oxley's first trip west from Bathurst in 1817, that settlement had reached the Lachlan. And, even more important than the actual achievement, the example had been set. If the flocks could go west, and in the face of such a mountain-barrier, they could obviously push north and south. The first feeling of hugeness—of vastness that could not be attacked—had gone; and the colonists were ready and eager to face the most appalling obstacles to reach 'new country'.

The next move was to the south. Macquarie had always turned an eager eye to the lands beyond the Cowpastures, and especially to his settlement at Illawarra, the home of the cedar-men. He commenced to grant lands there in 1817, and even emphasized Jervis Bay, twice as far distant to the south. Throsby, a free settler, ranged all over this country, and entries in the Governor's manuscript diary show how thrilled and how consistently interested he was in what he called 'the New discovered Country'.[3] Throsby, too, found an easier way to the West by making a detour via the Wollondilly (1819), and his road replaced Blaxland's steep and narrow pass. The entire county of Camden was thus opened, and Macquarie prepared for its occupation by a more intensive settlement of the lands near the Nepean and by laying out such townships as Appin and Campbelltown. He himself visited the new country in 1820 and emphasized it above the other regions.

Indeed, it was his personal pressure that concentrated the flow of settlement in this southerly direction, because practically no advance was made in his time towards the north. He even provided Hall with men and materials, and sent him south far through the new land of Argyle and over the bogs to Lake Bathurst. When he left, therefore, apart from the development of the old core of Cumberland and the laying-out of roads and townships in it, settlement had gone to the west beyond Bathurst, almost to the Lachlan, and to the south into Argyle, which was the centre of attraction when the new Governor came.

The position and the prospects of the colony, indeed, had been

[3] Macquarie's MS. Diary, 29 April 1818, 16 October 1820.

transformed in these years between 1810 and 1820. Much had been done, and even more important was the general atmosphere of optimism and agressive confidence in the future. With stock nearing the reed-beds of the Lachlan and tramping down the mud of the Argyle flats—with the west occupied and the southern frontier being pushed further and further out, it would have been difficult to have felt otherwise, and it was a far call to the old days when the Blue Mountains offered an impassable barrier to settlement and plunged the province into a gloomy barrenness of outlook. A quarter of a million sheep were ranging on, and a third as many horned cattle trampled the new lands.

But the wonders continued to appear, and another phenomenal advance came with Governor Brisbane. First, it had been the passage of the mountains, and then the occupation of the south; now, it was the turn of the hitherto untouched north—the spread along the Hunter. There, 120 miles up the coast from Sydney, the river came down to the sea through a gap between the two mountain-systems, and, flowing through river-flats which resembled the best country of South Devon, debouched at Newcastle, the site of the old convict coal-mines. To colonists accustomed to the less attractive lands of the South, these alluvial flats, only three days on horseback from Sydney, opened a new world. This region absorbed all attention in the twenties, both for agriculture on the river-banks and for the inimit-able cattle-walks in the rougher country beyond. Both banks were thrown open for selection at the close of 1822, three years after John Howe had crossed the unknown territory north of the Hawkes-bury and found meadows strikingly English in appearance. The line of the Hunter was at once rushed, 50,000 cattle grazing there by 1823. Within four years, 372,131 acres were granted, and, if a new settler wanted land, he naturally went to the Hunter, to the cedar-flats. A new class of settlers sprang up there—the richer feudalistic holders who for two decades were the butt and the envy of the democrats. By 1828, when the Counties were declared, agricultural life centred on this river, for as much land was alienated there as in the rest of the colony together,[4] and already the unlicensed stock were further out—over towards Wellington and up beyond the Man-ning, tapping at the inaccessible mountain-lands to the northward. Lieutenant Lawson had made four expeditions to open the country between Bathurst and the new settlement, and every stockman looked longingly towards the Liverpool Plains that Oxley had dis-

[4] The position is clearly shown in *Colony of New South Wales for the Year 1828*, p. 175.

covered in 1818, but which seemed cut off by the ranges. The barrier resisted their effort for years, and, though cattle were carried to Dubbo in the west, the sweep of the Ranges kept them confined to the Hunter, the burning Mount Wingen appearing as a guardian watcher of the inner country.

Here, matters rested when the Counties were declared—when, in other words, the squatting era proper commenced. Newcastle was a town, Maitland had been a small settlement since 1825, and Merrima, inland, almost up to the ranges, was the fringe of effective pastoral occupation. Further out, Mudgee had been settled—an isolated group of grants; there was a Government post at Wellington Valley which marked the extreme limit the administration would recognize for settlement; but there were no other grants. The land between the Hawkesbury and the Hunter was sparsely stocked and not at all granted; and the stockmen rested round Scone and Merrima, seemingly thwarted in their northern advance, with three stalwarts beyond Wellington Valley, on the present site of Dubbo. The Hunter round Maitland was obviously the centre of settlement, though the newer men were concentrating on the Goulburn, which continued the plains inland. The natural grasses there were less verdant than on the Hunter itself, and the carrying-capacity much less (for each head of cattle needed seven acres); but these disadvantages were offset by the wider choice available for settlers of small capital. The result was that stockmen filled in the gaps after 1825, leaving the ironbark country and slowly filtering north. By 1828, then, the frontier-line ran from the coast near Port Stephens, across through Dungog and Merrima to Wellington Valley, with everybody's eyes on the Liverpool Plains, which Oxley had approached from a different direction ten years before. They were waiting for the northern connection— for the new step that would open fresh provinces for them. The Government, however, viewed the barrier of the Liverpool Ranges as an indication that there, settlement was to end, just as, in the west, the naturally indicated limit seemed to be the Lachlan.[5]

In the south, the position was not so clearly defined, although another forward step had been made. Macquarie had left settlement in the north of Argyle County, with a few subsidized farmer-explorers scouting towards Lake Bathurst. This lake had been discovered in 1818, when Throsby's expedition had penetrated the south in two directions. He himself had gone from Cumberland to Jervis Bay, while Meehan, a subordinate, had turned west and discovered the lake

[5] Series of articles in *Maitland Mercury*, 1895-6, tell the story of the Hunter occupation.

and the Goulburn Plains. Macquarie visited the new land, called it
Argyle, and saw how it could link up the hitherto scattered settlements. Now, it was known that good plains swept round from the
west of the mountains to the '*Goulburne Downs*', and even to the
coast at Jervis Bay. But settlement was slow to follow. The Hunter
flats offered better opportunities, for who would wade over almost
impassible country to Lake Bathurst, taking three weeks to do it and
losing half his stock by the way, if he could ride gently to the Hunter
in three days?

Of course, a few settlers trickled in. Throsby himself settled at
Bong Bong in 1819, and, though only eighty miles from Sydney,
seemed in a state of desolate isolation. Two years later, Hume and
Broughton formed a station at Lake George, only thirty miles from
the Murrumbidgee, and discovered the Yass Plains; and, in 1823,
Currie and Ovens found the high plains of Monaro, and cattlemen
made outposts right through the County of Murray to the Lachlan.
But there the southern stream paused, and Yass was not reached
until 1829.

The south-east (also the future County of St Vincent) remained
vacant, and the only advance was in the coastal part of Camden.
The cedar-cutters had been at Lake Illawarra since the early days,
but the coastal region was not effectively settled until 1822. Berry,
an adventurous Fifeshireman, who had served in India and traded
with the Maoris, explored the Shoalhaven in 1820, secured a large
grant there, and, in the face of sneers of friends and enemies alike,
founded the town of that name, just north of Jervis Bay (1822). With
Hamilton Hume (a modestly recurring name in the history of the
south), he sailed a small coppered cutter down the coast and settled
a few men in the heavily-timbered region of Coolangatta. He cut a
road over the mountains from Illawarra to bring cattle, dug a canal to
the Crookhaven, and slowly consolidated a rude settlement in the
face of all manner of difficulties. He opened this inhospitable part of
the coast and, for his reward, received the confiscation of part of the
land he had so assiduously improved! His settlement for long remained
the outpost, so that, when the Counties were delimited in 1829,
Shoalhaven was the limit of pastoral occupation, though outsiders
were inland to Yass and, as in the north, were awaiting the conquest
of the beckoning new region—in this case, the cold tableland of
Monaro and the Murrumbidgee which tantalizingly flowed past their
holdings into the interior.

It was at this stage that the Government defined the settled lands
and introduced the stereotyped division that directly gave rise to the

squatting movement, as it came to be known in the thirties. They saw that settlement had reached the Hunter in the north but was halted by the mass of the Liverpool Ranges; that the line of the Lachlan in the west indicated a point beyond which the stockmen did not want to go; and that, in the south, the mountains again indicated the line from Yass to the sea as the ordained limit. They even consented to be generous and extended the northern frontier from the Hunter to the Manning (because a huge Company was agitating for this land), and the southern from Jervis Bay to Bateman's Bay. This region they enclosed in a sweeping line—from the Manning, round inside the Liverpool Ranges to the Wellington Valley post, and then down the Lachlan past the Bathurst settlements, and curving round Yass (already reached by graziers) to Bateman's Bay. *From the Manning to Moruya from the Lachlan to the sea*—they drew the line in 1829, and said that here was the colony of New South Wales, here the only lands that could be legally occupied, here the fringe of occupation obviously ordained by Nature—here, in effect, were 'the Settled Lands', 'the limit of settlement', 'the Nineteen Counties'. Here the colony ended and the bush began !

In this spirit, Darling divided eastern Australia into two regions, the settled and the unsettled, and gave legal sanction to a meaningless line that was to affect the entire course of settlement for decades. *'Beyond the boundaries'* henceforth became the most commonly-used expression in the colony. Everybody knew what was implied in that statement. The imaginary line of 1829 divided two different worlds. Within, land could be alienated, settlement was officially encouraged, police protection was provided, roads were made, and provisions existed for local justice and the like; but, without, no land could be granted or sold, occupation was positively prohibited, and any man who dared to trespass had to rely entirely upon himself. To go beyond the boundaries practically meant placing oneself in the position of an outlaw and consciously depriving oneself of all communal facilities. Nor was it simply negative—the Government not only refused to aid such transgression—they positively punished it, and the squatter who went beyond had to view any official as an enemy.

It is difficult to realize the complete negation of Government effort beyond this boundary-line. The administration at Sydney only saw *the Nineteen Counties—the Settled Lands*: the great part of Australia outside those limits had no existence in their eyes. The stockmen might push out, but, as far as the Government was concerned, it was just as if they had gone east from Sydney Harbour into the sea ! They were entering a land where Government influence did not run, and the very existence of which, indeed, was denied in official documents. Beyond the Manning and Moruya was No-man's-land, and nobody could mention it to the Government.

Every pound spent on development, therefore, went into the Nineteen Counties. In Brisbane's time, Oxley had commenced a survey, and now Major Mitchell, who gave Australia the first map made from a trigonometrical survey, completed it in 1831. He it was who laid down the three trunk-roads of the colony—the new Western line across the Blue Mountains, and the Great North and the Great South Roads—the three routes which dictated the course of settlement for many years.

The theory was that settlement was to take place only in the Nineteen Counties so delineated, but the flocks were moving on even before the warrants for the survey were issued; and, by 1830, they were to the Liverpool Ranges in the north, and well down the Murrumbidgee, past Jugiong, in the south. The Counties might spell recognized settlement, but it needed an irrevocable damning of Nature to set up actual limits. The only deterrent the pioneers would recognize were impassible ranges or deserts and, as long as they found or could carry water and could pierce even the bad country, they pushed on in the hope of *something better further out*. So it was that, even while Mitchell was directing his survey, interest was focusing on people like Henry O'Brien, the pioneer of the Murrumbidgee, and Semphill, the first squatter of New England. Even Major Mitchell himself attracted far more attention because of his explorations of Port Phillip (1836) and the new country he found for squatters. The Major's *Survey* might be very good, but it was *the Major's Line*—the track he took on his overlanding expedition—that every man spoke of, because this was deciding the course of pastoral settlement. The emphasis was wholly on expansion, however much the Government spoke of the old shibboleth of *Concentration of settlement*; and, in the early thirties, the squatters were moving down the Murrumbidgee and up the rampart-faces of New England, and even the *farmers* were seeking the county of Argyle and, before a decade, had passed the lands beyond Yass—even they were outside the Nineteen Counties!

II   *The Move to New England*

Of the two great lines of march, it was the Northern that first attracted attention. There, the cattlemen had been held up by the Liverpool Ranges, though they knew that good land—Oxley's

land of 1818—lay beyond and came out to the sea at Port
Macquarie. But the curve from Scone to Dungog saw them tied
down, tantalizingly held off from the promised land, with Mount
Wingen barring the way, burning and smouldering.

The problem had been partly solved in 1823 by Allan Cunningham, the botanist-explorer, who had set out to find a way across
Oxley's plains, especially one that could be traversed by horned
stock. Five weeks of failure, five weeks of buffeting in the maze of
nearer mountains were crowned by the discovery of an easy pass—
Pandora's Pass, so called because it opened on a land of plenty. But
the connection with the back-country had not yet been made, and
it was not until the expeditions of 1825 and 1827 that the way across
the marshes was found. In the course of these wanderings, Cunningham had discovered the westward-flowing rivers of the plain—the
Gwydir, the Dumaresq, the Condamine, all watering good stock-
country.

In the interim, another factor had entered this northern region. In
the years of speculation in England, a million pounds were sunk in a
huge concern called the *Australian Agricultural Company*, which,
in some way or other, survived the bubble and commenced the work
of colonization in earnest. In January 1826, the Company's Agent
settled at Port Stephens, just beyond Newcastle. Though actually
wasting money in an unproductive swamp, he was theoretically
undertaking the colonization of the new county of Gloucester and
extending the boundaries of the colony from the Hunter to the
Manning. The initial confusion lasted for years, and the Company
seemed about to dissolve, when they started schemes for an exchange
to better land. The first settlement had been on useless coastal lands
and on the wet Gloucester flats, whereas the Company had actually
been set up to produce fine wool. It was clear that they had to have
suitable dry lands, but the trouble was that nobody had penetrated
beyond the ranges. The Hunter region was already fully taken up,
so that there was no alternative on the southern side of the cor-
dilleras. Yet settlement had not passed this line in 1832, and the two
standard maps had blank spaces to the north. Mitchell prated of
Moreton Bay, and Cunningham of the Darling Downs he had penetrated in 1827, but neither knew anything of the country immediately beyond Gloucester.

The Company therefore sent out a series of expeditions, covering
the country from the Hunter to the Hastings, and unveiling the
mystery of the rugged ranges. They were seeking half a million acres
of land, and so could afford to spend time and money on such

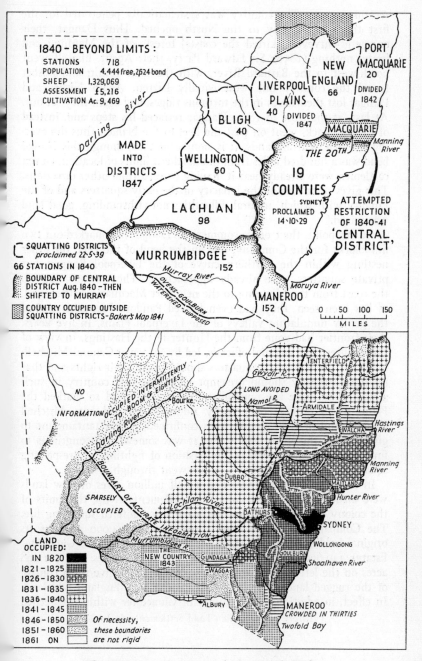

1840 – BEYOND LIMITS :
STATIONS 718
POPULATION 4,444 free, 2,624 bond
SHEEP 1,329,069
ASSESSMENT £5,216
CULTIVATION Ac. 9,469

Darling River

PORT MACQUARIE 20
DIVIDED 1842

NEW ENGLAND 66

LIVERPOOL PLAINS 40
DIVIDED 1847

MADE INTO DISTRICTS 1847

BLIGH 40

MACQUARIE

Manning River

WELLINGTON 60

THE 20TH

19 COUNTIES
PROCLAIMED 14·10·29

SYDNEY

LACHLAN 98

ATTEMPTED RESTRICTION OF 1840-41 'CENTRAL DISTRICT'

LIMITS OF LOCATION

SQUATTING DISTRICTS *proclaimed 22·5·39*

66 STATIONS IN 1840

BOUNDARY OF CENTRAL DISTRICT Aug. 1840 – THEN SHIFTED TO MURRAY

COUNTRY OCCUPIED OUTSIDE SQUATTING DISTRICTS – *Baker's Map 1841*

MURRUMBIDGEE 152

Murray River

OVENS-GOULBURN WATERSHED-SUPPOSED

Moruya River

MANEROO 152

0 50 100 150
MILES

NO INFORMATION

OCCUPIED INTERMITTENTLY TO BOOM OF EIGHTIES

Darling River

Bourke.

Gwydir R.

TENTERFIELD

LONG AVOIDED

Namoi R.

ARMIDALE

WALCHA

Hastings River

BOUNDARY OF ACCURATE INFORMATION

Dubbo

Lachlan River

Manning River

SPARSELY OCCUPIED

BATHURST

Hunter River

MAITLAND

SYDNEY

Murrumbidgee R.

THE NEW COUNTRY 1843

GUNDAGAI

WAGGA

WOLLONGONG

GOULBURN

Shoalhaven River

LAND OCCUPIED:
IN 1820 ■
1821–1825
1826–1830
1831–1835
1836–1840
1841–1845
1846–1850
1851–1860
1861 ON

Of necessity, these boundaries are not rigid

ALBURY

MANEROO *CROWDED IN THIRTIES*

Twofold Bay

The squatting occupation of New South Wales

reconnaissances. The country was systematically penetrated for the first time, and a way to the North opened. Thus Dangar, their energetic surveyor, skirted the coastal forests of the Manning and found nothing (1830); Sir Edward Parry, their Agent, himself went north-west to the Barnard River, with the same result; and Nisbet found the country due west equally barren. Again Nisbet and Dangar lost themselves in the tortuous ridges, and again they set out. At last, at the close to 1831, Dangar retraced his steps and, instead of turning back, went on past the Peel to the Namoi, thus discovering the rich Warrah lands. It is significant that, though this Namoi bend was a hundred miles from the northern limits of location, eleven cattlemen were already near it, having entered from other directions. This gives some idea of the tenacity of the early squatters and of the rapidity with which, natural difficulties notwithstanding, good land was seized.[6]

At this point, the trouble commenced. Dangar had marked out two fine blocks for the Company, one on the bend of the Peel, the other nestling within the northern curve of the Liverpool Ranges; but private squatters were already approaching. They were going up the coast from the Manning to the new Port Macquarie district, and, as has been seen, they had even braved Pandora Pass and reached the gently undulating valleys of the Liverpool Plains. In five years, their frontier had gone from the Hunter to the Hastings. In view of this progress, the colonial officials, led by Surveyor-General Mitchell, held that the individual squatters should retain their rights and that no stock-company should pre-empt all of the best country in such a way as to leave the remainder useless. They had so marked the Plains as to exclude only rocky ridges of gnarled box, Mitchell claimed; and, if their grants were confirmed, it was tantamount to giving them the entire Plains. But it was somewhat incongruous to find the Surveyor-General in the position of fighting for trespassing squatters; and the Company's grants went through.

In this fashion, over three and a half million acres of new lands were made known, a new squatting settlement set up, the limits of the colony extended, and an organized force entered squatting life. The Company finally obtained three grants—464,000 acres of its original holding from the Manning to Port Stephens (the Gloucester Estate); 249,600 acres at Warrah, just across the ridges; and 312,298 acres on the left bank of the Peel, so chosen as to give them control of the rugged lands stretching back to the New England tableland. In effect, in addition to the county of Gloucester within the Settled

[6] *History of Australian Land Settlement*, ch. I (1).

Districts, they were given a practical control of all the land of the Liverpool Plains—everything from Pandora Pass to Bendemeer. A principality was alienated, and the boundary of the colony extended from the south of the Liverpool Ranges to the fringe of New England. The old bogey of the Liverpool Plains was at length laid, and, however one may argue about the advisability of such extensive alienations to a company, all that mattered for the moment was that the breaking-open of this country meant the advance of squatting to NEW ENGLAND—the conquest of one of the most difficult layers in Australia. Viewed in this light, the Company's work between 1830 and 1835 was distinctly progressive, because their organized explorations achieved results that benefited the entire squatting movement.

Within five years, the development of these huge areas was proceeding apace. The Company, despite the opposition of Bourke and Mitchell, secured 350 convicts (Glenelg even authorized 500 in all!), and, with the aid of 150 freemen, stocked the Peel River with sheep and Warrah with cattle. The mountainous nature of the country was overcome when Peruvian mules and asses were imported; and it was no unusual sight to see South American muleteers picking a way down the tortuous defiles to the Hunter Valley. The positive results for an expenditure of £300,000 by 1834, it is true, were disappointing, because the Company had only 46,000 sheep, and Bourke showed how five private settlers, on less that a fifth of the ground, had double the stock and gave employment to far more labourers.[7] But such a summary ignored the Company's greatest service— in opening up new country, in starting communications, and in putting English capital into unproductive developmental works. The Company was usurping the place of the Government in the thankless task of pioneering, and, though its shareholders suffered, the colony prospered by the opening of the North. Moreover, huge sums were spent on French and Saxon merinos whose influence spread throughout the North. The Company commenced stock-sales, first at Maitland, then at Stroud; and between two and three hundred squatters would gather from all directions to improve their flocks by the pedigreed leaven that was thus available. These sales remained a permanent feature in the pastoral life of the colony for decades, and it must not be forgotten that much of the superiority of the New England and the Darling Downs sheep was directly attributable to them.

More immediately, from the viewpoint of pastoral occupation, the Company's activities meant that the Namoi had fallen, and that

[7] Bourke-Glenelg, 22 August 1835.

the *north countree* of the squatters' songs was beckoning. The
squatters knew from the explorers what lay beyond, Cunningham's
tracks were fresh in their minds, and the Company's officials had
performed the yeoman service. The individual, under these circumstances, had but to move on. All of the flat-topped Liverpool spurs
had been looked over, and the grassy levels of the plains proper—
excellent sheep-country—were soon covered. The Company's explorers had already found a few cattlemen on the Peel when they
were making their reconnaissances in 1831, in the blackbutt and
white-gum country; and it was obvious that the turn of New England
—the higher plateau-lands—had come.

Settlement had been erupting in this direction for some time. As
early as 1826, stray nomads had set up transitory stations over the
Liverpool Ranges, but it was not until six years later that the
removal of stock from the low-country estates to the New England
plateau began. The coming of the Company had established such
settlements, and the occupation of the Peel grant meant progress
to Tamworth. Exactly on a level with this, but slightly higher, is
Walcha, the commencement of New England proper. There, Semphill (Semple), a Scot from Edinburgh, moved his tent from the
Hunter in 1832 and set up the first station on the flat tableland that
Oxley had seen fourteen years before. The lower ward of New
England was rapidly filled. The high country round Walcha, once
the squatters had avoided the kidney-shaped obstruction of the
Mount Boyd Ranges, looked tantalizingly down on the Macleay and
the coastal fringe; but, for most of them, the black earth beckoned
north—north to the frowning buttresses of the New England Ranges.
Between 1832 and 1835, therefore, the stockmen crept along the
plateau-top to Armidale, where they stood facing the last and highest
crests of the cordillera. Cory discovered a pass over the Moonbi
Mountains, thus once more prolonging the track to the North: he
was the first to venture up the Moongap and formed the road over
the mountains—now the great northern line. He settled at Salisbury,
others came all round him—Tilbuster, five miles from Armidale,
being the furthest point out in 1835.

All the land to Armidale was thus taken, and then commenced
the occupation of the second great layer of New England—the five-
years' struggle for the belt up to Tenterfield, the highest land of all.[8]
Peter McIntyre, another Scot, climbed up to Guyra in 1836, the first
land in the four-thousand-feet belt; and the Macdougalls and Camp-

[8] The story is best told in *Gardiner MSS.*, vol. I, p. 17.

bell, passing Dumaresq's first tents at Tilbuster, came from the Namoi-source to the neighbourhood of Guyra, where they ran cattle. Scarcely a day passed without the signal-fires of the natives smoking down from the peaks to denote the arrival or movement of the whites; and the tribes, in this district very strong, withdrew muttering and troubled, before the approach of the cattle.

Alexander Campbell, who camped at Bundarra, where the range sloped westwards, had been constantly importuned by the blacks to go further north. As a result, his party drove out their drays, saw the Macintyre for the first time since Cunningham, and occupied Inverell. He had tried the crest-lands of the range, but had been deflected west by the menacing Ben Lomond to the lower slopes and settled on the river-land. That was either in 1836 or 1837, and, at the time, he was acting as agent for the McIntyres of Aberdeen. But later he took up a run for himself at Inverell—'the meeting-place of the swans'—and founded the well-known squatting family that still survives. All of this country had been found by two stockmen of Dumaresq's, who had struck through to the lower country in scouting from the Tilbuster cattle-run. Such men as these two—Chandler and Duval—bearded and unkempt, were much in demand at that time, when the rush of capitalists north from the Hunter was setting in. The newcomers wanted, above all things, guides or natives to lead them to unoccupied spots, and such men as the tracking shepherds—such '*beardies*'—were at a premium. In this case, graphically enough, the district they opened was named after them 'the land of the Beardies'—and so the land around Inverell and Glen Innes is known today!

A year after the occupation of Inverell, came the turn of the higher country round Glen Innes—back once more to the core of the range. Thomas Hewitt, an ex-employee of the Great Company, took up Stonehenge for Archibald Boyd, an English capitalist, in 1838. This station was then fifty miles out from the nearest neighbour and was completely isolated. The blacks were powerful and hostile, the ruggedness of the country offered a perfect hiding-ground for marauders, and, since the Clarence and the coastal side were unknown, the only communication was with the Hunter, far to the South. Yet, undeterred by all this, Hewitt set out with a compass and a black boy to mark a track across the ranges to Grafton, down in the coastal plain—and did it!

Other stockmen picked favoured valleys on the ridges in 1839, and, by the end of the next year, Tenterfield, where the northern fringe of the central range ran down, could be termed the outpost of settlement. In May 1839, the Government had so far recognized the occupation of this district as to appoint a Commissioner of Crown Lands to supervise all pastoral matters in 'New England', and George Macdonald, the first holder of this office, settled at, and named, Armidale as his centre. Early next year, Patrick Leslie, another of this band of indefatigable Scots, passed north on his Hegira from Collaroi to the Darling Downs, in modern Queensland. Passing on his way to the meadow-lands Cunningham had found long before, Leslie encountered the furthest outstation in New England at Gordon and Bennett's in the low country. The squatters had already filtered through the whole of the ranges, for this one was on a branch of the Severn River, some twenty or thirty miles north of the Beardy Plains. Thus, by March 1840, the layer to Tenterfield—that is, to the Queensland frontier—was filled in.

At the same time, other squatters, avoiding the main line of march across the mountain-systems, had been working quietly up the coast, from the Manning to Grafton. The Macleay district was extraordinarily rich, but for many years the authorities reserved it for convicts and would not allow free squatters to approach it. Major Innes, however, possessed an outstation at Rolland's Plains, between the Hastings and the Macleay, for many years, and had run a track from that post to the convict settlement. But no further encroachments were made for about ten years, when the cedar-sawyers came and the village of Kempsey, on the Macleay itself, was laid out. From that moment, the number of cattle rapidly increased, both over the timbered plains and up the inviting foothills of the ranges themselves. As has been seen, stockmen who had gone up top on the range-country cut ways down to the coast, and so, in this interlocking way, the coastal and the mountain-settlement went on concurrently. Run-seekers in 1839 even chartered a ship and attacked the Clarence estuary, further north; and a settlement grew up round the nucleus of Grafton, where the timbered river-flats seemed as if prepared for intensive exploitation.[9]

This rapid progress meant that, by 1840, the conquest of New England was virtually complete. A line drawn from Tenterfield to the Clarence would have marked the boundary of actual settlement —in other words, the flocks and herds had gone north, both by mountain and coast, up to the boundary of modern Queensland.

[9] Rudder MS., Mitchell Library (1887), or Journal of Australian Historical Society, 1921, vol. VII, p. 177.

Indeed, Patrick Leslie's expedition was somewhere north in the Downs, across that line. They were nearly five hundred miles from Sydney and were indescribably remote, cut off from their fellows and the Government alike. A ton of flour would cost £100 to transport to them—that fact best shows their position, although, to make the picture complete, the smoke-fires of the *myall*-blacks and the rigours of the climate have to be taken into account.

III   *The Murrumbidgee*

But all of this occupation had taken time. In an age when pastoral settlement was going on by leaps and bounds, five years seemed a long period; and, long before the New England mountains were occupied, attention had been diverted elsewhere. In the early thirties, the slopes of the Liverpool Ranges and the activities of the great Company had attracted most notice; but it had soon become evident that any success in the mountain-zone up north had to be hardly won, and the squatters turned with eager eyes to the South, where amazing news was filtering through! There, as will be remembered, the flocks had reached Yass on the Murrumbidgee by 1830, and were filling up the country round Lake George and the Shoalhaven. This was all in the settled lands, in Darling's *Nineteen Counties*; but, from 1830 onwards, they were across the boundaries of location and well into the forbidden lands beyond.

The Murrumbidgee, which came by extension to mean the whole of the southern river-system, was the nerve-centre of this movement, and expansion towards it was aided both by Government activities and by the comparative ease with which occupation could be effected. In that direction, Hume and Hovell had crossed from Lake George to the western bay of Port Phillip in 1824-5 (though they imagined themselves at Western Port), and, though they met great difficulties in the mountain-country, they were enthusiastic in speaking of noble downs and perfect pastures. Controversy had kept this expedition alive in the newspapers, so that it was generally believed by 1830 that rich plains lay waiting beyond the southern rivers. Then again, Captain Charles Sturt of the Dorsets had left the drought-stricken regions of settlement in 1829, and followed the Murrumbidgee and the Murray to the sea. This cleared up the old problem of the rivers, but its most important effect was to direct attention to the Murrumbidgee, just beyond the Yass holdings. Sturt had found a rapid stream, fed from the mountains nearer the coast, and, though he found the drier country further out parched by the drought, it was evident that the squatters could go on towards the Riverina plains—towards the vast new water-ways.

Nor were they long in seizing the opportunity.[10] Hume and Broughton had occupied Lake George since 1821, and, though a few turned aside to Murray County and towards the Shoalhaven, most of the new settlers followed the Murrumbidgee. In a sudden rush of 1829-30, the banks from Yass to Jugiong, where Henry O'Brien formed the first sheep-station on the river, were seized and split up; while less stable runs were taken up even out to Gundagai. O'Brien had settled at Doura, a site embracing the later township of Yass, shortly after Hamilton Hume had discovered the Yass Plains in 1821, but his rapidly increasing stocks had forced him out. Accordingly, he had mustered a thousand head of store-cattle, loaded a bullock-dray with sufficient provisions and utensils for a year, and set off down the Lachlan. But he found all of the suitable lands already occupied, so rapid had been the flow of settlement; and, not liking the grey mulga and saltbush plains further out, he turned towards the Murrumbidgee, secured two of the best fattening runs on the lower river, and became the largest stockholder in the district. Henceforth, he was a force, as revered as powerful, in the life of the new frontier-province. He was scrupulously fair to his employees in an age of exploitation, and soon became accepted as one of the squatting authorities of the State. No Commission of Enquiry, whether on land-matters or immigration, overlooked his evidence, and often proceedings were stayed long enough for this man to come to Sydney from 'the New Country' down the Murrumbidgee. Even financial committees asked his opinion on the effects of contemplated changes on the pastoral community. In short, O'Brien of the River was the uncrowned king of the self-made squatters.

When Sturt passed in 1829, on his way down the rivers to the sea, O'Brien's post of Jugiong was the largest station on the Murrumbidgee, though Warby's cattle-run, at the junction of the Tumut, was the furthest-out on the right bank of the river. Sturt's last sight of white men was at Stuckey's post of South Gundagai—a far-out station as yet not permanent. This region was even more fully selected in the next few years, a narrow strip of occupation driving down to Wagga (1829-33). The Thorns took up the Wantabadgery land, with Gordon across the river, and next year (1832), the Tompsons were at the present site of North Wagga. Other squatters in this

[10] Gormly, Exploration and Settlement in Australia (1922)—collection of articles by a river-pioneer.

strip took up stations with very long but euphonious native-names, from Yass to Wagga; and no room remained for newcomers after the first few years, because the nature of the country seemed to render a river-frontage necessary, and few cared to face the arid plains further out. All of their runs, except Oura and Wantabadgery, have now been converted into small farms, but at that time, they constituted the furthest fringe of settlement—'the back of beyond', where the plains ran out to the flat desert.

Still, venturesome stockmen, crowded out in the nearer ranges, dotted themselves down between the firstcomers—late in the race by a few months! Best, for example, came from Parramatta to the new Wagga in 1832, and Jenkins 'sat down' on Tooyal, fourteen miles below; Taafe, O'Brien's rival as the biggest stockholder in the West, came to Cooney's Creek in 1834: and even 'old hands', like the Macarthurs of Camden, sent cattle to Nangus. But the rush was not very pronounced. The plains here were too dry, in the opinion of those early stockmen, and they did not relish the utter dependence on the Murrumbidgee. Settlement on the river therefore paused suddenly, and a line from just below Wagga to Tarcutta would have marked its effective end between 1834 and 1840. At Tarcutta Creek, Mitchell saw the furthest-out stock in 1836—and there were no more until he reached the Hentys' at Portland Bay! The first settlers had divided the river-banks, and the time was not ready for any further movement. The north had swung back again into public favour, and for some years, the occupation of the South paused at Wagga. A little attention was directed to filling up the back-country—the Yass plains, the Tumut junction, and even the mountains of Monaro— but these were all desultory movements, and it seemed as if the occupation of the great river had ended, especially when its bed ran dry with drought.

IV Port Phillip

Just at this moment sensational news again came out of the South. The Northerners were finding the New England ranges slightly too difficult, and the men of the South were checkmated by the aridness of the plains: no sufficiently large field of pastoral enterprise was offering, and yet the hungry flocks were increasing at a phenomenal rate. The Old Colony was in a state of crisis, and Bourke saw that a definite limit would be set to advance unless new grazing grounds were opened up. It therefore behoved the Government to take steps out of the *impasse*, whether the Colonial Office approved or disapproved of the dispersion of settlement. Urged by the logic of these facts, Bourke invoked the aid of Mitchell, his Surveyor-General. Mitchell, as it happened, was dissatisfied with the success of Sturt—a mere civilian and amateur!—and wanted to annex the country between Sturt's river (the Murray) and the sea as his own preserve. An intensely dogmatic and selfishly proud man, he needed just this spur to goad him to his best effort: and the colony prospered by his choler. He had formerly explored the Upper Darling country in the north, and cleared up several uncertain questions about the great river-system of the interior. But nobody then knew whether the river he had been tracing beyond Bourke was the noble stream Sturt had found flowing into the Murray far to the south: and this he was sent to find out.[11] Yet not only this: Bourke's explanatory despatch also definitely mentioned the supposition of '*fine pastoral tracts*' on both sides of the Murray and down to Port Phillip, and Mitchell's instructions included the wider commission of determining the general nature of all the land between the mouth of the Murray and the Australian Alps—a gigantic task, but one on which would depend the future of pastoral settlement, which was then facing a crisis.

So urgent was the occasion that Mitchell's was practically the first expedition of discovery to be adequately outfitted by the Government. No previous party had had the material means of success that Mitchell's twenty-three men possessed when they left Sydney in March 1836—bound for the junction of Sturt's river with the Murray. Their first point was soon settled: the Darling undoubtedly joined the Murray where Sturt had found it. But what interested the squatters was Mitchell's next move. By some lucky chance, he followed the Murray upstream when he crossed it, thus avoiding the inhospitable scrub of the Mallee, an entanglement which would certainly have changed his whole interpretation of the country! Missing this desert, he struck the Loddon River and the beautifully grassed plains—'different from anything I had ever before witnessed, either in New South Wales or elsewhere—a land so inviting, and still without inhabitants'. So the land ran on to the Grampians, after which he again traversed rich river-plains, those of the Wannon and the Glenelg, finally coming out at Portland Bay. Here, he was utterly amazed to find unauthorized squatters—the Hentys who had settled this isolated spot from Van Diemen's Land almost two years before. From the bay, Mitchell struck north-east and traversed modern Victoria in quite a different direction from that in which he had come.

[11] Bourke-Glenelg, 15 March 1836.

First, the rich loamy plains of the west, and then the land from Mount Alexander to the Murray seemed unbelievable: and, from the top of Mount Macedon, whither he had made a detour, the Major saw the shores of Port Phillip, where still another set of squatters had camped.

Mitchell thus crossed Victoria in two directions, found the various sets of plains, and grasped such outstanding natural features as the Grampians and Macedon. Before he reached the outstations on the Murrumbidgee, he had laid open to the gaze of the squatters by far the richest and the most extensive province that had fallen to their lot. His expedition of March-October 1836 was therefore the turning-point in the history of pastoral occupation, and was alike the most successful and the most important journey of inland discovery in Australia. To the squatters cramped round Tarcutta, to those despairing before the ranges of New England, and to those who were braving the snowy pastures of Monaro, he brought news of a region of temperate and well-watered plains—the best land imaginable for sheep—and easily accessible for wheeled traffic. He got back in October: by the end of the year, the colony was ringing with the news, and the flocks were mustering on a thousand tracks for 'the Major's Line'. His deeply furrowed track was henceforth the axis of squatting occupation: it led to the heart of the new lands, lesser roads radiated from it, and runs were defined by their position to it. This surly, dark-faced official, who quarrelled with every Governor and was so solicitous of his own insanely developed pride that he went out of his way to resent implied attacks upon it, had proven the greatest possible benefactor: and, however unattractive his personality, the squatters at least had reason to be thankful for his skill in his work. His efficiency had given them a new lease of life— literally so, because now they had prospects that would have seemed visionary day-dreams only a few years before! Mitchell had transformed their position, and to his expedition of 1836 is due the rapid settlement of Port Phillip and, in no small degree, the pastoral growth of the forties. One has but to think of the worked-out Murrumbidgee, the bad lands in the settled counties, and the tremendous natural difficulties up north, to get his work in its proper perspective. To men in that position of hopelessness, he offered millions of acres of perfect pasture, with not the slightest drawback. It was a dream he was placing before their dazzled eyes, but a dream firm-set in hard fact. So that once again the bullock-drays were yoked, once more the store-cattle and the travelling flocks mustered, and the roads re-sounded afresh to the droningly insistent 'Roll up your blanket' of the stockmen. The second phase of the squatting occupation of Australia was starting—the phase of the new lands, of 'the Major's Line'.

The move to what was later Victoria had already commenced. Apart from the southern settlements at Melbourne and Portland Bay, the squatters, who had been halted by the unattractiveness of the Murrumbidgee beyond Wagga, had shown a tendency to turn south. Before the end of 1835, therefore—months before Major Mitchell left on his expedition—a squatter had crossed the Murray. Wyse, a stockman employed by Ebden, had left Tarcutta in the spring of 1835, and formed two runs, one on the present site of Albury, and the other across the river, on the Victorian side, at Bonegilla. Practically at the same time, George Mackillop had set out from the mountain-pastures of Monaro to open a track to the head of Port Phillip. On the way, he discovered the lovely plains round Lake Omeo, in wild isolated country, and at once stocked them. Wyse at Bonegilla and Mackillop and a friend at Lake Omeo were the only squatters in the northern part of Victoria in 1835, although more trickled across very early in the following year, and the trickle quickly became a torrent when the Major returned in October. The firstcomer was Charles Huon, a French refugee, on the Wodonga run, next to Wyse; and, before October, when Mitchell returned and the first overlanders came, a whole cluster of slab-huts had been erected and runs claimed for miles along the river. Spalding's party advanced to Thologolong, John Waite to Bungil (twenty-five miles above Wodonga), and Jubbins to the Mitta Mitta junction. Lesser stations were formed around, and someone even went to keep the Omeo exiles company. A loosely linked chain of runs was thus established between the neighbourhood of Albury and the head-quarters of the Snowy River in the mountains, and, spasmodically placed as they seemed, they constituted a permanent settlement.[12]

In October, a new note entered. Crossing the Murray between the stations, Hawdon, an enterprising stockman of the older dictrict, attempted to take stock overland to Port Phillip. He had with him Gardiner (a speculator who had been with Gellibrand in the Norval when that ill-fated vessel had carried sheep from Van Diemen's Land and lost practically the entire cargo) and Hepburn, a typical old sailor who had lost his life-work through the sinking of his coastal vessel. Gardiner was the only man of the party who had seen the infant settlement of Dutigalla, as Melbourne was known, and it was

[12] In detail in A. Andrews' The First Settlement of the North-East of Victoria, or Victorian Historical Journal, vol. III, 1916-17, p. 19.

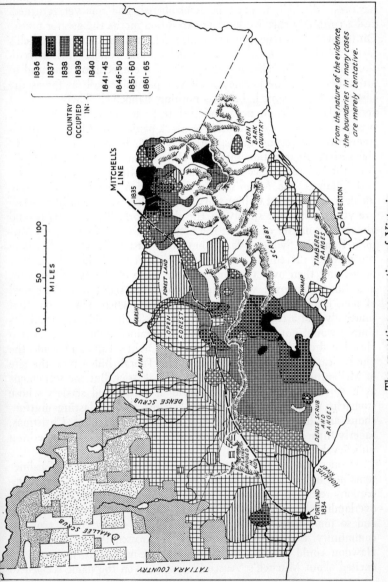

The squatting occupation of Victoria

on his word that the party was forming its ideas of the Port Phillip pastures. Mitchell, it must be remembered, had not yet returned, and accordingly this overlanding expedition merits the greater praise. On the way, it is true, the overlanders fell in with some of Mitchell's men at Gundagai, on the Murrumbidgee, and verified their expeditions of *Australia Felix*; but the origin of the expedition belonged to an earlier date. The journey itself was painfully dull, as far as the historian is concerned, because nothing happened. There were no spectacular incidents, no wonderful feats across swollen rivers or precipitous peaks, no mutinies or stock-panics—nothing except an uneventful succession of marching-days, all, however, testifying to the perfect organization involved. Hawdon marched for a fortnight from the Murrumbidgee runs to the flooded Murray, crossed it easily, and followed 'the Major's Line' for three more weeks. The only incident that seemed to him worth mentioning was a smashed axle—everything else was simply in the day's work. Thus, casually and almost as a matter of course, the first stock came into Southern Victoria from the Sydney-side.[13] They went east to Daylesford, where the mariner carved his mark on a virgin tree and chose his future home; and then over the ranges to the edge of the Werribee runs, and thus to the town, which consisted of a few slab huts and a crowd of men intoxicated with optimism. At first, when news came that somebody had arrived with cattle from the Sydney-side, the residents simply would not believe it, and they remained dubious even when Hawdon drove his tired animals across Dight's Falls and made the pioneer cattle-station in Victoria on the Toorak hills—now the site of Melbourne's most exclusive residential district. But the settlement as it stood boasted only fifteen head of cattle; and settlers whose stomachs were openly in rebellion against the everlasting mutton-chops and damper, and conscious of the approach of Christmas, eagerly turned to Hawdon's prime cattle, though still as to something unbelievable.

At once, the new route overland was filled with stock. Gardiner remained on his urban run in the Yarra-bend, while his two companions returned to Sydney for more stock. But so clearly had his overlanding brought Port Phillip into touch with the older colony, and so immediate was the effect of Mitchell's news on a crowded community, that three more parties had crossed the Murray before Hawdon could return. The Murrumbidgee-men were now greatly excited about Mitchell's '*Australia Felix*'—even the name seemed to

[13] Hawdon's journal is in *Letters from Victorian Pioneers* (1898), p. 44. This is the primary source for all of the expeditions to Port Phillip.

breathe hope. When Mitchell returned, therefore, and Bourke recognized the Melbourne settlement and authorized the location of settlers in Port Phillip, the effect can be imagined. A long drought was setting in to emphasize the disadvantages of the older districts, while the continued influx of English capital combined with the existing spirit of speculation to make the settlers pay ruinously high prices for stock, so keen was the mania to go south. With sheep at 60s. and rams at £6, it should have been evident that a speculative disease was abroad in the land; but each newcomer argued that, if the squatters could pay such initial prices for stock and borrow capital at 12 per cent and more, then the returns from sheep, especially in the now southern lands, must be enormous! They argued from inflated premises, treating them as true indices of the position, and thus went, in the jargon of the time, from puff to puff. Under these conditions—and especially in the middle of 1837, when the mania became almost a communal mental derangement—there was a continued rush to the rivers and plains of Port Phillip.

The first to pass the limits after Hawdon was the striking figure of C. H. Ebden, formerly noted for his tandem and his social proclivities in George Street, later as a Melbourne representative in Sydney, and ultimately as a Cabinet minister. Odd in manner, sparklingly epigrammatic in speech, and with a general air of *hauteur*, 'the great Mr Ebden' was a well-known colonial figure, especially for one of his sayings that was so often repeated by colonists of all degree as to play the part of the music-hall quip of a later date—'*I fear I am becoming disgustingly rich!*' But, in addition to providing popular catchwords, Ebden effectively settled new lands. Even in the forties, it required some organizing skill to become 'disgustingly rich', and Ebden possessed it in plenty. Early in the new year, he led a huge expedition towards *the Major's Line*—9,000 sheep, nine drays, and 30 horses, by no means an inconsiderable venture with ordinary wethers at £3 a head! Cladding himself in an elaborate Crusoe-beard and hairy fur-skins, Ebden turned his delicately lively face to the new task of setting up a sheep-station north of the Dividing Ranges —the first time this had been attempted. After a preliminary assay, he came down to Carlsruhe—for the stage was already shifting from the Murray to the Goulburn, and it was little exaggeration to say that, in the latter part of 1837, mobs of sheep could be seen every few miles along *the Major's Line*.

In May, Henry Howey, the next large settler, found himself cramped in the Goulburn Plains of New South Wales, and settled at Gisborne, on the east side of Mount Macedon—close to where the runs from Melbourne were coming up. Howey's life was in many ways an epitome of colonial growth at that time. A respectable Northumberland man, he had arrived twelve years before with four hundred golden sovereigns and £200 in tools, and, by dint of unremitting effort, had become a wealthy landowner in three of the Settled Counties. Now, not content with this, he was setting out for completely new lands. Thus, he settled south of the Ranges, and eventually bought city-lots at Melbourne's first land-sale. But the risks of colonial existence took a hand at this stage, and Howey was lost at sea in June 1838, on his way round from Sydney. His settlement was carried on by his brother, though his stock were auctioned in the July after his death—with results which are interesting as indicating conditions at the time. Though in quite new country and thus the pick of the land, his 'right of Station', as it was termed, was bought for £95—so limited was the tenure and so uncertain were the prospects of the squatters. His ewes, however, run-down and unequal as they were, realized 32s. 6d. on an average, while horses brought up to a hundred guineas without any trouble.[14]

Eight weeks after Howey's party, Alexander Mollison founded a squatting dynasty by settling on the Coliban. Mollison, a Londoner of three years' colonial experience, had visited Port Phillip from Hobart and, having satisfied himself as to its prospects, went round to bring stock overland. In April of 1837, he quitted his run of Uriara on the Murrumbidgee with 5,000 sheep, 662 cattle, and 49 men. Fortunately, his manuscripts have survived, and from them, in quite a spontaneous fashion, it is possible to get some idea of the degree of organization implied in each of these early overlanding expeditions.

The organization for this large party, with its unwieldy stock and mutinous *personnel*, was extraordinarily wide in its ramifications; every such expedition was practically a small army on the march through unknown country, with a premium on the numberless hazards of bush-life. Mollison's *Diary*, for instance, is one long chronicle of unexpected and unavoidable mishaps. Held up for six days at the commencement by a drunken smith, they encountered trouble after trouble. Their convict-servants did every conceivable thing to embarrass their masters, and frequently endangered the very safety of the party by a spirit of unreasoning caprice. One man was lost for ten winter days in the bush, others strayed from time to time; and the expedition could advance only by painful degrees. Open mutiny or ill-concealed acts of sabotage were met at every step,

[14] Howey's story is in *Victorian Historical Magazine*, vol. VI, pp. 82, 121.

especially when the men were asked to do anything out of the ordinary. Then, in addition to the human difficulties, the natural ones mounted up. The Murrumbidgee, for instance, was crossed by a bridge which Mollison built of drays, sheep-hurdles, and logs, with bush and clods to fill up the interstices; the Murray, too wide for a repetition of this experiment, could be crossed only by boats made of the dray-bodies, with water-casks lashed all round them. Thus perilously and tediously, forty sheep a trip were conveyed across, and the expedition resumed. Coming upon Ebden's track of a few months before, Mollison followed this through the forestlands to the Ovens, where, annoyed by the slow rate of progress, he made a lambing-camp for the sheep at Indigo Creek and went on to Melbourne with eight men and two drays. A canvas-punt and a whale-line got them across the Goulburn: then they passed Yaldwyn's and Ebden's stations, and finally Howey's new huts at Macedon, on their way to the settlement. Having satisfied himself afresh as to the actual position, Mollison set out to return to his main body, harassed this time with drink-sodden men, spoiled by the metropolis. Arrived there, he found the chapter of his miseries still being written. The servants were going from bad to worse, and his stock continually straying. To recover their *morale* at all, the leader had to set the entire expedition in motion towards the Goulburn. All the time, the record of misadventures read like a dirge, until provisions finally ran out and the overlanders were forced to make levies on the scattered stations round them. In the end, Mollison, heartily sickened of his mishaps and the eight months of turmoil, scouted ahead over the country from the Campaspe to Werribee, and chose the fertile granite-hills of the Coliban (December 1837). There, he lived with his men in reed *mia-mias*, and, by a rude pioneer-life, built up one of the finest of the old runs.[15]

From the time of these three early outposts, the tale quickened. Clarke's run of February 1837, on the Goulburn, had carried the frontier out to that river: now, and all through 1838, runs were formed as far south as Seymour and covered the good lands between the Dividing Range and the Murray. The flocks came more rapidly than before, expeditions assumed larger and larger proportions, and 'the Line' became almost one continuous track of dusty sheep. In January 1838, one strong combination set the new tone, when a veritable 'waggon-train', similar to those which were even then crossing the Indian Territory in the United States, passed the Murray.

[15] Mollison's diaries are in the possession of the Historical Society of Victoria (see their *Magazine*, vol. IX).

Hepburn, the sailor-member of the original overlanding party, having gone back to Sydney to gather stock, set out from the County of St Vincent with the flock his tiny fortune could buy—a meagre party of two drays, ten convicts, and some 1,650 very ordinary sheep. He was going to re-locate the tree he had marked on the western mountain where Daylesford now stands, and there stake out new country. Hawdon, his more unsettled partner, accompanied him, but with no intention of definitely squatting; and soon, the expedition gathered size. Coghill joined with a flock of 2,000; then William Bowman added his 5,000, both for convenience and protection, because the Ovens natives were showing themselves militantly disposed. The three parties together mustered nine thousand sheep and about forty men, so that it appeared as if the normal expedition were tending to increase, rather than be split up into smaller and smaller parties. This particular party, after an uneventful traverse, crossed at Hume's Ford, passed Ebden's establishment at Carlsruhe (the last cattle-station on their route), and, though attracted by the lands between the Ovens and the Goulburn, decided against runs on the main-road and so far from a port. Continuing still further into country they did not know, they met and passed Harrison and Hamilton on the Goulburn. Bowman, the last to join, chose first, and split off to camp in the saucer-like depression of Castlemaine: then Hepburn crossed towards his former spot and, with his ever-present telescope, picked out the precise tree, round which he settled Daylesford, up in the colder lands (April 1838). The Coghills, going further, reached and settled at Creswick, while the two men they had passed *en route* chose Sugarloaf and the Plenty in turn—the choice giving some idea of the lordly way in which these pioneers ranged over hundreds of miles of territory. One of a party of two chose a mountain-run near the Murray, his fellow would go down to the fringe of Port Phillip, while others would divide the north and centre between them at will. At least, they had imagination and not a little sound practical sense: thus, they viewed distance as one of the least important matters, and that is why, when only seven flocks of sheep had crossed the Goulburn (as they had, at the time of this joint party), the newcomers dotted themselves over lands separated by hundreds of miles.

So the process went on, the choice of the later-comers naturally being more limited. Towards the middle of 1838, despite the two-years' drought, runs were creeping over the unbroken forest-country to the Campaspe, where Mackay and Faithfull had already lived for three months. The Faithfull expedition, one precisely the same as many others, was fated to cause a stir that made history. George Faithfull, gathering his stock and leaving the settled land in February 1838, had followed the usual route to the Ovens, and then, making a detour to the Oxley Plains, had sent his brother to the Broken River with sheep. Here occurred the event that the squatters had always feared. The Ovens natives, roused by the misdeeds of another party, attacked and obliterated the camp, killing seventeen men in all. The colony was stirred to the depths but, save for a larger degree caution and a more ruthless treatment of the natives, the squatting invasion continued as before. Faithfull himself, despite his brother's death, remained close to the Oxley and, though fear of the insurgent blacks scared away most servants, the surrounding country was occupied almost at once by such well-known men as Bowman, Reid, and Mackay. In such manner, all of the Ovens country was disposed of, and even the land running from the head-waters of the Murray and Mitta-Mitta to Omeo, in the far mountains.

The drought now was unparalleled, and racehorses were trained in lagoon-beds that have never since been dry: but the occupation still held, because, bad as things were, they were still worse in the cramped settled lands that lay across the river. By the end of the year, then, newcomers had to go as far as the barren lower banks of the Campaspe, and the country around was so occupied that already some subdivision was taking place. Bushrangers harried the riverlands, and native-raids were alarmingly frequent, but, as the settlers said, the pioneering stage was passed—the district was becoming civilized. They even had an overland mail to Sydney, and were there not five police-posts in the North-East, with four troopers at each? All of the available north-east and the land down to the coastal ranges was taken; and, in 1839, the outposts moved to the Loddon, and then next year over the country west to the Pyrenees. From river to river they went, never leaving the safe waters of one until the next in turn became the base of attack, until, in the five years after 1840, they had to start the painful task of turning on their track and then, very slowly, moving over the lands north from Mount Tarrangower to the Murray.

The Sydney-siders had thus covered the land from the Murrumbidgee to the Victorian Ranges, and had even penetrated to the huts of Melbourne. But, in the interim, the second large stream of pastoral settlement had radiated north from Melbourne itself. From the first days of settlement, observers had tended to scorn the sandy wates of Victoria and look on the island of Van Diemen's Land as a dream of fertility. A soil of sand, with thin miserable timber—thus Collins had described the dried-up Port Phillip; and the impression held. Tasmania overshadowed the mainland for a third of a century, especially when it became the granary of New South Wales. But events changed rapidly in the thirties, and the island-settlers found themselves in difficulties of all kinds. The land-regulations, especially an onerous *Impounding Act* of 1834, prevented active effort; and even licensed occupants (as apart from freeholders) had to fulfil quite impossible clearing obligations. In addition, the island—so densely mountainous and timbered in most of its area—was proving too circumscribed for a rapid increase of stock, and, for lack of available space, the prices of sheep and cattle fell rapidly. Thus, just at the moment when Port Phillip was being opened, political conditions and the shortage of good land there turned the eyes of stockowners across the Straits. This tendency was not quite new, because the Van Diemen's Land Company, which monopolized the north-western corner of the island, had been considering a mainland-settlement since 1826, and John Batman had actually applied for a grant at Western Port in 1827.

Batman, after forming some of his friends into a body called the 'Port Phillip Association', renewed his claim in 1834, and, in the official delays, simply 'squatted' without permission. After maddening storms in which the tiny ship 'jumped about like a kangaroo', he landed with nine Sydney blacks at Corio Bay—on a land of grassy wattled hills with kangaroo-grass waving like young wheat. Very satisfied with this, he continued to the head of Port Phillip and there, round the mouth of the Yarra, found treeless plains on all sides. For a few trade-goods, he secured several straggling marks on an already-prepared 'treaty'—purporting to be the consent of the Darebin chiefs for a cession of '600,000 acres, more or less'. On his return to Tasmania, the *Association* requested Governor Arthur to give them enough land to graze 20,000 sheep.

While the slow negotiations dragged on in London, the squatters once more forced events on the spot. Batman had crossed again in August 1835 with Wedge, a surveyor-member of his group, and found that his men had built three sod-huts on the site of Melbourne. Wedge roamed over the surrounding lands of Werribee, found the best sheep-land he had ever seen, illustrated his diary with child-like sketches that still survive in the Melbourne Public Library, and returned to the Yarra to find the clumsy little *Enterprise* there, with Fawkner's rival band of squatters. Before leaving, he again scouted, this time north to a ridge near Macedon, thus getting some idea of the *Association's* lands both west and north of the settlement.

Actually, they claimed 680,000 acres, divided into seventeen allotments (one for each of the members), and including all of the land immediately around Melbourne—all within a line running through Geelong almost to Gisborne, then across to Morang, and south direct to Melbourne—a princely establishment, giving them control of the colony.

The rush set in at once. In October 1835, when pioneer squatters had already crossed the Murray in converging on Port Phillip from another direction, Batman's party brought the first sheep in the *Norval*, a little barque of 300 tons: and four private stockmen accompanied this first squatting expedition to the mainland. The members of the *Association* had divided their lands by the end of the year, and the four private squatters were looking beyond this boundary, which was roughly the Barwon. Since the *Association's* absurd claims could not deter private adventurers, several founded runs, even during the long negotiations with Governor Bourke. In the new year, while the Murrumbidgee-men were working south, various parties of stock crossed from Van Diemen's Land. Gellibrand, the unofficial head of the *Association* and one of the best-known men in Hobart, crossed in January to look after his Corio lands; but this was one of the *Norval's* ill-fated trips, and practically all of his stock were killed either by storm or mismanagement. Like Wedge, he found the best land he had ever seen in the Barrabool Hills, and, returning to the dozen houses of the settlement, sent 2,500 sheep to the Werribee plains almost at once.

In the first half of 1836, at least eleven ships were plying between the island and Port Phillip and, in 48 crossings, brought in some 20,000 sheep. These flocks spread over the nearer West from Melbourne and Geelong, and even to the north. Wedge, the surveyor, was the first holder of Chirnside's famous station on the Werribee, and became rich: John Aitken took a renowned stud-flock to the site of Sunbury in March, and rose from his bark-hut to be one of the first men in the land; and others followed them. Of course, there was the other side—the new land wreaked its full toll of disaster. Franks, Aitken's friend, was killed with his shepherd by the Werribee blacks, and Gellibrand himself perished miserably in the Otway bush. Many, less spectacularly, encountered adverse conditions and defeat, and it is little exaggeration to say that many went down for each man who rose. But nobody thought of this aspect, when throngs of sheep were everywhere in the western scrub, and new lands called further out. Cowie and Stead, two of the private passengers of the *Norval*, were the first to settle in Geelong: Stieglitz, from the same boat, sat down immediately next to them. In March 1836, two local syndicates appeared, when David Fisher, for the *Derwent Company*, marked out runs at Indented Head and inland on the Barwon; and the *Clyde Company*, through George Russell, had two stations on the fringe of occupation—the then little-known Leigh, a tributary of the Barwon.

Thus, the Barwon was claimed by squatters, while Melbourne was fighting for its first recognition. Pastoral disputes led to the first private tribunal (June 1836), when, at the first public meeting of the colony, the sixteen squatters of Port Phillip elected Simpson as a judge to settle disputes. In the same month, the Governor at Sydney, intrigued by the game of these unauthorized squatters, secured Stewart's report on the settlement. The play had clearly become reality, because Stewart found 170 persons with £80,000 worth of stock, and eleven vessels busily plying the Straits, Under these conditions, Bourke had no alternative than to authorize the location of settlers. This he did by a proclamation of 9 September, and next month, Captain Lonsdale arrived as official Police Magistrate. Surveyors, Customs-officers, and a squadron of troopers came too: so that, by the end of the year, the squatting camp had become a recognized colony.

The rush of squatters continued all through the year, accelerated, of course, after the official recognition. In July, the three Manifolds and Stieglitz ascended the Barwon, and others chose various sites in the Barrabool Hills, so beloved of the early surveyors. All of the land within a twenty-five miles' radius of Geelong was claimed by the end of the year, and connection had already been made with Sydney, because Hawdon's overlanders had brought fat cattle in time for Christmas. Early in the next year, permanent settlers had come down from the North and met the islanders going in that direction from the coast. The *Association*, as was just, lost most of its land in the long fight, because it was intolerable that a closed ring of men should own all the land from the Yarra and Barwon to the hills. Perceiving this, the Government accorded the *Association* a little compensation, and threw their lands open for settlement.

Early in 1837, therefore, the squatting occupation of Port Phillip had definitely assumed its shape.[16] Melbourne was settled, and, though the southerners were emphasizing the western district more than the north, connection had been made with the overlanders coming from the old colony. Dryden had settled at Mount Macedon, when a few had passed the Coliban; and Howey had gone still a

[16] *Letters from Victorian Pioneers*, especially map of the West. Ross tells the story in *Victorian Historical Magazine*, vol. I, 1911, pp. 51-71.

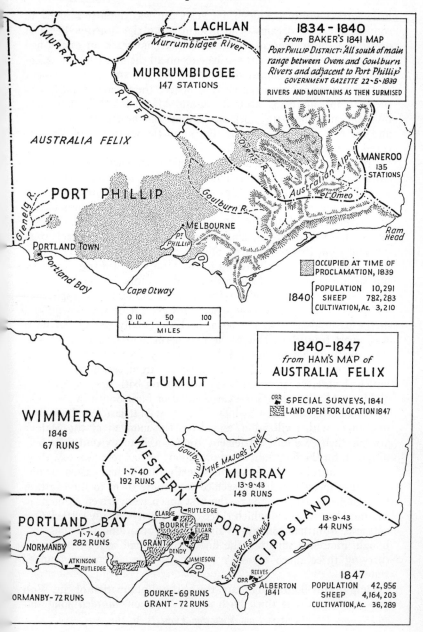

MURRAY

LACHLAN

Murrumbidgee River

MURRUMBIDGEE
147 STATIONS

1834 - 1840
from BAKER'S 1841 MAP
PORT PHILLIP DISTRICT: *'All south of main
range between Ovens and Goulburn
Rivers and adjacent to Port Phillip'*
GOVERNMENT GAZETTE 22·5·1839
RIVERS AND MOUNTAINS AS THEN SURMISED

AUSTRALIA FELIX

Ovens R.

Australian Alps

MANEROO
135
STATIONS

PORT PHILLIP

Goulburn R.

L. Omeo

Glenelg R.

MELBOURNE

Ram
Head

PORTLAND TOWN

PT
PHILLIP

Portland Bay

Cape Otway

OCCUPIED AT TIME OF
PROCLAMATION, 1839

1840 { POPULATION 10,291
SHEEP 782,283
CULTIVATION, Ac. 3,210

0 10 50 100
MILES

1840 - 1847
from HAM'S MAP *of*
AUSTRALIA FELIX

TUMUT

ORR SPECIAL SURVEYS, 1841
LAND OPEN FOR LOCATION 1847

WIMMERA
1846
67 RUNS

WESTERN

Goulburn R.

THE MAJOR'S LINE

1·7·40
192 RUNS

MURRAY
13·9·43
149 RUNS

PORTLAND BAY

CLARKE RUTLEDGE
BOURKE UNWIN
ELGAR

PORT

GIPPSLAND

13·9·43
44 RUNS

NORMANBY

1·7·40
282 RUNS

GRANT

DENDY

JAMIESON

'STRELESKIES RANGE'

ATKINSON
RUTLEDGE

REEVES

ORR
1841

ALBERTON

1847
POPULATION 42,956
SHEEP 4,164,203
CULTIVATION, Ac. 36,289

ORMANBY- 72 RUNS

BOURKE- 69 RUNS
GRANT - 72 RUNS

Victoria, 1834-1847

little further south to Riddell. Howey's run was the first actually to connect the two streams—the first to make the junction between north and south. Hereafter, with the overland track an established reality and with permanent settlements on all the best lands on either side, there remained simply the filling of crevices and the curtailment of the first principalities, especially where they had assumed such preposterous limits as around Mount Macedon. Definition, sub-division, and adequate stocking became the orders of the day—and the first occupation of the south and the north-east of Victoria could be said to have finished.

Concurrently with these two streams from north and south, a third had commenced, though not as feverish or spectacular in its later development. Edward Henty had reconnoitred Portland Bay as early as June 1833, and, passing the sheds and huts of the whalers, had struck inland to the site of the present township. Having applied for a grant of this land, he claimed that he had 'a tacit com-mission' from Downing Street, and, in November 1834, after thirty-four days of continual buffeting in the Straits, landed from Launces-ton with a comrade and five indentured servants. From his Antipo-dean Noah's Ark, he landed seine-nets and guinea-fowls, apple-trees and dogs—everything except sheep. However, if he was no squatter in the pastoral sense of the term, he had actually settled—in what was, apart from the whalers, the first permanent settlement in Vic-toria. Nothing happened until August two years later, when a party of strangers prowled with menacing arms from the north, and re-vealed themselves, after much explanation on both sides, as the men of Major Mitchell, the Surveyor-General of New South Wales, who had come overland from Sydney. The Hentys at last felt themselves in contact with civilization, and, from the moment of the Major's arrival, their Western settlement commenced to expand. Mitchell, in return for the hospitality and provisions he had received, told them of the beautiful downs, forty miles north, that he had passed beyond the dense forest which had seemed to confine them to the coast. A year later—in August 1837—the first sheep were driven through to *Merino Downs*, round which three of the Hentys finally settled. One of these, Muntham on the Wannon, was, according to Fetherston-haugh, himself a squatter, the finest run he had seen in Australia, carrying three sheep to every two acres, even in an unimproved state.[17]

Despite this flourishing start, the pastoral occupation of the West was very slow. The thick bush of the Wannon afforded admirable

[17] *Letters from Victorian Pioneers*, p. 263.

cover to the blacks, and for long, native inroads harassed existing settlers and deterred others. There was, it is true, a gradual widening of the circle round Merino Downs—in 1838, the squatters moved over towards Hamilton, and the Winters took up Tahara and Murndal. Henty himself told of many new settlers in the next two years, 'until all the country immediately around us was taken possession of', while one of the brothers even crossed the frontier to Mount Gambier. But the Portland settlement remained essentially a coastal one, and there was no expansion until 1840, when the Hopkins and the tract between the upper Glenelg and the Grampians were attacked. The movement from the east offered a greater return with less trouble, so that newcomers hastened to take part in the move from Melbourne westwards—up to beyond Ballan and Mortlake in 1839.

By the end of 1836, as has been seen, runs stretched round Geelong in a semi-circle of 25 miles. Next year, these early holdings were stabilized and new strips taken up, with a pioneer as far out as Colac. The *Western District*, which is practically the pick of Australia, was rapidly being encroached upon, especially after the early months of the year, when the expansions from Geelong and the Yarra met, and the joint effort was turned westwards. Now that the Werribee plains were fully stocked, the Colac country was a goal. At this time, Swanton's sheep on the upper Leigh were the furthest out, though, inside his holding, a whole series ran to W. J. T. Clarke's (the first Australian millionaire's) run on the Werribee, and so round to the settlement. Clarke's little flock of 2,000 at Station Peak had become 80,000 within sixteen years, yielding him £20,000 a year. The Bacchus Marsh lands were now occupied: and so the circle swept, late in 1837, from Clarke's run round to Ricketts and Armytage high up on the Barwon, where the Otways came down—to the giant forest country where Gellibrand had been lost, and where the savage Colac blacks were supposed to hide.

So matters stood when the Governor, Bourke, first visited Melbourne, and when the first land-sales were held. It was not a little ironical that, when the first land was officially alienated, permanent settlements with 100,000 sheep had been made! Ricketts was the furthest out; but late in the year came the turn of the Colac district. McLeod of Tahara had explored these Western lakes, but had withdrawn closer in and left the new lands to Hugh Murray, the Lloyds, and a handful of others. This was in September 1837, but nobody disturbed the firstcomers for at least six months—until the rush started in 1838, the great year of the West. Port Phillip was now seized by the boom-conditions that had raged in the older settlement, and, both now and in 1839, 'a spirit of speculation as hare-brained as ever the world saw' seized upon everybody. One observer described it as a general mental inebriety, while even the moderates spoke of 'the insane spirit of speculation'. Sheep soared up to £3 a head and beyond, and everybody was agog to avail himself of the too facile accommodation offered by the banks and then either buy town-allotments or pay crazy prices for stock and set out for the West.

With these conditions prevailing, it is easy to understand why more land was occupied in the West of Victoria in 1838 than in all of the other years together. The year started with a rush to the head-waters of the Leigh and the Buninyong country. Learmonth in par-ticular pushed out from the Barwon, even to Mount Misery and the foot of the Pyrenees. Throughout the year, new men occupied all of the vacant spots from the Otways to the central range (where the northerners were even then establishing themselves), and as far west as Camperdown and Beaufort. The nearer West was already crowded, and there were great quarrels over the gentleman's agreement that determined the boundaries. '*Three miles per man!*' was the under-stood limit in settled country. 'There was a tacit understanding', wrote Learmonth of the Barwon, 'that no one was to take up a station nearer than three miles to another person, the intervening ground being equally divided.'

Ballarat and Beaufort, the lake-country in the west, and south to the timbered coastal ridges—the stream flowed on in 1838, and ran into other streams. The northern overlanders had already met the men of Port Phillip round Macedon: now, further west, Clarke's shepherd's on the ridges of Creswick met the northerners deploying down from Daylesford—Hepburn and Bowman, the old stalwarts; and the Coghills. By the end of the year, the West was indeed conquered, and only consolidation was lacking. Another layer was added in 1839—past Mortlake on the plains, and Ballan in the later potato-land up north. The land south of the Grampians, for some reason or other, they avoided like the plague, but this was an excep-tion. Everything else was occupied, and in 1840, the Hopkins saw the meeting of the expansions from Portland and Port Phillip.

Thus the period ended. Settlement from the Murrumbidgee had come up to that from Melbourne: further west, overlanders from the northern rivers had met those from Geelong, and more slowly, the expansion had crept east from Portland. Now, these movements achieved, the heart of Victoria (from the Hopkins to Albury, and from Avoca to Western Port) was occupied by a race of squatters, at first with no title at all, and later on yearly sufferance. More explicitly, the outer line of settlement ran from the head of the Glenelg to the headwaters of the Goulburn, and then up that river to the Murray; while the other limit was from Western Port due north to the line of the ranges. All of *the Major's Line* was stocked, except the plains near the mountains—avoided for some queer superstition. The whole of the West was taken, except the scrubby ranges of Otway, and the line of occupation curved down from the Glenelg to the Grampians. Northward, the open plains and forest—the drier lands—north of Bendigo, were being attacked in a desultory manner, but the Goulburn was the limit of effective occupation. The northern river-lands, of course, were firmly held, but the squatter of 1840 was apt to pass scathing remarks on Mitchell's glowing descriptions of the lower reaches of these rivers, and to restrict his own efforts to the lands farther away from the Murray. The Wimmera, the Mallee, and the lands along the Murray were still free, and, on the southern side, Gippsland retained its virginal isolation. Squatters had reached Western Port, and Macmillan, even in this year of 1840, was forcing a way from Monaro to the coast: but the mountain-barrier still resisted attacks, except in the cluster of hill-posts round Omeo.

But all of these unconquered lands were merely the uninviting outskirts, where desert or mountain exacted too great a toll: the centre of the land had all been taken, and the fact that the squatters had reached the fringe of Gippsland and the Mallee indicated, not the limits on their expansion, but the vast extent of territory over which they had flowed. The first squatting onrush was over, Port Phillip was now a settled colony. The metamorphosis is one of the most complete in Australian history (even Queensland was on a much smaller scale in its earlier stages): and, taking these results into consideration, it may certainly be called the *apogée* of the Australian squatting movement—its justification, and its revelation to the English world of what it meant and the vast forces it implied. Unauthorized squatters could make the colony like the Victoria of 1840 —or, as it was then called, *the Southern District of New South Wales*—in five years—the fact was sufficient of itself!

V   South Australia

In the meantime, while the squatters had been crossing Victoria and even entering Queensland, a new colony had been built up round St Vincent's Gulf—the nucleus of South Australia. This was the model colony of the Wakefield school, the first-fruits of systematic colonization, the demonstration of how to colonize. After years of violent criticism of former projects and seemingly endless preliminaries, a South Australian Association was formed and received practically *carte blanche* in founding a colony on the south coast. They advertised themselves to the point of nausea in the early thirties, and reiterated their claims so often and so dogmatically that Parliament, the Colonial Office, and the public came to believe them and see in them the prophets appointed by reason to lead the practical colonizers of all time into the paths of colonial infallibility. By reason of these long agitations in England and the influence the Wakefieldians exerted on colonial policy in general, their schemes were much discussed in the existing Australian colonies, especially when they bore such fruit as increased land-prices. The Wakefieldians were thus more an influence on colonization than colonizers, and their connection with squatting was primarily in the direction of keeping the Colonial Office to the doctrines of high price and concentration of settlement. But, over and above this doctrinal assertion, they founded a colony themselves and encountered precisely the same squatting difficulties which they had so heartily condemned everywhere else.

After much bother, the first of the Company's ships moored opposite the wastes of Kangaroo Island in July 1836, but afterwards moved up the Gulf to the northward and established a colony at Holdfast Bay. From that moment, however desultory the preparatory steps had been, the colony leaped into life. Fifteen vessels arrived in 1836, land-values at once boomed, and a general air of urban excitement characterized the new settlement. With the struggles between Company and Government—with the speculation and prodigal expenditure that passed the colony through boom to crisis, this survey has little to do, beyond mentioning that the squatting expansion took place against this background of inflated conditions within the town.[18]

It was at once evident that the pastoral future of South Australia was not to be compared with that of Port Phillip, or even New South Wales proper. Sturt's rhapsodies of 1829 had been largely responsible for the site of the colony, but the settlers dumped at Adelaide found themselves little helped by his accounts. '*My eye never fell on a country of more promising aspect, or more favourable position,*' he had written on going down to the Murray-mouth. To the contrary, all that the settlers could see were the hills that confined Adelaide to

---

[18] The chronology of South Australia is given in Hodder's *History of South Australia* (1893), or R. C. Mills's *The Colonization of Australia, 1829-1842* (1915).

the sea and that stretched north indefinitely like a cleft stick. Sturt's lands between the Murray and the Gulf might be there, but they seemed very remote.

Moreover, the new colony was curiously agricultural from the start. The emphasis was far more on labour and reaping than on run-seeking and sheep. South Australia had a large artisan-population and stood for small farms and crops. Everything was on a small and intensive scale—small farms, small runs, small flocks. The Eastern colonists despised farming (hence the almost complete dependence of New South Wales on foreign grain, even in the forties!), but, with South Australia, it was very different. It was the first mainland-colony to become a self-supporting granary, for it was practically self-sufficient even during the crisis in 1841.

With this emphasis, it was only natural that pastoral occupation should be slow and chequered until the artificial fillip of the gold-discoveries. South Australia stood apart from the general squatting fever of the late thirties, and, save for the numerous expeditions 'overlanding' stock from the newly-opened Port Phillip, the squatting repercussions there affected general Australian development very little. Practically nothing was done until the Rivoli Bay country—Sturt's lauded plains—were opened in the later forties, and there was again a quiet period until the gold-rushes in Victoria led to the stocking of the country north of Mount Remarkable. There was no feverish occupation of new country, as in Victoria—no surge over the inland, as in New England and the Murrumbidgee—no feeling of optimism, as in the Darling Downs of the same period. Every successive step was slow and dubious, and the results were those to be expected from such a combination of patchy country and disconnected effort. By 1840, when the main settlement was consolidated, the South Australians were convinced that their country was not one for unlimited pastoral occupation, and, having been lured there by Sturt's optimism, they were now prepared to accept Eyre's doleful experiences in the north as typical of what the interior in general offered them.

The first few years saw a very restrained effort. After Kangaroo Island, the Commissioners had become almost poetical about the thinly-wooded meadows that reached out from Adelaide, especially when Morphett first crossed Mount Lofty to the Mount Barker country on the east in 1837, and found gradually rising land with undulating bottoms of the best alluvial soil and good silky grass. Land seemed to stretch out ready for the taking, but idle land-jobbing in the town offered easier prospects when the average settler was dreaming only of amassing a fortune quickly and easily. The fancy of a few turned to the Reed Beds, to the new lands of Mount Barker, and even to the two hundred miles of the Murray valley, which was a kind of terrestrial dream to the South Australians for decades.

But actual enterprise lingered, because, apart from the boom in town-allotments and the frenzied speculation, both capitalists and small men were more concerned with wheat nearer town than with sheep and cattle beyond the mountains. The South Australian Company, it is true, attempted to aid pasturage (its circulars repeatedly called it 'the staple'), but they proceeded on an artificial plan. Each lot had 640 acres of pasture-land attached to it, and the Company's Agent envisioned neat holdings dotted mathematically over the interior—purchased paddocks with square grazing areas round each. The colony was to be a series of squares, with each settler separated from the next by a large grazing-area. Naturally, occupation in a new country cannot follow such a plan, and the leasing-project accomplished little. More practicable were the sheep-stations—'No. 1', 'No. 2', and so on—that the Company dotted over the Glenelg Plains, where the suburbs now stand.

The first real impetus to squatting came in April 1838, when overlanders arrived from Port Phillip with stock.[19] At that time, nothing had been done beyond a few desultory explorations, so that the note of enterprise sounded by the Victorian squatters burst like a resounding clarion. Joseph Hawdon, the first of the overlanders to Melbourne, now in turn drove three hundred cattle from the Goulburn to the Murray-bend, and then across to Mount Barker and Adelaide. His journey was as uneventful as his first one to Melbourne had been, and as successful, because only four head of cattle were lost. A month later, Edward John Eyre left to strike straight across and avoid the Murray, with its truculent savages, but the difficulties he encountered made him fall back on Hawdon's tracks. Sturt followed a few months later, and then, in March 1839, Bonney, who had accompanied Hawdon, left the Henty's establishment on the Glenelg to try the coastal route. Past the sheoak marshes, he forced an arduous way over the hundred miles of sandhills to Lake Alexandrina, and, difficult though the trip was, he succeeded in opening a route only a quarter as long as Hawdon's, and incidentally in directing attention once more to Sturt's original land of the south-east. Meanwhile, Eyre had again crossed, this time overlanding a flock of sheep (the first so to be driven) as well as his six hundred cattle: then, eleven more parties crossed, and so many followed that overlanding came to pass

[19] G. Williams, *South Australian Exploration to 1856* (1919), ch. VI.

as an unnoticed episode in a squatter's existence. The filling of South Australia by stock overlanded in this way from the other colonies was one of the most remarkable features of the time, and it was typical of the age that such ventures were treated so casually. Mundy and Hawdon, who seemed quite irrepressible by this time, even drove tandem from Melbourne to Adelaide in 1840, and, of course, after that, nobody could take overlanding in the heroic manner.

In this fashion stock came to South Australia, and, naturally, a squatting expansion followed. Cattle-stations were thirty-five miles east of Adelaide by the middle of 1839, and 120,000 sheep were shorn. The links with the eastern colonies were growing every month, and cramped stockmen, like Henty, were advancing on South Australia from the outside—a spread facilitated by Eyre's demonstration that sheep could be driven to Port Lincoln by land.

By 1841 then, the further settlement had reached Horrock's cattle-station,[20] ninety miles from Adelaide, in the Hutt survey, though the spontaneity of the overlanding time seemed to have somewhat abated. The squatters were depressed, alike by the grave crisis in the colony and by the pessimism of the explorers. Sturt and Eyre had both been hardly-met in the north, and Eyre's fresh attempt in 1840 had only confirmed his first impression. In view of this, only a few bold spirits—most at the time called them heedless—moved north. J. and W. Chambers were first, passing to take up Pekina (afterwards one of the richest runs in the province and resumed by the Government for agriculture), but seventeen months without water induced them to move to Lake Bonney. Then, Captain Chase, on foot, explored further, and well-known runs like Arkaba and Wilpena were taken up near the ranges he found. But this was already past 1840, and even then, no one went beyond Howannigan Gap, which was for long the most northerly post. By this time, it must be remembered—when South Australia had only dabbled with the north and had not touched the east—the Port Phillip squatters had covered all of their land up to the fringe of the Mallee and even to the mountain approaches of Gippsland.[21]

Thus, when the occupation of Victoria was almost complete, and when the older colony was moving to the grey-bitten mulga lands of the far west, the South Australians still rested inert—and it was not until the Downs of Queensland were being encroached on that

---

[20] Morphett's letter in *S.A. News*, 15 February 1842.

[21] Details in Bull's *Early Experiences of Life in South Australia* (1883), p. 95, *et seq.*

they moved to their good lands. Farming was more than ever the cry, and little could be expected of a colony when the largest flock was Dutton's 11,000 sheep—when the Victorians were accustomed to overland flocks of that size! Realizing this inertia, the South Australians turned, in the forties, to their south-east, two hundred miles away.[22] These were the lands boomed by Sturt and again brought before the public by the overlanders. Since Government effort was relied on more in this colony than elsewhere, Governor Grey went there in 1844, and found almost uninterrupted good land from the Murray to the Glenelg. The north was now known to be dry, and the west desert: therefore, this new land of Rivoli Bay came to be the centre of attention all through the decade. Henty had built the first cattle-hut there in 1841, squatters had arrived in 1842, and all the land from Bordertown west to the coast was taken up before 1850. The sheep were 'increasing beyond all calculation' at this time, so that the need of pasture was severely felt, especially in a country like this where, despite the huge area, only isolated patches of the interior were at all useful. The undue emphasis on the south-east, with its straggling little township of Robe, can thus be understood—in itself, it emphasizes the general paucity of South Australia's effort.

There, South Australia rested in 1845. The papers were full of Rivoli Bay—which was what the *Southern Australian* called 'a nobleman's park on a large scale'—and were exultant over the occupation of Mount Bryan, a hundred miles north of Hallett's previous outpost, itself one hundred and forty miles from town. The boundaries of permanent settlement, however, were much nearer in, being practically one hundred and thirty miles north and sixty south of Adelaide. The far north was not very much esteemed, and the lands nearer town were full, so that attention was concentrating more than ever on the East—the safety-valve of the colony. East of Encounter Bay, were sheep and cattle runs, and then along Lake Victoria and for a hundred miles up the Murray; and Rivoli Bay was still booming. In all, the colony had 30,000 acres cropped, 400,000 sold and about three-quarters of a million sheep. There were some 12,000 farms or stations, and the agricultural settlements, especially round Mount Barker, were models for Australia. But, impressive though these results were as far as agriculture was concerned, the fact could not be gainsaid that the good pastoral land seemed at an end—and that with only a two hundred-mile strip north and south from Adelaide, and a young settlement in the south-

[22] *Southern Australia,* 27 February 1844: detailed account by Talbot in *Royal Geographical Society,* S.A., 1919-20, p. 106.

east! It was evident that the squatting movement here was to be of circumscribed limits; and history emphasized this conclusion in the next twenty years.[23]

With the move to Rivoli Bay, the period dealt with in this monograph was practically over. No expansion at all was to be chronicled before the boom of the lands beyond Mount Remarkable in 1851, when the gold rushes forced prices up. Other factors occupied attention throughout the forties—first the crisis, then the labour troubles, and then the attempts at small farming. Land was now offering a-plenty for agriculture, commercial confidence was restored, settled counties were proclaimed (1842), and the lodes of Glen Osmond and Burra Burra revived the former optimism: but, of squatting, there was practically no mention.

Not unnaturally under these conditions, the squatter of South Australia was a far different person from his eastern fellows. His life was strangely mobile and unstable. He could only erect a turf hut and moveable hurdles, because he was always liable to be warned off. The declaration of a county would imply that his tenure immediately ended, and that the small settlers had come: and, as late as 1845, a famous case, *McKenzie* v. *Stocks*, decided that squatters had no claims against even the smallest purchaser.[24] Till 1847, they could be turned out of their huts by purchasers or eaten out by intruders, and thus had no prospect of permanent settlement. Hence, they had few improvements and no expansion, and, by deduction, no privileges and no political power. By 1850, they numbered only two hundred and ninety-three, and ran a million sheep over 12,000 square miles, but they were not very prosperous. The price of labour was determined by agricultural conditions, they had to pay high rates of interest after the crisis (because theirs was a discredited occupation), and they were hit by the low price of wool in Europe. All in all, South Australia made a poor squatting story at this time, especially after the magnificent conquest of Port Phillip and the competition of Queensland. Not till the gold days were there squatting kings in South Australia—not till then were they endowed with a position and outlook at all resembling those of the easterners. In the late thirties and through the forties, their history was one of baffled effort. Circumscribed by Nature and overshadowed by the magnates of New South Wales, they were in no position to fight, and were overridden by the small farmers time and again. The South Australia of that

[23] For position of settlement, see *S.A. News*, 11 November 1844; *Southern Australian*, 29 March 1844 (Rivoli), and 14 May 1844 (Murray).
[24] Report in *Adelaide Observer*, 7 June 1845.

time chose its destiny by emphasizing small men: but it was the squatters who paid, by long years of repression and neglect, both implied and actual.[25]

VI   Queensland

After the rush to Port Phillip and the discontent in South Australia, the squatting interest moved to Queensland, where boom conditions existed throughout the forties. Here was new country awaiting the occupant—not sandy desert like the Victorian Wimmera, and not difficult country like the New England ranges, but gently undulating downs and grassed plains. The pastoralist of that era thought that such meadow-land was the best for sheep: the day of the dry plains had not yet come. They were still arguing from the European analogy, and sought for even dampish land, so long as it was richly grassed and watered. It did not occur to them that other factors than a mere bed of greenery had to be considered, that, perchance, much of the drier land they had passed over in their first onrush might be far and away the best sheep-land under Australian conditions. Flat land, thickly verdured as a lawn, was what they desired—let him have the rocky lands, scant-grassed and wind-bitten, who would! To such men, the Downs were naturally a dream of richness, a Dutch meadow prepared for them by Nature.

The existence of such country, moreover, was no secret. It was known to all. Cook and Flinders had been on the coast, and Oxley, seeking the site for a convict settlement far from Sydney, had entered the Brisbane River in 1823. A penal colony had at once been started, under a certain ubiquitous Captain Logan, who appeared to divide his time between studying the physiology revealed by flogging his charges, and charting the botanical specimens in his neighbourhood. Neither of these diversions helped pastoral occupation to any extent, and it was not unnatural that the district seemed, for a time, 'to sleep the dead sleep of inane criminality', with various Commissioners doing nothing but torturing convicts and grazing a few head of stock. However, forces were slowly tending towards free settlement. Cunningham, by pushing through the Downs in 1827 and finding 'extensive tracts of clear pastoral country', had made this inevitable because there was scarcely a hemmed-in pastoralist in the southern colony who did not ponder his map and speculate on the northern lands. In 1828, too, Cunningham had connected his new

---

[25] 1849 *Report of Crown Lands and Emigration Commissioners*, p. 61, for peculiarities of South Australian position.

regions with Moreton Bay, thus giving his discovery a port: and what did a squatter want beyond a new region of downs and a road to a port, even a convict-port forbidden to freemen?

But here came a surprising fact in Australian settlement—a gap of thirteen years before these lands were utilized! It was not for lack of knowledge, because Cunningham had published his diary and widely circulated his maps; and it was certainly not for lack of incentive, when the squatters were being forced to the arid west of New South Wales, to the Mallee, and to the patchy lands north of Adelaide. At first, of course, the Murrumbidgee and Port Phillip distracted attention, and nothing could be done from landward until the New England ranges were pierced. But these conditions had disappeared some time before the actual settlement, and, moreover, there was always Cunningham's track to follow, or, as an alternative, the seaward approach which he too had pointed out. It is true that the Government forbade the approach of any freemen within fifty miles of the convict settlement, but the squatters did not usually pay so much regard to the letter of the law. The delay was simply incomprehensible, accounted for—but not justfied—by the difficulties of the mountain approach and the adequacy of the land between Armidale and the border. It was an exception in the long tale of how the squatters faced opportunity: here, on the other hand, opportunity waited on them, fairly beckoned to them for years before it was grasped.

Nothing actually happened, nor was the fifty-miles' cordon really broken until the forties, although Gipps had slowly worked for free settlement. While he did not go as far as laying out a township or lifting the ban on occupation, he, at least, stopped the criminals in 1839, and, next year, sent the chainmen for a trigonometrical survey. At last, in February 1842, he proclaimed the new order: henceforth 'all settlers and other free persons shall be at liberty to proceed thither in like manner as to any other part of the colony'.[26]

As has been seen, the squatters had spread over the northern ward of New England in the five years before 1840. From Glen Innes, the land of the Beardies, they had gone to the border: and now, in January 1840, an expedition of Scotsmen followed a track of thirteen years before, past the station of Gordon and Bennett's on the Severn, on to the north. They were the Leslies of Collaroi, looking for Cunningham's *Darling Downs* of 1827, and relying only on a rough copy of his map. Patrick Leslie was an enterprising Aberdonian, in

[26] Coote, *History of Queensland*, 1881, p. 23. Documents are in Gipps-Glenelg, 1 July 1839, or N.S.W. *Government Gazette*, 15 February 1842.

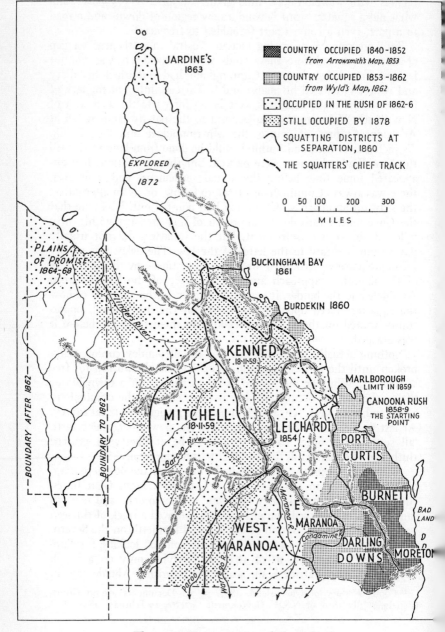

The squatting occupation of Queensland

many ways the very type of squatting pioneer. Absolutely fearless and something of a rough jewel, he was active and energetic, 'hail-fellow-well-met' and 'the prince of bushmen'.

He had obtained full particulars of his project from Allan Cunningham before setting out, though the loss of a certain map left him uncertain of anything except the exact location of Ben Lomond, the roof of New England and the nuclear guiding post of the whole north. He set out with his brother, a friend, and two convicts, but soon left the main party and scouted ahead with Peter Murphy, a Dublin *lifer*—Leslie's inseparable friend, 'the best plucked fellow I ever came across in my life, and as good a servant as master ever had', he records gratefully. Two days on from Gordon and Bennett's, he was satisfied that he had found a serviceable route and returned for his stock. This—the first stock expedition to enter Queensland, apart from the convicts by sea—consisted of

400 breeding ewes, 100 ewe hoggets, 1,000 wedder hoggets, 100 rams and 500 wedders 3 and 4 years old. We had two teams of bullocks (24 in all) and 2 drays, a team of horses and a dray, and 10 saddle-horses. We had 22 men, all ticket-of-leave or convicts, as good and game a lot of men as ever existed, and who never gave us a moment's trouble—worth any 40 men I have ever seen since.

The broken language of Leslie's Diary serves to heighten the picturesqueness of his effort, and it requires little imagination to see the cavalcade, winding down the mountain tracks and so across the plains—'wedders and hoggets' and drays and convicts!

Tracks had to be cut in advance in this rough country, for even a span of a dozen yoked bullocks could not drag drays over such difficult virgin lands. Despite this, Leslie reached the Condamine in less than three weeks, without, in his own words, losing a hoof or breaking a bullock-chain. As with so many of those hard-bitten old pioneers, he unwittingly knew how to be picturesque, although his main concern was to eliminate any trimmings and concentrate on his task of bringing his motley crew of convicts and sheep to where the food lay on the Downs.

There, in June 1840, he formed the first station at Canning Downs, claiming a principality of some hundreds of thousands of acres—'from the bottom of Toolburra to the head of the Condamine'. But obviously no one man could hold such an area with the few stock that Leslie had, and he had to concede Glengallan to the Campbells and Rosenthal to others.[27] Leslie's claim to be the pioneer of Queens-

---

[27] Leslie's journal is in Russell's *Genesis of Queensland*.

land has not remained undisputed. One John Campbell, later of Ipswich, claimed to have been on the north bank of the Severn when the sheepmen came over from New England and to have set up a cattle camp there in January 1840: and there is much to support his contention. But Leslie's was the recognized expedition, it was his track that the later-comers followed, and his was the first permanent settlement.

A ring of rivals encircled him almost as soon as he 'squatted' at Toolburra, jostling for the best sites. The Middle District was still facing drought and a crisis, and Port Phillip was full, so that attention quickly turned to the reopening of the fabled north. Hence, although shepherds asked £100 to £150 and rations, and could scarcely be found at this price to face the isolation and the blacks, an early rush occurred in 1840-1. Sir Arthur Hodgson, a cultured *dilettante*, took up Eton Downs and surrounded himself with a *Round Table* of well-bred jackeroos, fresh from home Universities. Then the Campbells, who followed Leslie, had Glengallan 'given up' to them. One cannot picture Leslie cheerfully acquiescing in this, but presumably the new occupant was of the same breed as that Campbell who had fought for a Byron Plains run in a fistic combat that still stirs memories amongst the 'old hands' of the Beardy Plains! Most of these Downsmen, it will be noticed, were Scotsmen, and this is the more obvious as one goes down the list!

Dalrymple got Goomburra, another bit of the original Leslie holding; the Gammies took and held Talgai; Thane named Ellangowan; and Campbell, Leslie's rival claimant, went a little further out to Westbrooke. Most of these holdings were the pick of the Downs and have since either reverted to the Crown or been resumed for closer settlement. Still more flocks crossed every month. Scougall of Liverpool Plains, the fame of the new country spreading, sent Henry Dennis exploring, and he took up the huge Jimbour run for his employers and the richer Jondaryan for himself. In addition, this 'eye-picker' chose Warra for Irving and Myall Creek for Coxen, a connection of the ornithologist Gould (1842). To conclude the tale, two runs, the size of large English counties, were settled by the Gores— the well-grassed Yandilla and Tummaville. And thus the Downs were filled. The first wave of pioneers, claiming absurdly large runs, had secured one of the natural gardens of Australia and opened a fertile region for the more intensive settlement that was bound to follow.[28]

[28] The occupation of the Downs is told in Sir A. Morgan's paper in *Queensland Geographical Journal*, 1902, vol. XVII, p. 87. Gipps's account is in despatch of 4 May 1842.

But their settlement was not a mere hectic rush. There was much Scotch caution and still more tenacity in the way that early holdings were consolidated in the forties and held against all-comers—neither of them easy tasks. Difficulties massed up against them. Their settlement shared in the depression of Sydney in the early years of the decade, when capital of any kind was beyond their reach: they found the labour problem almost insoluble: and they had to encounter bad seasons until the three-years' stretch which started in 1844, and even those coincided with the new imposts of Governor Gipps. However, by 1842, they were strongly enough implanted to warrant the appointment of Commissioners and the declaration of two squatting districts—*Moreton Bay* and *Darling Downs*, under Simpson and Rolleston respectively. The last military commandant had gone by this time, and the police magistrate come. Gipps himself arrived to see the new squatting stronghold in May 1842, and, not a little amused in his grim way, pondered on the 45 stations he found there, and the 1,500 bales of wool they were shipping that year—all in territory officially closed to free settlement until three months before!

Occupation rested at this stage during most of the period dealt with here, although, avoiding the bad lands directly north of Brisbane, the squatters gradually pushed up the coast to the Maryborough region by 1850, and to the edge of the Downs out west—but in a very slow, controlled movement, because the land suitable for sheep in Queensland was far from being unlimited. Occupation was a difficult task at every stage. The squatters on the Downs, for instance, were barred from the ports by the frowning coastal range, and had to combine in voluntary road parties to hew a passage. No man 'out back' could hope to keep good shepherds, and all had to face escapees in the bush, and in particular, the numerous and recalcitrant natives. Still they went on. Russell and Glover formed the first station on the Burnett in 1843 (the bad year): and others soon camped on the upper Burnett and the Mary River— adding a fresh layer to the settlement. This brought them to the Dawson, the northern outpost when this survey closes (1850); and all rested poised to attack the great north road from this nucleus—north to the Burdekin, and out to the Warrego.[29]

The early fifties thus passed: then came the sixties with the greatest of all pastoral booms. The main body of Queensland was filled, from the Maranoa to the Plains of Promise on Carpentaria (with the Jardines at the very tip of the continent), and out west

[29] For the northern occupation, see Palmer, *Early Days in North Queensland* (1903), p. 86, *et seq.*

past the dry Paroo and Barcoo into 'the dead heart'. It was in this rush that central and western Queensland fell—twenty years after the stage of this book. As far as this survey is concerned, Queensland meant Moreton Bay and the Downs, with the pioneers further out on the Burnett and reconnoitring towards the Dawson. Mitchell discovered the Fitzroy in 1846; and that was *the new land* of the time. *Wide Bay, Burnett,* and *Maranoa* were first proclaimed in 1849 —these were the official outposts, although even officials 'knew of thirty stations taken up in the previous couple of years outside the most distant licensing districts'.

The Queensland squatters, for the rest, were a noisy band, for ever holding indignation meetings against the Sydney Government, and clamouring for cheap labour from Timor or English gaols or anywhere else! But they had, as yet, occupied only a fragment of their State. *Moreton Bay,* as their settlement was called, was a very tiny colony in the forties. Theirs was rather a matter for the future, though the existence of so much unoccupied land meant much in the general squatting outlook of eastern Australia, especially once a base on the Downs had been established. For that reason, the Queensland settlement could not be neglected.

VII   New South Wales and Victoria, 1840-1850

In the meantime, while South Australia and Queensland were being stocked, the pressure of the flocks was reopening the older routes, and the western trend was resumed again in New South Wales, and the move to the inhospitable corners of Victoria. The forties, though belonging primarily to the Rivoli district of South Australia and the Darling Downs, saw much persistent striving in these less-favoured zones. The fight there was becoming too strenuous in proportion to the reward, but with the monopoly of the more settled districts, a newcomer had no choice.

In New South Wales, the first rebound of the Victorian rush was felt on the Murrumbidgee. Those river-runs had stocked the new districts of *Australia Felix*: now, the latter offering few more prizes, there was a turn back to the source. Incidentally, the lands thus despised at first in New South Wales were afterwards known as *the Riverina,* the best land in Australia for merino flocks!

Settlement had been stagnant below Wagga for some time. Nothing was done until the rush south was over and until the Murrumbidgee had recovered from the drought and was again running in its bed. Then the rush to *the New Country* began, from Deniliquin up the Lachlan. The vacant spots south and south-east of Wagga soon filled, and some sheepmen even went to the Lachlan and Murrumbidgee junction. The first there was Hobler, an old Tasmanian who settled at Paika, and who effectively opened this region,[30] although the great crisis of the forties and machinations of land speculators, like Wentworth, drove him out to California. Thence, the runs crept along to the Murray junction, and up its northern bank to the Darling. John Scott followed Hobler to Canally, the Jacksons first ran cattle where the Murrumbidgee joins the Murray, two boys went above, and a few months later, stock ran on the present site of Mildura. The river-runs divided the land to the Darling, and, in 1850, even up that river to Wilcannia. Tapio, near the junction, was taken, and a number of Scots—never far behind in the search for new country—roamed up the Darling, exploring its banks, and marked out superficial runs in hundreds of square miles. During 1850, for instance, MacCallum settled at Menindie, on the bend, and the boy Morey went still further, with McKinley, the third of the band, below him. The runs were already creeping up to Bourke.

The new runs were soon crowded, at least according to squatting ideas. Tyson, the prince of Australian squatters, went to Buckland in 1844 and found all the land on the Murray occupied.

A new man coming along in search of land was looked upon by most of the squatters as worse than a highwayman, and he could seldom obtain information as to the boundaries of the runs, for most stockholders claimed all the land to the nearest neighbour.

Tyson, however, managed to squeeze in on the Billabong Creek, near Urana, and started to found his huge fortune. Gormly had found the Murrumbidgee fully taken in 1843, and could not get in at all: and Crisp, three years later, had to go back to the lower Lachlan. Even townships were coming, first at Gundagai, then Albury, and then Wagga Wagga (1847). The south-west was passing from the squatters' stage to what they derided as civilization.

Further north, in the centre, an equally intensive movement was taking place between the Lachlan and the Queensland boundary. For many years, the arid lands out west had restrained settlement round the native reserve of Wellington Valley, although the land round Dubbo went in the thirties. The diamond brand of Judge Wild was first seen at Gobolion, Palmer took Murrumbidgee and its Macquarie Falls, and Tollemache, an old Commissariat soldier, occ-

[30] In Gipps-Stanley, 21 January 1846. An excellent account of this region is by Baird of Dubbo in *Daily Telegraph*, 14 September 1912.

upied Guyulman and Geary. Dalhuntly seized the town site of
Dubbo itself, and others went on up the Macquarie. By 1840, they
were already far up that river and down to the Lachlan, and even going north up the Bogan (1846-7). Here, the blacks were bad, and the
west was slow to forget the seven men massacred at Willaroon and
raids on practically every station in this northern river system. But
the Bogan fell, then the Namoi, and lastly the Barwon, where Jones
settled on the site of Walgett township in 1839. A report of the Commissioner, Roderick Mitchell, showed that Turnbull, on the Namoi
junction, was the farthest out in 1845, and that the Darling had
already been menaced from this direction.[31] The lands of the north,
between the Namoi and the Gwydir, came under a ban, like the
Pyrenees in Victoria: but, with this superstitious exception, the
march went on, even during the long crisis. Unfortunately, the
drought and the financial breakdown ruined many of the pioneers,
because, at a blow, all credit was withdrawn and an end was put to
the system of 'orders' (credit *chits*), on which the economic structure
of bush-life was built up. Stock fell ruinously and runs were abandoned.
Sandy Creek, for instance, was sold at one stage for a pound of
tobacco and two gallons of rum, and sheep could be bought anywhere
for a few pence. Lured by these conditions, the hands of speculators—
the type of Boyd and Wentworth, the so-called *People's Tribune* in
Sydney—seized upon the desirable spots of the west, and bought out
or forced out many of the pioneers. The crisis of 1842 was a boom
for such speculators, and the men who had fought every difficulty
of distance and adverse conditions too often had to submit to the
capitalists of Sydney. Some of them, like Hobler, fled the country
in disgust, but many, scraping together a few store stock, simply
started afresh and turned west to '*better land further out*'—now,
alas, the saltbush lands.

By 1850, then, the bulk of the available west had been stocked,
and settlers were up beyond the Darling Bend and approaching
Bourke along the northern rivers. They were menacing the far west
beyond Menindie and intermittently stocking its fringe; and now,
if a man set out for new land, it was no longer Port Phillip or the
Downs, no longer the Murrumbidgee down to the Darling, but the
mulga desert, where the curious vegetation twined in a tracery of
death. In 1850, for instance, Mitchell left Mungabeena for 'the then

[31] Hobler's MSS. are in full in the Mitchell Library—wonderful documents
for squatting days, but with their rusty ink fading. See Gormly for the whole
story, especially *Wagga Wagga Express*, 10 April 1815, 5 February 1816,
19 August 1816.

outside country' and, to find this, had to penetrate the ghastly stillness of the red country and the grey-blue mulga land, pale and desolate. Sheep can survive for six weeks without water—in these lands offering in 1850, they certainly needed such a capacity! The Darling alone remained, and its back-country on either side. Governor FitzRoy had already made the Lower Darling into a district, and now, in 1851, had to subdivide it into two regions. It was there and beyond that the newcomer had to go, if he reckoned up his chances and decided on the suicidal risk in this sandy desert with its terrifying pallor of soil and vegetation. It was clear, under such conditions, that the work of the squatters was practically over. They had penetrated as far as they might, in reason, go.

In Victoria, the case was very similar. Here, too, the pick of the good country had been settled in 1840, and there remained only the inaccessible corners or the refuse disdained by the first-comers. Thus, cursing Mitchell for his optimistic descriptions, the squatting scouts seized every available spot. By 1840, the northerners had occupied the belt from Bendigo to Avoca, and even to Ararat: now, by 1845, they spread over the dense scrublands of the Loddon, overrunning the river banks between Mount Tarrengower and the Murray, and seizing every likely spot on the Avoca. Thence they moved northwards to the Wimmera. Starting with Foster's run on the Avoca in 1842, they filled the entire Wimmera two years later, and thus stood on the edge of the Mallee scrub. In 1845, they waited at Dimboola, Brim, Wycheproof, and even Swan Hill, and wondered if the sandy plains of the Mallee were worth taking up.[32] Since there was no good land behind them, they moved over the *open* Mallee in the next five years and took up the whole of the Murray bank, right up to Euston where the seventeen-year-old Morey had settled in 1846. This left only the scrub land beyond the river fringe, and its turn was not to come for another twenty years.

With the west thus disposed of, only one portion of Victoria remained—the isolated timber-lands of Gippsland, stretching back to the almost inaccessible Australian Alps. Most of this country was useless, but it was rich in parts, and the mountain squatters, in particular, wanted some egress to the sea through it. A strange feature of its occupation was how difficult the approach was made. The two obvious ways of penetration were from the infant settlement at the head of Port Phillip or from some other point along the coast line, but, strangely enough, the first entrants chose the much more

[32] Kenyon in *Victorian Historical Magazine*, 1914-15, vol. IV, p. 122, an important account.

difficult overland route—over the Great Dividing Range. It was thus disconcertingly surprising to find stockmen as far in as Lake Omeo early in 1836, and to see all the triangle from Omeo to Mount Hotham, the very heart of the ranges, taken in 1838.

The first man actually to enter Gippsland was Mackillop, of Hobart, who moved from Monaro to Omeo in 1835, though he was soon followed by roaming outlaws, to whom the sanctuary of the Ranges appealed. The long drought encouraged a more reputable class to come in their tracks, and, by 1839, cattle were to be found in Gippsland itself. Andrew Hutton, the first man in point of time, came along the coast to the Lakes in 1838, and Bayliss and Wilkinson followed to Buchan. More important was Angus Macmillan, the rightful claimant to the title of Gippsland pioneer. He was a hardy native of Skye, dour and rugged, with a hard face ringed with beard, and with the Scot's peculiar capacity for winning the fidelity of the natives. In February 1839, he crossed from the southernmost Monaro runs, past the three settlers alone at Omeo in the mountains, to Ensay or *Numbla-Munjee*, where he formed a cattle station for Lachlan Macalister. He discovered Gippsland with the aid of a compass and a copy of Flinders's map, disdaining such civilized articles as a tent, and relying on one single native boy— who tried to murder him in the night! Next year, he made what he called 'a fearful journey' to *New South Caledonia*, the plains on the coast, and reached Port Albert after three attempts in 1841. He was twice attacked by natives, but, despite such hindrances, succeeded in the almost unbelievable task of connecting the port with his original run by a road one hundred and thirty miles long—and the reward for this was the privilege of dying in poverty.[33]

Meanwhile, in March 1840, a Polish adventurer, Paul de Strzelecki, had left Macmillan's station on the Tambo and crossed the timberlands to Western Port—a passing expedition for which, important though it was, he received too much credit, owing to his own conduct in tending to overshadow Macmillan's prior effort and emphasize his own feat. As the country existed, however, neither Macmillan's nor Strzelecki's paths were of much practical utility, save by demonstrating that the real entry to Gippsland was from the west. Hence, the emphasis came to be on the movement from Melbourne, as contrasted with the eastern approach through the mountains. In 1838, for instance, all of Mornington Peninsula was taken up to the

[33] Greig, *Beginnings of Gippsland, in Victorian Historical Magazine*, 1912, p. 1. Macmillan's journal is in *Letters from Victorian Pioneers*, p. 254, cf. p. 199.

swamps, but this side of the bay was not greatly favoured, because the western district was so much richer. During the great land boom, when smiling pastures would have been made out of much worse land than Gippsland, various 'special surveys' were taken out for large areas. Routledge, Orr, and Reeves all invested large sums of money, and the Port Albert project flared up and sank in fiasco, like a burst of fireworks. These coastal settlements were failures, but gradually the cattle trade rose in the interior, where Glengarry, the picturesque chieftain who had left the Highlands with all his feudal retainers to recoup his family fortunes, had set up the first station.

The country was so difficult to traverse, and so little of it was of any use, that the task seemed hopeless. In addition, the natives were bad, protection of men and stock was difficult, and the Tambo and Snowy were happy refuges for the bad characters of the Continent. Hence, by 1844, when the first Commissioner, Tyers, came to infuse order into the scattered holdings, Gippsland could muster only three hundred and twenty-seven people, who ran about 200,000 cattle and, perhaps, three times as many sheep on their twenty stations. Yet, already, complaints were widespread that the land was overstocked, and it was said to take three weeks' search to find a run. By 1850, under such conditions, the occupied land could have been fitted into a circle round the Lakes from Bairnsdale to Moe, and then to Alberton, with the intervening ridges vacant. It was a sparsely-peopled cattle land, not suitable for the conditions of the squatting period, and offering little to the stockmen. With it, the occupation of Victoria was ended, save for the very remote Mallee. Ranges and desert alone remained, and it was a foolhardy squatter who ventured on to either. The newcomer would henceforth find nothing in Victoria—he would have to go north to Queensland.

VIII *Conclusion*

In this manner, while the Government at Sydney had recognized only the settlement of Melbourne and still viewed Moreton Bay as a closed convict preserve, settlement had flowed over eight squatting districts by 1840. New South Wales was taken down the Murrumbidgee to the Murray junction, and even the colder mountain pastures of Monaro were uncomfortably filled and flowing over to the Australian Alps. The drier lands behind the Lachlan still set the western boundary, but, up north, first the Liverpool Plains, then New England, and lastly the Darling Downs had fallen to the slab huts and moveable hurdles of the sheep-tenders. The entire east of

New South Wales was occupied. In Port Phillip, all the good land was squatted upon: indeed, the only land of any kind at all, good or bad, was in the Wimmera and the Mallee, the dry northern rivers, and in the mountains of Gippsland—that is, all of the heart had gone and only the outskirts remained. The squatters had taken all of the land that was to be settled for tens of years, and were even then moving their sheep on to the most arid of the north-western plains and up to the *transhumant* mountain pastures of the east. Connection had also been made with South Australia; many parties of Victorians had overlanded stock; and a few (like Stephen Henty at Mt Gambier) had settled on South Australian runs. But South Australia itself had not gone far in the direction of pastoral occupation. The northern stream reached only ninety miles from the capital, and the fertile south-east had not yet been touched, despite the crossings of the overlanders. Further west still, Swan River was still languishing from the early excesses. The York and Toodyay regions were stocked, and people were talking of King George's Sound and of grazing in the interior. But the colony still meant the tract around Perth and had only 30,000 sheep. *To all intents and purposes, pastoral Australia, in 1840, meant a patch around Adelaide up to Pekina (which was stocked in that year), and then one continuous belt from the Victorian border, sweeping up between the Lachlan and the sea to the edge of the Darling Downs.*

Thus matters stood in the period of this book. At the end—that is, about 1850—the earlier region had all been more closely settled and often subdivided; but, in point of new territory, the squatters had moved forward very little. There was nothing approaching that invasion which had swept over the interior in the thirties, and had converted the *Nineteen Counties* into four large colonies. The forties, in short, saw far more consolidation than advance into new lands: it was the time when new elements were being added to the population, and when the claim was rather on the nearer settled lands than at the outskirts. It was a decade of readjustments, of new alignments of forces, leaving the first squatters in a defensive position.

Nevertheless, there had been some expansion in the forties. The northern line was forced almost to the Dawson, Victoria was picked over from sea to sea, and South Australia had settled the only province available to her. The squatters now stretched from Mt Remarkable (north of Adelaide) round to the Dawson and almost to the Fitzroy in Queensland, but with the significant difference that now, in the middle part of the belt, they ranged out to the far west. They were almost to Bourke, both up the river and from the eastern side. *They had occupied three States and the centre of another.* They were up to the ten-inch rainfall belt, and, in parts, beyond it; and had gone so far that it was only a matter of time when they would reach the furthest mulga and saltbush lands.

They had spread loosely over the fertile parts of Australia in 1840: ten years later, they had consolidated their occupation and advanced over most of the habitable parts of the continent. The first pastoral occupation was over: they had gone as far as they could go under the given conditions—almost too far in the inland: and already, dawn was breaking on the day of the fight with the new city populations. The farming selectors were making themselves heard—*the cockatoo farmers*, who were already hovering, just as their namesakes were screeching on squatters' outposts and looking over the lands within. No longer pioneers, the squatters in 1850 were hearing the cries of monopoly and *'unlock the land'*. The wheel had clearly gone round! One squatting age—that of establishment—was over: and another was at hand—that of maintenance and concilia-tion with the newer classes of colonial society. But the basic fact could be gainsaid by none—*the squatters had already covered the face of Australia!*

7

THE GREAT CRISIS: 1841-1844

I *The Course of the Crisis*

ONE OF THE turning points in the squatting movement was the great crisis of the forties—*the bad old times*, as they were known for a generation when every foundation of the colony tottered. No crisis of this magnitude was felt again until the land boom half a century later, and even that could not have the same effect, because, by that time, colonial life was more diversified. But, with the earlier one, and with a society in which any extraordinary happening affected Government, townsmen, and squatters alike, everybody in the colony was directly troubled by such an event. The colony suffered from the simplicity of its structure.

The trouble was that nobody had thought of a possible check in the thirties. Many remembered the bad year of 1828, when the English *company bubble* swelled over to Australia and coincided with a long drought: but that was when the colony was in its infancy and before its trade and squatting had really grown. All through the thirties, the future was faced without any fear—and indeed, unquestioningly. The price of wool was soaring, English capital was coming in, land was awaiting the squatters, free emigration was starting in earnest, and new colonies were springing up along the south coast. The man who grumbled under these conditions, it was held, simply lacked energy to seize the opportunity held out to him. Any decent man could obtain a loan from one of the Banks or the new Loan Companies, and, buying a flock of sheep, could push into the interior to make his fortune. The wool would quickly repay his loan and even allow him to invest in the town sites offering at Port Phillip: then, both of these investments would increase in value, and so the process would be repeated, being without limit so long as the feeling of buoyancy was there, and until someone pricked the bubble.

Governor Bourke, in a despatch of the first day of 1837, had testified to this position. New South Wales, he said, was in a state of unexampled prosperity. Nor was this a mere figure of speech, because the larger settlers literally had more money than they could use, and knew that they could obtain as much more on their personal signature. This surplus cash, not wanted in their own industry, went into the newly-opened Crown lands, especially after the spirit of speculation seized upon the real-estate world. There seemed no limit to the possibilities of Port Phillip and Portland Bay, and rumours spread that the Clarence and Moreton Bay were to be thrown open to rival them. Everybody had seen Port Phillip jump up meteorically and this afforded some concrete justification for the boom conditions. But the colonists became practically insane in the valuations they placed on the land. It was a disease that grew on itself. As long as there was one man to increase already foolish bids, the delusion was maintained, and values were fixed solely by this intoxicated form of demand, and not at all by the intrinsic worth of the properties offering.

Matters were worst at Port Phillip. There, the proceedings appear utterly foolish on paper. Land changed hands again and again, with such feverish fears as would scarcely have been justified had oil gushers been spouting all over Melbourne. The mere possession of land-scrip was thought to constitute riches, and the hardest old colonial vied with each newcomer in swelling the boom. Blocks in the city increased a hundred-fold in a few months (in 1839, allotments bought for £150 changed hands at £10,224);[1] and speculators were as ready to buy at Carpentaria as at Sydney, blaming the Government for its *Ships Chandlers' policy* in not throwing open all of the interior for sale. The Land Fund received by the Government soon jumped up to over £300,000 a year, and it seemed as if the periodical opening of new lands would prolong this state of affairs indefinitely. Nothing could stop the emotional disturbance that produced this speculation. The minimum price of land went up from 5s. to 12s. an acre in 1839, but this only had the effect of stimulating the competition, and the large sales went on until the crisis. It was a fictitious prosperity, based largely on a turnover of capital that had not been produced within the country, with each successive handling of the same money accentuating the general state of economic madness which was making the colony so distraught.

Capital was pouring in faster than it could be absorbed in legitimate business, even taking into account the squatting expansion. England, now discovering the Australian colonies, was reacting to the Wakefield propaganda by this export of capital—an export unaccompanied by equivalent supplies of labour, and so destined to be

[1] *Port Phillip Gazette*, 10 August 1839.

frittered away. Before Bourke's time there had been only two Banks: now came two more (the so-called *Mammoth Banks*) with English capital, three loan-companies also financed from England, and two colonial Banks. Between them, they provided an inflated amount of accommodation for a population of 150,000 and they were forced by the competition to enlarge their operations so as to cover more and more unsupported investments. The law of the time prohibited them from doing anything beyond discounting bills, the result quickly being that money was available on the smallest security. Hence arose a spirit of reckless speculation, because money so easily available meant little to the borrower.

Soon, every branch of colonial life became marked by boom-conditions, with very little actual foundation. The competition for land became ridiculous; the squatting rush led to ordinary scraggy ewes realizing 60s. each; and the import of needless luxuries swelled until it was a by-word in English trading circles. This was the age when the auctioneers lavished champagne and chicken on any who cared to attend their land sales, when the Governor found the roads leading from Melbourne strewn with gold-topped bottles, and when even the bullock drivers were wont to break bottles of champagne into their buckets and swill what they called their *gentleman's brew!* Every imaginable excess was tried with the money that circulated so freely, and all the vices of the *nouveaux riches* were found in these new colonies. 'The years from 1839 to 1842', wrote Judge Therry who lived through this time, 'may be described as marked by prudence in no quarter, unbounded credit and extravagant speculation everywhere.'[2]

Everybody seemed to have too much money. The squatting movement would probably not have been possible, and certainly would not have assumed the proportions it did, had not English capital been so lavishly sent to the colony in these few years. Squatting was a costly business, with sheep at £3 and horses up to a hundred guineas apiece: and no small capital was invested, say, in a mixed draft of 10,000 sheep, with the other appurtenances necessary for a station. Therefore, if money had not been waiting for any newcomer on practically no security, the movement would have been confined to the rich families—that is, a minority movement, and not the general exodus it became. The Banks had to invest their money and cared little if their clients spent it in flocks or in city allotments. The interest was all that concerned them for the moment, and their

[2] R. Therry, *Reminiscences* (1863 suppressed edition), pp. 226-7.

primary business seemed to be to secure a field of investment for all the money. It was literally a competition between the various Banks for clients to whom to lend money—an attempt to keep up the turn-over of loans as compared with their competitors, especially the new loan companies.

The Government felt this boom at an early stage. In an essentially small community, it was obtaining too much money from the invest-ment of large sums in land. At the end of 1836, for instance, it had two-thirds of all the specie in the colony—some £340,000 worth. Of this, it kept two-thirds in its vaults, lying idle, and lent the rest to the Banks.[3] Since it obtained first 2 per cent, and later 4 per cent to 7 per cent on these deposits, the inference was that a Bank had to extend its discounts with every instalment of Government money lent to it, and, in the later stages, at such an increase over 7 per cent as would allow it to make a profit in the ordinary way of banking business. The money thus lent out by the Government would find its way into circulation again, the security being less carefully scrutinized each time, and the borrower pledging himself to pay any-thing up to 20 per cent. To recoup himself, he bought lands, and thus the money went back to the Government, which in turn lent it again to the Banks, who in their turn started the ball afresh. It was a merry little game, as long as it lasted, and as long as the spirit of optimistic speculation prevented a real analysis of the situation.

Meanwhile, the price of wool—the only firm basis for the whole structure—commenced to fall; but nobody took very much notice, because the land speculation was still at its height, and money was still abundant (1837). The boom continued to grow through 1838 and 1839 and in most of 1840. But, towards October and November of that year, the first signs of commercial distress began to disturb thinking people. Nobody exactly knew how it happened: all that was obvious was that questions were beginning to be asked. The three-years' drought was still prolonging its devasting course, and the English wool market was weaker; but, then, neither of these factors was new. They had been there when the boom was at its height: the explanation must lie somewhere else. Those engaged in commerce were no longer certain—that was the crux of the situation. Some-thing was affecting trade, but nobody could analyse it. Then prices began to fall, especially those connected with the luxury imports, and the land revenue dwindled at a terrifying rate, sinking from £316,000 in 1840 to £85,000 in 1841. Finally, at the beginning of

[3] Bourke-Glenelg, 1 January 1837.

1841, Gipps dropped his bombshell, in declaring that a million pounds were outstanding in bounty orders and constituted a charge that the colony would probably have to meet.

The changed atmosphere was first noticeable in November, though prices had started to fall two months before. Rather troubled speeches in Council, on the proposed Insolvency Law, next made speculators pause, while the bounty revelation indirectly led to the reckoning which it did not, of itself, warrant or cause. It was the spectacular event that made the colonists reconsider their position and determine what real foundation they had for their inflated values. Gipps, in reporting the bounty position in February, also mentioned the commercial embarrassment, but saw in it nothing alarming. It was precisely on a par with those crises that occurred in England after any period of over-trading, and sprang, he said 'from an excess of speculation or over-trading, or from the undue extension of credit, and the facility with which our Banks have been in the habit of discounting mere accommodation paper'.[4] Two classes of traders were affected in this early stage—millers and corn-factors were hit by the great fluctuations in grain prices in the previous three years, and those importers who had introduced goods on speculation, against paper discounted by the newly established Bank of Australasia in London. But Gipps was not greatly perturbed. The crisis, he somewhat blandly stated, was worse at Port Phillip than at Sydney, because there the madness had been more pronounced: but in both places it would probably exercise a salutary influence by putting an end to the dealing in fictitious capital. Under these conditions, he could see no need for any legislative interference: he even went further, and contended that the recent Council debates had served a bad purpose, by opening the eyes of the Banks and the public too suddenly.

This particular despatch, labelled *Confidential*, was curtly analytical and read much like a modern economists' view of the situation: but, in general, Gipps paid little attention to the unparalleled distress that started in 1841. It is altogether impossible to procure an idea of the situation from his dispatches, because he claimed a right to give a personal opinion on an issue, irrespective of documents, and then deem the matter closed. This was especially the case when, at one period in 1840 and in the bulk of 1841, he practically stopped sending despatches, presumably because he disagreed with the Whiggish politics of the Secretary of State. He had to be reprimanded for his neglect by Lord John Russell—and this at the very time that he was unauthorizedly engaged in pledging the colony's credit to the extent

[4] Gipps-Lord John Russell, 1 February 1841.

of a million pounds! Still more serious was his interpretation of the various channels of opinion. The voluminous documents attached to the Council proceedings at least allow of a reconstruction of the entire situation, but the Governor's despatches were very *ex parte* and ignored anything that he did not countenance. Nor did he consider the newspapers, which, at that time, were surprisingly virile and political—nor the more or less inarticulate sections, like the squatters or the new class of immigrant labourers. His reports home, therefore, were singularly devoid of information on general conditions and, of themselves, would be quite inadequate as historical sources for this time.

In reality, the first commercial disquietude soon changed into a positive crisis, affecting all classes of the community. The commercial constriction led the Banks to reconsider their advances; and immediately the bottom fell out of the land and stock markets. Lastly, as a consequence of the general panic they had themselves evoked, the Banks had to give way, and a general failure of credit institutions put the seal on the colony's sufferings.

By the close of 1841, the commercial distress was worse, and observers spoke of a 'state of distress and embarrassment, unparalleled within the memory of its oldest inhabitants'.[5] Next year, the settlers fared worse than the merchants, but in 1843 ruin was widespread— amongst traders, squatters and bankers alike. A quite general collapse had replaced the first commercial tightness, and now, no section could be described as better than any other. There was a perfect equality of misery.

Real property, of course, was entirely useless. The values that had been fixed by the feverish demand of a few months before were seen to be quite unjustified in most cases. The intrinsic worth of an acre of bush land was very little—scarcely the 12s. fixed by Government, and certainly not any of the fancy prices, which would have been ridiculous in the heart of London. But, however much justification there was for this collapse of land values, it is clear, when one reads of an equally great fall in the price of stock, that the people had succumbed to a new form of disease—a pessimism as absurd in its premises and reasoning as was the baseless optimism it replaced.

The squatters had already found it difficult to cope with the falling price of wool and the high rates of interest they had to pay on the capital so easily borrowed a few years before: and they were just recovering from three or four seasons of drought. When to these occupational difficulties was added a calling-up of their loans and a

[5] *Votes and Proceedings, Council*, 1841, p. 402.

complete absence of demand for their increase (because who had money, now, to commence squatting?), they were quite ruined. They soon realized what the crash meant. The failure of the first big Melbourne commercial house early in 1842, for instance, was an ominous harbinger. So they came in from the outposts, down from the mountain rivers and along the great north road, trying to secure readjustments over the crucial stage that was at hand. Edward Curr, a type of the best of them, came galloping the hundred and fifty miles from the Murray on a broken Valparaiso mare in two days, and passed many others travelling on horseback or in light curricles. The bush was giving up its debtors, the city throttling the pioneers!

The towns they found must have seemed strange places to them— barren nests of despair, where the inhabitants seemed to revel in the intensity of their hopelessness. Extravagance was at an end. No more bottled beer and champagne were left lying round at auctions; no more dashing squatters scattered traffic by dashing hither and thither on their blood steeds, with little servant boys on their croups; and no more extravagant equipages wound through the streets. The towns, instead, were places of ghosts.

Melbourne [wrote Russell in March 1843] is no longer Melbourne. No money, no credit, no trade, nothing but failures—the Sheriff's Officer is the only active man in the community. Even the lawyers can scarcely succeed in getting paid. Land is worthless, and cattle and sheep little better.

There was a steady march towards insolvency. Persons with only colonial produce, like wool or wheat or lands, had no other refuge, and, according to Gipps, 'were driven in crowds to the Insolvency Court'.[6]

The prices were ridiculous. In 1839, when the drought and over-lambing had brought the price of sheep down to 12s. 6d., observers had not been able to conceive of anything worse; but, now that the great bubble had burst into nothingness, sheep came crashing from 60s. to 1s., even with eighteenpence worth of wool on their backs. In 1843, anybody could buy up good, sound sheep at sixpence a head, or, according to the current lament about the fate of *Billy Barlow and the Sheriff*:

> He took them and sold them; I am sure 'twas a sin,
> At sixpence a head, and the station given in!

At times, there were even more farcical happenings. The sheriff

6 Gipps-Stanley, 11 August 1843.

simply had to realize, if he gave the sequestered stock away. Threlkeld, for instance, sold his 9,000 sheep at the rate of a shilling a dozen! One New England station, with 4,680 sound sheep and 207 head of cattle, was disposed of for £505, the wool given in! Fat cattle came down to 50s. and then to 7s. 6d. Sixty-guinea Arab horses could be had for 18s., and so many luxurious curricles were offered at a sixtieth of their value that a new form of transport appeared in the Sydney streets—*hackney coaches*. No wonder, under such conditions, that bankruptcy was almost universal and that no shred of confidence remained. 'The whole community seems horror-struck', wrote a western pioneer out on the Murrumbidgee mouth, after being forced to file his schedule,[7] 'and nothing that can be now foreseen can avert general bankruptcy.'

The period from February to December of 1843 resembled an economic nightmare, with everything breaking down in almost unbelievable failure. Nothing had ever been like it in the colony, nothing could have been worse. Practically everybody of note failed. Wentworth, for instance, estimated that nine-tenths of all houses and land were mortgaged up to their full value, and it was notorious that a squatter owning 10,000 sheep, worth a clear £30,000 a couple of years before, could not obtain credit for a chest of the Hysong tea he used! As Wentworth told the Legislative Council, in arguing that the depression simply could not be exaggerated:

The insolvent-list in fifteen months had swelled to nearly two millions, the dividends of the insolvents amounting to 6/1½ in the £, and, in most cases, no dividend paid at all: while, in the six months previous to August, 1843, six thousand writs had been issued out of the Supreme Court at no less an expense than sixty or seventy thousand pounds. The merchants were without custom, traders without business, and mechanics and artisans were pining for want in the streets.[8]

The Government was feeding hundreds of distressed labourers, and hundreds, too, were shipping off to Valparaiso. The city was lifeless, the country worse, and it was difficult to see whence relief was to come. At one time in the year, the price of sheep appeared to firm, but soon broke again, leaving the pessimism more deeply implanted than ever. The squatters were coming in, broken men: the merchants had already fallen: and labourers, both in city and bush, were practically starving.

At this juncture came the final blow—the failure of the Banks.

[7] *Hobler Manuscripts* (Mitchell Library, Sydney), entries for 3 April, 15 November 1843.
[8] Gipps-Stanley, 1 September 1843, 4 November 1843.

Three of them gave way early in the year, and a run on the Savings Bank started in May. A failure of the latter would have been 'fearful to contemplate', said Gipps, because most of the artisans were living on the savings they had deposited there, and any loss of these would have meant starvation and, inevitably, riots. Hence, Gipps came to its aid to prevent a further run, which it could not have withstood.[9] The most serious failure was the Bank of Australia, the old *Pure Merino* concern that was noted for its aristocratic *clientèle*, and which lost all its capital. The Sydney Bank went, the Port Phillip Bank accompanied it, and the four surviving institutions in the middle of 1843 held two millions in discounted bills—that is, they had parted with the whole of their subscribed capital and held only bills, the drawers and endorsers of which were daily flocking to the Insolvency Court. The last reserve of the colonies had thus disappeared, and, by the end of the year, the crisis was at its worst. Practically every vestige of the normal economic structure had disappeared; and colonists of all classes were left without valid assets. With every ray of hope gone, the full significance of the departed bubble was being brought home to them, and, all alike in the tumbled *débris* of their hopes, they were reckoning up their debts. Thus dawn broke on 1844.

II   The Causes of the Crisis

Such was the course of the severe crisis—its passage from prosperity, through inflation to the climax of a ridiculous speculation, and finally, after questioning, to a crash and a sane evaluation of the remaining resources. The causes, however, are more difficult to ascertain. It is comparatively easy to make lists of contributory factors, and say that over-capitalization, too rapid immigration, high land prices, a fall of wool, wasteful extravagance, and a score of like things combined: but such an aggregation of causes and symptoms does not explain the basic reason for the crisis.

There were, doubtless, many minor causes that aggravated the boom conditions, once they had started; but, in so far as one single root cause may be discerned, that was clearly *the entry of surplus capital* in the thirties. Gipps insisted on this time and again (though tending to ignore other factors that had an influence), and even Bourke had anticipated some of the evils in his time. Gipps in as many words said that the crisis was due to

[9] Gipps's General Report, 19 August 1843: *Government Gazette*, 9 May 1843.

the reckless activity with which Capital of all sorts, but especially Banking Capital, was poured in, seeking greedy gains at usurious interest, between 1834 and 1840, the mischief beginning with the commencement of business by the Chartered Bank of Australasia in 1836.[10]

In 1834, for instance, there had been only the two Banks—the emancipist Bank of New South Wales that had flourished since 1817, and the Bank of Australia, which had followed a somewhat stormy career since 1826. But, by 1840, there were seven banks (with a paid capital of £2,300,955), and two English Trust Companies which were lending money on mortgage. The Governor protested against this state of affairs: no population of 150,000 needed a banking capital that approached three millions: but, the very day he was penning his protest, Lord Stanley, the Secretary of State, was also writing to him, asking if he would consent to the incorporation of still another loan company, with a capital of a million pounds?

The English investors thus provided the material: but the colonial Banks now played their part. They cannot be looked upon as mere agents, despite the almost impassioned protests of their managers to the 1843 *Committee on Monetary Confusion*. Instead of acting only as distributing agencies for the money thus made available, they deliberately and continuously swelled the turnover.[11] The excess of capital, as has been pointed out, meant that, to compete with their rivals, they had to accept less and less security. To win business became the primary aim of their existence and they discounted paper more and more readily. Thus, by 1843, they had issued notes to the extent of only £189,016 and had £456,000 in coin in their coffers, but, as against this positive business, they held over two and a half millions in discounted bills, not to mention an unrevealed amount in accommodation or bad paper. The Banks were clearly too liberal. Their directors shared in the current optimism, and, by making money too plentiful, added to the excessive speculation. In face of this, to say that the Banks were only the instrument—mere machines for keeping the process going—seems absurd. They were led astray by the facility with which capital came to them from England, and by the general feeling of prosperity within the colony: and, quite apart from the degree to which they were forced into reckless discounting by the competition of other concerns, eagerly embarked in a debauch of spending in which they *believed*. Partly the victims of circumstances, they were only too glad to join in that tendency, in which, willy nilly, they would have had to acquiesce.

[10] Gipps-Stanley, 6 May 1843.
[11] W. H. Hart's evidence, p. 2; and Gipps's speech to Council, 10 May 1842.

First the English investors, and then the Banks had thus erred:
now came the turn of the Governor. Sir Richard Bourke had found
it difficult to dispose of the revenue received from land-sales, and now
his succesor had to manage a Land-Fund of over £300,000 a year. At
first, Gipps had divided the money between the Banks and charged
2½ per cent for it, but, later, the deposits being large, he demanded
the same rates as were allowed to the public—from 4 per cent to 7
per cent. The Banks, confident that they could lend as much money
as they could obtain, accepted these terms, and, from this time,
had to secure interest of more than 10 per cent, and, in some way or
other, lend out all of their rapidly enlarged capital. A feverish
search for clients commenced, although, since the lenders looked to a
high rate of interest rather than the security offered, the rates did not
go down. To the contrary, as in the American banking-boom just
before this time, they soared up to 15 per cent in Sydney and 20 per
cent in Melbourne.

The amount of such Government money in the hands of the Banks
increased just when the boom was at its height. Through 1838 and
1839, for instance, the total had never exceeded £90,000: thereafter,
it doubled between February and May of 1840, and then went up
from £188,000 in July to a maximum of £281,000 in October.

Even more serious was the action of the Government in the next
few months. Gipps had accelerated the reckless spending by allowing
Government funds to be used: now, at the moment when some outside aid would have been useful in bolstering up the structure thus
erected, he withdrew his advances without notice. When the commercial crisis was several months old and when the community was
beginning to doubt, he forced the Banks to pay back what he had
lent them! If he had previously aided the boom, he now caused the
failure, without stopping to consider what results might attend his
action. He argued, of course, that the advances were temporary and
that he needed the money to meet the immigration-bills; but might
have considered the general background a little more, and pondered
on the results that would follow any drastic action, or even utterance,
at such a moment. Instead, he withdrew the advances at the beginning of 1841, made special deposits of £15,000 at a high rate of
interest with each of the eight Banks for a few months, and then,
in the year following November 1841, drew £260,000 from the Banks
to finance immigration—a procedure which, while not causing the
crisis, at least acted as that outside spur which was necessary to bring
it into existence.

The Banks were compelled to restrict their discounts as suddenly as they had hitherto increased them, and the money-market, already wavering, received its first downward impulse. The Governor had left too much money in the Banks at one time, and, at others, had demanded it too rapidly—both unwise courses of action. He himself averaged the advances over the period since 1837, and explained them away as too little to affect the course of events; but this evaded a minute consideration of the transactions in the few crucial months, when his actions were a deciding factor.

Everybody so far had erred on the side of extravagance—the English speculators who had provided the basic capital; the Banks which had recklessly spread it over the colony and accepted far more paper than even their inflated capital warranted; the Governor who lent the proceeds of land-sales to go into the vortex once more and swell the speculation; and the colonials who paid such extravagant rates of interest on little security and sacrificed their sense of reality to an unfounded speculation. Granting the original money with which to dabble, such a course of events was perhaps inevitable, but the colonial exuberance was in itself a distinct mania. There was an extraordinary temptation and an extraordinary folly on all sides—and the entire proceeding grew on itself at every stage.

Through various other causes have been adduced as explanations of the crisis, it will be obvious that the above chain of tendencies was quite sufficient. Thus, though other events may have built up a favourable atmosphere, they were indirect and contributory rather than actual causes. All of them counted towards the aggregate, accentuating both boom and crisis, but they merely hastened something that other events had made inevitable.

Apart from the excess of capital, due both to imported specie and wool-sales, the group of causes most stressed was that concerned with land and immigration. At this time, the minimum price of land had been advanced to 12s., and then £1, an acre, and the colonists bitterly complained that money was thus needlessly diverted from profitable employment. Town-speculators and settlers in the Nineteen Counties were in the forefront of this agitation; but how little foundation the allegation had in fact is readily ascertained. The trouble was not that the Government was putting an undue check on land-alienation, as the plaints ran. To the contrary, the evil lay in the huge sums paid by colonists for land which they did not want, but for which they paid enormous sums to forestall competing speculators. They paid too much at auction for needless lands, and, over and above that, bought and re-bought land already extravagantly high.

Yet it was impossible to convince the colonists of this. They argued that the Government, through land-sales, was drawing specie into its vaults, and then paying it out in bounties for immigrants—the money thus being lost to the colony, and the land saddled with needless workmen. That they were crying in the same breath for more labour, and accusing the Governor of not using the whole of the Land Fund for its legitimate purpose of migration, did not appear to them a contradiction : nor was it obvious to them that they were paying for all of their land-speculations with money advanced from the Banks, and thus mainly coming from England.

All that the average observer saw was that the Government was receiving £320,000 a year from land, and that, at the beginning of 1841, the country was pledged to pay a million sterling to meet outstanding bounty-orders. These facts and the crisis, to them, were cause and effect, for they did not stop to carry the chain of connected events back still further. The Secretary of State supported this argument, too, because Lord John Russell gravely censured Gipps for having so many bounty-orders afloat at such a time of commercial crisis. Doubtless, the amount was unduly large, and, certainly, Gipps was not tactful in bursting the news on the colony just when the commercial difficulties were acute. But beyond that—and it must always be remembered that the million represented a potential rather than an actual debt (because the entire amount would almost certainly not be taken up)—it is difficult to see how the emigration position could be said to have caused the crisis. The real point was that the excess capital was in the country and had to be absorbed in some way or other. That the squatters and the townsmen speculated in land-values was unfortunate for them, but this was simply a medium of getting the money to the Government; and that they wasted much in useless extravagance was also simply a stage in the game. It was unfortunate, too, that the Banks were left with so many liabilities—'holding the bag', as the newly popularized Yankee phrase went; but they, like the speculators, were simply the middlemen of the game. Stripped of unessentials, the position was that the money, with these various side-movements by the way, had gone from the English investors, and partly from the wool, to the Government, which in turn was using it to further immigration. Gipps may have accentuated the pricking of the bubble by the fear he aroused regarding the bounty-liabilities, but this expenditure—the so-called 'sending the money out of the country'—could not have been the direct cause of the crisis, because, if anything, it was a productive use of capital. With many losses by the way, the original capital imported from England was going back again—not to those who had advanced it, but to the shipowners who were bringing out bounty-emigrants. In effect, then, the cycle of the crisis meant that English investors were paying for bringing labour to Australia. Indeed, such immigration was the only positive progress during the whole of the crisis—the only tangible result of all the heedless expenditure and waste of money.

This being so, the prodigality of Gipps must be termed an accessory rather than a primary cause. He had the land-revenue, contributed voluntarily by the speculators (because it must be remembered that no land was being sold in the squatting districts at this date), and had to do something with it. The normal thing to do was to bring in migrants, because, with the increase of the flocks, the colony had been crying for cheap labour for years. To call the provision for immigration the original evil thus seems unjustified. Gipps was partly responsible for the excessive migration of 1840-1, though, even there, he could not have been expected to foresee that the land-revenue would fall to one-twentieth of its amount in two years; and throughout, he was only yielding to the clamours of the Council and the populace, and, if anything, slackening the demand rather than stimulating it. Moreover, as Judge Therry recorded at a later date,

It should be borne in mind that it was not *he* who advised the importation of unsaleable consignments, or the influx of excessive capital, or the granting of mortgages on insufficient security, or the extravagant extension of discount by the Banks, or many of the measures creating a thousand ills to which the Colony was subsequently a prey.[12]

All that he did was to utilize the money that came in to him. Had he reduced the price of land or made no provision for immigration, the evil of the position would have grown rather than diminished, and, as for drawing capital from the colony, that was precisely what was wanted. Thus, while party politics of the moment may have blamed Gipps in this regard, the charge cannot be maintained in the light of after-events. The simplest justification of his position was that, by July 1842, all of the emigration-claims were met, and he had £30,000 in the Treasury, the only entry on the debit side being an issue of debentures to the extent of £49,500. Gipps certainly lost his presence of mind in announcing the extent of the bounty orders and in predicting their effects, but this figure shows how easily the claim was met. After all, the mere narration of the colony's sufferings sufficed to keep off most of those who had a right to avail themselves of the bounties. The whole matter was grossly exaggerated, because, al-

[12] Therry, op. cit., pp. 229-30; Lang's skit in appx. 7 of his 1875 edition.

though a few hundred artisans had temporarily to be supported by the Government, the colony was not suffering from too much labour in the forties. The 16,000 new hands who came in 1841 were readily absorbed, and only reduced the price of shepherds from £25 to £22. Nothing could be clearer than this.

Then came an array of lesser causes, which the panic-stricken colonists repeated in their misery. Most argued that the fall in the price of wool from two shillings to one (1839-41) was a primary cause of the trouble, but, depressing though the continued fall was, it had commenced in 1837, and had continued throughout the period of extravagant prosperity! Of course, the squatters received less for their products, but squatting could still pay with wool at a shilling a pound. They could hold out until the money lent by the townsmen was called up, after the commercial panic. It was then that they were hardly hit—when, in addition to having to pay up their liabilities, their stock became unsaleable. As long as they could sell their increase to the newcomers who were spreading over the land, financed with city money, they could make a profit: but, once no more money was entering the squatting world, once they could not dispose of their lambs, no way out remained for them.

The factor they all stressed—more even than the fall of wool— was the lack of a market for their surplus. In the middle of 1842, for instance, when the crisis was well advanced, half of the squatting witnesses before the *Immigration Committee* of the Council could still pay their way, even with the low price of stock then ruling; but, when they could no longer sell their stock at any price, they had to kill their increase and stop operations. It is true that they had previously erred on the side of optimism, and that, at the time of the great squatting expansion, they had based future calculations on a continuance of the existing price of 3s. a pound for wool. They had built up their industry on inflated expectations and could not withstand realities.

The other causes, important enough in the aggregate, did not count very much. The witnesses before the *Committee on Monetary Confusion* in 1843 enumerated long lists of causes, but most were obvious. All agreed on the excess of English capital, the ridiculous accommodation of the Banks, the speculative mania, the boundless extravagance of all classes and the fall in price of colonial products: and all added lesser reasons. The end of transportation in 1840 was said to have provoked a labour shortage and deprived the colony of the money spent by the Commissariat: but Gipps denied this, and claimed that free labour was coming in and that the colonists were not greatly affected by supplies for the convicts.[13]

A cognate complaint concerned the high price of labour; and there, the ground was safer. The price of labour had certainly increased after 1840, but that was rather a result of boom conditions than a cause.[14] The real labour crisis had started in the years immediately before that date, when the sheepmen were flowing over the new country and when the new level of £20 a year, with rations, had been reached. It rose to £25 a little later, but the arrival of the immigrants at once brought it to £22. These increases were not unreasonable and could not have mattered greatly either one way or the other. In the towns, the fluctuations were greater, a labourer receiving 18s. a week in 1830-3, 21s. in 1836, 24s. in 1839, 30s. in 1840-1, and 34s. in 1842: but this increase was directly due to the boom. Prosperity meant a tremendous building activity, and, at one stage, the Government had even to curtail its public works, in order to satisfy private demand. Wages, therefore, were obviously an attendant factor and scarcely a cause of the inflation.

The seasons, too, were blamed, especially the long drought of 1837-9. Rather more to the point, however, would have been a statement to show how the colony had neglected agriculture and was quite incapable of feeding its population, so that, in times of drought, vast sums had to be paid out for grain from India and South America, and even for Chinese rice. Money was drained from the colony for the essentials of life, and settlers complained, in addition, of the grip of local monopolists. Sellers, with money advanced from the Banks, combined to buy up every successive shipment of tea or grain, and thus added to the economic ills of the country. But, as compared with the huge sums wasted in speculation and extravagance, this legitimate grievance constituted a mere bagatelle. Rather more pertinent were the imports of luxuries, sent on credit by the new Banks in London, which inflated the colony's trade in certain directions, whether the inhabitants wanted it or not.

Another feature that received much attention in 1843 was the high rate of interest. Normally 10 per cent, this was, in many cases, double that amount, so that the settlers, apart from large sums on mortgage, were paying more than £200,000 a year on discounts alone. They thought they could easily bear this rate, and tended to increase their loans to be better able to do it. It was soon obvious

[13] Gipps-Secretary of State, 9 September 1841, 19 August 1843.
[14] Table in 1842 *Immigration Committee*, report, p. 20.

that there was a big disproportion between the return from capital and that from industries of any kind, the former being far greater. The discount rate was clearly too high, because the scale of profits after 1839, when labour began to rise and wool to fall, could not justify such overhead claims. As C. W. Roemer, a German who had been a Bank director, reported to Windeyer's Committee,

persons have been mistaken in the profitableness of certain pursuits, and have, in consequence, taken erroneous measures: they have not been correct judges of what they were doing, either with regard to the present time or prospectively.[15]

If the merchants were thus induced to pay too much for money the problem was worse with the squatters. Under the peculiar credit conditions then pertaining, they were forced to obtain their money from the merchants and thus doubly to pay a high rate. In an age that was primarily pastoral, there were no facilities by which the squatters could obtain money directly from the Banks—an anomaly that will always remain one of the incomprehensible features of the squatting system. All of the Banks' representatives, without exception, told Windeyer's *Committee* that they preferred the paper of merchants or shopkeepers. '*We rather avoided settlers' accounts*', said one; and, if that was the position with regard to the freeholders, it can be imagined where the stockmen were, when they had only a yearly licence to offer as security! The Banks considered that they had no landed security to justify a loan, that their life was so mobile that they could easily evade their obligations, and that mere stock formed too floating an asset. A squatter needing an advance, therefore, had to go to a merchant and rely largely on his personal influence and integrity.

Usually, then, the merchant would secure money from the Bank at 10 per cent and lend it out to the squatters with whom he dealt, adding a premium for the risk he ran and for the lack of tangible security. There was no secret about this. Roemer, the director above-quoted, in the course of his very clear evidence, said of the Banks in general:

I think they would have had a better chance of safety in trusting to settlers than to a certain description of merchants: there is no doubt that many settlers would have been accommodated, if the Bank had been less anxious to support Sydney speculators and adventurers; but, *as a general banking principle*, settlers are not the proper parties whose bills the Banks should hold, as settlers' property is less speedily convertible into cash, and they seldom keep money to meet their wants.

[15] *Report of Monetary Confusion Committee*, 1843, p. 39.

Moreover, the further out a squatter was, the less supervision there could be of his real position. As Wentworth did not hestitate to say, 'Why, they are certainly a very irritating set of persons, as regards the payment of their promissory notes and bills!' and capitalists financing them would naturally expect a larger return. The upshot was that the squatters had to pay far larger rates of interest even than the merchants, and thus, in an industry demanding much original capital, especially with sheep at 60s., they were burdened from the commencement by almost unbearable overhead charges. This was no small factor in producing their particular crisis, but, by its nature, was inevitable until the stabilization of squatting assets by some more permanent tenure. It did not, however, cause the boom or hasten the collapse: it simply contributed to the weakness of the staple and thus accentuated the general crisis.

Thus the excess capital was the comprehensive reason for the inflation and collapse. Even if the mania for speculation and waste within the colony was needed to produce the full height of the boom, it went back, in its turn, to the facility with which the colonists could obtain capital. They were like a set of children playing with small crackers and suddenly obtaining access to barrels of gunpowder which would allow them to make unlimited quantities—and probably perish in the attempt! Hand in hand, the excess capital and the spirit of inflation worked through the various stages of unbounded prosperity, sweeping along the existing prosperity of the squatters in its train, until the bubble burst and everybody went down, squatters included. There was one generic cause both for boom and failure, and masses of contributory causes or agencies; and it was the colonial inflation that infused the whole with its life, and that, leaving it, accounted for the depths of despair. Practically everybody aided the course of events—Governors, Banks, and colonists of all classes: none can be freed from the stigma of undue optimism and lack of foresight—and yet booms of a later period have shown, again and again, how easy it is thus to be swept along and how impossible it is to resist such a current.

III   The Recovery From The Crisis

The crisis continued unabated until the close of 1843, although, in the previous few months, the first of the ultimate remedies had been emerging. Squatters had begun to wonder whether a sheep was worth more than the few pence the Sheriff was realizing. It seemed ridiculous to let so much wool and flesh and bone go for a small a sum, and, in despair, they reduced the sheep to a mere aggregation of component chemicals. Hence came the expedient of popping the poor animals into huge boiling vats and keeping them there until nothing remained except what might be called a collection of residuary parts— a process aptly termed *boiling down*. The meat, under the conditions then ruling, was obviously worthless, and the bones nearly so, but what of the fatty portion? Tallow was worth from £2 to £3 a hundredweight in London, and a sheep even in moderate condition could realize from twelve to fifteen pounds. In all, with freight at 70s. a ton, eight hundred tolerably fat sheep would cost £109 to boil and deliver in London, where the receipts would be £350. That is (argued Henry O'Brien of Yass, the pioneer who first popularized the scheme), every beast was worth 6s. in the worst conditions. He published this information in June 1843, when conditions were at their worst, and predicted that the possibility of converting sheep into tallow meant a standardization of values—a level below which the price of sheep could never go.[16] To people who were wasting their flocks at sixpence a head and even less, the significance of *this great safety valve* may be easily realized. Newspapers throughout Australia had leaders on the new staple and an immense excitement spread through the land, because here was something tangible in a period of falling values—something that required no special process, something that was not dependent on Sydney capitalists, but which simply meant providing a margin of safety for the primary industry of the land, whether in drought, financial panic, or crisis of any other kind.

One newspaper alone, the conservative *Sydney Gazette*, failed to perceive the implications of the discovery and ponderously warned the colonists not to be led away by such chimerical wealth. 'It can be scarcely necessary to descant upon the ruinous absurdity of the scheme,' went on this senior of Australian papers, 'for, as long as the flockmaster can realize 7½d. per head for the fleece of one sheep, he must be an arrant fool to sell the principal, so to speak.' But such an attitude meant a passive acquiescence in ruin, and the boiling vats were soon bubbling merrily round the chief towns. A ring of tallow houses tainted the breeze in all directions (New South Wales boasted fifty-six of them within the year), and the colony had a new staple in the list of exports. Colonists could rejoice with a later writer:

---

[16] *Sydney Morning Herald*, 22 May 1843. Hamilton and Ebsworth preceded him on separate occasions, but his was the effective effort.

> Here is the song of the Taller,
> Likewise the chanty of 'Ides,
> Greasy and dirty and yaller,
> Gritty an' stinkin' besides—
> 'Ides and Taller, Taller an' 'Ides!

—obviously not aesthetic, but the means chosen to retrieve the squatting industry, both then and later.[17] The squatters' assets had increased twelvefold at a bound, and their prospects were quite changed by the certainty that never again could the past depression be rivalled. Nearly 200,000 sheep were boiled down before 1844 was out, and the squatters sang ribald refrains about making candles of their flocks, rejoicing the while in the knowledge that the scrubbiest ewe could bring 6s.! More than 750,000 went to the vats in 1845, and by 1850 over two and a half million a year, with 260,000 cattle in addition. During the crisis, ingenious tallow men built huge boilers to hold three hundred sheep at once, so that literally the flocks marched into the tallow vats. Optimists also tried to salt the beef and mutton that was left over, but this was expecting too much from Providence, and the pastoralists had to rest content with one gift from the blue.

This was the first and greatest relief—both in itself and because of the frame of mind it engendered. Soon afterwards, the operation of the *Insolvency Act* cleared the air. Once the speculators had faced their problem and written off what they could, they were in a position to start afresh. The process of insolvency was thus in the nature of a beneficent purge, clearing away the accumulation of past ills, without which there could be no healthy facing of the future. During the crisis, in 1842, a new *Insolvency Act* was passed—the famous *Burton's Purge*. Under this act, Sydney had 1,356 cases of sequestration and Melbourne 282, before the close of 1844. Filing a schedule ceased to be a disgrace, because it had ceased to be any distinction! In all, there was said to be £10 lost to the creditors for every man, woman, and child in the colony—almost two millions sterling.[18] What wealth remained in the State was changing hands too rapidly and at absurd prices: and it seemed far better to allow a harassed debtor to start his life afresh, without being forced to dispose of his property in a falling market.

[17] *Southern Australian*, 11 July 1843, leader: Bonwick, *Romance of the Wool Trade* (1887), pp. 130-1. Details are in T. Southey's *The Rise, Progress, and Present State of Colonial Wools* (1848), p. 42.
[18] Gipps-Stanley, 1 January 1844.

Under these conditions, the Council passed a *Solvent Debtors' Act*, to enable a debtor to continue in possession of his property if it was clear that he could ultimately pay.[19] Gipps was not at all sanguine about this, holding that it was bolstering up persons in a tottering condition: he accepted it only as an unwelcome *pis aller* to even less desirable happenings.

I was, moreover, and still am, persuaded that a restoration of high prices, such as those which prevailed in the Colony from 1836 to 1840, is neither to be expected nor wished for; and that the Colony cannot recover a healthy state until a large portion of the agreements entered into, whilst those high prices prevailed, shall be cleared off, as they only effectually can by the operation of the Insolvency Court.

So far, Gipps accepted the idea of the beneficent purge. But there was a limit, he went on to say.

Nevertheless, when I saw the ruinous prices at which property was occasionally sacrificed by forced sales, I felt myself compelled to yield, and (though reluctantly), gave my assent to the Act. Land has been sold as low as 1s. 3d. an acre, full-grown oxen fit for the butcher and weighing from 6 to 7 cwt. at a guinea, and sheep with a year's wool upon their backs at 2s. each.

Since it seemed desirable to prevent such waste at any cost, Gipps tolerated a measure which he could not improve, though clearly realizing its faults.

At the same time, Wentworth (the author of this relief measure) had proposed the famous *Lien-on-Wool Act*—now so accepted a part of Australia's pastoral life that the quarrels attending its introduction seem curiously unreal and remote. The principle was very simple. A stockholder could make a preferable lien on his wool from season to season: he would guarantee a merchant, early in the year, that he would sell him his clip at the end of it, and would get an advance, usually eightpence a pound, on the coming clip. In effect, a squatter could obtain mortgages on stock, without delivering them to the lender. Simple as this seems—in fact, almost inevitable as it appears in any system of pastoral economy if the stockmaster is to be allowed to raise money—it caused a considerable hubbub, both in the colony and at home. It was obviously not reconcilable with the English law regarding the alienation of things moveable, but its need must surely have been evident. A squatter could not mortgage his station—that was decided during the discussion, because the right of station was not worth much, and because too, that would have meant mortgaging

[19] 7 *Vic.*, No. *iv*. Gipps-Stanley, 7 October 1843.

Crown Lands. But this being so, since he could not hand over the stock which he had to use in earning his living, he simply had to be able to forestall his product.

In point of fact, the safeguards proved easily enforceable, moveable though the security was; and the measure was one of those very simple things, like boiling down, that make the observer wonder why they were so long delayed and so greatly opposed. Gipps, for instance, adopted a deprecating attitude towards it, saying that 'no very salutary effect is expected from it by any party'. He failed to foresee the tremendous part it was to play in Australia's rural development. At home, the opposition was even clearer. Earl Stanley intimated that it was so irrevocably opposed to English law that he would have disallowed it completely in any other colonial circumstances. Why, he argued in effect, of course it would encourage improvidence and imperil the lender! *'It is a law,'* he wrote, *'which will place society at the mercy of any dishonest borrower, and which will stimulate the speculative spirit which it is so important to discourage.'*[20] If commercial security and public morals were to remain, such laws in favour of debtors (and there had been a whole sheaf of them in the foregoing year!) could not become permanent. But, the crisis being what it was, any relief was to be temporarily welcomed, and he would, therefore, accept the law, as long as it was repealed before July 1846. Neither Gipps nor Stanley thus realized that they were acquiescing in something permanent.

Accompanying these two measures—and all three were discussed in the first two months of the new Council—Wentworth proposed the third of his legislative panaceas, a measure far less defeasible than either the *Solvent Debtors Act* or the *Lien-on-Wool Act*. He wanted a *Usury Bill*, to fix all interest at the rate of 5 per cent. He even introduced a retrospective provision, so that it would have violated 90 per cent of the existing agreements between man and man—a principle so obviously unfair that the Council, interested body though it was, rejected it at the second reading. A less stringent *Act* was passed, by a single vote, in the following year, but both Governor and Secretary of State rejected it, because it interfered with the freedom of trade and would have aggravated the already grave mistrust of Australia in England. But, strangely enough, the agitation had its effect, because, immediately on the rejection of the first measure, two of the four surviving Banks voluntarily reduced their discount rates by 2 per cent![21]

[20] Stanley-Gipps, 28 October 1844; Therry (1865), op. cit., p. 236.
[21] Stanley-Gipps, 16 June 1845.

So far, one positive advantage had followed the Council's efforts. Squatters could henceforth raise loans on their clip and stock; and that, coupled with boiling down and the good season, was sufficient to reinstate their industry. But the Council (newly met this year) was ambitious and dabbled in a further scheme for rehabilitating the whole economic life of the State. A *Committee on Monetary Confusion* was appointed, under Richard Windeyer, the Council's David Hume, and an authority on English Parliamentary procedure. After examining several bankers and merchants, and gathering such economic theories as the colony could muster—some of them very high-flown and ridiculous—he wrote a horribly over-punctuated report which, though confined to two and a quarter foolscap pages, included a scheme that would have upset the whole colony.

Briefly, Windeyer came to the conclusion that, though the crisis was due to a combination of most of the causes adduced by the several witnesses, its joint and most aggravating manifestation was in the restriction of currency. Since Gipps had pricked the bubble of excessive credit by calling up the Government funds in the Banks, credit facilities had shrunk abnormally—an obvious evil had been remedied by going too far in the opposite direction. Two colonial Banks had ceased operations in the previous year; various Loan Companies had restricted their issues; the notes in circulation had diminished by a third in two years; and all the circulating medium, except silver, had disappeared. The settlers could no longer secure even a warranted supply of accommodation, and the *orders* or personal notes of squatters, which had been practically the only form of money in the country districts, had entirely gone. Along with the feeling of trust, all loans or money on a personal basis had disappeared, and the colony was practically stripped of credit and currency. This annihilation was quite as bad in its effects as the previous inflation, and Windeyer especially directed himself towards securing both of these facilities in normal quantities. Without this, it was argued, even solvent persons would have to go, because one of the first results of such a general constriction was that property values fell far more than the crisis warranted. New South Wales was far from the commercial world, and its transactions depended on credit: with this gone, and with little money in the colony, everything would continue to decline in value, making the crisis worse confounded.

'Under such circumstances,' wrote Windeyer,[22] 'your Committee do not hesitate to recommend the intervention of the credit of the

[22] His Report is in the *Votes and Proceedings* for 1843. Comments are in Gipps-Stanley, 29 November 1843, 14 December 1843.

colony, in favour of all those who are in a position to give adequate security.' His method of intervention was most peculiar. One of the witnesses who had lived in Prussia dilated at length on the *Pfand-briefen* or *pledge certificates* which the Prussian State lent to its landowners, and Windeyer took the matter up, as a grain of solidity in a desert of verbose theory. He proposed that the colony should issue unlimited quantities of such *pledge certificates*, which would be somewhat like the English Exchequer bills, but issued on specific pieces of land at a third the valuation placed by the Government on such land. The Government was really to become a provider of credit for the whole community, although, in theory, Windeyer foresaw a profit, because, while it was paying 6 per cent on such bills to the holder, it was to receive 7 per cent from the mythical mortgagor !

That was to deal with the scarcity of credit. To cope with the lack of currency, Windeyer amplified his already too ingenious scheme by tacking on to it a proposal for *Land Board Notes*, also an emanation from Prussia. These were supposed to offer all the good points of a paper currency without its evils. Such notes, to the extent of £100,000, were to be issued in lieu of *pledge certificates* for that amount, and, though inconvertible, were to be legal tender. To safeguard the Government, half of the revenue was always to be paid, partly in coin, partly in such notes, so that liabilities might always be met.

But abstruse problems of national credit are not solved so easily; and both press and mercantile interests rose against any such amateur interference in complicated economics. The amazing point is how the colony leaned towards this plan. Indeed, it was even passed by the Council, and the Governor, though opposing it, took it quite seriously. He did not trouble over its economic fallacies, but was simply concerned with the attempt to make the Government the Mortgagor-General of the colony—an old device of Wentworth's. Accordingly, he withheld his consent from the Bill. It was all a rather tragic business—to have a representative Council glibly attempting to solve the most complicated economic problems in the same spirit of *a priori* enquiry that a little boy uses with a new toy: it reads like a travesty, and yet was painfully serious at the time. The Council were prepared to risk the whole future of the State on it, so certain were they that their own ingenious minds had produced something that the world's economists had not. As it was, the restriction of credit and currency passed away as naturally as the inflation had done: it was obviously a form of the crisis, and passed with the crisis. Credit facilities were soon found to keep pace with the opportunities offering. It was the lack of confidence that was the root of the evil, and no legislative enactment could produce that. In 1825-6, the British Government had found that its Exchequer Bills were unnecesary to restore confidence, because, though authorized, credit was restored without them: and so it was in New South Wales.

The last clearing of the crisis remained in the banking field, since it was the breakdown there that had produced the final and the gravest crisis, in 1843. The failure of the trading-firm of Hughes and Hosking, which at once involved the fall of the Bank of Australia, produced the ultimate crisis in every field; and the clearing away of that *débâcle* still remained. Something had to be done to restore the public confidence that had been so shattered by the failure, because this firm and Bank occupied a peculiarly important place in colonial life. Hughes and Hosking had married the co-heiresses of old Samuel Terry—'the rich emancipist', as he was always called. He was the richest of the old convicts, and it was his wealth that had so excited the surprise of the *Transportation Committee* of 1838. The firm of merchants and general agents that he built up was supposed to be the most solid in the colony, and the Bank of Australia unquestioningly advanced as much money as they wanted. As Gipps wrote, it was because of

the strange delusion which long prevailed in the colony in respect to the supposed enormous wealth of Hughes and Hosking, for it was under a delusion of this sort that the Directors entered into engagements which virtually identified the affairs of Hughes and Hosking with those of the Bank.

The connection largely accounted for the supposedly impregnable position of the Bank in New South Wales—the other Banks might be safe, but the one linked up with Hughes and Hosking, why, its position was as safe as the continuance of Sydney! Therefore, when the shutters went up on its Market Wharf buildings and when the trading houses suspended operations, the entire basis of colonial credit seemed shaken. The unthinkable had happened; and the Bank closed its doors, too, in March 1843, although its profits were reputed to be 20 per cent, and, as late as 1840, a 45 per cent premium had been obtained for its shares!

At once, the reckoning had to be made. The Bank had been founded on the joint-stock principle, so that each of the one hundred and seventy-six shareholders was liable to the full extent of his property, and, since this was the aristocratic Bank, the leaders of the land, already embarrassed by the crisis, were faced with ruin. Bowmans, Coghills, Campbells, Jamisons, Parrys, Throsbys, Wentworths —all of the familiar names were there, all of the pillars of the colony and the squatting world. To dispose of its assets in such a time of depression, Wentworth, one of the most interested persons, with his usual disregard for the separation of public and private concerns, proposed a lottery. The bank held vast tracts of unimproved country which nobody would buy; but a chance in a lottery was a different proposal to most men. Hence, the Council passed the Bill by a large majority. But the Law Advisers of the Crown had already pointed out that no colonial Legislature could sanction such a gamble, so that both Gipps and Stanley issued their fiat against the measure.[23]

The Bank, however, far from being disposed of, continued to play its leading *rôle* in these years of reconstruction. The Bank of Australasia had advanced it £150,000 in its time of travail, but it had forthwith repudiated the promissory notes, on the contemptible ground that its directors had no authority under their charter to borrow in this manner. At the trial[24]—incidentally, the only *trial at bar* ever held in Australia—the whole of the local legal talent was mustered, and nothing else was in the public eye at the moment. What could be, when the fate of Hannibal Macarthur, the chairman, and most of the *pure merinos* was at stake? After twenty days, the jury found for the plaintiff Bank, but the Court, on a point of law, reversed this; and the old exclusives breathed afresh. But, ultimately, the Privy Council reversed this, too, and the Bank of Australia had to meet its debts, although the principle of unlimited liability led to the irreparable ruin of many of its shareholders. Strange as it seems, this spectacular trial did much to restore confidence, because the revelations clearly showed how much of the crisis was due to the gross mismanagement of the Bank directors and the undue facilities they offered. The long evidence showed the colonists the disease from which they had been suffering, and, by inference, convinced them that the ill was not primarily in the colony itself.

By this time, the colony was recovering. The banking panic had been largely checked by Gipps's decisive action in supporting the artisans' Bank, and by the end of the year the more solid features that were to tide the colony over could be discerned. The community was quiet, and everybody was pulling what was left from the mire. Indeed, as nobody felt in the mood for agitations, this was probably the quietest time New South Wales ever had. The Council, too, had

[23] Gipps-Stanley, 1 January 1845.
[24] The first trial was in April 1844, the trial at bar in June 1845.

done its best, although, by the end of the year, the public agreed with Gipps 'that the Colony cannot, by any direct legislative enactment, be relieved from the depression under which it labours'.[25] Much more was expected from the curtailment of the hasty expenditure of the recent years and from the newer outlook of the squatters. The worst year of crisis had been a good season on the land, and, at the same time, wool-prices recovered in England. This combined with the new *Lien Act* to put squatting on a sound basis once more, and the colony could not but react to the prosperity of its primary industry. The flocks rapidly increased, and those sheep which could not be used in stocking new country were boiled down. Moreover, the squatters were combining and felt so organized in 1844 that they were ready to plunge into the great fight for security of tenure. Freed from the huge rates of interest and the other adverse factors affecting their clips and increase, they were regaining their vigour; and two successful years reinstated their former buoyancy.

A similar change more slowly crept over the towns. There, the necessities of life were cheap and abundant: the crisis had reduced prices all round, and the expense of housekeeping in 1843 was less than half of what it had been three years before. Naturally, this aided all wage-earners, especially the new immigrants who had been brought out during Gipps's rush of bounty orders, because the fall in wages was more than counteracted by the low prices. With mutton at a penny a pound and wheat at 30s. a quarter, labourers could live on a wage of 2s. a day; and with the start of the hay harvest at the close of 1843, and the subsequent revival of squatting, the demand for labour soon grew.

It is true that the merchants and speculators still suffered; but the colony in general was progressing, and Gipps was not far wrong in urging that, in some ways, good had emerged from the evil.[26]

The Mania, whilst productive of many evils, has at least had the good effect of adding 50,000 souls to our population, and of changing, in the almost incredibly short space of six years, the whole character of the Colony—of converting it, in fact, from a convict colony to a free one. Had there been no Mania, the Government could only have got these 50,000 souls by incurring a debt of perhaps £500,000: but, by aid of the Mania, and the intervention of Banks and Loan Companies, the Government has got them in exchange for land.

Though he achieves this result from a somewhat fallacious dis-

[25] *Votes and Proceedings, Council*, 1843, p. 253.
[26] Gipps-Stanley, 17 January 1844.

tinction between the welfare of the community and that of the individuals, there was much truth in his arguments: the State had benefited.

By 1844, then, the colony was once more on the road towards progress. It recovered from the crisis almost as rapidly as it had gone into it: indeed, the rapidity and extent of the recovery are somewhat incomprehensible to observers who cannot realize the rapid changes of fortune that are possible in a community dependent on so volatile a staple as wool. One good year can obliterate the accumulated arrears of several bad ones: and it is well to remember this extraordinary recuperative power of a pastoral polity, for otherwise, one would be tempted to ascribe much of the distress of 1842-3 to a facile exaggeration. To the contrary, the evil was there, as depicted; and the recovery can be equally accounted for. A young and rich country, with resources practically untapped, and an industry as phenomenally lucrative as squatting was in its good years, combined to effect the metamorphosis, because, in last resort, it was only a shackling understructure, due to something extraneous, that had to be removed. That gone, and the factors making for successful squatting coming back, recovery could naturally be rapid. Hence the prosperity of the squatters and the townsmen in 1844-5, and the extreme vigour with which they could throw themselves into the struggles that characterized the rest of the forties and that contrasted so strangely with the anaemic and despairing quietness of the years of crisis. Healthy once more, the infant could stretch its growing limbs and fight—and the record of the next few years showed how effective the struggle was!

8

THE STRUGGLE WITH SIR GEORGE GIPPS

I *The Two Sides*

A S SOON AS the great economic crisis had run its course, the colony was plunged into the far more virulent crisis of squatting tenure —an issue which concerned not only the future of the squatters themselves, but the very directions of Australia's development.

The position was very involved. In the east of Australia, nearly seven hundred licensed stations were spread over the land beyond the boundaries, from Moreton Bay to South Australia: and 1,334,000 sheep and 371,000 cattle were grazed in this land where Government influence could only slowly follow in the track of settlement. All that the Government could do was to charge not less than a penny a head for this stock, divide the lands so occupied into fifteen districts, and send a Commissioner of Crown Lands and a small force of Border Police to look after each. The control, by its very nature, was frequently nominal, and, as Gipps reported in 1840, the squatters often remained unknown to the Commissioner until some positive happening, usually a conflict with the aborigines, brought the station concerned to his attention. Such men usually followed pasturage, paid the licence fee of £10 and the small head tax if they could not avoid them, and built homes despite the Government and their neighbours. An average run was probably 5,000 acres, though already some squatters held over half a million acres, and cries were heard every year that monopoly was increasing.

Under these conditions, it was absurd to speak of *a theory of concentration*. Sir George Gipps had clear ideas of the rights of Government, but he was the first to insist that the configuration of Australia, by allowing any settler to go into the interior and graze stock with little outlay of capital, consigned any adverse schemes to realms of inapplicable theory. He warned Lord John Russell, in bringing the squatting problem to his notice:

Let the evils of dispersion be what they may, they must be borne with: our flocks and herds already stray over a country 900 miles long by 300 wide; and I hesitate not to say that any attempt to bring them within the limits even of our twenty contiguous Counties would end in failure, if not in the ruin of the colony ![1]

The counties might mark the limit beyond which no lands could be sold, but to go from that, and argue that they marked the close of legitimate settlement, would have been absurd. Settlement ended, not on the fringe of the counties, but in the new districts of the Clarence and Moreton Bay in the north, and down to Twofold Bay and Port Phillip in the south. Why, he exclaimed in effect, there was a town at Portland Bay, sixty-six known stations were on the New England ridges, and every river running westward was dotted by runs for some three hundred miles, and Macalister and Strzelecki were in the heart of the Gippsland Ranges! Already in 1840, it would have been extremely unstatesmanlike to have evaded this situation: and Gipps dinned into the ears of the Secretary of State again and again that the problem, already huge, was becoming more unwieldly with every postponement. It had to be settled—it was practically insoluble at the moment, but to delay it was equivalent to a withdrawal of Government control.

The two points of view were clearly opposed, and the trouble was that each had reason on its side, as far as it went. A squatter who had settled in unknown country and built up an establishment, with no aid at all from the Government, naturally desired to retain it: but all that he had was a yearly licence and a clear statement that he could obtain no property rights at all. He had no right to renewal, no safety in his improvements, no opportunity to buy his homestead: he could not legally make a permanent settlement, even if he wanted to. As a corollary, he lived in a rude hut and stunted his industry in many ways, for no reasonable man would spend money on a place if it was to go next year to the Government or to some favoured rival. 'I make only such rude improvements as are absolutely necessary,' Dalhunty, of Wellington, told the *Immigration Committee* in 1842, and he would not dream of building 'a house for a respectable family'. In 1842, judging from the array of such evidence, the squatters wanted some security over a period of years, first and foremost: with this was to go a right in any improvements they might erect; but beyond that point they were slow—extremely slow—in going. Questioned on their views as to a right to purchase their homesteads and water holes, they hesitated. Sheep farming would not pay on purchased land, they argued: a lease would give them the security they wanted, without involving additional expen-

[1] Gipps-Lord John Russell, 28 September 1840—an important despatch.

diture. They, therefore, confined themselves to demanding a long licence or lease, with perhaps a safeguard for any expenditure they might make on permanent improvements. Beyond that, they would not go. The crisis was still running its course, and they were not prepared to pledge themselves to ambitious projects.

As against this, the Government expressed its point of view. Three million acres of land were practically alienated for a yearly payment of £7,000, and sheep grazed at a penny each on Government land. This was ridiculous—the charge could be five or six times as high, and still be absurd, wrote Lord John Russell—but, when it was considered that the squatters were so firmly ensconced in practice that the land was virtually theirs, the position became tragic, in so far as its implications on the future were concerned. The estate which was to go to the millions of small settlers of later ages had been effectively grasped by 700 station holders, whom already not all the power of the Government, not all the redcoats of England, could evict! Already, by 1841, one Lieutenant-Governor, La Trobe, had urged a pre-emptive right for them, on the grounds that they were legally authorized settlers and were developing the country: and soon, if this went on, all that would remain for the Government would be to acquiesce in something it could not prevent, and issue grants in fee simple for the runs occupied! Events were forcing the hands of the Crown, it was clear; and a halt had to be called at some time or other.

Gipps had seen this in 1840: next year, even during the crisis, he upheld what he considered to be the rights of the community against an encroaching minority of 700 stockmen, and absolutely refused to accept La Trobe's advocacy of homestead rights for them. The squatters had no rights against the Crown, he said dogmatically —they were there from year to year, could be evicted at will, and had no redress and no claim in their improvements. Such improvements, he went on, have been 'in fact always regarded as certain though remote advantages accruing to the Crown, in return for the easy terms on which the occupation of them is allowed'. Gipps therefore viewed the squatters as legalized intruders—as men not committing any legal fault, yet trespassing as a matter of privilege (and a revocable privilege!) on what did not belong to them. The claims of the Port Phillip squatters implied the possession of rights held by them against the Crown, he argued: and that was false in fact and absurd in logic.[2]

But the matter was not as simple as this. The Governor's views

[2] Report in *Historical Records of Australia*, series I, vol. XXII, p. 254: or correspondence in Gipps-Russell, 24 February 1841.

may have held in practice at the moment squatting started, but they were already seven years behind the times in 1842. The gap between law and practice was too great to be ignored. Some compromise was inevitable, as even the Colonial Office realized. The newly appointed Crown Lands and Emigration Commissioners, for instance, held that the problem should be systematically considered, because what would happen when no more land remained for sale within the boundaries, and the squatters were claiming the whole of the outside? They were thus inclined to cede some pre-emptive right to the squatters in 1841, though, having made the biggest sacrifice, they hesitated at the minor one and would not hear of any claims for compensation.

All sections thus agreed on the need of solving the problem, and all believed that delay only added to the difficulties. A pretext was all that was wanting: and this came in August 1842, in the midst of the financial crisis, when the Governor refused to renew the licence of one William Lee, in the western district. The case was undoubtedly hard, because Lee had been forced out by a combination of drought and native attacks, and had himself been away from his men at the time. Eight magistrates supported him (because he was a man of proved courage), and a meeting of the neighbouring graziers at Bathurst drew up a petition against such insecurity of tenure and presented it to the Council. The Governor reiterated his statements and said that occupation had to be continuous: but the squatters were convinced of the injustice done to one of their number and were not inclined to acquiesce in such ultra-legal views. They declared that the Executive was consciously depreciating the value of live stock in a time of crisis, and that security had to come either by persuasion or force: *and the fight was on*. From this moment, the urgency of the crisis notwithstanding, there was no pause until Gipps withdrew, a broken man.

II The Conditions and Leaders

In the struggle, the colonists were now provided with an adequate means of expression—the new Legislative Council. The old Council had been a body of officials and Crown nominees, with no elective element, and in general, had been a vague ghost of a Legislature—it was only an ornamental registering Chamber, reflecting official opinion. But the colony had long outgrown this: indeed, the statute of George IV which had set it up (and which had expired in 1836) was avowedly so inadequate that it had been given new life only by yearly renewals, the understanding being that the new Act was to be introduced as soon as possible. After long delays, Lord John Russell sent a draft of a proposed Bill in 1840; but two more years elapsed before Stanley's Ministry passed the final Act based on it. This reached the colony on the first day of 1843 and set up a Council which was in existence throughout the period dealt with in this book.[3]

Briefly, the body so instituted was a representative one, as distinct from the old nominee Council, but its powers did not reach to responsible government. It was to have thirty-six members, two-thirds elected, but the only electors were to be those living in the Nineteen Settled Counties, and were to be freeholders—that is, all of the squatters who dwelt beyond the settled districts were disfranchised, together with the leaseholders within the counties. Anybody within the counties who possessed a freehold worth £200 or yielding £20 in annual rental, could vote—whether he was an emancipist or a free man. Ex-convicts thus received the full rights of freemen, but squatters were deemed unfit for this privilege! The only recognition of the extension of settlement was in allowing five members for Port Phillip (modern Victoria), while the concentration in the towns was met by giving Sydney two members and Melbourne one. In this way, the electoral districts and the franchise were rigidly limited, though the Government thought itself liberal in allowing a majority to be elected representatives and in retaining only half of the nominated places for officials! The powers of the new body were not numerous in the *Enabling Act*, but rapidly swelled in practice. They were allowed to make laws, providing that land matters and land revenues were not touched; and to appropriate taxes, providing they did not interfere with *the three Schedules*, which left £81,600 a year for the civil, judicial and religious services. Beyond this, they were free, although the Governor could propose or amend laws (and thus act as a second Chamber) or withhold his assent until he consulted the Colonial Office.

In practice, the powers conferred on the Council were not unreasonably small, taking into account the stage of development reached by the colony. If they co-operated with the Governor, they could make laws and appropriate two-thirds of the revenue; and naturally, the Crown had to safeguard itself in such a colony of convicts and squatters by leaving reserve powers against a recalcitrant Council. The Act would allow a body that worked with the Governor to control practically everything, except the vital services—

[3] 5-6 Vic., clxxvii—An Act for the Government of New South Wales and Van Diemen's Land.

that was its significance! The colonists, however, in an attitude that was typical of their unreasonable claims, could not see the extent of the powers opened to them in practice, and loudly clamoured against what was withheld from them. The Act was most unpopular. It set aside £80,000 a year from the Council's control—more than in the rebel Canada! It made the chief executive officers independent of the Council! It allowed the Governor to override the Council at every stage! It withheld the land revenue from them! It failed to adjust the old quarrel of the police-and-gaol expenditure in their favour! It had not given them responsible government, even to the degree of passing laws not repugnant to those of England—and yet Canada had this! It had ignored the existence of the squatters and the leaseholders! It had given Sydney two members to represent a fifth of the population, and all the shipping, commercial, and trading interests! It was so arranged that three-fifths of the population had a third of the members! And it had given ten sections to providing for the Governor's favoured District Councils, though the colonists did not want these or the new taxation implied in them! In short, it was a tricky device, bred of Downing Street, Gipps and the Attorney-General: and the colony would have none of it! The colonists wanted complete self-government, both legislative and financial, and were not prepared to recognize any gradual development in this direction. Their general attitude, however, was such as to justify the criticism that the constitutional Act erred rather on the side of liberalism than of conservatism—that a handful of 9,300 electors were given far too many opportunities for hindering administration and far too much power without the political education that was a necessary preliminary. Nor were after-events slow in demonstrating this.[4]

The old Council had its swansong for a few days in January, and then the preparations for the election started—against a general background of crisis and failure. The Bank of Australia fell during the agitations, and the colony lost its confidence and swooned down to the nadir of its depression. Quietness was not to be expected under these conditions, although certainly, the actual upheavals—wide-spread riots which caused the loss of two lives—seemed a little ebullient for an electorate newly enfranchised for its supposed general progress! Mob passions (and it must be remembered, these were largely those of a convict mob) were let loose, and thus the first Australian representatives were forcibly exuded out of the mire and

[4] For details, see *General Grievance Report of 1844*, or the *Franchise Committee*, in *Votes and Proceedings*, 1844, vol. II.

assembled in a detached wing of Macquarie's general hospital as the new Legislative Council. *'Some rioting took place'*, Gipps mentioned casually—and from such statements, one realizes how aloof despatches are from actuality and how difficult it is to grasp currents of opinion from them.

As assembled, the 43 representatives were a peculiar body—as Gipps went on to imply in a despatch that radiated his obvious disapproval of this result of 'shooting Niagara' (18 July 1843). Only one Government officer was elected, and only one of the unofficial members of the former Council—the people certainly left no doubt as to their regard for officials and for their former representatives. Of the others, at least fifteen were squatters, and all were opponents of the Government. The elections had been held when the colonists were distressed and inclined to attribute their distress to such acts of the Home Government as the abolition of free grants and assignment, and the rise of land prices. Moreover, the existence of the nominated element meant that the people would elect nobody but avowed enemies of the Executive. The very constitution made the Treasury and opposition benches coincide with the nominees and representatives respectively, for did not the existence of the nominees, it was asked, mean that English and colonial interests were of necessity opposed on some matters? Otherwise, why were they there?[5]

As a corollary of this, the situation came to mean that the opposition were always in a majority. The Ministry, if such the official element could be called, could not be displaced, but their opponents had a clear two-thirds majority: and, since the elected men were usually squatters, it followed that the Council was a squatting stronghold—a veritable garrison held by them against the Government.

The Governor had his six officials and (whenever they chose to support him) the six private men he could nominate; but since three of these were old patriarchs from the previous Council and the other three were self-interested capitalists of no particular personality, this help was at all times precarious and never very strong. The Bishop and the Chief Justice, both strong supporters of the Government, had gone with the old Council, and there was only Deas Thomson, the Colonial Secretary, to lead the Council from the Government side— and he was too courteous and polite to cope with his rowdy opponents. Gipps, too, was no longer a member, so that his brusque force could not galvanize the Government supporters into unanimity and strength.

The Council's antagonistic attitude was soon manifested and was

[5] Leader in *Atlas* (Lowe's organ), 7 December 1844.

maintained without a break until Gipps left the colony four years later. Any form of co-operation, however desired by the Governor, was put out of court, and Gipps, of necessity, was forced into a partisan attitude. He wanted to approach the problems from something like a national standpoint and to consider the community of interests involved; but they insisted on regarding him as an advocate of one side only—as an opposition paper said,[6]

As the authorized interpreter between the wishes of the colonists and the will of the Ministers—the Imperial private-watchman—the keeper of so much of the Secretary of State's conscience as we may consider dedicated to this portion of Her Majesty's Dominions!

Moreover, Gipps was not a person to wear down such continual opposition in a tactful way: his motives once doubted and his integrity impugned, he was inclined to meet opposition by opposition, and bludgeon his way through his opponents' ranks. He had given them a fair opportunity, he would argue, but, having rejected that, he would give them some cause for their unjust aspersions! Each wave of opposition, therefore, irritated in direct proportion to its injustice, so that the Council practically ended by compelling him to be what they had pre-judged him—an autocratic Crown advocate! Given the defects of his personality, the tigerish vindictiveness he would exact for attacks on his honour, and the hopelessly partisan views of the Council—and the upshot was inevitable: and it was against this background of mutual misinterpretation and hate that the colony was swept into the midst of the squatting trouble.

The primary blame, however, must be attributed to the Council. They had the excuses of immaturity and lack of political education: they were bound to err in the same naïve way that all newly constituted legislative bodies do; and they wanted to exact some retribution for the long years in which they totally lacked expression—but these explain rather than justify the stand they took. The first thing they did was to pass *an humble Address* to the Governor—a pure matter of form: as an amendment, they voted that the word '*humble*' be expunged! Their next task was to elect a Speaker, and that was taken to be the first step of the Opposition's strength. Gipps had proposed one Hamilton, a capitalist who had been in the colony for three years, and whose chief claim to recognition seemed to be in having an Under-Secretary as an uncle. As against him, the Opposition raked up the aged M'Leay—the leader of the official clique under Darling, and Bourke's inveterate enemy—and aroused him from the reminiscent dotage of a man of seventy-seven in order to dump him

[6] *Atlas*, 20 November 1844.

in the Speaker's chair. That achieved, they went on to defy the Governor time and again. Gipps was excluded from Council deliberations and could only sit in Government House, send innumerable messages to the Council down the street, and veto—for ever veto! Even his nominees deserted him. The Attorney-General was out of the colony, Deas Thomson was chronically ill, Blaxland invariably opposed him, and Berry very frequently forgot that he owed his place to him. And Lowe (whom 'I have appointed solely in consideration of the support which I think he will be able to afford to my Government') answered his patronage by becoming his most bitter opponent.

The Council, thus completely unchecked, went from rudeness to rudeness. They protested against the reserved *Schedules:* they refused to grant the essential services any more than the Act provided: they cut down salaries by a trick of casuistry: they revived the preposterous old claim that England should pay all their police and gaols expenditure, and even presented a bill for £793,034 as back payments: they said that the Governor's *Messages* were breaches of privilege, and, for every *Message*, retorted by clipping something from an official salary: and they claimed powers to legislate for Crown lands and give security to the squatters, although the enabling Act had specifically withheld these matters from them! In a word, they seized every opportunity to harass the administration and thrust forward their own class-interests.[7]

A complete list of the claims they advanced would be the most telling argument against an uneducated democracy; but enough has been told to show how irrevocably alienated they chose to be from the Governor, and how impossible it would have been for any self-respecting Executive to have worked with them, without sacrificing his integrity and betraying those Imperial and communal interests which he had sworn to uphold. The Council made itself a hindrance to the development of the country: but, after all, the greatest dereliction was not in anything the members did (a strong man like Gipps could neutralize that!), so much as in inducing a strained and abnormal attitude in the Governor. Their opposition made Gipps a sick man mentally, and the colony suffered more from this than from any other of the Council's misdeeds. He was prevented from giving the entire wealth of his sagacity to the service of the State—there lay the evil!

The first session thus ended with the atmosphere fixed for 1844—

[7] A sagacious analysis of public opinion is in Gipps-Stanley, 28 October 1843. For history of financial trouble, see this or despatch of 30 September 1844.

one of unrelenting antagonism between Governor and Council. The Council had tardily passed an *Appropriation Act*, but had defied Gipps on the wider issues. As a result, he had been constrained to appeal to the Secretary of State, because they had attacked the *Schedules* (and thus by implication, the *Constitution Act*), and as Gipps wrote, the *Schedules* 'are absolutely necessary to the form of Government which has been given to the colony'. Lord Stanley, at home, while not realizing the nature of the questions involved, insisted on the *Schedules* and informed Gipps of the statesmanlike idea he had himself evolved. If the Council would not reform, allow the essential services to break down, and thus, by leaving the convicts without restraint, make the colonists themselves suffer! In the course of a very odd and impersonal despatch (29 March 1844), the Secretary of State criticized everything—the indiscretion of an untrained Council; the pugilistic and abstract nature of the Governor's *Messages*; and the general attack on the Crown's rights.

With the passage of the months, events resolved themselves into a three-cornered duel between Gipps and two members of the Council —Wentworth and Lowe. Colonial life in the forties came to centre round these three disparate personalities. They were the outstanding characters in the colony, and it was their characteristics and the reactions between them that gave the squatting issue the intense form it assumed in those years. Gipps has already been explained— with his over-conscientious idealism thrust down by a grimly implacable fighting spirit. Opposition brought out his best and his worst points, and events doomed him to a continual opposition. But, right or wrong in his immediate actions, and however human he was in hating his opponents, he was the least self-interested and, it must be insisted (though he himself would have hated such sentimentality!), the most idealistic of the three. He stood for *Crown, colony and the future*: and, though he may have been often wrong and frequently indiscreet, these interests remained throughout in the forefront of his mind. Viewed from any approach, Gipps had an integrity and a persistency that no one in the colony could even remotely rival. The moral nature of his fight placed him poles apart from his opponents.

Even the crudest of his actions was transmuted in the fire of this sacrificial idealism, even his most errant impulse stands out from the dross, and, almost a century later, is explained by the general *motif* of his integrity. Gipps was not a likeable man, not a personality to rhapsodize over: there was something coldly inhuman in his aloofness. In all, he had the elements of greatness—this strange, isolated figure who stood for disinterestedness in a colony of selfish class-interests and for abstract principles in a *milieu* in which they were quite unintelligible. Brutal in his manner and often coarse in his characteristics, he was yet too fine to be understood by the Lowes and Wentworths and M'Leays. Unknowingly, he had the soul of a martyr, and he quite literally gave his life for the fight he had undertaken. A rude man masking a strange fineness of spirit—people judged Sir George Gipps by his gestures, whereas they not only hid his real self but were consciously exaggerated by him.

Gipps erred, he made mistakes worse by his defects, and he was obstinate in his own way: but he was a great man. One of his opponents became a Chancellor of the Exchequer in England, another the so-called *Father of Australia;* but an impartial historian must come to the conclusion that neither, for greatness of spirit or fineness of character, could bear comparison with this early colonial Governor. He lacked the defects that so much aid worldly success and died a broken man, his enemies successful and his policies reversed, but the judgment remains—in his work and character, Sir George Gipps was a great man.

With Wentworth, the case was far different. William Charles Wentworth made no pretentions to idealism or to fineness of character: he was a gruff, self-made man who had bludgeoned his way to the position he had attained and cared not who knew it. He had done sterling work in the colony—work that was evident to all —and by the forties, was inclined to base his omniscience on his past record. That record was almost entirely constitutional, for Wentworth, *The Australian Patriot,* as his admirers called him, had given the country its constitution, in so far as it could be described as the work of any one man. As a youth, he had been one of the first party across the Blue Mountains. Then he had gone to Cambridge to study law, and, while still in his twenties, published a well-written account of Australia that ran to several editions. Returning to the colony with liberal ideas and an intense personal ambition, he at once found himself in opposition to the Government. He came to a land where trial by civil juries was unknown, where there was no Parliamentary representation, no agreement in taxation, no freedom of the press: and all for these he fought in a struggle that knew nothing of mercy for his antagonists and no restraints, even of good taste, in his own methods. He was always a social tyrant, an intellectual egotist in a land of social bondage and uncouth colonists. But, despite his obvious personal faults and perhaps the not disinterested nature of his aims, the reforms he achieved were very real.

He co-operated with Dr Wardell in the campaign of the *Australian* that wrecked Darling; he led the *Patriotic Association* that was formed to wrest constitutional advance from the executive; he fought consistently for trial by jury; and he was undoubtedly the driving-force behind the fifteen-years' agitation for a representative Council. This great bulk of work was rounded off, however, by 1842, so that, when the first Council met, Wentworth was in the position of an undoubted autocrat. Any act of his, however retrogressive, could be excused by reference to his democratic struggles in the thirties, and his position, since it was based on the unmistakable achievements of these earlier years, appeared to be unassailable. He had entrenched himself behind a wall of privilege and thus answered all attacks by evading them.

As leader of the Council, he had no rivals. The opposition (that is to say, the majority-party) were at his beck-and-call, and nobody even remotely rivalled him. He was an autocrat, and comported himself as such. An essentially coarse figure, this species of autocracy became him, though it developed the grosser aspects of his personality. Wentworth lacked fineness and susceptibility, although as a brutal driver, he certainly revealed great strength, as long as he could dominate any given situation. Accordingly, his figure came to symbolize the opposition. Interested as he was in squatting now that he had left the local Bar, he affected the bushman even in his city costume and usually took his seat in the Council-chamber in an ill-fitting morning jacket and soiled corduroys. Once seated, he lolled down, hands in pockets and head thrown back, openly contemptuous of the Council and deliberately rude to the permanent officials opposite him. His speeches were bad. As the perhaps over-frank account of a contemporary news-sheet described them—he spluttered and growled and glared, called for his 'extracts', fumbled with his clumsy spectacles, and then would suddenly rise into a broken sublimity of language, then stutter afresh, retrieve himself by his inevitable appeals to *the Great Dead*, and wind up with much cheap clap-trap. He has left no great speech, no clearly analytical essay: the essential part of his utterances was in the brusque force of his personality.

By 1842, Wentworth, now a man of over fifty, was no longer the fighting young Radical of even ten or five years before. He had achieved a place and, that once attained, seemed to have forgotten the people in whose name he had so strenuously waged the fight. He was already rapidly tending towards Conservatism and, in fact, became a violent reactionary. It would almost appear as if he had considered his own interests the whole time: and it certainly remains a moot point (to which his subsequent actions give a decided answer) as to how far his constitutional fight was due to the fact that it benefited the country, or to the equally obvious fact that it took power from the Governor and placed it in the hands of himself and his friends. It is curious how the occasion and his interests always coincided. Having achieved the position he desired for himself, he deserted the people: his Radicalism seemed in inverse proportion to the attainment of the privileges for which he had fought. Already by 1843, he was the hated *Tory of Vaucluse*—the head of the Conservatives—the man who had built up his reputation as a liberal patriot, and yet was supporting the claims of a landholding minority against what he now chose to term the excesses of democracy! It was a strange transformation, but one so borne out by a long chain of events that its existence could not be denied—so many were the instances that converted the quasi-rebel editor of the *Australian* of 1832 into the hidebound reactionary who yearned to become *Baron Vaucluse* in 1852!

His position in 1843 was especially despicable, because, on a recent occasion, he had deliberately sacrificed community-interests to his own mercenary opportunities. As a fighting reformer, Wentworth had consistently opposed Governor Darling and had even threatened to escort him to the foot of the gallows; but he had for the most part supported Governor Bourke. Gipps, therefore, on his arrival, deemed Wentworth to have become sufficiently moderate to enjoy a seat on the Council and nominated him for one.[8] In the interim, however, Wentworth had proposed to grab the whole Southern island of New Zealand at a penny a hundred acres and had openly thwarted the Governor's attempts to win over certain Maori representatives then in Sydney. Negotiations that may have changed the whole position of New Zealand were ruined because Wentworth wanted to make money out of nothing. Gipps, as became his position, had to attack this false conduct, which he denounced as worse than all of the various 'jobs' achieved or attempted since the time of the Stuarts! Wentworth thereupon resigned his magistracy and became the Governor's inveterate enemy, though hitherto he had shown every disposition to work with him. Though entirely in the wrong, he turned away and determined the whole of his attitude to the Governor by this unjustified personal animus—because Gipps refused to cede him an island of New Zealand for a couple of hundreds of trading-truck! Somebody had written of the base alloy mixed with

[8] Gipps-Glenelg, 3 April 1839. Wentworth's defence of 30 June-1 July 1840 is reprinted in a pamphlet.

the fine gold of his masterful personality: this mixture was clearly evident in 1843.

At the time of the squatting fight, therefore, Wentworth was the master of the Council and spokesman of the squatters. Though he temporarily found favour with all who opposed Governor Gipps, he was distinctly unpopular. He was so much against the new city-immigrants and so intent on his own self-interest that even those who appreciated his old fight were forced to reconsider their position. Even as a democrat, he had opposed the emigrants: now, as a conservative and a capitalist, he spurned all crowds. Once he had favoured the convicts, and then dropped them, because he found that he could use them against a certain Governor. Once he had upheld the people against the Government on a constitutional matter: now, he was fighting for minority rights against both Executive and people. Further, from the very inception of the Council he had done so much to bring into being, he sullied his reputation by a long string of actions based on personal interest. He wanted to dispose of his estates by a lottery, and even proposed a Bill for that purpose, quite oblivious to the fact that he was accentuating the improvident instinct of the people at a time when gambling had already produced a national crisis. He made a speciality of tendering for pioneers' runs, by the information he was able to glean in Sydney; and, to his shame, thus outbid the Darling pioneers on Paika and five other runs.[9] He refused the Speakership in 1846, because the Council would not double the salary or give him additional 'dinner payments' twice a week. He prevented the town of Parramatta from obtaining fresh water, because, when they wanted a few of his barren rocks for one end of their reservoir, he made them buy all, and *as a legislator*, voted for this scheme that would so obviously aid his own interests.[10] As a squatter, and despite the fights of the rising democracy, he wanted to bring in Asiatic labour, and was thus assailed as 'Coolie' in the great Sydney election of 1848. He attacked railways as 'an outrage on ancient usages and vested interests', which, said even the *Sydney Morning Herald* (the most Conservative organ), 'this generous son of Australia will spare no pains to prevent!' When gold was found, he demanded half an ounce a day from all diggers on his run, whether successful or not: and Sydney was afforded the delectation of seeing the People's Tribune illegally trying to force diggers from land to which he had no other claim

---

[9] Entries in *Hobler MS. Diary*, 30 March 1848, 9 September 1849. *Sydney Morning Herald* supplement, 27 June 1850.
[10] *Sydney Morning Herald*, 15 May 1850.

than a lease, or, as an alternative, securing £2 a day if they were not earning, and two-thirds of their reward if they were.[11] In the same year, he recommended titles for Australia's successful men— but his career of rabid conservatism need be carried no further than this. Wentworth had deliberately dissipated his great heritage of the thirties, and it would have been far better had he never known his anti-democratic and squatting days. Before them, even if his principles were questionable, the work that he achieved more than counteracted them: but now, both acts and principles were of the same species, and Wentworth, the opponent of Gipps, could hardly be described as the same man as Wentworth, the opponent of Darling. The one was a self-seeking reactionary, the other had been a fighting figure advancing the cause of a nation.

Yet these defects could not utterly take away his power, and Wentworth was still the leading politican throughout the forties. His acknowledged position, his vigorous dialectics and impassioned power of attack were all there, as Gipps's party found to its cost: and his harsh abruptness and violent gestures still swayed the Assembly. Wentworth, conservative or liberal, could hew a way through his opponents, and Gipps had to count him his arch-enemy in launching any new scheme. His voice that sounded 'like sweet bells jangling out of tune' and his rough growls could be counted on to harass any of the Governor's moves: and it may be said that the driving power of this 'rough diamond' and his bullying command of his followers were the strongest force the squatters possessed. Wentworth was the leader of the combination that wrecked Gipps, and there is no doubt that, had he retained his early democracy and joined the Governor in upholding the smaller freeman against the minority who wished to lock up the lands, the two would have carried the day. No combination could have resisted Gipps and Wentworth, and the history of Australia would have been far different, and Wentworth for ever an unsullied *Father of the People*, instead of the patchwork figure history must now needs judge him.

One day in the new Council, late in 1843, the third figure in the trilogy made its dramatic entry on the colonial stage. Wentworth, as has been seen, was the practical Tsar of the Council—the leader of squatters and Conservatives. The despot of Vaucluse, his position of supremacy secured by long years of fight, simply sat back with his feet up on the rail in front of him, and loudly exuded his complacent breath. He cared no longer: his reputation was made, and even his delivery could become as slovenly as his manners, and nobody would

[11] Ibid., 11 September 1851.

question him. That he *could* do things properly if he wanted to was doubted by none: the fact that he did not deem the effort worth while simply served as a further testimony to his position of un-challenged—and, he would grant, unchallengeable—supremacy. Under these circumstances, he assumed the manners and methods of a Tammany boss—whom, indeed, he rather resembled in appear-ance.

Then came the bombshell. The Council had appointed a *Committee* to enquire into the causes of monetary confusion in the colony—in other words, the crisis; and had recommended some obscure German system of Government-debentures—the *Pfandbriefen* of Prussia. This was being duly hustled through the Council, Went-worth not even taking the trouble to speak on the matter, though he had condescended to become the last witness and make a few dogmatic remarks to the Committee shortly before. The matter was seemingly closed. The opposition had made known its wishes, those wishes were being clad with the necessary formalities of going through Council, and the squatters were thinking of their next move to plague the Governor, when a young man whom Gipps had nominated to the Council ('Who is this Mr Lowe?' the leading news-paper had asked) jumped up and, peering shortsightedly from right to left and rubbing his nose on his notes, loosed a flood of reasoned oratory very unusual in that Chamber where Wentworth's uncon-sidered growls set the tone of debate. This, to the contrary, was the touch of the Oxford Union—a delicately thrusting stiletto against Wentworth's bludgeoning cavalry-sabre. Moreover, probably because the presumptuous young man was mentally as well as physically myopic, he was actually attacking the Wentworth *régime*—opposing the Bill! Governors' representatives were simply supposed to behave like gentlemen and automatically vote in their minority: but now one was actually comporting himself as an individual and opposing the popular majority as if he believed what he were saying and not simply earning his sponsor's approval.

Wentworth sat up, first in amusement, then in pained seriousness. He tried flippant condescension, followed by weighty attack. He started in a gently patronizing way,

The efforts of *the Hon. Member for Horbury-terrace*, smelling of the lamp as they did and highly considered as they were, were nevertheless efforts of no small merit. But all the opposition emanated from persons who were comparative strangers to the land, ignorant of its wants, ignorant of its history, and ignorant, in short, of everything connected with it.

To this, Dr Nicholson, a Port Phillip representative, dutifully added his praise of the beautiful peroration; and fully two-thirds of the Council had a great day's amusement in laughing at the heckled newcomer. Thus, Robert Lowe, barrister-at-law, entered Australian politics, *en route* for the British Chancellorship of the Exchequer.

Wentworth, as has been seen, has had his real character hidden beneath an evaluation based on his earlier days, and then translated to the entirely different personality and events of the forties: by a somewhat similar inversion, the actions of Robert Lowe in Australia have never really been considered by themselves. The observer has read backwards into the period the personality of Viscount Sherbrooke, Gladstone's right-hand man, and estimated Lowe's worth by a scale of values distorted by the greatness he later achieved. Just as Wentworth was never considered apart from the veiling superstructure of his earlier years, so Lowe could never, it would appear, be torn from his later years. What is needed is to consider Wentworth, not as he was earlier or as he might have been, but as he was at the moment—in the early forties, when the squatting struggle was in full swing—and Lowe, not as he afterwards became, not even as the Chancellor in embryo, but as the rather chameleon-like young solicitor of that moment. Lowe's future had nothing to do with the squatters, and it seems absurd for later commentators to interpret the forties of Australia in light of his later career in Whitehall, and to claim that, because Lowe became one of the leading English statesmen, he must naturally have been dominant in the local matters of a mere colony. His official biographer, Martin, for instance, claims that no man could rival Lowe's importance in solving the constitutional problems of Australia in the forties, and that Lowe, merely on his way for the English Cabinet, devoted a few years to straightening out Australia's problems—that, of course, is arrant nonsense and bad history. What happened was that Lowe landed in Australia, poor, unknown, and practically blind—was given opportunity by gubernatorial patronage—won, by not altogether praiseworthy means, a place of pre-eminence and rivalry with Wentworth in the colony—secured notice and riches—and left Australia at the earliest possible moment for the wider field he so much desired. To him, Australia was but an episode, so that naturally his career there was tainted with a desire to seek his own personal ends: but, none the less, he became one of the colony's leading figures and played a fundamental part both in the great squatting crisis and later.[12]

[12] The standard life of Lowe is by A. P. Martin, 2 vols., 1893, and there is a shorter but more critical essay by Hogan (1893).

Lowe, at this time, was a strange, and in many ways a pitiable, figure. After a miserable time as a Winchester commoner (a kind of Dotheboys-Hall existence), he had spent eleven years at Oxford, mostly 'selling his life-blood' tutoring, and then, as a briefless young barrister of thirty-one, had sailed for Sydney—to what he later called 'the reminiscences of a penal settlement' or 'an ignorant, vicious, lazy and degraded community'. He arrived in the middle of the long crisis, unknown and unattractive, to set up 'the wretched trade of an advocate'. Fortunately, the Governor helped him, and even kept him at Government House until he found his feet. Once started in his law, he had to follow false medical advice about his eyes and wander round, practically penniless, for nearly nine months, unable to read or write—a time of stress in which Gipps again came to his aid and again kept him at Government House. The Governor, however, could not provide him the position he begged for, and he once more resumed his practice. By this time, his fortunes had turned, because Gipps now found him a place in the new Council. The Government party there was singularly weak, especially in the light repartee of debate, and was continually flinching before the gruff assaults of Wentworth and the lighter but more salient thrusts of Richard Windeyer, 'the David Hume of the Council', Gipps particularly and specifically gave Lowe the seat on condition that he would support the Government,[13] and for a time—until he had established himself in the public eye—he remembered his benefactor.

He soon became one of the leaders of the Council, because his clear flexible style and his wealth of rapid allusion marked him out in an uneducated Assembly. His strange figure was soon as well-known as Wentworth's. At Oxford, he had been mistaken for an old gentleman with snowy hair, so bent and aged did he appear. A born albino, he had a total absence of colouring matter—his eyelids were always practically closed, and he could scarcely read. Once seen, his red ferrety eyes and white eyelashes could never be forgotten—bank-tellers remembered his peculiar peering expression half a century later. When, in addition, he affected a strange shield-like device for his eyes, and a long stockwhip and shady Panama hat, the *gaucherie* of his appearance can easily be imagined. But all of this was forgotten once he started to speak. He would break into a rapid delivery, and pour out an elaborate speech garnished—perhaps almost florid and turgid—with rhetorical ornaments, and thick with allusions covering all languages and all history. His efforts may have smelt of the lamp, as Wentworth said, and they were certainly

[13] Gipps-Stanley, 10 November 1843.

somewhat flamboyant, but they none the less overrode the Council
of the forties and carried their point even when they were not
understood. Disraeli, at a later date, followed Wentworth in ridicul-
ing his set speeches as the literary exercises of 'an inspired schoolboy': and several critics complained of his mixture of flippancy and
ornament and 'rhetorical fury' as each insulting the listener's intelligence and as savouring of the mountebank: but none could deny the
effect of his speeches. Just as later, when a Liberal member of Parliament in England, he had the Tory benches screaming with delight
at his attacks on his own party's Reform Bill, so in New South
Wales, his rasping voice and torrential flow won the Assembly and
gained for him the applause of the crowds, almost at once. But the
trouble was that his listeners were carried away at the moment by
what would scarcely bear analysis afterwards, and usually ended by
admiring the frenzied verbosity which they began by half scorning:
amused, they became convinced, though still knowing in a sneaking
kind of way that the dialectic did not ring true and that they should
not be lured by it into betraying their saner, but not nearly so
vivacious, predilections.

As a result of his debating powers, Lowe, in a couple of months,
had been transformed from the unknown barrister twitted by the
Sydney Morning Herald, into one of the colony's foremost public
figures. Gipps had given him his seat in October 1843—in the following August, he resigned, with some over-elaborate remarks that he
was a slave if he voted for the Government and a traitor if he
opposed it.[14] He did not quite see, so myopic was everything connected with him, that he was both traitor and place-hunter if he
deserted his benefactor under the strained conditions of 1844. Gipps
had made Lowe: now, in the bitterest moment of the Governor's
struggle, he was abandoned by the man he had saved from starvation
—and for no reason that had not pertained at any previous moment
since Lowe had arrived in the colony!

The truth was that, in the interim, Lowe had acquired considerable
interests in land and had joined the *Pastoral Association,* because he
could see an opening future by taking up the cudgels of the opposition against the harassed Governor. This, however, was not so bad:
he may, perchance, have honestly changed his opinions since the
time of his arrival. What was inexcusable was the stand he took
against Gipps personally, reviling him in the lowest guttersnipe
manner and submitting him to the most caddish attacks in the *Atlas*
periodical, of which he was the founder and practically the editor

---

[14] *Atlas,* 22 March 1845, or Gipps's report of 27 July 1844.

from November 1844, to the middle of 1845. In anybody, these attacks on a man who was so tied by his position that he could not answer them would have been despicable: but to come from Lowe, who had been Gipps's *protégé* ('the veriest place-hunter that ever arrived in the colony never followed a Governor's tail so constantly as Mr Lowe did that of Sir George Gipps', said the Conservative journal), they were simply unspeakable. No heat of conflict, no temporary passions can excuse them: they were inhuman shafts to direct into the quivering flesh of a bound man. It were almost as if Lowe, before the eyes of his victim, experimented in the coldest manner on an anatomical dummy, preparatory to inserting them in the helpless flesh. Whatever Lowe became, and however he developed, the stain of 1844 must remain—not for the desertion (that is the least of the charge), but for the manner of its taking and the method of the revenge he exacted—the more bitterly because he knew that he had no cause for revenge.

By August, then, Lowe was in opposition and editing the squatters' most powerful organ. He was elected unopposed to the Council in April 1845, and, because of his defection, was thrown into the hands of the man he hated—Wentworth. Together, they attacked every scheme of Sir George Gipps, and where they could find no actual issue to combat, concentrated on personal abuse. Speaking of his host and benefactor, whom he knew was at the moment a physical wreck in his labours for the country, Lowe said, in March 1845:

Hope nothing from this Governor: his whole attention is taken up in scraping together, by every disgraceful expedient, a revenue which, being emancipated from the control of the representatives of the people, may serve the purposes of the Colonial Office. For you, he cares nothing, and will do nothing.

Wentworth, at least, had some grounds for attacking the Governor, but Lowe had no excuse whatever, and, in addition, an education and a training that should have taught him gentlemanly restraint. No wonder that Gipps, in his moment of travail, wrote home that 'Mr Lowe's appointment to the Council is one of the acts of my Government, which I have had most reason to be sorry for'; but Gipps did not live long enough to know that, in Lowe's case, just such apostasy to his patrons, just such unblushing trimming of his sails to his own interests, opened the way to the Cabinet. Gipps had hoped so much from him and had leant on him as a friend—that made the admission of his defection the more poignant. That Lowe did not even have the usual excuse for his betrayals—that he was

not forced to change by changing events—heightened the offence:
events were as they had been, but Lowe had so strengthened himself,
both financially and in popular acclaim, that he could now experiment in desertion as he pleased.

But he could not be satisfied even by his changes to date. He
seemed to find positive pleasure in his *volte-faces*—this political Dick
Swiveller who was constant only in his inconstancy, and who seemed
to suffer from some intellectual *malaise* which viewed loyalty as
something to be directly attacked wherever it threatened to manifest
itself. Thus, he felt himself uneasy in his squatting allegiance, the
more so because the loathed Wentworth was the natural leader of
the squatters and, after Gipps's departure, had been 'transformed
from the suppliant into the master', as Lowe said. It seemed clear,
therefore, that the path of ambition was beckoning in other directions, and, in 1846, Lowe once more joined the anti-squatting camp.
What he now called *the squattocracy*, 'the petty aristocracy of the
colony', the vanquishers of gum trees and kangaroos, the graspers
of the people's patrimony, became the butt of his biting irony. He
was a popular idol once again, this time against both squatters and
officials. '*I have been consistent in fighting for liberty: the squatters
have been consistent in fighting for money*', was the pap he fed them;
and that accounts for his popularity with the Sydney masses during
the great election of 1848. He had aided Gipps and abandoned him:
he had aided the squatters and abandoned them: he was aiding the
artisans now, and was destined to abandon them very shortly—
a career of transformations.

By this time, his income consolidated and the great days of adver-
tisement over, the colonies could offer little more to him. By coming
out, he had lost much ('I have sunk into the slave of those who were
once my equals', he even said in public), and now awaited the
opportunity to return. As the popular leader, he headed the crowds
against the *Hashemy* convicts, though a few years before, as a
member of Wentworth's *Committee*, he had not shown any particular aversion to them—one last change of opinion. Thus, since he had
alienated everybody except the artisans of Sydney, and had little
hope from them, he left Australia (1850), and could tolerate the
name only in addressing the receipts for the unearned increments in
Sydney-land that enabled him to win fame in England. From this
stage, he belonged to national history, and the way was easy to the
Ministry of Health under Palmerston, the Chancellorship of the
Exchequer under Gladstone, the peerage, and the nation's inner
councils. But this book is not concerned with Viscount Sherbrooke,

the friend of Gladstone and Selborne and Jowett—but with the early days of struggle when a quaintly deformed young solicitor was, for the nonce, using his gushing flow of oratory and his malleable principles in fighting the cause of the squatters against Gipps. Of his importance in that early period, there can be no doubt: with Foster, he was the outstanding protagonist of land matters for fully five years after 1844—and therein, rather than in the development of his somewhat chequered personality, was his importance for Australia.

These three men clearly dominated the stage of the time—Gipps, the dauntless but perhaps obstinate incorruptible: the self-seeking Wentworth, but a gruff force which the observer could understand and which left no doubt as to where it stood: and Robert Lowe, flashing and ever-changing—the personification of brilliant inconstancy. But they were supported by an array of personalities, lesser, it is true, but strikingly well-developed for such a young colony. Perhaps because the stage was so small that few persons were in the public eye—perhaps because the work was so large (they were shaping a continent), their personal peculiarities seemed abnormally developed—Lowe's stockwhip, Wentworth's corduroys, Boyd's extravagant curricle, and the rest. Certainly, there seemed a very large proportion of fine characters in public life at that time. There was Deas Thomson, the old Colonial Secretary, always plain, courteous and business-like—the very type of a Crown official: with him worked Riddell, the Treasurer, equally conscientious, but pilloried by Lowe as being able, indeed *to sign his name* with consummate skill and some velocity!

But the Government side lacked driving power and aggressiveness, and so much more was heard of Wentworth, Lowe, and their lesser aids like Richard Windeyer, the great forensic orator whose stinging satire so affected Gipps. Windeyer had consistently fought for the people from the time of the Corn-law struggles in England, and never deviated from his task until his death. He was the financial and educational authority in the Council, and the soundest, if not the most obvious, debater. On the same side, if his inveterate egotism and quarrelsome nature could enable him to be described as one of a party, was Dr John Dunmore Lang—'*Dr Spluttermuch*', the Presbyterian cleric who, despite his faults, was for ever noisily smelling out abuses and fostering immigration schemes: but in these years, he was not certain if he hated Gipps or the squatters most, and so found his effectiveness curtailed! Cowper, another of the band, was Lowe's second-in-command, and steadily upheld the Liberal cause, though keeping a close eye on Wentworth and Deas Thomson. 'A strange mixture of pious predilections and mundane practices', he was jocularly described by Lowe (who really esteemed him more highly than any other public man in the colony) in this phrase—'if Cowper saw the Gates of Heaven thrown open, he would not walk straight, but would wriggle in'. Then there was the squatter Forster, later a Premier, but at the time the most bitter satirist in an age when political satire was particularly acrid, and one of the keenest opponents of Sir George Gipps. His piece, *The Devil and the Governor*, in the *Atlas*, remains the strongest shaft that met Gipps, and it was remarked at the time that Gipps feared Forster's satire outside as much as he did Windeyer's debates inside the Council. Lastly, on the squatting side, was the wirepuller *par excellence*—Benjamin Boyd, member of the Royal Yacht Squadron, English capitalist, importer of *Kanakas*, general speculator, worker of the marionettes in the Colonial Office, and the biggest squatter of them all. All of these, except Deas Thomson and the nonentity Riddell, were arrayed against Gipps: they had the personality, the position of expressing themselves in the Council, and money from the sheeps' back to speak for them at home, and before their phalanx, Gipps had to fight a losing action, where even his frontal attacks were by their nature primarily defensive. They had him so borne down by numbers, position and power (especially when they won over the Colonial Office) that it was impossible for him to prevail. That was the tragedy of it all.

III The Proposals of Gipps

Confronted by this situation, Gipps had to take some positive steps. Despite the opposition, he felt in his mind that any longer delay was unfair to the country. All that the squatter paid under the 1839 Act was one licence-fee of £10, and for that he could run as many stock as he liked anywhere. Some paid a halfpenny for each cow depastured, others 7s.; and, on the average, the general charge for using the pick of the Crown lands amount to much less than two per cent of the annual return from the sheep. To counteract the inequality of this general charge, there was the supplementary assessment on each head of stock, but this was not enough. Where, for instance, one man could occupy from ten to thirty runs on the Darling and could seize as much land as he desired, irrespective of the amount of stock he placed on it, something was vitally wrong. The Crown was obviously not receiving its due; and, though Gipps had postponed any action hitherto, because of the distress and the constitutional changes, he could not allow a policy of negations to go on for ever—as he had intimated in his speech of September 1842, on the Bathurst case, a speech which he thought so important that he took the unusual step of printing it and spreading it throughout the land on his own authority.

His standpoint was quite clear.[15] He agreed that easy occupation of the soil was desirable under Australian conditions, but *that* was afforded by the Squatting Act, and there seemed no reason why the occupants should want a fee-simple over the patrimony of the future! The Councillors, he said, ridiculed a Secretary of State who did not know that every sheep needed three acres, and who wanted 20s. for every acre of rock or scrub: but the Governor retorted that every fool knew that sheep raising wouldn't pay on purchased land, and that the Government, far from valuing its worst land at 20s. an acre, as the opposition implied, was simply determined not to sell any land that was not worth 20s., and certainly not to give a few sheep men the best of the land at what it was valued for pastoral purposes. He had said in September 1842 that he was 'an advocate of sale at a comparatively high price, or not at all', and the passage of time only confirmed him in this opinion. The squatters argued that the existing price was absurd in a grazing country: Gipps retorted that licensed squatters had no concern with freehold, even at a few pence an acre. The proprietor of the sheep need not necessarily be the proprietor of the land—indeed, squatting was of so peculiar a nature that dear land seemed a kind of corollary to cheap occupation. 'The high price of land and the squatting system seem to me to naturally go together, the one supports the other, and either would be indefensible without the other', he wrote. Price has so little to do with present use that such a criterion at the moment would reduce land values until they became 'less per acre than the smallest coin in use in the colony'. It was the possibilities of the future that counted, and Gipps was not prepared to admit that value for sheep was the final value. To the contrary, holding that such lands should be kept intact for the future, he would rather stand against all alienation. Why, he expostulated, they should be thankful for the right of occupation they had, and should bless Nature for the fact that every acre of unimproved land would produce a pound of wool a year. From the point of productivity, they were far better off than they would be in Canada, even though land there was only eighteen-pence an acre!

[15] Gipps-Stanley, 17 January 1844, and 16 April 1844—very long and important statement of his own views, especially the former.

This represented the stage reached by Governor Gipps in January 1844. A few years earlier, he had denied all rights to the squatters. 'I will not allow them to secure any title at all to the land they occupy, or to occupy land where they please, or to sell their right of station', he said in September 1842. But *rights of station* soon became articles of common sale, worth up to five hundred pounds, and city dwellers developed a system of 'thirds', under which they received a third of the produce in return for their capital. Under such conditions, the squatters spread from Wilson's Promontory to Harvey's Bay, a district 1,100 miles long, with 9,885 inhabitants, 573,114 cattle and over three million sheep.

As these new provinces were developed, Gipps began to modify his opinions. He suddenly realized the implications of all this life beyond the boundaries. A new race was springing up under conditions which threatened a reversion to barbarism, women were beginning to go into the bush, children were growing up there—yet there were few ministers, no churches, and no schools. To his credit, Gipps placed these social and humanitarian arguments in the foreground, whereas his opponents were concerned only with profits and cheap labour. He recognized that the social problem of squatting was emerging, although neither Government nor individuals could move to solve it. The squatters, uncertain in their tenure from year to year and liable to be ousted at the caprice of a Commissioner, would have been madmen to have erected permanent improvements. Most of them, even in 1844, were forced to live in bark huts; it was only here and there that dwellings worth the name of cottages were to be found. Crops were non-existent, and a garden was a luxury, the talk of the countryside for miles. The children of men who were, themselves, mostly educated people of the upper middle class were thus being reared in an atmosphere of savagery with no redeeming features and no prospect of future change.

Under this new emphasis, Gipps accepted part of the sheepmen's claims. He realized that they had to have some permanency, if only to combat the growing social ills, and his despatches of 1844, choleric and disjointed as they were as compared with previous ones, reflected this changed approach.

Independently, therefore, of any considerations of Revenue, [he wrote in a despatch of 3 April of that year] the time seems to me arrived, when some alteration is required in the Administration of the lands of the Crown beyond the Boundaries of Location, in order to relieve the Government from the reproach, not simply of allowing the continuance of such a state of things, but actually of prohibiting amendment; and, to do this, not only should a portion of the lands now occupied by Licence be opened to location in the usual way, but facilities should be afforded to squatters in general of securing to themselves *a permanent interest in some parts of the lands they occupy.*

To point this decision, it must be remembered that, while he was thus proposing to yield the squatters more than they wanted, the colony was rent with vituperation of him, and men in the bush were speaking of loaded bullets in their carbines and of holding the ranges by force! While he was weighed down under these torrents of unjustified abuse, the transport was pushing its slow way to England with the Governor's revolutionary proposals, not only to give security, but even a partial freehold, in order to facilitate the spread of civilization in the outback lands! The juxtaposition of these events is one of the little tragedies of history—between these clashing forces, Gipps was caught, powerless and unable to respond.

Already, in December 1843, he had sent circulars to the fifteen Commissioners of Crown Lands, seeking their views on any changes: he wanted a symposium of the ideas of the men in the field, before he made up his own mind. Actually he received little aid from these men. The problems of general reconstruction seemed too wide for them, and their only unanimous recommendation was in opposing a uniform licence fee of £10, irrespective of acreage or stock. In the first set of regulations, therefore—the *Occupation Regulations* of 2 April 1844—the Governor proposed that each run should have a separate licence; that no run was to exceed twenty square miles, save under exceptional circumstances; that not more than 4,000 sheep or 500 head of cattle were to be depastured on each; and that abuses were to be severely punished. Beyond that, he did not go, and yet the publication of these regulations aroused a *furore* throughout the colony.[16] A *Pastoral Association* was immediately formed, and an organized campaign stretching to London and India and Scotland was launched, on a scale hitherto unheard of in Australia. The upheaval was out of all proportion to the actual cause. One would have imagined Gipps an arch-schemer deliberately cutting at the existence of squatting, whereas all that he wanted to do was to eradicate the obvious abuses and charge a sheepman a little more than a halfpenny a year for a sheep, or a fifth of a penny for an acre of Crown Lands!

The riotous portents continued and even grew until the morning of 13 May when the *Sydney Morning Herald* published what purported to be a second or supplementary set of regulations—the so-

[16] *Depasturing Correspondence, 1842-44,* asked for by Council, 5 July 1844.

called *Purchase Regulations*—which Gipps had drawn up on 3 April, and sent away by the *General Hewitt*, the same ship that had his *Occupation Regulations*. As published in the newspapers, this set provided for a completely new principle in Australian land legislation—for the alienation of land *beyond* the official boundaries. Each squatter was to be able to purchase a homestead of 320 acres, provided that he had occupied his holding for a term of five years. He was to receive the value of his improvements, but the land itself was to be sold at not less than £1 an acre.

But a quite new principle entered at this point. So far, the squatter had received a homestead and compensation for his improvements. Gipps, however, did not stop there: to this concession, he attached an obligation. Any squatter who bought a homestead was to receive security over all of his run for a period of eight years, if he took out the usual licences, but, at the end of that time, if he wanted an additional eight years, he had to buy another 320 acres, and so on. To the homestead proposal, Gipps had appended the idea of periodical purchases, which meant in effect that the squatter had to pay £320 every eight years for security—a bonus of £40 a year. It was practically a recurrent tax, payable in advance; and the sting lay in the fact that, if the squatter refused to buy, any competitor could do so, and the rest of the run was to go to the man who bought the homestead. Even granting the desirability of the original homestead, therefore, every squatter had to pay £40 a year in addition, for land that he did not want, and face the constant menace of the auction room.

This plan seemed far removed from Gipps' stand of even the year before, and it is important to know how it had developed. The *Occupation Regulations* were clearly justified, despite the popular outcry against them: and the homestead idea had little against it, save the possible argument that it was conferring over-large privileges on a few sheepmen: but whence had come this idea of periodicity— of the recurring purchase of blocks that were clearly not homesteads, and yet not wanted by the squatters?

Gipps had stated that he had evolved two supplementary sets of *Regulations*, both sent home by the *General Hewitt* on 4 April; but a study of despatches proves that this was not so. In saying so, he was either deceiving the colonists or crediting himself with a clarity which his views had not possessed at that early stage. What happened was this. Gipps sent home the *Occupation Regulations* as they were published; and, in the same despatch of 3 April, proposed to give homesteads to the squatters. He still professed himself opposed to any right of pre-emption (if only because it was contrary to the Imperial Act of 1842), but thought that the squatter might receive compensation for any of his improvements and might even buy 320 acres in freehold after five years of occupation. While this gave them a homestead, there was still no mention of periodical purchases.

On the same day, Gipps sent off a *Separate despatch*—a private one as distinct from the public document above. The *Separate despatch* was concerned with what might be termed matters of higher importance—with constitutional ways and means, should the squatters prove recalcitrant. Gipps realized that any plan of his, however mild and moderate, would at once raise the entire colony against him. He warned Lord Stanley:

It is most essential to bear in mind that the Squatters form by far the most powerful body in New South Wales—that in fact, almost anybody who has any property at all, is a Squatter. This, I would submit, is the chief ground on which the interference of Parliament might be called for, should the Squatters at any time seek to appropriate to themselves the Lands of the Crown.

He was afraid that the colonists would resort to extreme measures and was seeking a discretionary power to override the Council—that was the whole purpose of the despatch. He wanted to produce a mandate from the Secretary of State making him the master of the situation, though, to do this, he really proposed to upset the principles of the new Government Act of 1842. The actual point was that the local *Squatting Act* was due to expire in June 1846, and both Gipps and the Executive Council (that is, his officials) were certain that the Legislative Council would not renew it. That, in turn, implied the loss of the assessment on stock, the abolition of the Border Police, and the paralysis of Government action in the squatting districts. Confronted by this situation, Gipps was practically asking for power to take the matter entirely away from the Council, despite the Act of 1842, and settle it by an executive action.

This, of course, was very much in the nature of a reactionary *coup d'état*, but the point for the moment is that the secret despatch of 3 April was concerned solely with this matter and did not mention the details of the new squatting *Regulations*. Neither of the despatches sent off by Gipps on 4 April mentioned periodical purchases—nothing was envisaged beyond the limitation of runs and the concession of a single homestead—with a request to override the Council in time of trouble. The current story that Gipps sent the depasturing regulations in one despatch, and those for periodical purchase in another despatch of the following day, was thus obviously a *canard*. In so far, the whole fight of 1844 was based on a false document.

As a matter of fact, Gipps was perplexed on the matter. Though he used tabular forms and thus clad his statements in a cover of conciseness and clarity, he was really very confusing. He made contradictory suggestions as to what would happen if a crisis emerged, but proposed nothing beyond restricted runs and one homestead for each man. The auction idea, the periodicity idea, were both absent: and it would appear as if Gipps was either befogged in his own mind or withholding something from his readers. What, for instance, must Mr Under-Secretary Stephen have thought, when he received these two despatches, and read them side by side with the files of the leading colonial papers, with the references to rebellion and the Canadian example? There was obviously faulty *liaison*-work, and, so far as the colonists were concerned, not a little deception in presenting to them regulations that were supposed to have gone by the *General Hewitt*, but which contained vital matters not mentioned in the despatches sent by that vessel!

What happened was that Gipps published his *Occupation Regulations* on 3 April, and sent them away, as published. The same day, he proposed to give a homestead to the squatters—though what afterwards became known in the colony as the '*General Hewitt Regulations*' contained far more than this. At once, however, the *Occupation Regulations*, published alone, had evoked an unparalleled uproar in the colony. This upheaval was on so large a scale that Gipps felt himself obliged to reconsider his position. Therefore, on 1 May, he sent an explanatory despatch by the *Gannott*, telling of the rebellious spirit evoked by the notice of 2 April, and justifying his action, because the outcry

shows how completely the occupiers of these lands have accustomed themselves to look upon them as their own; and how urgently some declaration on the part of the Government was necessary to check the growth of opinions such as those that were proclaimed at the meeting [of protest].

Undoubtedly influenced both by the extent and the unreasonable nature of the opposition, he enclosed in this despatch a *Memorandum* by himself. This purported to take each of the homestead proposals of 3 April in turn and to give comments on them: but, in effect, in his last comment, Gipps introduced the vitally new idea of periodical purchases. Even now, he was not clear. All that he wrote was that, after the purchase of his homestead, a squatter should be allowed to hold the unpurchased parts of the run, on the same terms, or rather under the same understanding, that a new run would be held by the person forming it; that is to say, he should, under ordinary circumstances, remain undisturbed for eight years; should he, during the course of these eight years, desire to extend his purchase, the Government would afford him the opportunity of so doing, and every purchase (if not less than 320 acres) would virtually act as a renewal of an eight-years' lease of the unpurchased parts of his run.

That was all—periodical purchases were still not compulsory, they were still not an obligatory tax, but only an optional aid made available to the squatters.[17]

On 11 May—ten days after this despatch, Gipps deemed the time ripe to tell the squatters what he had been doing, and, for lack of better means, gave a *Memorandum of the Purchase Regulations* to Thomas Icely, a leading mercantile man of Sydney, who held a nominated seat in the Council, with instructions that he could make it public.[18] Next day, it was in the *Sydney Morning Herald*— supposedly as the *Purchase Regulations* Gipps had sent on the *General Hewitt* on 4 April, to supplement the *Depasturing Regulations* of the day before. In reality, as has been seen, they were not the *General Hewitt* recommendations, not even the proposals of the Memorandum of 1 May, but the views Gipps had reached some time between 1 May and 11 May, in which time the germ of periodical purchases had so developed that it had grown into a plan for a compulsory purchase of blocks of three hundred and twenty acres every eight years. Gipps did not mention the changes in the interim, either in disclosing the *Purchase Regulations* in their final form to the public, or in the covering despatch with which he sent the *Icely Memorandum* to England—thus certainly dealing very cavalierly with the dictates of clarity and straightforwardness.

His conduct is open to two interpretations. Either he was a person so statesmanlike that he was prepared to jettison plan after plan, and publish no final scheme until he had painfully evolved it by slow process of change and addition: or he was clumsy and undecided, the lack of a concise idea producing what the opposition papers called 'a wretched patchwork mode of proceeding'. As far as cold facts go, the criticism of Lowe's *Atlas* was entirely justified—that

first he publishes a series of *Regulations*, to all appearances intended to be of a permanent character, and the next day writes a despatch to Lord

[17] Gipps-Stanley, 16 April 1844, 1 May 1844 (in *Atlas*, 5 September 1845).
[18] Enclosed in Gipps-Stanley, 17 May 1844. For Governor's vacillations, see *Atlas*, 12 July 1845.

Stanley, recommending a new series of proposals on the same subject. A meeting is called a few days after the publication of the *Regulations*, and then he writes a *Despatch* containing what purports to be a commentary upon the proposals which he has already forwarded, but which is, in effect, a new series of proposals.

And, the *Atlas* might have added, ten days later, he makes known a finished code which is still different again!

The truth was that Gipps was rapidly breaking up. His despatches had become much more disjointed and choleric since the beginning of 1844: and he seemed suddenly to age when the concerted opposition of the squatters flared up in April. His reports read more and more jerkily; he had lost his conciseness, and he talked like an old man, of his six full years of Government and of the feeling that, if he wished to do anything, he must do it soon. From this moment, he was a sick man, fighting a growing opposition with his own resources steadily diminishing. The despatch of the *Gannott* in May was really a painful one. He admitted that he had the necessary conconstitutional power in his hands, but said that the licence question was of such magnitude in the colony and so extremely onerous to the person dealing with it, that he begged the Queen and Parliament to relieve him of it—or at least, lay down rules for his guidance. A little earlier, Gipps would have stepped briskly towards the conflict: now, his old prowess was gone, and he was beaten to his knees.

By the middle of May, then, the warfare was open: the armies had been mobilized, and the issues at stake clearly outlined. The Governor offered security and a homestead to squatters, and in return, demanded limitation of their runs and a periodical tax (disguised as additional land purchase) of £40 a year.

IV   The Opposition in the Colony

Against the Governor were the solid masses of the squatters: practically everybody, except Gipps and his friend, Bishop Broughton, seemed grouped in a fighting opposition against *Regulations* which they chose to interpret as direct attacks on their liberties. In some way or other, the squatting and the constitutional issues had become linked. The same persons were fighting for liberalism in both spheres, and the one agitation became tinged with the popularity of the other.

Oddly enough, it was the first set of *Regulations*—the *Occupation Regulations*—that provoked the whole commotion. A few days after their publication (9 April), three hundred and fifty squatters, no small proportion of the whole, flocked to the famous meeting at the Royal Hotel, and there, in the smoky rooms, drafted the text of the protests that were to keep the stockmen united until they had wrested a permanent hold on Australian land from the Crown. Argument on argument was adduced amid clamorous applause: the regulations, it was said, were *unnecessary*, because the *Squatting Act* was already producing £25,000 more than the expenses it was intended to cover—*unjust*, because the squatters all contributed to the general revenue—*unreasonable*, because of the great crisis and the colonial distress—*oppressive*, because the general profits of pastoral pursuits were too small to admit of extra charges—*injurious*, because they would check the export of wool and the increase of stock—and *unconstitutional*, because they involved a taxing power that should have been vested in the Council. Four resolutions were passed without opposition. Wentworth, appropriately continuing his *rôle* of constitutional reformer, opened by moving that the *Regulations* involved unconstitutional acts on the part of the Executive. They implied a right of levying unlimited imposts on occupants of Crown Lands, and thus rendered the Council's powers in taxation practically nugatory: and in addition, he concluded,

these regulations, if persisted in, must not only be ruinous in their immediate operation, but are calculated to strike a blow at the future of the colony, rendering the tenure of the squatting licences precarious, inasmuch as they would be subject to the uncontrolled decision of the Governor, and preventing any accession to the population or wealth of the colony by the influx of capital or labour.

It is difficult to see how a mere insistence on Crown rights and paying £10 for every run would have brought about these manifold results; but the squatters were led away by the exuberance of their own verbosity and went on to endorse an equally rambling and, indeed, overlapping, resolution of Benjamin Boyd's, the largest of their number. Boyd's special contribution was in demanding leases for a long period of time—in fact, anything that would obviate the ruinous uncertainty and caprice of the existing regulations. Kemble, a merchant, added his note in emphasizing the dependence of the traders on the squatters, and their strong support of the opposition against anything that would shackle primary industries.

One man at this stage proposed that £10 was a fair and equitable licence fee, because it amounted to less than a tenth of the quit-rents that would have been due on grants of equal area, even under the old free-grant system: but this was only Alderman Macdermott, leader of the masses! He was later a popular figure in the fight for responsible government, but the squatters saw in him only a pestilential advocate of the city emigrants who were organizing to spoil the country with their demands. Besides, ran the punch-thickened titters through the hall, who was this democratic merchant who had been a mere sergeant in a marching regiment? Had not Lowe refused to fight him, on the ground that he had not always been a gentleman, and had he not the effrontery to call a large public meeting in defiance of the Council? His absurd motion therefore fell for lack of anyone to second it. Nevertheless, Macdermott was significant in that assembly—he was the representative of the future at a time when the squatters were being transformed from pioneers into land monopolists. Despite his interruption, however, the meeting went on and closed with the drafting of a petition for the Queen and both Houses, and the formation of a *Pastoral Association*. For the first time, the squatters in New South Wales were organized as a body: for the first time, they were making political capital out of their grievances: and, for the first time, they were arrayed, the Council behind them, openly against the Executive.

At the same time, the men of Port Phillip had come together. One day, notices were broadcast—a clarion appeal running through the countryside like fire in dried gums—

The squatters of Australia Felix will meet on horseback upon Batman's Hill (Melbourne) on the First of June, for the purpose of forming a Mutual Protection Society. From the Murray to the sea-beach, from the Snowy Mountains to the Glenelg, let no squatter be absent!

The *Port Phillip Patriot* published the regulations of 2 April in a thick, mourning border, called them 'the copestone on the ruin of Port Phillip', and turned with renewed bitterness to the cry for separation. The long lines of mounted squatters duly filed up through the marshy valley to the hill overlooking Melbourne, and passed resolutions similar to those of the Royal Hotel meeting in Sydney.

Gipps, writing on 17 May, had to report meetings of protest at nearly all the towns in the colony, with resolutions based on those of the capital. Maitland and Mudgee up towards the northern ranges were on a par with Yass and Goulburn at the edge of Monaro, and even the inner centres—Camden and Penrith and Bathurst—were not for the moment scorned by the outsiders. Regional differences, for once, were swept away in a single blaze of protest: the 'boundaries of location' simply did not exist: plainsman joined ranger: and everybody outside the labouring classes seemed naturally to combine, irrespective of rank and (despite Dr Lang in the *Chronicle!*) even religion.

'Too *much for a purchase, too much for a lease, too much for a squatting licence'*, they moaned, as they went on to more and more spectacular excesses. They planned to send forty petitions to the House of Commons, each by a different member: they deluged the remotest clubs and coffee-houses of the British Isles with their almost rebellious papers: and they conducted propagandist campaigns in every colony that could conceivably affect English opinion.

If wool falls, they went on; no alternative was left 'between ruin or rebellion', and the men going inland paused on this new note. They were dabbling now in grave things, and the papers openly preached a kind of sedition. Lowe's paper (though he should have known better than to stimulate such a spirit of dissidence) printed rebellious speeches, and told of squatters who had held that raising the republican flag 'is the natural and perhaps necessary course of affairs in such a crisis',—that the Council should turn itself into a *Convention*—that 'this is an impracticable country for an invading force',—that 20,000 armed insurgents could not be hunted down in a country of nearly two million square miles! Threatened with coercion, one squatter was reported to exclaim—'Pah! Pah! Only give me twenty good stockmen, and I would defy any regiment in Her Majesty's service!'[19] Little wonder that the London *Morning Chronicle* of 14 September described Australia as in 'an indescribable ferment', with its papers 'almost as menacing and excited as the Canadian'; or that Gipps, in June, sent a confidential despatch dealing with the question of the colony's defence, and curtly advising against any reduction in the troops stationed in Australia until the squatting agitation had been dealt with! Sixteen members of the Council, three of them Crown nominees, had attended that first squatting meeting—this fact showed the seriousness of the question and the general hold it had on all classes of society. Whatever the cause, eastern Australia in 1844 was emotionally insane, and even sensible pioneers were gripping the stocks of their saddle carbines and openly speaking of rebellion—and when men on the land do this, and when the upper classes in society stand firm to speak of armed sedition, the position is serious, however minute may have been the cause that produces such intensity of feeling!

On 28 May, in the midst of the renewed uproar due to the recently disclosed *Purchase Regulations*, Gipps opened the Council, in full expectation of a lively session after the continued opposition of the previous year. He was certainly not disappointed, for this was the Grievances Session *par excellence*. Wentworth and Lowe and

[19] *Atlas*, 19 July 1845.

Windeyer were now working together in Chamber and press, and no loophole was left untouched by the joint influence of their skill and prestige. Gipps made a non-committal speech, saying that the public finances were in a sound position despite the crisis, and that the ordinary revenue was still in excess of the expenditure chargeable on it. To this, the Council responded by appointing two Committees—Wentworth's, to consider the constitutional issues, and Cowper's, to examine the squatting trouble. Cowper, with his usual unscrupulousness masked by piety, certainly made the most of his opportunities. He examined twenty-six witnesses, all well chosen; circularized every magistrate, one hundred and twenty-two in all, because he knew which class was standing firmly in his support; and finally, after seven weeks' labour, produced a long report that was a model of painting a picture by emphasizing certain half-lights so that the remainder were in obscurity.[20]

This Committee, it must be asserted, despite the comprehensiveness of its enquiry and the force of its report, was an *ex parte* body from the commencement, composed of men whose minds were already firmly made up (all seven of them were squatters), and examining only witnesses who were prejudiced in their findings. Indeed, they did not claim to be anything else, but, after ninety years, a document put forth under the full authority of the Council tends to be taken at its face value and not as a mere stage in a campaign against a Governor.

As was natural under the circumstances the Committee followed the *Pastoral Association* in its protests. The *Depasturing Regulations* on 2 April were 'impracticable in principle and oppressive in detail, and ought to be recalled': while the *Purchase Regulations* nominally dated 3 April were 'founded on principles which cannot be worked out without the utter ruin of the grazing interests'. The licence fee should be restricted to the amount necessary to maintain the Border Police, and even that body was denounced as impotent for good as it was efficient for evil, with its convicts and blackfellows! All of the new proposals, that is, were to go, and the old charges to be reduced: and, in addition, such parts of the shackling Imperial Acts as controlled land matters were to be repealed, and the management and revenue of Crown lands vested in the Governor and the Legislative Council. That done, the newly empowered body was ordered by this Committee (and the Council quickly accepted its views in

---

[20] *Report on Land Grievances* (250 pages)—a fundamental collection of evidence on the squatting position. (*Votes and Proceedings*, 1844, vol. II.) Appointed 30 May, report printed 20 August.

September) to frame long leases for the squatters, to give them a right of pre-emption over all of their runs, and to allow compensation for their improvements.

Gipps may have been a little premature in his scheme, but he was not even as remotely innovatory as this Legislative Council, which, in December, once more approved of the above findings and embodied them in a petition to the Queen. In the same month, they were passing claims about responsible government, judicial appropriation, and financial matters that were so absurd that the Council itself was the most powerful advocate against the views it was adopting!

At the end of the year, therefore, quietness was once more over the colony. Gipps had sent his proposals and was inclined to allow the unreasonable colonial tumult to work as his best argument: and the Council, after a session of excesses, had sent petitions to England demanding constitutional and land claims so advanced that they were equivalent to setting up a distinct State! The matter had gone to extremes, the colony had exhausted itself, and everybody was awaiting the answer of the Tory Government.

V *The Opposition at Home*

Meanwhile, such vested interests as the squatting classes in the colony represented at home had not been passively submitting to what they deemed exploitation. The first agitation was that of the newspapers, and it was at least interesting to note that any colonial matter, whatever its import, could attract notice in that early-Victorian period. Viewed in the light of the usual colonial indifference, the campaign of 1844-5 was unusually widespread in its ramifications, because industrial interests felt themselves so threatened by anything that would interfere with the supply of wool that they rallied the newspapers. The *Colonial Gazette*, a Wakefield organ, naturally upheld the class of gentleman-colonists, the *Morning Chronicle* and the *Sun* and even the *Times* joined their respective weights: and, strangely enough, the *Morning Herald*, a Gladstonian publication, conceded that the demands for security were justified. As a result 'the watchword, *Security of Tenure*, is now as firmly raised in the precincts of the Colonial Office as it was last year in every district of New South Wales, from the tablelands to the sea'![21] So marked was the degree of systematic energy behind the campaign that papers as far afield as the *Madras Athenaeum* joined in it!

The colonists were organized to the point of rebellion, and England

[21] *Atlas*, 4 January 1845.

knew it. They made their grievance a matter of metropolitan politics, broadcast it in the daily press of all parties, and appealed to interested business men all over the country. For example, they sent across one of the most powerful of their numbers to keep the agitation at fever point and to provide funds lest it should die of sheer inanition. One day, in the midst of the coldness of 1842, a vessel of the Royal Yacht Squadron had drawn through Sydney Heads—a sumptuous vessel with piano and curtains and bookshelves and a long brass eighteen pounder amidships; and one Benjamin Boyd stepped ashore. He had already been heralded by the three steamers and the schooner he had sent out, and now, with a city reputation based on nearly twenty years of stockbroking and with some £200,000 in debentures, he opened a Bank on Church Hill. A strangely grandiose figure, his mind was filled with all manner of huge schemes, and, from now until his death nine years later, the colony rang with his unbalanced projects; and none know whether he was the financial genius he claimed to be, or the slightly insane charlatan his actions would appear to make him. The one obvious fact was that he had money to develop the wildest schemes, and he flung it round in all directions. He speculated in his Union Bank; he bought nine whalers; he made a town on the shore of Twofold Bay, with Gothic church, Elizabethan hotel, and sandstone lighthouse all complete; he imported *Kanakas* to fill the labour shortage; he built a long road to develop the Monaro uplands; and he became the largest squatter of his period. By the time of the squatting crisis, he had land in eight districts and ran over 300,000 sheep. Not unnaturally, such a capitalist was in the forefront of the squatting ranks, and Boyd can be termed the organizing genius behind the protests of 1844-5. Wentworth growled, and Lowe scintillated in the papers; but Boyd provided the business acumen and the intensive organization that were necessary for such a campaign on both sides of the world. He had two aides—Robinson, the Quaker representative of Port Phillip in the Council, and his brother, Archibald Boyd, who was the agent chosen by the squatting bodies to go to England in 1844 and direct their campaign there.

Archibald Boyd was astute enough to see that colonial injustice *per se* was of little concern to English interests, and realized that he had to place the matter on a business plane. He therefore showed how the new *Regulations* imperilled the supplies of colonial wool and, at the least, meant a tax of a farthing a pound on wool. Peel and Gladstone, it was argued, protected raw materials from taxation in the northern hemisphere, while their subordinates taxed them in the south. 'Manchester and Leeds', it was argued, 'are more formidable antagonists than New England and Monaro', and so the colonial squatters called a new bogey into existence to redress metropolitan indifference.

In May 1845, therefore, a meeting of interested business men was held at the house of Messrs Boyd, in London.[22] Lord Polwarth presided: the largest importers of colonial wool were there in force; city bankers and merchants attended; and anybody connected with the squatters of Australia filled the ranks. In all, a strikingly important group of people converged on Princes Street on that gusty May day, and resolved to approach Lord Stanley in favour of a twenty-one years' lease for the sheepmen of the Antipodes. They elevated the matter from one of local to imperial concern, and placed it in an entirely new light by stressing the effect on English industries. Four days later (26 May) their deputation waited on Stanley, and similar influences, though not achieving as much as they would have liked with Stanley himself, at least won over Gladstone and Peel to the cause of the squatters. Stanley, however, had ideas of his own on every conceivable subject, and tended rather to support Sir George Gipps—a position the easier for him to adopt since he had continually insisted on maintaining all of the Crown's rights in Australia. All that the deputation got from him was a smile at Boyd's reply to his query whether a lease would satisfy the squatters:

> My Lord,
> It sounds more clever,
> To me and to my heirs for ever!

But he would not incline to their wider claims and left them in the dark as to his intentions.

The squatters, in the interim, had turned to the wider auditorium of the House of Commons itself. The Council of New South Wales, in a moment when they wished to embarrass Gipps still further, had sanctioned a resolution appointing a special representative in the British Parliament—in order, as they specifically stated, that the Government could receive impartial statements on Australian matters, as contrasted with the biased representations of the Governor's despatches! Benjamin Boyd therefore chose the Hon. Francis Scott as the type they wanted. Men like Charles Bulwer or Bulwer Lytton were put aside as too philosophical or literary, but Scott was the very man. The brother of Lord Polwarth, a director of the South-Western Railway, a barrister of standing, and unassailably Conservative and Protectionist in his principles, he was ideal for their

[22] London *Colonial Gazette*, 31 May 1845.

purpose. Edmund Burke had represented New York before the War of Independence, Roebuck had fought the cause of the Jamaica planters; and now, Scott was to organize a party in the Commons to watch the Colonial Secretaries and afford justice to the squatting and moneyed interests of New South Wales. To develop their idea, the Legislative Council appointed a Committee of fourteen to correspond with their English Agent, and, by sitting through recesses, to secure permanent relations. The matter was held in abeyance for some time, because Gipps and Stanley objected to such an important matter being settled by a mere resolution of a Colonial Council, but Scott commenced his duties from the time of his appointment and effectively protested in the English Parliament against the squatting *Regulations* of 1844.

By all of these agencies—press, business associations, private and group influence, and a Parliamentary representative—the colonists waged their fight in England in the last part of 1844 and the next year: and so powerful and well-directed were their batteries that the upshot was never long in doubt, despite Gipps's recalcitrance. The Governor was outclassed, once recourse was had to stronger weapons than abstract justice, and once the industrialists and politicians of Great Britain were invoked against him. From the moment of the Polwarth gathering, the actual decision was only a matter of time and political juggling. The opposition had been too resourceful for Gipps, and the issue came to be settled, not by its own significance on the spot, but as an interlude in the wider problems of England.

VI   *The New Stage of 1845*

While this backstairs opposition was gathering force in England, Gipps was fighting his losing struggle in the colony, at times lulled to security by a false victory, but usually being borne down by adverse events. He thought that the publication of the *Sales Regulations* on 11 May had somewhat allayed the excitement, especially amongst the smaller squatters, but the financial weight of the larger and less reconcilable men forced the lesser fry to a new allegiance, and the effect of the *Committee's* report was to consolidate them all once more. Only one paper in Sydney, the *Herald*, supported the April *Regulations*, and even it was not consistent. The *Atlas* was raving the whole time, hiding its partisan unfairness beneath a real literary merit; the *Australian* had fallen to Benjamin Boyd during the crisis; and, in Port Phillip and the country-districts, the unity of the press was even more striking.

But Gipps fought on. He showed how self-interested the squatters were—how Benjamin Boyd had stated in public that all of his 380,000 acres of picked lands were his for all posterity, as long as he paid his £80 a year in licence-fees (though quit-rent alone, had they been granted him in fee-simple, would have been £3,175 a year!)—how one man, Walker of Willerowang, held 27 stations under a single licence and had no less than three million acres—how, at the most, even counting the land acquired as freehold as useless, his charges would not have taken more than £66. 13s. 4d. a year for 4,000 sheep—and how absurdly large the agitation was in comparison with the cause for it! He even showed that he was willing to modify his proposals—not so much because they were unjust or untoward in themselves, but as a concession to bad times and the intensity of the opposition. Gipps admitted that he may have chosen a bad moment to introduce the extra charges, and that it was not a wise policy to impose additional burdens on the staple industry when it had not recovered from drought and financial crisis; but he would not go so far as saying that he had been maliciously inclined towards the squatters or that his plans had been unsound at base.

His last views, as amended by the long agitation and the report of the *Squatting Committee*, were enclosed in a despatch of 9 September 1844. To give an impartial opinion, the Governor enclosed a *Minute* by Bishop Broughton, who had been in the colony for fifteen years and was one of the few persons in New South Wales who had no interest in sheep. Broughton (who, it should be added, was a personal friend of Gipps), rapidly disposed of the *Committee's* report. Emanating from a body every member of which belonged to the *Pastoral Association*, the report was at variance with facts, and its opinions were no more than bare assertions. Moreover, it offered no alternative scheme that would consider the Crown's rights, and thus was solely destructive. Gipps, he said in effect, had realized that no grazing system could be founded on the purchase of the soil, but, on the other hand, a system which involved no property-rights had already been shown to involve vast moral and social evils. The new *Regulations* surmounted both of these problems—they gave occupiers sufficient rights in their runs to secure the desired ends, and they were only equitable in making the larger man pay more than the smaller.

In this presentation, Gipps entirely concurred. He still favoured homesteads in fee-simple, and was prepared to acquiesce in preemption at a fixed figure (thus abandoning auction)—because he knew that he could not hope to gain his own views in the face of the opposition at home. 'Though I cannot take on myself the responsibility of recommending the measure, I am prepared to acquiesce in it.' He retained all of his earlier objections to long leases, he still thought the arguments against his proposals to limit areas frivolous, and he had come to believe that some fixed agistment (so long as it was determined by an Act of Parliament) was preferable to either rent or assessment. In other words, the investigations and agitations of the intervening six months had made him abandon most of the extreme parts of his earlier programme and accept the much wiser and practical aims he now enunciated—no long leases, pre-emption at a fixed rate, homesteads for all, fixed payments for the use of Crown lands, and fixed appropriation of the moneys so derived. By such a system, the squatters would obtain security and a reward for their efforts, while the Crown would still retain sufficient power to intervene in case of abuse and could still uphold the interests of later generations. But Gipps realized that the stream was passing over him: and all that he could do was to plead for a consideration of the common welfare (as apart from such sectional interests as those of the Council), and, in particular, to pray that the lands that were Australia's greatest gage for the future should not be locked up in the hands of a few hundred graziers whose motives had been so strikingly revealed by their actions of the preceding six months. On this high note, he closed his last appeal to Downing Street, and, the while, went back to encounter the reverses he was receiving in the colony.

In this spirit the new year—1845—ran its course in New South Wales. The outburst of the previous year had worked itself out. It had been so intense that it could not last very long without constant additional fuel; and, once the appeal had been made to the Colonial Office and the fight was on a wider front, the colonists relapsed into their usual groove. The new year, therefore, was reasonably quiet, although the opposition had in no sense abated. If anything, their claims became more absurd, but there was no longer the fevered unhealthiness of the early stages. It had become a settled part of their lives now, and not the all-absorbing passion of a moment.

Gipps's work was really finished. He could not make his views any clearer and could do no more with the Council under his existing powers. Tired of the ceaseless struggle and the lack of appreciation of his work, he was eagerly awaiting his recall. Six years was the normal period of a Governor's rule, and his term had expired on 23 February 1844—so that he was unrelievedly pleased when the packet *Graham* brought Earl Stanley's despatch of March 1845, announcing that he could come home with the full approbation of the Government. He received this news in August: ten days before, in opening the new session of Council, he delivered what was really his swan-song—showing how the colony had weathered the storm; how the general outlook had improved; how the exports of 1844 had for the first time exceeded the imports; how the decline in revenue had been more than met by a decreased expenditure; and how there was every prospect of improved prosperity.

A few weeks before, he had received Stanley's approval of his squatting *Regulations*, and, from then until January 1846, he was an old man, resting on his laurels—the fight, as far as he was concerned, over. What mattered it then, that the opposition rejoiced over his recall by what they termed a Colonial Office clerk, or that they parodied a ditty of the time and sang

> He has crouched to the Crown as to something divine,
> Till his fulsome compliance has sullied its shine:
> He has sought to perpetuate Wakefield's mad scheme
> Till an empty Exchequer has ended the dream:
> He has crippled our commerce, retarded our clips,
> But his days are now numbered—*Good-bye, Sir George Gipps!*

He knew that he had held the fort and that, even if the final settlement had not been reached, he could do no more.

The year thus passed. The squatters had been prepared for the worst in the matter of their appeal to Downing Street, because they were pinning their hopes not so much on winning over Stanley as in getting a new Minister. They knew, too, that further quarrels in the local Council would not help their cause at the moment. Consequently, their leaders dropped hints that the new session might be quiet if the Governor desired it, and he was sufficiently astute to make his opening speech conciliatory—a tone made the easier by the defeat of the extremist Archibald Boyd at Port Phillip. The colony was recovering from the agitations of 1844, primary industries were flourishing after the long crisis, and individuals were more tempted by Puseyism than politics.

Save for a few intrenchments on the Crown revenue, therefore, and a few more of the absurd claims that were now staled by repetition, the session passed quietly. The Council wanted renewed immigration, reduced charges—but these were old cries now. In November, rumours of Gipps's recall spread, and the reception of Stanley's Bill to confer leases roused the almost dead embers of opposition for a moment. But this was rejected by a House too uninterested to notice it, and the colonists thought Gipps so emphatic in his denial of responsibility for it that he must be speaking the truth: it was all a trick of that 'fiery ettercap', Stanley, 'the factious chiel' whose days were running out. Not even the publication of the comments Gipps had sent to England on the report of the Squatting Committee could arouse any energy. The papers were so hard pressed that they had to fall back on the French atrocities and the Jews, but the squatters scarcely noticed, because they were too busy making money and eschewing political agitation. Lowe, it is true, was somewhat noisily quarrelling with the Parramatta District Council, but nobody took any more notice of the fiery albino's tilts. The slumbrous quietness paralysed all public life, Gipps was more restrained and less actively unpopular, and the Council—'the Macquarie Street farce'—ended in November, without causing trouble over vital matters.

Everybody knew that the front was no longer in the colonies but behind the scenes at Downing Street. The whole tendency, as foreshadowed in Stanley's Bill, was towards a lease, and the colonists were more hopeful when Gladstone, who favoured their cause, replaced Stanley in December 1845. Gipps had recognized this no less than the squatters and, despite Stanley's support, had not carried the new Regulations into effect. He knew of the backstairs influences at home and resolved not to complicate matters further by premature actions in the colony! The Colonial Office had taken matters in their own hands while outwardly supporting him—very well, he argued in effect, he would await their decision! As soon as he received the approval of the Occupation Regulations (June), he published all the relevant documents and made a few changes favouring the squatters: but he acted more slowly in the matter of homesteads. The July despatches authorized him to act in this direction, but his numerous consultations with the Executive Council were still running their course, when news arrived of independent action by the Colonial Office and the proposed Bill for leases.

Nobody worried greatly over this delay, because the squatters did not want homesteads. They were not concerned with anything beyond a general safeguarding right of pre-emption which they could use if threatened, and were not at all anxious to spend money at the moment. When the draft of the proposed Bill arrived, therefore, nobody was averse to a stop being put to colonial action. Gipps at once suspended the Executive Council and contented himself with hastening the survey. The new Bill proposed seven-yearly leases without competition for the homesteads, but with auction for the rest of the runs. It was thus diametrically opposed to all that Gipps had fought for, in the way of purchase. Though realizing this, he made a last plea in January 1846 for his old homestead idea, urging it concurrently with the scheme advocated at home. If they *would* give grazing leases for seven years, despite his advice, let them at least safeguard the Crown rights to some degree, and make the squatter buy his homestead at auction! But matters had long since passed this stage. The co-partnership of Gipps and Stanley was several stages past in the negotiations: now, Gladstone and the squatters were at the helm in Downing Street, and it would appear as if they were devoting all their plans in 1846 to upsetting everything for which Gipps had stood.

Gipps soon realized this and, in a confidential despatch of 12 January 1846, foretold the new state of crisis that must inevitably arise in the colony in the coming year. The postponement of the English Act would mean that he must call the Council and ask them to renew the hated *Squatting Act* for one more year: and he knew they would not do this, and that, once assessment and the dependent police went, the Crown would have no power beyond the boundaries. It was all very well for the English Act to take over the situation, but at least the executive on the spot had the right to expect that Parliament would either expedite its passage or do something to enable the Government to survive the interim in the colony. As it was, their changes left Gipps, discredited and powerless, to face the freshly recalcitrant squatters in the Council. Hence the quite different atmosphere in 1846 and the last bitter session of Council before Gipps left. He was already long overdue, but he could not expect his successor of the ducal House of Grafton to hurry; and so there was the last dreg of bitterness, with the Opposition, now supported at home, humiliating him on the eve of his departure for all of their pent-up reverses of the past. The Colonial Office had betrayed him, and the gods had played him a scurvy trick in leaving him so completely in the hands of his enemies.

The public had not expected that Gipps would have to face a new session, but the expiry of the *Squatting Act* forced him to convene the Council in May. Of course, they refused to renew the *Squatting Act*, every elected member voting against it, and Lowe, in particular, making a ringing speech that defied the Governor to broadcast his writs throughout the colony and try to eject the massed squatters. 'That Sir, is a struggle from which Englishmen never shirk. It is a struggle in which they have never been beaten. If your Excellency thinks the prerogative sufficient for your purposes, try its power, and we shall be prepared to contest it!'[23]

The opposition, it was said, came together disunited and full of mutual mistrust, but Gipps forced them into harmony by emphasizing the only matter they held in common. Partly true, this statement is mainly beside the point, because Gipps clearly had to consult the Council and at least try and secure their consent. They had previously complained of Stanley's 'most insolent despatch' in rejecting their extreme demands, but now they forwarded the following *Address* to the Governor—and it cannot be deemed either modest or tactful! They rejected the new Act, they said

1st. Because we are not disposed to continue summary powers which have been used to support a claim to tax by prerogative alone, the validity of which we, as the representatives of the people, can never recognize.

2nd. Because Your Excellency has repeatedly held that Her Majesty is the absolute owner of the Waste Lands of this territory, and that her prerogative is sufficient for their management, proposals which, if true, render the interference of this Council unnecessary.

3rd. Because we do not feel justified in imposing any particular tax upon the squatters, so long as Your Excellency claims in the name of Her Majesty a right to tax them to any extent you may think proper.

4th. Because the powers conferred by this Act of the Commissioners of Crown Lands are most arbitrary and unconstitutional.

5th. Because these Acts were passed with the understanding that the licence-fee should not be increased—an understanding which had been disregarded by Your Excellency in the regulations of April 2, 1844, and in subsequent despatches and regulations.

6th. Because Your Excellency's new regulations were made without consulting this Council, and have been carried out in spite of its most earnest remonstrances.[24]

Gipps refused to reply to this *Address*, saying that its 'studied discourtesy' placed it outside the pale. The Speaker presented it, and the Governor was said to reply:

I am happy to say that this is an Address which requires no reply, nor do I intend to give any. I thought it right to give the Council the opportunity of passing the Bill, if they thought fit. Perhaps I thought they would not pass it, and they have not; but I do not see why, on that account, responsibility should be cast on me.

[23] *Atlas*, 6 February 1846.
[24] *Votes and Proceedings*, 1846, vol. I, p. 37: *Atlas*, 16, 30 May 1846: for documents, Gipps-Gladstone, 25, 29 June 1846.

Somewhat discomfited, the Speaker withdrew with Windeyer and Lowe, who had been responsible for the *Address*, and returned to the Chamber to devise other schemes of upsetting the Governor. They were sufficiently astute to see how Gipps's rudeness had aided them. The Attorney-General explained it away by saying that even Governors have feelings, but the *Sydney Morning Herald*, Tory as it usually was, demurred against this human fallibility and insisted that, since the *Address* was concerned with vital matters of land administration and the protection of life and property in the interior, it *did* require an answer, Gipps to the contrary!

This took place on 9 June. The same day, Gipps sent down the financial *Minute* for the year, and Wentworth gave notice that he would adjourn the next day until 21 July—until Gipps left. In a word, the Council refused to have anything more to do with the Governor. On the 13th, the *Sydney Morning Herald* ironically suggested that perhaps Gipps would save the Council the trouble of adjourning by proroguing it! Next day, in a *Government Gazette Extraordinary*, he did!

Of all of this episode, Gipps's despatches, written almost while he was packing, give a very incomplete account. He barely relates the events and says nothing of the motives or results of his actions. Perhaps the fact that Gladstone had replaced Stanley may have had something to do with it—but, however this may be, Gipps's attitude is of giving casual official summaries to someone who cannot be expected to know what it is all about and who cannot be interested in what is primarily a personal struggle between the Governor and his adversaries. In the despatch, for instance, he baldly states the fact of prorogation, without hinting how it would checkmate the Opposition. All that he wrote was that he welcomed the adjournment, because it had given him an excuse for prorogation—that he would extend it if necessary—that the Opposition (though this sounds extremely unlikely) did not expect such a rapid move—and that the events of the preceding six weeks had left him as strong as ever.

Having prevented the Council from functioning, Gipps turned to the matter of licences. The Commissioners and the Border Police, of course, had to go, now that there was no law to authorize them; but the licences and fees would go on as before. The Commissioners could not settle disputes between occupiers, they could not call for returns of stock, and they could not remove intruders: but the fact remained that it was still unlawful to occupy Crown Lands without a licence—though no powers existed for enforcing this. Gipps, however, still clung to the prerogative and announced on 30 June that any squatter not paying his licence fee as before would be viewed as an intruder! The position was absurd. The law said they had to pay £10, but each squatter could please himself, because there was no power to compel him—no officials or police whose powers ran beyond the boundaries![25]

With this parting shot, Gipps left the colony on the *Palestine* on 11 July 1846—his enemies dumbfounded, the Council still in prorogation, the Commissioners still exercising many of their functions, the Act of Parliament not passed, and with his own dramatic actions surrounding him with a general atmosphere of triumph. But all of this implied a corresponding increase of his own unpopularity. The Council, on 12 June, had gravely debated Windeyer's motion to thank the Queen for the recent changes in the Colonial Office, incidentally linking Gipps with Stanley in their abuse; and even the City Council—Gipps's 'own pet bantling'—refused to vote him an *Address*. On his sailing day, the *Atlas*, Lowe's paper, sped him in these words:

This day is one likely to be memorable in the annals of New South Wales —for it is the day on which His Excellency Sir George Gipps leaves our shores for ever. After eight long years of despotism and mis-government, the incubus that sat so heavily on us is removed, and we can breathe freely once more. We have often said, and what is more, have often proved, that Sir George Gipps is not only the worst Governor that we ever had, but the worst that could possibly have been selected—and that assertion we now deliberately, but not maliciously, nor sorrowfully, repeat!

Even the Conservative *Sydney Morning Herald*, generally a Government supporter, repeated in italics that Gipps was the worst Governor the colony had ever had—'a blind guide, straining at a gnat and swallowing a camel'—and repeated this, *verbatim*, in another issue lest any of its readers had failed to see it! To the queries whether he had been impartial, or actuated by good intentions, it gave a decided negative.[26]

Thus Gipps, ill and broken in the colony's service, was sped on his way! On that Saturday morning in July 1846, Sydney was *en fête* with joy at Gipps's departure. All the Government offices and most trading places shut at eleven, and the Governor was escorted to the wharf by a guard of honour and the band of the 11th Regiment. Awaiting him there, the 99th were drawn up, and a hundred men

[25] Gipps-Gladstone, 30 June 1846.
[26] *Atlas*, 11 July 1846: *Herald*, 3 July 1846, repeated three days later.

of each regiment formed a red-jacketed lane for him, from Government House to the stairs of the Customs House. An address of some 5,800 signatures was given him by Darvall, and sadly he held his last *levée*, and left the wharf with the Chief Justice and the loyal old Deas Thomson, and those who had assembled to do him honour. The crowd cheered him on leaving his house, and once or twice by the road, and again as the boat left the wharf, for it was their rights he had upheld against the squatters! Gipps entered, and, as the barge shoved off, nineteen guns boomed out from Macquarie Fort, and another salvo sounded from H.M.S. *Castor* as she rounded the point. The eastern side of the cove was thickly dotted with people making holiday, and innumerable rowing and sailing boats flaunted their colours, none knew whether in derision or honour! Soon, the smaller craft dropped away, then, some miles out, the *Thistle* and two venturous yachts fell back, with a last cheer; and by sunset, the *Palestine* was hull down from South Head, and the Governorship of the broken invalid who had gone aboard was over. The fitful sunshine of that cold, wintry day had turned to a leaden greyness—and Gipps wondered contemplatively of it all—of human nature and human endeavours; and turned below, his broken body and seething mind both in protest. The day of Sir George Gipps had obviously gone down in a chilly greyness—and only the chill was to remain for him.

Perhaps he went over that struggle in retrospect on the long voyage round the Horn, and read the estimates the colonists placed on him—read Forster's satire on *The Devil and the Governor*, or the version of the *Atlas:*

> Such, oh such, art thou, oh! Gipps!
> Never resting, ever toiling,
> Ne'er repenting, ever sinning—
> Meddling still, and still embroiling,
> Fighting oft but never winning.
> Ah! the flaws of head and heart,
> Making up the thing thou art;
> Tinsel reason, boorish wit,
> Still to graze but scarce to hit.

> Shallow judgment, flippant style,
> Artless art and guileless guile,
> Which had given thee note and vogue
> As a smartish pedagogue,
> Or had raised thee from the dark,
> As a pettish kind of clerk!

Perhaps he thought of the desertion of the *Sydney Morning Herald* and of the Council's attitude in that last impossible session. He may have recalled his despondent suggestion to suspend the constitution for ten years and revert to the old non-representative Council, until the people should have shown themselves politically educated in some way or other. All the humiliation of defeat preyed on him in those eventless months, and he may have gone over the old fights again, this time altering his moves and with his later actions less querulous, less personally bitter, and more tolerant.

Certainly, they could not have been pleasant months, and he landed in England a broken man. Though the Colonial Office at once consulted him, he felt that he belonged to the past—and was not yet ready to forget that, when he was fighting, back to the wall, at the Antipodes, it was this same Colonial Office which had refused to support him and had played into the hands of his enemies. He realized that he may have come down somewhat from the pedestal of magisterial aloofness which he had occupied before the middle of 1845—but one does not wage war in a spirit of philosophical calmness, and he thought, not so much of his own failings as of the lack of support he had received from England. Nevertheless, he advised the new Secretary of State, Earl Grey, on the drafting of the *Order in Council* of March 1847, though this meant the reversal of everything for which he had stood. He was trying to lighten the blow given to Australia and to minimize the locking of the land to which the leases must lead. Finally, the *Order* was issued, in Grey's words 'after obtaining the approbation of Sir George Gipps, than whom no one had on this subject a more accurate and extensive knowledge, or a sounder judgment'.

This completed—this sop given in his defeat—Gipps was offered and accepted the command of the Royal Engineer Department of the Tower Hamlets, but, on the eve of assuming command, died suddenly, at Canterbury, at the age of fifty-six. Heart disease had found him out, aggravated by the strain of administration in New South Wales and the consequent neurasthenia. The man who had tried to introduce an Imperialistic idealism into the Australia of the forties had gone—almost, the outside observer might say, in a pathetic anti-climax, but really with his integrity and wisdom justified more than in the heat of conflict. He had striven for the future, and he had died in harness—defeated perhaps, but rising to a certain greatness in his adversity, and with history reversing the judgment and giving him a place none of his colonial contemporaries could aspire to have in the history of Australia.

9

LEASES AND THE LOCKING OF THE LAND

I have no doubt (said the gentleman in Downing Street to his Under-Secretary) you will get through the business very well, Mr. Hoaxem, particularly if you be *frank and explicit*: that is the right line to take when you wish to conceal your own mind and to confuse the minds of others.

Disraeli, *Sybil.*

WHILE GIPPS WAS FACING the tumult in the colony, Lord Stanley had replaced Lord John Russell when Melbourne's Ministry fell before Peel's attack in 1841. Stanley, fortunately for Governor Gipps, had a decisive, if somewhat highly strung, personality. *Autolycus Hotspur*, as Aubrey de Vere called him, was a brilliant gladiator of debate and a very convinced young man with views on everything. His inconsequential brilliance was a perfect foil to the loose pomposity of Peel. But, while his restless, impulsive oratory marked him out at once, he would sacrifice everything to effect. He was said to dispense with actual knowledge, because he was so dexterous in debate that he could get all he wanted from his opponents! Hence the speciousness of his eloquence and the lucid inconsistency of his position. It was commonly thought that he was too clever to be trusted—*he is a boy, and a spoilt boy*, said the *Examiner* of 11 October, 1845, *and will never be other than a spoilt boy, were he to live to the age of Methuselah.*

Yet, his impudence and impetuosity to the contrary, he was obstinate enough once he had made up his mind; and it was this side of his character that was most felt in Australian affairs. He certainly brought order into Australian administration and adhered to his opinions in the face of opposition. It was Stanley who gave the general plans—he passed the *Government Act* of 1842, he secured the first general land act for all Australia, he aided decentralization in colonial government, and he proposed the very elaborate system of convict punishment known as *the five stages*. He may have been brusque and challenging and dictatorial, but it needed the vagueness and circumlocutory evasion of a Gladstone at the Colonial Office to demonstrate the utility of any positive standpoint.[1]

[1] *London Examiner*, 11 October 1845: *Times*, 13 June 1846: *Colonial Gazette*, 4 January 1845, or G. H. Taylor, *Autobiography* (1885), vol. I, p. 330.

Aiding him were the permanent officials, at this time under the control of Mr *Over-Secretary Stephen*—James Stephen, who had remained untouched by the passage of a succession of Secretaries. In reality, however, the clerk in charge of the given local affairs decided matters unless some principle was involved. The Australian clerk was one Gardiner, beloved of colonial cartoonists. He usually doubled one corner of a despatch and referred the answer to the Under-Secretary, who was practically the *ultima linea rerum*. The Secretary of State would usually interfere only when some outside agitation reached Parliament: and then, as with the squatting issue, he would have to cram himself with all the relevant despatches. Then, through the Under-Secretary and the unknown clerk, the matter would filter through to the Governor. On the way, the Board of outside experts set up in 1840 to supersede the Colonization Commissioners of South Australia—the Colonial Land and Emigration Commissioners—would exert as much influence as they could. These three—Torrens, Elliot, and Villiers—were convinced Wakefieldians and could always be depended upon for a mass of theoretical arguments. By this tortuous channel, the details of colonial administration were arranged in the forties, usually, as with Gipps's squatting *Regulations*, some year and four months after they had been sent! It was admitted that lumbering bureaucracy held sway there, but no protest seemed to prevail. Buller had moved an antagonistic motion in the Commons in 1845; Sir Edward Cust's pamphlets had shown the evils of the system; Saxe Bannister's fugitive writings were repeatedly making their points; and the weight of Roebuck was felt at intervals in the House. But the old system groaned on, and was enlivened only by Stanley's brusque interventions.

It will readily be evident, under these conditions, how the viewpoints of Gipps would survive only up to the point at which the theories of Park Street Commissioners and the outside influence of the squatters' capitalistic friends entered—and it was precisely in these two directions that Gipps lost. This explains why, although Gipps's squatting *Regulations* were approved, the Colonial Office went on at the same time to introduce a *Bill* setting up a quite different system. The confirmation of Gipps's plans meant the grinding official side, the new set marked the effect of the outside influences.

At first, it appeared as if Stanley would support the Governor. He had, of course, consulted the Colonial Land and Emigration Commissioners. But all that they suggested, instead of Gipps's idea to leave the squatters undisturbed for eight years, was to give them security for that term—*a licence!* Thus, baldly and casually, they proposed eight-yearly leases—the first official mention of such a scheme![2]

Stanley concurred in their ideas, except that he would not make the idea of a lease compulsory. He signified his cordial approval and left the matter for the Governor's discretion. He was studiously polite to Gipps, honouring his sense of duty in issuing the *Regulations* ('a step which you could easily have avoided taking'), and was conscious of 'their justice and propriety', although his own prepossessions were in favour of the gentlemanly squatters. Between the lines is clearly a castigation of Gipps for having needlessly raised the question! As opposed to this, he resisted the general arguments of the extreme squatters. There is, there can be, no question of the Government's *right* to issue such *Regulations*—he said—however much their reasonableness and timeliness may be questioned.

With the Commissioners, therefore, he could see nothing wrong with the *Occupation Regulations*—it was absurd to protest against a licence fee of £10, because, if anything suffered under the scheme, it was the interests of the general public, and not the squatters! About the *Purchase Regulations*, he was not so certain. He realized the evils of the existing system and he felt that the squatter had to have his improvements; but, as against these, there were the rights of the Crown. The principle of giving freehold for the improved sections and compensation for improvements, he fully concurred in; but, perhaps, it would be better to leave the details of execution to Gipps! With this last evasion, he followed the Commissioner in approving *en bloc* of both sets of *Regulations*, and closed his strange analysis with some florid remarks about his duty to the Empire and his sacred trust!

These long-delayed despatches, finally sent off on the *Bussorah Merchant* on 30 January 1845, were amazing documents. Stanley needed only one printed page to dispose of the *Purchase Regulations*; he made no attempt to discuss details; and he gave no indication that he realized what was implied in the homestead scheme or the auction plan or the proposals as a whole. The answers to Gipps show how far the English authorities were from realizing the facts of the situation, or from measuring the issues involved, or estimating the difficulties of the Governor's position. Their views were circumscribed by their indignation at the Council's presumption in questioning Crown rights, and they would accept anything as long as the old Wakefield theories remained intact. But, as they always had a strong capitalist bias in Park Street, they were not averse to helping

[2] In Stanley-Gipps, 30 January 1845.

the large squatters, to whom they proposed to yield millions of acres. Little wonder that Gipps marvelled even in his triumph—for they gave the squatters all they wanted—*and a lease in addition!*

But this was not the end. Stanley was now thinking of settling the matter by an *Act of Parliament*, and he wrote to the various Governors in August 1845, announcing his plans. He had wanted to legislate in the previous session, but had awaited the reports of the local Committee and the numerous discussions with interested persons. Thus, velvet hands in London were veering the Colonial Office towards the idea of a long lease; and the *Bill* of Under-Secretary Hope meant a solution quite different from that of Gipps. It meant turning to the remedies proposed by the interested squatters—or rather, by those financiers in London who had controlled the destinies of the colony since the introduction of the English trust companies. Five days after Gipps wrote his moderate paean of triumph and related how the accession of the reserves afforded by Stanley's despatch had enabled him to re-establish his front line intact, Stanley sent his new factor—the draft of Hope's *Bill*.[3]

The original *Bill* had aimed only at removing any doubt as to the Crown's ability to grant leases and had authorized a fixed agistment for all stock depastured; but the report of the *Squatting Committee* had arrived in the interim and the *Bill* was amended in the light of all this fresh evidence. It thus came to propose leases, without auction, for seven years, the general idea being to make the Crown Lands productive without infringing the Sales Act. Stanley again mentioned that he had been swayed by interviews with gentlemen connected with Australia; and obviously, a clasp of the hand was worth more than a screed from the bush. These gentlemen had told him that Gipps's *Regulations* would fall to the ground because the squatters had not sufficient money to make use of them; and, in commiseration, Stanley obligingly murmured that he would not be averse to leases of *up to twenty-one years!* But the squatters themselves were loth to run the risks of the auction room. They saw the immediate risk rather than the ultimate security, and so accepted Stanley's alternative idea of seven-yearly leases *without* auction.

The amazing and quite unexpected change in the squatting problem was at once accepted by the Colonial Land and Emigration Commissioners. Indeed, they had been reconsidering the matter since January. Early in August, they had reiterated their support of Gipps's proposals, but since then a great mass of evidence had reached

3 Stanley-Gipps, 7 August 1845.

England, and, in particular, ran their report,[4] *they had communicated with returned flockmasters* and were only beginning to realize the difficulties of the problem. In view of this, the gist of their advice to Stanley was to retract his former affirmation and do nothing!

The Commissioners still did not believe that £10 to run 4,000 sheep was excessive but, rather than any local charge, favoured a fixed agistment irrespective of area, imposed by an act of Parliament —the solution Grey had adopted in South Australia. As for the *Purchase Regulations*, squatters, so far from viewing them as a boon, were protesting against such an unprofitable expenditure of capital; and it was not possible to deny their plaints. Some experts said that 1,000 sheep gave £400 profit, others less than £100, and each case was so local that profits could not be averaged. But they could pay at neither rate, and the only certain fact was that all squatters opposed the *Purchase Regulations*.

To overcome this, the Commissioners were insistent on the proposal for a lease—an idea which they again claimed as their own![5] But they had not reckoned on the force of local opposition. Gipps and La Trobe both opposed it, and not five of Gipps's fourteen Commissioners returned a favourable answer. The Commissioners, therefore, advised Stanley to halt, here too, and make no specific promise. In all, they proposed the principles of Hope's *Bill*, leaving a discretion to Gipps to have either a fixed payment on the stock or one on the land—to continue his *Occupation Regulations* if he pleased— and to see if his views on the *Purchase Regulations* were modified— surely an excellent hint to drop them.[6]

Stanley concurred in this advice and asked Gipps's opinion on the issues at stake, because the threatened expiry of the local *Squatting Act* was looming nearer and nearer. He made it clear that he thought homesteads without runs were useless, and once more asked if Gipps would approve of leases over the whole run for seven years? The drift was clearly towards leases over whole runs, with no homestead and no auction, but a safeguarding right of pre-emption over the whole—and the Governor was asked to conform or (as the very reiteration of the suggestions indicated) be overridden.

Gipps, deserted even by the Conservative Government, realized

[4] Enclosed in Stanley-Gipps, 8 August 1845.

[5] Boyd had first suggested a lease at the meeting of April 1944, and the London meeting had embodied it in their memorial to Stanley on 26 May 1845.

[6] Stanley-Gipps, private and confidential, 31 August 1845.

that he could do no more. He replied on 10 January 1846 that he always had two ideas in view—to give the squatters homesteads in fee-simple and to avoid giving long leases. He even *italicized* this latter point—a most unusual thing in despatches. But he saw that he was defeated and admitted, after repeating his full condemnation of the lease idea:

I think it right and freely to say that I think the time is now arrived when the granting of them must be conceded. It is scarcely necessary for me to add that I greatly prefer leases of seven years to leases of any other period. I believe I may pretty safely assert that a Lease for 21 years would in New South Wales be, in the great majority of cases, a lease for ever.

And that was exactly what happened!

His old homestead scheme was dying hard, and he still fought for it.

The scheme for the sale of homesteads was brought forward by a sincere desire to confer a boon upon the squatters, and only remotely or contingently as a means of increasing the revenue of the Crown. It has, with some degree of adroitness, been turned into an attempt to compel persons to purchase lands which they do not want; and I therefore am well satisfied to find that it will, under Mr. Hope's *Bill*, form no necessary part of the system to be established.

Moreover, he had yet to hear of any alternative means of fostering the growth of villages or even of durable dwellings!

By this time, Stanley had gone (Gladstone had succeeded him in the previous month), and Gipps was preparing to go. Gipps's homestead plan now belonged to the limbo of past discards, the squatters had won the Colonial Office, the lease was a definite proposal, and Australia was entering the period of land monopoly. The squatters had turned the corner and the officials were offering them the land—and every time opposition occurred (as in England in 1846) Scott was able to organize the wealthy and aristocratic friends of the squatters and call forth his phalanxes of Edens and Eliots and Trevylvans—and on such names depended the fate of Empires! But now, Gladstone had gone as he had come, after seven months of uncertain liberalism. He was connected with the Victorian squatters through his cousin and namesake (who was a partner in a squatting run) and so was not averse to aiding their cause.[7] He was supposed to be too immersed in divinity to descend to sublunary matters at this stage, but, though his despatches breathed an air of turgid metaphysics, his actions were sufficiently concise.

[7] Correspondence in Hogan's *Robert Lowe* (1893), pp. 68-71.

Thus, when Earl Grey followed him in July 1846, the tendency was well-defined. The squatters wanted leases, fixed by an Act of Parliament—and two Secretaries of State had already worked in this direction. Earl Grey was that Lord Howick who had proposed a minimum price of £2 an acre to the South Australian Committee and was an inflexible Wakefieldian. Very able and a terrific worker, he was too scrupulously rigid and too clear-cut in his conceptions. But such qualities at once produced order out of the chaos of the various *Bills* and rushed the Australian leases to their conclusion. A few months after his accession to office in November 1846, he settled the matter with the new Governor. Using enormously long sentences to write all round the problem, he devoted most of his space to a defence of the high price of land, but there was so much theory and so little practice that it was all very difficult to understand! Once delivered of his favourite theory, however, he went on to admit that, since wool was the great Australian staple, the *sheep and cattle farmers* (to such had the squatters degenerated!) should be given every opportunity. Two things he abhorred—alienation below the existing purchase price, and the yearly tenure that banned improvements. This being so he naturally turned to long leases.[8]

Descending to practical details, he enclosed the Act passed in the session that had just closed *(9-10 Vic. c. civ.)*.[9] This proposed leases of not more than fourteen years, with compensation for all improvements. But Grey was still hesitant about the actual regulations. He had communicated with the various squatters then in England and was awaiting the return of Gipps, but, in the interim, authorized the Governor to classify the land into three districts—*the unsettled lands* (with leases for fourteen years); *the intermediate lands* (with leases for eight years); and the *settled districts* (where only yearly licences would be allowed). It was all very confusing. In one part, he said that leases could be for not more than fourteen years, implying variations below that level; in another, not less than fourteen years, adding distinctly that the Crown could not interfere before that date. He had the same uncertainty about the intermediate belt—the whole despatch, indeed, was very unbusinesslike. Not content with giving away Australia's lands, Grey could not even say what he meant— and thus involved the colonies in endless litigation and the tying up of much extra land. But, after all, the distended phraseology was

---

[8] Grey-FitzRoy, 29 November 1846: *Atlas*, 28 November 1846.

[9] Documents are in N.S.W. *Votes and Proceedings*, 1847, vol. I (including a summary of *all* land-regulations since 1831). The *Order-in-Council* of 9 March 1847, was enclosed in Grey-FitzRoy, 30 March 1847.

only an aggravation: the real evil lay in the cession of long leases.
The germ so idly cast forth by the Colonial Land and Emigration
Commissioners three years before had certainly sprung into a lusty
life, and hereafter Australian history came to be written in terms of
monopoly, blocking up the land, squattocracy, and the like.

It only remained to introduce the leases to the colony. There, a
vitally different hand was now in control. The man who had taken
two years and four months to relieve Gipps was continuing his reputation. Sir Charles FitzRoy was the scion of three ducal houses—that
was the only positive thing about him. Accomplished in the art of
doing nothing, he avoided the pitfalls that would have entrapped a
more active man. Caring nothing for the colony, he let it go its own
way, as long as he could get somebody else to do everything for him.
A junior clerk wrote his despatches, his speeches were a symposium
from scribbling subordinates, and he yielded to men of colonial
experience in every step. He had no opinions, left everything to the
Council and his officials, and, as was said, glided over all obstacles by
a combination of urbane temper and the impartiality of indifference.
His indolence was far too complete for him to interfere in politics.
To Lowe's request for his views on squatting, he replied that *he
hadn't any!* He introduced Grey's system and nonchalantly sat back
to let the squatters get rich, or the land be alienated, or anything else
happen! It was all on a par to him!

The colony was, therefore, very quiet in the last part of 1846,
because everybody was awaiting the leases. When news came in
November, nobody was quite certain about the project—even the
squatters failed to see how they were to gain and were still inclined
to look for the hand of Gipps and Broughton. Only one voice was
raised in aggressive clarity—that of Lowe, who had quarrelled with
the squatters and was fighting for the people. Wentworth and Boyd
were now his arch-enemies, and his fiery invective was directed
against 'two or three sheepholders who may have the temerity to set
all law and right at defiance'! He argued that he had opposed Gipps
because the constitution was ignored and taxes levied arbitrarily.
But, he went on, squatters were no longer oppressed under FitzRoy,
and, indeed, the few now threatened the many. He opposed the
partition of Australia for 'the inheritance of a few shepherd-kings',
for such men as Boyd with his 200,000 sheep. The new leases meant
undue concessions to a few capitalists and a locking of the land. A
difference of conduct under circumstances that had changed was not
an abandonment of principle, he went on; and, from September 1846,
he swung round so that he was working with Macdermott, whom

he had once refused to fight, and with the people, whom he had hitherto condemned. The *Sydney Morning Herald* reported that he loved effect like a stage-performer and that he would rather delight than profit, rather startle than delight![10]

Yet never in his Australian experience was he on so high a note as that sounded in his *Address to the Colonists of New South Wales on the Proposed Land Orders*, in which his words rang like a warning of someone who had seen the future:

Once grant these leases, and beyond the settled districts there will be no land to be sold—the lessees will have a right to hold their lands until someone will give £1 an acre for them. . . . Be the capabilities of these lands what they may, *they are to be a sheepwalk for ever!* . . . The squatter may make sure of his run at the end of his lease by buying up, in the exercise of his pre-emptive right, all the water-frontage, thus rendering it valueless to anyone except himself. . . . The price he has to pay for these privileges, counting three sheep to an acre, is a fifth of a penny per acre. Thus does a Government which is so niggard of its land that it will not part with the fee-simple of the most barren rock for less than £1 an acre, while that £1-an-acre-law remains in force, alienate millions of acres at a tenth of the rent which it received on its free-grants. The system devised for the protection of the waste-lands will end in their confiscation! (1847).

But the evil was done, and, as a *bonne bouche* for the New Year, news came in December of the passage of the Act that was to yield the land to the squatters in leases that were to prove unbreakable. Three months later, in March 1847, Grey was to issue the famous *Order-in-Council*, carrying out the principles of the Act; and the land was locked up. One stage of Australian squatting had ended: the pioneers had become a monopolistic minority: and the cause of progress had shifted to the immigrants landing from the lumbering old packet-ships and crying for land on which to settle. That day of 7 October 1847, which saw the proclamation of the *Order-in-Council* in the colony, was the last occasion when Australia's land-problems could have been attacked with something like justice to all sections. But once the *Order* was in force in every colony in Australia, it was impossible to put the clock back—monopoly had entered and could not be banished at notice, or indeed, at all. Earl Grey and those who had departed from Gipps had saddled Australia with an incubus that could not be shaken off, a problem that could not be solved—and the country has been paying ever since.

[10] Contrast *Sydney Morning Herald*, 15 September 1846, and *Atlas*, 3 October 1846.

10

THE SQUATTING LIFE

I The Town Background

To ANY IMMIGRANT arriving in the colony in the thirties, the experience was very similar. After a terrible buffeting of anything over four months from the English port, the sailing vessel, now thick-barnacled, would cautiously pass between the Heads, veer around the Sow-and-Pigs and then the hoary stones of Pinchgut, until an irregular township loomed on the left—Sydney. It was a town scattered over the hilly coves, with narrow, twisting streets and a skyline broken by numerous windmills. The houses, most of them cottages with gardens in front (for Sydney had few two-storied buildings till 1850), seemed clustered round on terraces or jutting promontories; and the only large erections were the military barracks right in the centre of the town and the huge Government offices of sandstone.

Pulled in at the wharf, the vessel was greeted by a mixed collection which might have stepped from a music-hall stage—villainous convicts—*canaries* in their appropriately sallow garb; poor settlers—*dungaree-men* in the cheapest of blue cotton from India; and, of course, the *cornstalks*, the lean, dishevelled *currency urchins* indigenous to the colony, and either tipsy or enlivening matters with a few brickbats. Perhaps a tattoo of the drums and fifes could be heard from the barracks—indeed, the military touch would be evident throughout, for officials were everywhere—for immigration control, landing, inspection, customs, police purposes, and several other reasons, and each naturally required the prestige of military sentries. The expectant immigrant, waiting with his carpet bag and elaborately bound sea chest, must have wondered at the clutter and fuss and military pomp—and still retaining his home reticence, would probably already have noticed the dram-drinking propensities of the colonists and the lewdness of the viragos who made every boat day a holiday, and the free bartering of men and women for immoral purposes, both on and off the boat. Even to a bewildered newcomer, it was soon evident that here was a world in which the old moral values, and even the secrecies called for by decency, seemed to have disappeared.

Once ashore the emigrant found his astonishment increasing. A *Wapping or St Giles in the beauties of a Richmond*—the standards of a gaol and a brothel mixed in a beautifully fresh environment, it was all incongruous. Reason might argue that this was a growing colony: but, at first, any observant newcomer must have been amazed at the contradictions offered by a convict metropolis—at the conditions in the centre of the colony. The people were so different— our average emigrant would realize that somewhere there was a Government House and somewhere merchants and lawyers and upper classes, but, rambling round the badly-lit hill-streets, he would see a collection which could only have come from a pipe-dreamer's idea of a seaman's *Lusatia*.

The redcoats and the *currency lads* were always quarrelling, the latter sticking clannishly in hives and forming the *pushes* of the time: while all alike joined with the convicts in going to the grog-houses which were then plastered thickly over the city. *Dram drinking*—taking the rum neat from wine glasses—struck the outsider more than any other single fact. Everybody drank the execrable Bengal rum, and all, even the women, smoked good old Brazil twist in *dudeens* or clay pipes sometimes scarcely half an inch long. In the lower districts, and especially along the steep ridge above the King's Wharf, the worst characters joined in unrestrained excess. Above the wharf was a kind of Limehouse, where, at places like *The Sheer Hulk* and *The Black Dog*, was to be found the refuse of a settlement in itself a sink for England's refuse—sailors, prostitutes, fences, drunken shepherds, and all the flotsam of a convict settlement.[1] Inns like *The Market House*, beyond the rail fence of the market yard, were comparatively decent, but, even there, one seemed to enter a *Thieves' Paradise*. Some of the motley crew wore the typical blue jacket of the English *lagger*, others short woollen frocks or even blue smocks, and still others the popular fustian jacket; and hat fashions ranged from straw-beavers to kangaroo skins; but the indisputable sign of a democrat was his footgear—not one workman in an average inn wore either stocking or sock! All that they were concerned with was in eradicating any freeman from England who dared to enter

---

[1] A good account of first impressions is in A. Harris's *Settlers and Convicts* (1847; republished 1964); a book dealing with the thirties and far more important than its unprententious exterior would indicate. It is a good account of colonial vicissitudes and squatting life, as seen by an observant mechanic— an unusual angle.

their *lagging* confraternity and claim the privileges of the initiated. Above that, they joined in discussing the iniquity of preventing illicit distilling in a community where 5s. a gallon was demanded for rum wholesale—and 6s. for brandy, and 4s. for gin!

Another stratum of society was encountered when one left the inns for the market place. King's Wharf, on the seaward end of the promontory, was the usual mooring place for sea-going vessels; but on the opposite landward side, lay the market wharf, whence came the produce of the settlers down the smaller rivers, and even the goods from the coastal boats, though these latter usually carried cedar from the timbered flats. On the high ground just above, next the long barrack wall, was the market proper—a walled paddock with old sheds disguised as stalls; and here the settlers were found. Usually, they were miserably poor, eking out a precarious existence on the poor land this side of the mountains and inveighing against *the lordly* men who had monopolized the Hunter and the Government that listened only to capitalists. All of them—even wives and children—were clad in the blue dungaree that was quite as distinguishing a mark as the canary cloth of the felon; and all of them huckstered with a little wheat, a few vegetables, and the bundles of coarse green grass that took the place of hay in the colony. So poor were they that it was quite a rule of their lives to sell their wheat and live on *dough-boy* made of maize and, at times, a little salt beef— a luxury costing five guineas a tierce, and rivalled by Irish pork, which worked out at four guineas a barrel. Most of these small men —who were really labourers on the land—felt no ambition. For them, the squatting problem did not exist (save to offer the safety-valve of a shepherd's life at £10 a year!), and even the lands beyond the mountains or on the northern rivers were beyond their ken. A poor, struggling lot, they were giving little to Australia—they, and their bark huts, and large families, and peasant-like existence!

Turning away from the market yard, past the barracks again, one found the streets (even Pitt Street had cottages with gardens in front in 1839!), with their two very different classes of workmen and merchants. The labourers, in 1835, were very disgusted. Those who were freemen found themselves cold-shouldered by the convicts and emancipists, and all alike were sceptical of the colony and its future. The papers were speaking of the new interior and immigrants were being deluded by the glowing tales of wages that were said to apply; but the small man in the Australia of this time had a hard lot. Work was very difficult to obtain in the city, and freemen were loth to go into the bush and doubly loth to lower themselves to the *hatter's* occupation of shepherding—convicts' preserve as that was. Skilled men could be absorbed, though even the best turner and joiner could not aspire to more than 6s. a day on an average: but, as a petition of disappointed immigrants stated in that year, the only shortages were for ploughmen, shepherds, and shearers—all at £10 or £12 a year and rations, and far up-country in the master's power. If a man happened to be a dairymaid, it was facetiously said, he was very favourably situated; but it was a far different plight for those who were mere mechanics or labourers. Work was scarce, convict competition always existed (and the fear of sinking to a convict level!), and conditions were hard. House rents were thrice as high as in England and most things were very expensive. With a wage of a couple of shillings a day—and usually intermittent at that—a man could not buy much bread at fivepence a two-pound loaf, or beef and mutton at fivepence, or sugar at threepence, or butter at 2s. 6d. or flour at 40s. a hundred; while such things as green tea at 1s., coffee at 1s. 4d., and foreign tobacco at 3s. 6d. were luxuries to be dreamed of![2] A small capitalist could coin money in the Australia of the late thirties, and even a careful mechanic with a good name and a hundred or so, could aspire to the squatting ranks; but there was little place for the labouring classes that had to live from week to week, especially if they wished to keep above the convict mire—and it was so tantalizingly easy to slip down and become one of the cheerful and dominant *canary* crew.

The other city dwellers—the buyers and sellers—were correspondingly prosperous. Trade was thriving, especially with the occupation of new lands in the interior, for the merchant's part was both to outfit the squatters and to advance them money at rates far higher than the accommodation rates they themselves paid the Banks. The squatters were generous and immigrants were coming in—all spelt additional turnover, and the Banks were ready to advance money for purposes of expansion. Something very like a boom was in full swing in the town. Some land had recently been sold at the rate of £10,000 an acre, Sydney had been declared a free port in the previous year, and imports were jumping up. The merchants were, therefore, becoming stout citizens, with a conservatism and a civic dignity adequate to their new prosperity—a prosperity that was to last until the crisis of 1841. Three Colleges had just been opened for their offspring in as many years (1832-5), they proudly asserted; and where would you find a merchant body as sound and esteemed as they were—the men in their plum-coloured swallow-tails and nankeen

[2] *Sydney Monitor*, 19 December 1835.

tights, and their womenfolk on display with their short skirts and high waists and elaborate sandals with no heels, and very, very careful to have long gloves to cover their arms completely, and very circumspect not to lower their social prestige in a convict community by showing too much of their *ears*! Reading of the estimable merchant class, one understands much of the irascibility of Governor Gipps, and why many preferred to pass over both the Sydney merchants and *the lordly settlers* on the Hunter flats, and go to the squatters and the convicts.

Above these classes stood the strangely isolated Governor in Macquarie Street, the official classes, and a few professionals. At the moment (1835), Governor Bourke was reasonably popular, though in the midst of various social struggles; the quarrel over the displaced magistrates was in full swing, and the emancipists were fighting the free men, through the columns of the *Gazette* and the *Colonist* respectively. Judging from the crude revilings of the press (when the papers devoted any space to some other object than criticizing rival editors), the country was a prey to social factions. But minor quarrels in the capital, though so prominent in the papers and the official despatches, counted far less for the future than the quiet penetration of the inland. Rightly speaking, the city was there mainly to facilitate the squatting onrush—to provide the capital, the goods, the labour supplies, and the Governor to direct. This, however, was heresy to a settlement viewing the squatters as bushmen—where even a free labourer would rarely think of going upland as a shepherd (*walking after sheep*, as they derided it)—and where anything was considered good enough for the country.

The Governor and the judges, for instance, pointed out time and again that education was stagnant, that there had been only one new church since 1821, and that the entire colony boasted only eight churches, and that, in a convict population of 40,000, seventeen counties had only five chaplains—but the townsmen refused to listen.[3] There were the three new colleges and the old churches for them, and the country people did not matter. If people were content to go up bush, and live in twisted bark huts, and *pig down* on sheep skins, and live on steaks and damper, why worry about religion and education and other social graces? The city wanted nothing from the inland except bales of wool and orders for supplies. In all, the township was a distinctly unattractive mixture of all manner of types, not yet blended into a community, not yet possessed of any civic institutions, and in no degree realizing its duties as the centre of the

[3] Glenelg-Bourke, 30 November 1835, enclosures.

colony, and indeed, of the continent. One might go even further, and say that the town had realized nothing—not even that its *raison d'être* was as the foil of the country, as the agency of those sheepmen it tended to despise.

II Finding and Establishing a Station

Assuming that our typical new arrival had a few hundred pounds, he would quickly realize where his opportunities lay. Everybody in the colony, save for the inveterate town dwellers, was smitten with the new stock disease—people talked of stock, traded in them, wrote of them, dreamt of them; and every unencumbered person, by fair means or foul, tried to join in the squatting rush. *Put everything in four legs*, was the advice given to newcomers. It mattered little if prices were already exaggerated, the turnover was so rapid and the profits so large that the most absurd prices and interest rates could be met; and, as for the land, a tract 1,500 miles long was not easily filled, and beyond that was still the great unknown. To stop in the town meant to become a mere trader in a tiny counting house or to sink into the ranks of a distressed proletariat: but the bush offered opportunity—and a free life to boot. Moreover, the *old hands* in the colony were far too practical to be carried away by mere chimeras, and the movement was joined by all who happened to be in the colony, native-born or newcomer, country gentleman or ex-convict.

But eastern Australia was wide and largely unknown, and other people had forestalled our newcomer in the most accessible spots. With emphasis on *the New Country* in the New England ranges and far down the Murrumbidgee, beyond Gundagai, it was not easy to locate vacant land without going far afield—and no fool's job even then. A man had to leave Sydney on horseback, the whole length and breadth of the continent in front of him, and find a space to run his stock, one good enough to yield large profits and yet without prior claimants. By the nature of things, profits largely varied with accessibility, but, equally naturally, the advantage in this direction lay with the early comers. A new hand, therefore, had to go a fair distance into the bush and evaluate his own land—both difficult tasks for an immigrant freshly arrived and acting on the vaguest of instructions. 'It's no fool's job', one of the old pioneers wrote feelingly, 'to traverse some hundreds of miles of rough, broken, and unknown country, and ride up to within a few hundred yards of a problematical gum tree supposed to have certain Roman numerals cut into it many years previously'—and yet that is how Gregory found Mitchell's blazed track on Salvada Creek in the north![4]

The immigrant in 1835, however, would probably have a somewhat easier task. He had three alternatives. He could become a pioneer and go *furthest out* beyond the last settlement; or he could wedge in somewhere in already occupied land; or (though this was not so prevalent then as later) he could buy a *right of station*. His course of action depended on his personality. Most people, now that so much virgin land was beckoning, preferred to ride out to completely new country and have their pick. In the *Hogan Manuscripts* in the Mitchell Library, one of the earliest squatters, in 1833, expressed this argument very clearly:

It is of great importance not to embroil the Establishment by disputes with neighbours, and (without, however, weakly giving away to unreasonable objections, and though distance is no doubt an objective), I think an extensive good Run, not subject to be encroached upon, may sometimes more than compensate for remoteness.

The average squatter thought little of an extra hundred miles or so for his dray, because, after all, the bullock teams only came out once a year with the wool and took back station stores for the following season, and it might as well be a long trip as a short one, if there were other compensations. To crowd into the southern Counties, with only inferior and limited land remaining, and with the certainty of perennial boundary disputes, was much less attractive than pushing out to the unoccupied fringe.

In the mid-thirties, it was the Murrumbidgee or New England, and, a few years later, all of Australia Felix or across Pandora Pass to the Downs and beyond. A man had simply to pass from station to station until he reached the outskirts: then, if he were not repelled by loneliness and a spice of risk, he could go as far as he liked and choose land according to his taste. Possibly, he would prefer to come to an understanding with the man already furthest out and settle the future by a rough delineation of boundaries. The established squatter would conduct the newcomer to the edge of his run, and say in effect—'*That river is my limit: behind it, on the rising ground I would advise you to settle, and there, high and sheltered, is the spot for your head hut.*' In this way, an interlocking phalanx of runs could be erected, the squatters' mutual interest being in holding the ground intact against newcomers. Or, according to temperament, the squatters already there might issue buckshot cartridges to their shep-

[4] *Nisbet Papers*, p. 32.

herds and solve the problem of boundaries in an elemental way. But the reverse was the rule in new country. Since a reasonable occupation strengthened everybody's position, there was usually a rough *camaraderie* amongst the firstcomers.

As time went on, however, and as larger numbers came to demand some share in the accessible lands, more men turned to wedging their establishments in between the principalities claimed by the first settlers. Naturally, at this point, the *camaraderie* broke down. In settled country, it was to a squatter's interest to hold as much of his run as he could against invaders, and a newcomer would find it extraordinarily difficult to elicit information of any kind, even as to the limits of the land already claimed. Shepherds might be bribed and squatters talk in their cups; but usually, the would-be aspirant was met by a conspiracy of silence, and, in country once picked over, he found himself treated like a bushranger, as Tyson was on the Murray. In the later thirties, in particular, the established squatters had almost to face a perpetual siege to hold their out-stations, by craft or force, against the successive waves of invaders, and naturally, the better and more accessible the run in question, the keener the competition. Any new man passing *en route* for the outer country made a bid for any especially succulent morsel: he lost nothing by the attempt, and always stood to gain. A herd of scabby sheep, the terrorism of a crew of convict shepherds, or a thousand and one tricks might serve the turn, and, anyhow, there was no harm done. Both sides had justice to support them. The pioneers staked out enormous areas without adequately stocking them; and the newcomers, knowing that the earlier men had no more rights than themselves to the land they could not use, naturally resented such attempted monopoly.

The inner country—and, in fact, any land once partitioned, however roughly—was thus the prey of *run hunters*. A man wanting to become a squatter would fill his saddlebags with tea, sugar, and tobacco, pack his flour, look after his quart-pot and tinder-box, and set out, blankets strapped to saddle and kangaroo dogs behind. Two days would get him beyond Bathurst in the direction of *the New Country* to the south-west, and his directions, gleaned from a bribed shepherd, would run something like this (these were actual ones):

Our directions to it (there being no roads across the country, except the two or three great ones to the principal ports) were up a certain hollow, through a gap in the range, and then across to a mountain on the distant horizon, by riding over which at the easiest acclivity we could find, a creek would be reached, and this creek followed down would lead to the run.[5]

It was all very vague, but, in most cases, the run hunters had to rely on even more nebulous information. Another day's ride would bring him to the edge of the New Country, but the secrecy of the stockmen would almost always necessitate pushing still further. Harris, for example, who had set out on the above directions, was compelled to scout over the Goulburn Plains for twenty-seven days, seeking a vacant spot. Half-starved stations with lazy convicts would be passed in the poorer belts, well-stocked runs in the river flats, and everywhere in the Plains would be well-guarded establishments, green and smiling. Dry flats would alternate with creeks and ranges; but still the squatters would prove reticent—even down to the Monaro Plains. Tired with the incessant riding and resentful of the continued suspicion, the horsemen would eventually reach the out-skirts and be ready to own defeat—either choosing poor land or starting afresh in a different direction.

If fortunate, as Harris was, he might hear of a run—in this case, a stockman told of a tract he located for his master in the Georgiana County, which was vacant now that the squatter in question had decided to seek less restricted spaces further inland. Harris, delighted, since he wanted a run on a modest scale, turned on his tracks for two days' hard riding to the spot indicated—and even then, it was 'one of the most solitary parts on the extreme verge of colonisation'. Past the last miserable flock of sheep, he rushed to the few stoney ridges not claimed for the moment, and then, leaving traces of his occupation, returned to settlement for his flocks. The procedure was usually in this way—a man ranged the countryside until he found new or abandoned land and came to some rough understanding with his neighbours, if any. If he were the outermost dweller, he would take care to choose his run by well-defined natural boundaries, such as rivers or mountains, easily held against later arrivals and giving a certain compactness to his holding. But, on the whole, for safety and other reasons, he would prefer neighbours with whom some agreement had been reached.

Save for the choicest spots, occupation was very fluid. A squatter was forever tormented by the dream of better country further out, and was for ever deluded by the vaguest rumours of travellers passing through. The average man, therefore, while securing one run either

[5] A. Harris, op. cit., p. 126. An excellent account of looking for a run. H. de Castella, Les Squatters Australiens (1861), p. 30, is also good.

by discovery or negotiation, would range the neighbouring country for better sites, since the best land was often hidden, especially in mountain country. Curr, for instance, having bought the right to occupy a rugged run near Heathcote (Victoria), roamed over the surrounding mountains in all directions, and one day, looking for lost bullocks, found good land on the Goulburn, eighty miles off as the crow flew. Naturally, he would desert the barren scrubs and the wretched creek where he had perforce established himself, and *trek* overland to this new region of promise. In this case, he had to face a mutiny of his convict servants, for the interminable scrub lands filled them with a species of nostalgia, and they had to be driven at the point of the carbine until the *wild* scrub changed to the plains which seemed to the temperamental shepherds *more homely*. Finding a run was playing a game of hide-and-seek in an unknown country of millions of square miles, without clues, but with the enticement always there in the possibility of rich prizes. A man could not say whether all the good land was behind until he was lost in a central desert or dying of thirst in the grey-white mulga lands: he could never be certain, and even his dying delirium would invoke mirages to make him totter on—and the irony was that, oft-times, the mirages might be real!

The average man, however, would probably find land somewhere within a month's scouting, unless he had resolved to go along *the Major's Line* to the farthest limits of Port Phillip or up the great north track to the plateaux. But, if he were not an overlander, he would choose a spot for a run and double back to Sydney to make the preliminaries.

The first task was to make an actual establishment—to make effective nominal occupation. He would have to arrange the financial end with the merchants or his bankers in the town. A frequent arrangement at that time was the system of *Thirds*, by which a Sydney capitalist would buy the sheep and finance the enterprise, receiving in return a third of the profits. This enabled the townsmen to participate in the squatting movement, and at the same time opened the way for practical overseers to establish themselves independently.[6] Usually, through the merchants, a squatter with an initial capital of £1,000 could buy on credit sheep for three times that amount, especially during the boom. A sound practical man or a small capitalist would have no difficulty in raising money in the Sydney of the thirties.

[6] *Piper Papers* (MS.), Mitchell Library, vol. II, p. 209—Balcombe-Piper, 3 June 1837.

Then he would buy his stock, improved by the new Saxon merinos if possible, and exercise the greatest care in his choice. Not unnaturally, with sheep so much in demand and with so many newcomers competing for animals at any price, not every deal was what it purported to be. Sheep bought in the peak period for £4 might be scrubby old ewes, and, of course, nobody bought *sight unseen*, with so much scab and footrot and the new-fangled catarrh around. Indeed, the best safeguard was to purchase from persons of known integrity, and especially from the neighbours near whom one had to live. Old ewes there would be of course, but a buyer's job was to see that his rams were good and that his flocks were well-balanced among two, four, and six-toothed ewes, with wethers and weaners of both sexes.

As important as the stock was the overseer, for on him depended the actual running of the station. Once retained, he would immediately commence supervising the stores and taking the preliminary measures. A bullock driver, shepherds, hut keepers, and splitters would all be enrolled, the numbers depending on the size of the flocks, and the salaries on the remoteness of the runs and the demand for the time being. In the late thirties, a shepherd would receive £20 a year and rations, and an overseer £40; and, with labour so short, one shepherd would have to mind at least six hundred sheep, with one hutkeeper or watchman to every two flocks. An establishment of 2,000 sheep, rightly staffed, would require seven men, especially in mountainous country. Food and all supplies for a year would have to be bought and loaded on the drays; and, finally, with a great cracking of rawhide whips, the cumbersome equipage would lurch forward, the flocks going ahead and the drays creaking behind, spewing the dust from their four-inch wheels—and still another squatting party would have set out for *the New Country*.

Once on the squatter's land, the actual buildings were begun. High and commanding land was chosen for the homestead, the closest attention being paid to the water. At this early stage, too many people met failure by preferring the low lands and forgetting the rapidity with which the floods came, while it was not uncommon to treat subterranean waters as permanent—a failing, it must be added, that this optimistic generation often neglected even with surface streams. The squatter of this time, too, was prone to couple green grass with flowing rivers in his scheme of things: and many years were needed to drive in the lesson that lushly-grassed country was not the best for sheep, and that the despised flats—the dry, burnt-up country of the salaceous vegetation—was oft-times far better.

First, the site for a head station would be chosen, by which time, if he had not brought sufficient hands from the settlement, stray splitters and casual wanderers would have been attracted from the neighbouring stations. A couple of bark huts, each of them of about twenty-five sheets at the most, would be hurriedly erected—within two days—to serve for the time being, and then the splitters set to work to get wood for the permanent huts. Sometimes these were of sod, but usually of rough poles, with shingles or a grass-thatch. The red beef-wood (known as *Botany Bay wood*) was especially sought, because it split, as the bushmen said, from heart to bark. A ten-foot by twelve-foot hut, with slab walls and a bark roof, could be erected quickly at a cost of £10: there would be one for the men and one, probably a trifle larger, for the master. Almost for a decade, the men in the bush lived in such erections of bark and slab, in a simplicity that reached the point of savagery. A rough bedstead of sheepskins or opossum rugs would suffice, and even of sheets of bark; while a bark table or, on occasion, a sea chest served every other purpose. The fire-place was of stone, an aperture cut in the slabs admitted air, and wool-packs were hung for the door. Furniture was not needed. A large tin dish would do for the leg of mutton at every meal, and a pint pannikin or a quart-pot for the tea. A discarded pannikin, filled with clay topped by mutton fat, gave light at night (the *fat-lamp* that was so universal)—and beyond that, the hut was empty. *Mutton and damper and something to lie on*—a squatter's needs were simple, and it was a sumptuous hut that boasted a few three-legged stools. Scattered round would be horse hobbles, a jar of tobacco twist, perhaps a gun, stockwhip, and almost certainly a *cabbage-tree hat* half braided, and perhaps a blue box of Seidlitz powders; but that was all. The squatter's immediate life was romantic only from a distance: seen in its monotonous verity, it reeked of mutton fat and smoke.[7]

Smaller huts would be built at strategic posts some eight or ten miles away from the head station, both to guard the run and look after the outer flocks. At each would be two shepherds and a hut-keeper, and at all, the sheep at night would require hurdle yards (made of split palings) and a watch box, built sentry-wise for the hutkeeper to mind the restless flocks. A rough wool shed, with a

[7] E. Curr, *Recollections of Squatting in Victoria* (1883), ch. III, gives a very good account of this side of squatting life.

wool press and a place for shearing, would also be required at the centre, or, if it were a cattle station, stockyards.

The average squatting establishment would not include more than that. There would be two slab huts and a tumble-down wool shed, a couple of rougher out-stations, and moveable hurdles and a watch box. No sane man would erect a permanent home or build extensive improvements when he had no security over his land: and, in bush country, the very roughness of the dwellings and the lack of luxuries were the best protection from pillage. Theoretically, a squatter would boast of his garden and his intention to plough some ten acres, and would dream of a small barn and a dairy, but these very rarely came to pass. Living conditions for long remained unbelievably hard and rudimentary—even more so than the uncertainty of tenure warranted. Even a prosperous squatter would be content to live in a collection of slab hovels, with hurdles moving from place to place as each became filthy, and with the inevitable heaps of sheep dung and sheep bones piled everywhere. It was a sordid, filthy existence, despite all the writers' eulogies of the free life in contact with nature and communion with the gums. The only real contact was with a few degraded convicts—mad *hatters*—and the eternal smell of sheep effluvia. Its sole return was monetary; in itself, it was a penal servitude of the worst type—there is no romance in monotony and mutton fat.

III   *The Commissioner's Part*

Before having gone thus far, the squatter, after 1836, would certainly have applied for his licence and brought himself against the ubiquitous officials of that era—the Commissioners of Crown Lands. The local Act of 1836 had divided the squatting land into districts, each under an official called the Commissioner. The amending Act of three years later somewhat defined their attributes and allowed each to have a section of Border Police to enforce his decisions.

The Commissioner was thus a person of considerable importance. Every stockman had to apply to him for a licence for his run: he determined the limits of each man's holding and settled the numerous boundary disputes: he could exclude undesirables: he collected Government revenue, and decided everything about the incidence of the licence fee and the assessment on every head of stock. In a word, the local Commissioner was the arbiter of everything connected with squatting life, except the price of wool. He was omnipotent, and there was no practical appeal against his decisions.

Doubtless, the position was very difficult. Here was a completely new province, with none of the institutions of civil government and overrun by truculent sheepmen. The Commissioner had both to safeguard the interests of the Government and secure equity between the individual stockmen : he had no aid except a few black or convict troopers, he was loathed by the entire countryside, and he had no fixed code or set of rules to guide him. Equity and his conscience were his only help, and, unfortunately, the facts of human nature somewhat limit these when a man, however conscientious, is placed in the position of a despot.

Of course, the Commissioner's unpopularity was predestined. A discoverer would make known a new tract of land, squatters from all directions would rush there, a guerilla fight would spring up between them, and the Commissioner would have to settle all disputes, give each man his property right, and restrict the absurd claims every squatter made. Squatters' estimates of the Commissioners, therefore, have to be largely discounted, but, even so, the record of these rustic *Bashaws* was a trail of officialdom which ranged from arbitrariness almost to corruption.

The Commissioners, from their command of the Border Police, affected the military in their costumes and manner. In the Melbourne of 1839, they were familiar figures. Usually, they resembled officers of irregular mounted rifles, with their magnificent chargers, dark-green uniforms, hessian boots and braided caps; and they seldom stirred without a clatter of military pomp—with orderly, sergeant, and troopers, bristling with carbines and pistols. Their holstered and be-canessoned horses cluttered the streets and rattled through the bush, and not all the exigencies of up-country existence could deprive the Commissioner of his military spruceness.

Unfortunately, fickleness tinged all their acts. No two runs presented the same problem, and nothing could be solved by mathematical rules determined in a Sydney Land Office : but, on the other hand, to view each problem as distinct meant a variety of decisions that could only seem contradictory to those interested. Moreover, any attempt to introduce the personal factor into each case (and each Commissioner evaluated the evidence by his own estimates of the character and desirability of the squatters concerned) made the confusion worse. The whole system worked in the direction of making everything personal—hence the undue dependence on the Commissioner as an individual. The decisions of one Commissioner were said, with some degree of justice, to depend 'on the proportion of bile in his worshipful stomach', and a luckless stirrup cup of sour milk was said to have cost one unfortunate his run.[8] Gipps had argued that equity was more important than hard-and-fast rules and that a practical man was needed to do his business roughly and summarily, with a minimum of red tape: but the Governor's equity soon degenerated into personal autocracy. The Commissioner lived in his district and held the economic existence of all in it within his hand, irrespective of justice or reason: he dwelt with a certain set of squatters, cultured or otherwise, and naturally would mostly hear the *ex parte* statements of his companions; and yet he would have to deal with important property rights concerning those to whom he was either hostile, indifferent, or friendly. Under the conditions, it would not be difficult to convince himself that justice pointed in the same direction as his inclinations.

The whole position thus became absurd, especially when the squatters came to have important rights of property in their holdings. A Commissioner was judge, jury, policeman, sheriff, treasurer, prosecutor, and even hotel licenser: and such undifferentiated vagueness could pertain only in a period of origins. As it was, however, the worst sides of the position developed. Even if a Commissioner convinced himself that he was maintaining his integrity and acting according to the facts of the situation and the dictates of his conscience, the nature of his work made self-delusion almost inevitable. He was a despot, cajoled and fawned upon, and, of necessity, developed the unstable caprice of an Oriental monarch. Few men, and certainly no group of men, could escape the influence of such surroundings, and the natural consequences developed—uncertainty, favouritism, personal jealousies, and at times positive corruption.

Even the best of the Commissioners were the evil genii of a squatter's life. They provided the greatest element of uncertainty, for a man never knew when he was going to be turned out of his run, without compensation—for none could stand against an adverse decision of a Commissioner, and no one could predict what a Commissioner was going to do next. Blacks might be repelled, scab stamped out, and nature withstood: the tricks of wool buyers might be condoned, falling prices tided over, and difficulties of labour and distance steadily overcome; but what means could be adopted to secure consistent decisions from a Commissioner, when he had no

---

[8] *Portland Gazette*, 30 June 1846. Confirmation of such incidents is in the evidence before the Crown Lands Committee of 1844 in full. For *Fighting Fyans*, referred to in text, see *Port Phillip Herald* 12 June 1845. For the difficulties of the Commissioner, however, see Westgarth, 1850, p. 98.

text-book or limiting rules, and only the caprices of his own personality to check him?

One Commissioner was dismissed in the Peel River district, because
he speculated in squatting holdings, misappropriated Government
advances, and neglected to pay the fees on his own stations. Written
to officially, he fined himself as an unauthorized squatter, and, as
Gipps said, was merciful, because he contented himself with a fine
of 50s., when it might have been £80![9] This man was dismissed,
but, usually, it could not be proved that a Commissioner's arbitrary
actions were caused by self-interest, because the problems were so
variable.

In last resort, if the individual squatter was wealthy enough and
could afford the time and money, and could get his witnesses to the
city, he could invoke the aid of the law; but this was much too
expensive and uncertain. The only redress in practice was when
the delinquencies were so flagrant that the Governor had to intervene, but this possibility was a remote one, because the Governor
appointed his personal *protégés* as Commissioners and naturally
accepted their versions against those of the squatters with whom he
was fighting so strenuous a struggle. A Commissioner was appointed
to control land the size of a principality, he was the virtual executive
governor—and scarcely any other fact counted! He allocated runs as
he pleased, irrespective of first occupancy; he could bring in outsiders and displace the pioneers; he could cut runs about in any way;
he could fine on the vaguest pretext and within the most pliant
extremes; and he interfered in every aspect of the squatter's life.

There was only one rule—a pastoral tenant had to pay £10 a
year and a half-penny on each sheep, and could not have more than
twenty square miles or run more than a given number of stock per
square mile. As long as the Commissioner conformed to this and as
long as he bullied his district into submission, the central Executive
was not likely to interfere. Later, the Courts decided that a squatter's
occupancy was good against everybody except the Crown, but it was
still the Commissioner who decided the terms and extent of that
occupancy! The Committee of 1844 was therefore not exaggerating
in saying that 'there is no functionary in Her Majesty's Dominions
to whom is entrusted such absolute power over the property of his
fellow-subjects', and certainly provided the most telling argument
that, while every witness before it censured the Commissioners as a
body, he was earnest and eager to except the official of his own

[9] Gipps-Stanley, 15 June 1843, 11 September 1844.

district, who was invariably a model of fairness and an exquisitely courteous gentleman!

Instances of their actions are not difficult to find. Every squatter's story reeks with them. Curr, a typical educated squatter, for instance, relates that, in all the applications for country, he never saw the Goulburn Commissioner mark a tree, take a compass bearing, or make a memorandum, and rarely did he send a detailed report. One instance Curr quotes is quite typical.[10] He had been at Colbinabbin for six months (having occupied the land on the Commissioner's assurance that he could keep it if he stocked it first), when two interlopers came, and an appeal was made to the Commissioner to define the boundary. After two or three months, along galloped a trooper to tell of the meeting-place. But Curr's rivals got in first and persuaded the official to divide the land midway between the huts of the rival claimants—a proceeding which, to him, appeared the perfection of equity but which, unfortunately, neglected the fact of prior occupation. Even this was not enough for the bush Solomon. Before the matter was finalized, an orderly pointed out a couple of emu on the plain, half-way to the ranges. Halloing his dogs and gathering his men, off the Commissioner was going emu-hunting, had not Curr rather brusquely reminded him of the business of which he had come. Then, looking round, with one eye on the emu, the *Bashaw* spoke:

You see that single tree on the plain: an east-and-west line through it will be the boundary on this side of the creek, and, on the other side, the blackfellows' oven!

and off he scampered, leaving Curr, the firstcomer, with a boundary two miles from his hut, even worse off than under the already unfavourable midway division! Yet Curr voiced the general concurrence of testimony in saying that even this autocratic and lax method of procedure was preferred by most to the cost and delay of anything more elaborate.

In point of fact, most of the Commissioners were just and reasonable men, who erred to so great an extent mainly from the impossible nature of their position and the vague cases they had to decide: and one heard far more of a blustering martinet like Foster Fyans in western Victoria than of a score of less spectacular, but more reasonable Commissioners. Fyans, the irresponsible militarist, was wont to say that he carried his holster filled to protect his dignity as well as his person, and was famous for his peppery indiscretions: but for-

10 Curr, op. cit., pp. 314-15. Compare *Atlas*, 21 June 1845, 10 May 1845.

tunately, he was an exception. Yet, attributing a reasonable degree
of fairness to such officials, it must be remembered that they were
autocrats, and that the Governor, on whom they depended, was
waging a war to the death with the squatters whose causes they had
to decide—a combination not favourable to the squatters. In all, the
song of the sheepmen (afterwards acknowledged as the work of
Robert Lowe) was a fair commentary on this position and on the
element which, after all, was the most important in the squatter's
life:

> The Commissioner bet me a pony—I won—
> So he cut off exactly two-thirds of my run;
> For he said that I was making a fortune too fast,
> And profit gained slower the longer would last.

> He remarked, as devouring my mutton he sat,
> That I suffered my sheep to grow sadly too fat;
> That they wasted the waste land, did prerogative brown,
> And rebelliously nibbled the droits of the Crown;

> That the creek that divided the station in two
> Showed nature designed that two fees should be due:
> Mr. Riddell assured me 'twas paid but for show,
> But he kept it and spent it, that's all that I know.

> The Commissioner fined me because I forgot
> To report an old ewe that was ill of the rot;
> And a poor, wry-necked lamb that we kept for a pet,
> And he said it was treason such things to forget.

> The Commissioner pounded my cattle, because
> They had mumbled the scrub with their famishing jaws
> On the part of the run he had taken away,
> And he sold them by auction the cost to defray.

> The Border Police were out all the day
> To look for some thieves who had ransacked my dray.
> But the thieves they continued in quiet and peace,
> For they robbed it themselves, had the Border Police.

> When the white thieves had gone, next the black thieves appeared,
> My shepherds they waddied, my cattle they speared:
> But for fear of my licence I said not a word;
> For I knew it was gone if the Government heard.

The Commissioner's bosom with anger was filled
Against me because my poor shepherd was killed;
So he straight took away the last third of my run,
And got it transferred to the name of his son.

The cattle that had not been sold at the pound,
He took with the run at five shillings all round,
And the sheep the blacks left me at sixpence a head,
And a very good price the Commissioner said.

The Governor told me I justly was served;
That Commissioners never from duty had swerved;
But that if I'd apply for any more land,
For one pound an acre he'd plenty on hand! (1845).

The position was complicated by the nature of the boundaries and the general uncertainty of squatting existence. Boundaries were vague and fluctuating, and practically every squatter's life was enlivened by fights with encroachers. The pioneers claimed such absurd areas—Batman, for example, wanted some 600,000 acres because of his treaty with the blacks; Russell claimed all of the Barrabool Hills in Port Phillip, because Buckley, the wild white man living with the natives, gave him as far as eye could see; a few men demanded all of the lower Murray; Patrick Leslie and the other Downsmen claimed whole provinces in Queensland; and, even in 1845, Gibson seriously wanted 100,000 acres in the new Glenelg country in Victoria, and seemed perturbed when the Commissioner insisted that he had to place 10,000 sheep on it. Under such conditions, there was a constant campaign of attrition against the bigger runs, and boundary fights became a normal part of squatting life. Most of every Commissioner's duty was to settle such disputes, and Gibson, for instance, fought for three years to keep his Glenelg runs intact, even holding his out-stations by force, and only reluctantly accepting the Commissioner's fiat.[11]

Everything was so vague. No land was surveyed, and there were no adequate maps. Any natural feature, therefore, served to mark the limits of runs—tree trunks, blazed poles, striking rocks, hills, and, in default of these, plough-tracks. The official definitions of the runs thus often seemed ridiculous. Edward Henty, for example, quarrelled with Whyte over the boundaries of Muntham, and the boundary finally decided by the Geelong Commissioner ran thus:

it follows Mr. Whyte's *ploughed line* as far as *a rock* described by Mr.

[11] J. C. Hamilton, *Pioneering Days in Western Victoria*, p. 20.

Grant as situated about 350 yards from a *tea-tree spring* (should it not touch the rock, to be drawn from the nearest point to it), then a straight *plough-furrow* to be drawn to the Intersection of Mr. Henty's plough-furrow with a *Creek or Marsh* laid down in Mr. Urqhart's survey.[12]

Native *tumuli*, ant-heaps, clumps of scrub, isolated sheoaks, or even notches in trees all served; and the officials did not seem to realize that ploughed lines could be altered, or blazes in trees removed, or natural landmarks obliterated. Often it was not as definite as this, and a description would read—*seventy-five miles from Albury on the Major's Line, between Smith and Jones' runs*—a vagueness delightfully pregnant of quarrels.

A normal squatter had thus to come to some arrangement with the Commissioner and then fight the matter out with his neighbours and the successive invaders, because, under those conditions, a clout with a waddy at an out-station or a charge of shot often counted as much as an appeal to a Commissioner who appeared perhaps once a year. But, however he settled them, a squatter had to count on boundary quarrels both with the official and with other stockmen, and he could be certain that any weakness on his part would quickly lead to the spoliation of his run. Rarely, indeed, could a squatter hold his lands intact: either by force or as bribes, he had to clip off his out-stations and submit to the dwindling of his pasture grounds; and, unfortunately for him, this necessity increased with the growth of population in the bush. His flocks would increase, his lands diminish —that was his dilemma.

IV Life on a Sheep Run

Once the squatter had built his huts, secured his licence, and arranged his boundaries for the time being, life became very monotonous. He divided his sheep into various flocks, and, for the greater part of the year, simply had to see that they grazed and escaped disease. The size of the flocks varied, usually becoming too large on account of the labour shortage. Whereas a flock of four hundred would have been ample, it was usual to have five hundred or six hundred ewes and up to 1,000 dry sheep, especially in clear country. But the larger the flock, the more trampled the vegetation became and the more difficult it was to feed all the sheep without making them go too far every day.

The various flocks were divided among the out-stations, two to

---

[12] *Henty Papers* (MSS.), Mitchell Library, letters 9 December 1845, 5 June 1849.

each. The two shepherds had to take their respective flocks to the grazing grounds, one easterly and one westerly, not more than an hour after sunrise; they would watch them and keep them slowly moving all day, and bring them back at night, when they were counted and put into the fold. The shepherd's duties were ridiculously simple. A man merely had to tramp after his flock or ruminate under the shelter of a tree until he became what the colonists termed a *hatter*, as lack-wit as his charges.

When counted, the shepherds handed over the sheep to the watchman (there was one watchman to every two shepherds), whose duty it was to protect them at night. The wild dogs *were as bold as hungry wolves*, and one of them working quietly amongst folded sheep, would mangle some seventy animals before he could be heard from the huts. To guard against this menace, the sheep were strongly folded, and the watchman slept with them. Yards were not usual at this time: in their place, were moveable hurdles, made of rough scantling cut from gums or swamp-oaks. Each bar was six or seven feet long, and there were usually five, placed close enough together to keep the young sheep from crawling through. From forty-four to forty-eight such hurdles (six feet by three feet six inches) could pen up to a thousand sheep, and each would cost from a shilling upwards. Rough logs and brushwood had been tried, but these lacked mobility and security, and the movable hurdle was soon accepted. Between the two yards would be a kind of sentry-box, a strange contraption on four legs, measuring about six feet by three feet by two feet six inches, and just large enough for a man to squeeze into. It had two projecting handles and could be moved with the hurdles so that, at night, each out-station presented the strange spectacle of two folds of densely clustered animals and this funny box sticking up between them, with the watchman inside, one eye open for canine marauders. The whole structure—hurdles and box—had to be moved every few days, the sheepmen of that time being inordinately afraid that yarding in one spot meant footrot. Yarding and moving were the basic articles in the stockman's creed—it was these they held essential for their success.[13]

The settler or his overseer would check their numbers once or twice a week, but, if no scab or footrot appeared and if his grazing grounds were not attacked by outsiders, he had little to do until the

[13] Good accounts of sheep-life are in the *Wright MSS.* (Mitchell Library): *Three Years' Experience of a Settler in New South Wales* (1838): the *Gardiner Papers* (Mitchell Library), for New England practice: Hamilton and Curr, op. cit. Details are in Appendix D to N.S.W. *Immigration Committee* of 1841.

outstanding events of the sheep-year—lambing and shearing. Lambing would occupy about six weeks from the end of June, but, unless
the weather was extraordinarily cold (as it became on the snow-
pastures of Monaro), all that was needed would be to assign two extra
hands to each flock. The lambs, of course, had to be weaned, dressed,
castrated, and *pitchbranded* with a mixture of tallow, tar, and lamp-
black; but these were all simple operations, and lambing was not so
much a matter of difficulty as an anxious gamble with Nature.

In October, shearing would commence, but, just before, there
would arise the most-discussed question on sheep-runs—the perennial
dispute about washing. There were no reservoirs, douches, soap or
soda in those rude days—the sheep had no summer toilet. Until
about 1877, it was the custom (now discarded) to wash the wool on
the sheep's back—it was only a fractious theorist who would want
the French or Spanish method of washing *after* shearing. An
Almanack of 1835, decrying this new-fangled idea, loftily said, 'this
has not been approved by the buyers generally, and particularly by
those who buy for combing purposes', and this attitude defied the
relevant facts for many decades. The sheep were simply washed in a
running stream or were made to cross a river: if the waters were in
flood, each animal was passed along from man to man and *ducked*,
but that was all. The triple spines of the Bathurst-burr and hundreds
of dirty excrescences might have accumulated on the sheep's back
during the months of grazing, but the current practice was not
changed, despite the almost frantic protests of British buyers
against the dirty state of Australian wools. 'I visited the sheep-shear-
ing and wash-pool,' wrote Sir Edward Parry, who managed the
estates of the Australian Agricultural Company in 1832, 'and am
still of opinion that the mode of washing is an excellent one, though
capable of much improvement'—and, if that was the attitude of the
wealthiest organization in Australia, it may be imagined how negli-
gent were the smaller squatters.[14]

Shearing, too, was much simpler then than later. A rough shed
served all purposes, and there was little fuss. A squatter deemed himself fortunate if he could secure a few extra hands at a remuneration
of £1 a hundred sheep and some four glasses of rum a day. All the
later paraphernalia of rouseabouts, machinery, and separate cooks
was unheard-of. Men simply turned up, and were given shears and
ointment for any cuts they inflicted. Sixty to eighty were considered
a good day's work, and the man who did ninety was usually the

[14] *Parry's Journal* (MS), Mitchell Library, 12 November 1822, 18 November
1830.

ringer or top-hand of the shed : a record of 120 was known, but such achievements were food for pothouse arguments. Then as now, it was an anxious time for the squatter, for already the peculiarly irresponsible qualities that came to distinguish peripatetic sheep-shearers had developed, and a squatter could never be certain when his men would down their shears for some pretended grievance and move on. A bad shearer, reprimanded for hacking the fleece by 'a second blow', instead of keeping the clip clean, would as like as not call out his friends, and the squatter would have to rely on his permanent shepherds and his family. Once the last obstinate *cobbler*, the last recalcitrant sheep in a catching-pen, had gone under the shears, and once the *board* or floor was cleared, the squatter breathed again.

Adjacent to the wool-shed was usually a rough wool-press of split-stuff—what Sir Edward Parry called a barbarous device, consisting primarily of a lever forced down by main strength. To *screw* the bales was unforgivable, because it was thought to cake the contents (and moreover, a screw-press cost £60), and the squatter was satisfied with this rudimentary pressing. The fleeces were packed in the German mode, spread one on the other, the neck of the second on the tail of the first, and pressed into bales nine feet by four.[15] Then, greasy and dirty, and of a filthiness that today would be incredible, the sagging bales were sewn and tied on the bullock-waggons, and the squatter's wool would face the long trip through scrub and mud and dust to the coast.

Simple as this round sounds, all manner of obstacles were for ever emerging to spoil its tranquillity. The difficulties of Nature and labour in themselves kept the squatter on the *qui vive* the whole year through, and in addition were many others—outbreaks of scab, footrot, and catarrh; the menace of other men's diseased flocks, encroachments of neighbours and travelling sheep; negligence at the out-stations; the frequent *boxing* (mixing) of the flocks so badly that perhaps a week would be taken in re-drafting them; and a score of other things. A sheepman's tribulations were the source of many a plaintive song of the period, and it was always said that every theoretical contingency would have to be considered, including the mad acts of the Commissioner, and that, even then, some new obstacles would turn up!

V *Life on a Cattle Station*

In the case of a cattle-station, the procedure was very different.

---

[15] *Australian Almanack*, 1835, p. 150.

After the squatter had brought his herds, he would knock up a rough yard of thick saplings, stout enough to resist the onslaughts of an infuriated steer. Twelve-inch rails, six-high, were none too strong for what the drovers called *a real Rooshian*—a bush *clearskin* that had never known restraint and that resisted the proximity and the smell of the other cattle. Log on log would pile up, and sometimes clumped sod fill the interstices, until a regular fortress of a yard was completed. It would take perhaps three months to make such a yard and the slab huts, and to get the herds in working order.

A stock-keeper would *tail* or follow the herd, keeping them quiet at night by a monotonously droned song, until some months had gone by, when all except the untameables—*the wild Bushians*—would be content to stop on their new grazing grounds. But if, at first, the stockman relaxed his vigilance even a little, at any time of day or night, off the herd would stampede in the direction of their old run, stamping down everything in their path. A stockman, perforce, had to be of a sterner mould than a shepherd—no half-witted *hatter* could hope to survive this more strenuous life. For that reason, to term a stockman a shepherd was to invite assault—there was always the clearest distinction between the two classes.

As soon as possible, the cattle would be branded—the blacksmith would make a monogram of the owner's initials or some distinctive sign peculiar to the station, and this would be burnt into the flank of each beast. The JW stock could thus at a glance be distinguished from the B-BAR-B or from the *Double Triangle*, though most owners contented themselves with their initials and rather scorned the fancier combinations. With the neighbouring squatters in attendance —there both to help and to watch—the herd would be gathered into the railed yard, drafted, roped, and thrown to be branded.

Cut into smaller batches, the cattle would be handed to their respective stockmen, who would henceforth be responsible for their feed and safety. At this early time, before fences had come and before even runs had been defined, it was a great temptation to have one's herd grow more quickly than could be accounted for by the natural increase. Cattle were not like sheep—a steer is an anti-social animal —and isolated cows or groups would stray into the most distant and remote spots. Their calves would be *clearskins* (unbranded), and their own brands could be altered, so that small herds often increased at an amazing rate. *Gully-raking*, as it was suggestively called, was an inevitable concomitant of the squatting movement until the runs were all fenced; and cattlemen in the thirties often complained that, though they themselves might be honest men, it was almost impossible for them to prevent *gully-raking* by their employees. The practice was universal, and it was a matter of pride with a stockman to vie with his fellows in increasing his charges. Harris, for instance, the squatter mentioned at an earlier stage, found that even respectably connected squatters had the most liberal ideas about branding straying cattle. His immediate neighbour rudely resented his intrusion until he accepted the tacit understanding to which every stockman in New South Wales had to submit at that time—the *live-and-let-live* principle, they called it; and his own stockmen thought *gully-raking* the most natural thing in the world, something even praiseworthy, if successful.

From time to time, either to mark the increase or to select beasts for sale, musters were held on each station, and it was always courteous to invite the neighbouring stockmen. With a terrific clatter and rush, the herds would be driven into a blind gully or the big stockyard. A lane, probably some nine yards by thirty, would be opened in the middle, and gates would lead into four or five other yards, according to the drafting. Group by group, the cattle would be yarded from various parts of the run and then *cut out*. Driving-in from the open country was simple as compared with this. First a swirl of gritty dust would arise on a distant slope; then a bow-shaped cordon of riders, yelling hoarsely and cracking long thongs, would get the animals started towards home; and the deeply bellowing cattle would crowd into the yard, thrusting hither and thither, surging against the yielding logs until they stopped, densely packed and exhausted, and awaiting what would come next. From this swaying mob, the drafting-men would allow each in turn through its appropriate gate, with an incredible agility, or horsemen would *cut out* unbranded cattle and work them towards the edge of the mob, where they would be taken over. Noisy, dirty, dangerous, but intensely skilful—this part of a cattleman's life was no child's play. The percentage of calves with uncut ears had to be ascertained, and *clearskins* sorted to their proper owners, if they could be determined.

Apart from such periodical drafting and branding, what was called *a bang-tail muster* was held every few years the idea being to take a census of the whole run. All the cattle would be yarded, and the long hairs of the tails shorn off square, so that an accurate toll could be taken and compared with the station-books. At times, too, would be the far greater excitement of a general muster for the whole of a given neighbourhood.[16] This was the acme of excitement

[16] An excellent account of such a muster is in the *Wright MSS.*, or R. D. Barton, *Reminiscences of an Australian Pioneer*, pp. 261-2.

in a squatting region, and stockmen would gather from far and near. In those days before the fences, when stock roamed as they chose in the virgin country, such a general sorting was very necessary. There was always, it is true, *the gentleman's agreement* that straying stock were to be passed on from man to man until they reached their owner, and it was agreed that things in the long run *evened up;* but nevertheless, the squatter was not averse to determining ownership by the more direct means of a general muster.

The cattle roamed for huge distances of their own accord under this system of the open run, and their spread was aided by the lack of water-improvements. There were no water-reserves, or conservation-schemes, or even Government-maintained stock-routes in those days: and in dry seasons, the claypans were only too often the only source of water. Stock therefore drifted further and further, and often the cattleman himself, once the holes in the plain had dried up, would be compelled to send his stock long distances to the rivers. In northern New South Wales, for instance, the Namoi and the Barwon were the *rendezvous* of stock from all the surrounding country: the stations far and wide would be practically deserted, the herds tramping away off in search of river-beds that were not dry.

To sort out such extraordinary mixtures, as well as the usual jumble on a smaller local range, general musters were of fairly frequent occurrence. Stockmen would often have to go sixty miles and more to a muster convened by one of their number: indeed, Wright tells of a typical one at Drildool (N.S.W.) much larger than this. The assembled men would camp on some central spot, in this case on an anabranch of the Namoi. More than a hundred riders had come together and had gathered round the sparse fires (this was a woodless region!) to boil their quartpots of tea—*Jackshays,* as they were called. Cold beef and damper satisfied them, and then the camp took on aspects which resembled only the life of the large caravan-parties that used to cross America for the Far West. Step-dancing, athletic contests, playing on all fours for *gombenes* of tobacco, and wild tales of bush cattle attracted various groups of men, while the larger owners would hold their council at a central campfire to decide the next day's programme. A man who knew the locality would draw in the sand and show just how the groups would spread out fanwise and muster all the cattle they could find on to a small low sandhill, some ten miles away. Then, at ten punctually, lights-out would be ordered, and each man would roll in his blanket under the stars, his saddle for pillow.

At daybreak, the black boys would find the hobbled horses and bring them to camp, and the groups would separate, saddle up, and ride out. Towards noon, the dust-coated riders would have reached the concentration-camp—perhaps with a muffled whisper that a *breakaway* steer had ripped up Jenks of Brinbool, and that a stumble of his horse had broken Paddy of Limerick's chest. But this was part of the risk, and now the champing cattle were demanding attention —a herd, in this case, estimated at fully 20,000 head, kept in check by a few sinewy cow-ponies, but sweatily billowing in all directions. Drafting would begin on all sides at once, a rapid scrutiny of earcuts or brands determining ownership. Every man would *cut out* his cattle and draft them in a group in an outer circle: perhaps there would be twenty separate groups on the outside, but they seldom showed any disposition to mix with other groups or go back to the swaying main-herd. Apart, too, would be a separate *cut-herd for strays*, which would be divided up later. This procedure would go in various directions, until each man had his stock drafted apart, and not a stray could be found within riding-distance. Then the musterers would disperse, each moving towards his own station, the stock slowly separating and being herded along the scant tracks. At night, the cattle would be rounded up in a convenient spot, four fires lit at separate corners, and a couple of riders, in various watches, keeping guard, gently crooning and watching if anything crossed the line between the corner-blazes into the outer darkness.[17] So shepherded, the cattle would move slowly until their home-station was reached, and there, once more, the general process of distribution and the inevitable straggling would commence afresh. Local musters to select beeves for sale or to stock a new station; run-musters for the annual branding; and perhaps a *bang-tail muster*—all would come in their turn, until, from another direction, a stockowner would send word of a general muster, perhaps down south this time, or over towards the cordillera.

Perhaps sometimes, a sterner call would go the rounds. The depredations of *duffers* (cattle-thieves) would have become too much to bear, or the menace of bushrangers who had thriven by neglect. Men *on the run* from the law may have been operating from their hidden lairs in the ranges, and the stockmen knew that they had to be their own vigilance-corps, and that the handful of Border Police could in no sense suffice to control the countryside. Licensing bush-shanties and collecting dues absorbed *their* attention, and the customary trooper—ex-convict as he was—had no lively interest in running bushrangers to earth. The country would therefore for a time have to

[17] Holt MS. (Mitchell Library), p. 5.

submit to what was called *a cattle-racket*—in other words, a whole-sale system of plundering cattle. The *duffers* either ran off strays, or, tempted by the impunity they seemed to enjoy, clipped the herds proper, or—still further emboldened—raided whole groups of branded cattle. The mountain-gorges would attract runaway convicts, and cattle were sufficiently valuable to tempt them, especially since brands could be so easily altered. The branding-iron was their weapon, the mountains their hiding place; and they could secure the connivance of some shady character pretending to live a normal squatting life. This went on until they aroused the local countryside, when word would go forth for a muster of stockmen at a certain point, with ball-cartridges in their carbines and lint for emergencies. This time, it was a manhunt, with desperadoes who knew that recapture meant the gallows and who were not in the least concerned about adding a few more deaths to their charge. Every region of Australia knew these happenings in the early days, even the Plenty Ranges, just outside Melbourne; while, of course, the almost inaccessible mountain-resorts of the Australian Alps and the New England Ranges had particularly bad records. Numerous were the tales of sieges, of pitched battles, and all manner of running fights in the bush; and not a few squatters, in their turn, fell before the bullets of such *duffers*, or, as they came to be known, bushrangers.

A cattleman had to count this menace as a certain feature of his yearly round, especially up north, where convict renegades led gangs of black outlaws. Many squatters had to write off a certain percentage every year from this cause—indeed, even after the time when the runs were fenced and the squatting world more defined. Duffing was inevitable where cattle were concerned, and especially under the system of *the open range*, where many shady characters could pretend to be *bona fide* stockmen, and where *Government men* (convict assignees) were so ready to afford shelter and obliterate tracks. Volumes could be written of these fights, and there are few books more typical of ordinary bush life—not some exceptionally romantic incident, but the ordinary, everyday world of cattle-country existence—than Rolf Boldrewood's *Robbery under Arms*. It is a history of this early period, rather than fiction. *Duffing*, indeed, was so common, so accepted a feature of existence, that when the first Queensland squatter (Gideon Scott of Mt Esk) issued notices for a general muster, he was viewed askance by his neighbours, on the principle that he who protested too much was himself suspect!

Another feature of cattle life was rounding up *wilds* in the mountains. The wide reaches of the Australian countryside were admirable refuges for straying stock, and the effect of a few years was to raise mobs of wild cattle and horses that had never seen a human being. Many a newcomer in the thirties bought herds of wild cattle that had never been mustered, and never could be! Wilder country always saw mobs of *clearskins* and *scrubbers* that had reverted to a wild existence. The mountains of eastern Victoria, all of Monaro and New England, and the newer districts of Queensland were especially fruitful homes for them. Hunting wilds in the mountain gorges and the back scrub country was almost universal before the fencing of the sixties,[18] and even today, *brumbies* (wild horses) range the Gippsland hills and untamed cattle graze in various parts of New South Wales and Queensland. Much of the headwaters of the Hunter, for instance, known as *Inside the Range*, was such a no-man's-land, even after runs had been defined hundreds of miles further out, and cattle roamed there as they pleased, wild and heedless of original ownership. The bush in parts of South Queensland swarmed with them, and, on scores of runs in the back country, the effect of the great slump of the forties was to allow the herds, now worth so little, to drift off as they pleased. Every young fellow in the middle forties, it was said, yearned to take a couple of *coachers* or decoys and comb the wilder lands for cattle to start a run.

Wild as hawks, such *ruggies*, as they were called, lived high up in the gorges and defied their hunters. To rout them out was as exciting a story as any in Australian squatting. Wright, an Etonian seeking a bush life in Australia, tells of a typical instance in his *Manuscripts*. With his two brothers, he resolved to gather such a herd, avoiding trouble by buying a mustering right from the squatter who claimed the mountains in question. For a trifle, they acquired ownership of all the wild cattle running in the head of the Isis River, but it was a far cry before their purchases could be brought to the city auction block. They collected five musterers and first built a high stockyard where several valleys came down to a focal point. High up in the gorges, red and dun beasts would signify the cattle outlaws, openly showing themselves as if in defiance of the smoke-twirl curling up from the valley to their fastness. First, a hundred or more of the semi-wild cattle of the lower lands would be caught and accustomed to the restraint of a stockyard and the smoking tang of the branding iron, ultimately to be used as *coachers*—decoys to entice down the main herds higher up. Every morning, after they had been turned out for some time, they would be driven from the yard away up the creeks for about eight miles, and then turned up the spurs to the side

[18] See entries in *Wright MSS.* and *Grant Papers*, 48-9, for extent of this.

of the main mountain. Left to graze there, with one horseman in charge, they would ramble round the lower heights and appear to be unsubdued cattle quietly feeding.

Then came the climax of the chase. The musterers would separate, out-flank the wild cattle, and appear behind them from the other side of the spurs—a procedure by no means as simple as it sounds. *Heads down, tails up,* the wilds were driven down the steep mountainside, into the waiting *coachers* or lures, and all stampeded at a breakneck rate down the gullies. But that was not all. To tumble the mob headlong into the creek at the bottom was only a stage, and it was no time for a rider to congratulate himself on not having broken a neck or having escaped the avalanche that would be coming down all round him. When the herd had reached the bottom, the musterers had to be *already* there to receive them—ready to gallop to and fro and shepherd them in the steadier march down the creek bed to the yard prepared for them. Two men would have to be in front, others on either side and behind, to prevent an uncontrollable stampede; and none of these were enviable positions with mob-maddened bush cattle, aware that something was wrong. 'I have been one of the men', casually wrote Wright in his *Manuscripts,* 'riding ahead of about two hundred rushing cattle going down a steep, timbered hill at a gallop: if my horse or I had fallen, we should have been trodden to death!' Run into the waiting yard, the mixed band—*coachers* and untamed bandits—would be left to quieten down, next day to be drafted and branded. The day following, another gorge or ridge would be worked in the same way, and the whole helter-skelter, but fascinating, process repeated.

But such episodes were comparatively few, and, save for the musters and drafting for sale, life on a cattle station had long periods of monotonous grazing. Round-ups were more in the nature of picturesque appendages than anything normal; and, for the most part, cattle-life was little different from a shepherd's existence in its deadly irksomeness—as the stockdrivers were wont to complain when they sat for hours braiding new hats or stitching opossum-skin rugs. The long, dull year was enlivened only by births and sales, or by going to Sydney with some fat beasts or occupying a new station.

VI   *Types of Squatters*

Hearing so much of the strange life and the resolute fight put forward by these early squatters, one naturally asks—*what manner of men were they?* It was soon evident that they could not be dismissed as convict escapees or uncouth bushmen—Bourke, as early as 1837, wrote that not more than a score of them had even been convicts, and Gipps their opponent, admitted that their ranks included the best-born men in the colony and that, socially, they were the types with whom he would have mixed under normal conditions. To realize what they were like as human beings—to be able to conjure up some idea of the strange mixture hidden beneath their hirsute frames—in short, to have the idea 'squatter' materialize itself into a vision of a few sentient personalities seems to offer a way of understanding far more fruitful than reams of documentary records of their fights or economic charts of their work. It was the personal aspect that decided the issues at the time, and their story seems bizarre and strangely inexplicable, unless one reconstructs their individual personalities.

Most squatters certainly looked alike. Not even the most casual account written in the forties was complete without a word-picture of these strange bush-beings who stamped and galloped round the central towns. Whiskers, beards, and moustaches of every description effectively protected or hid their faces in striking contrast with the clean shaven townsmen of those days, so that all of these pioneers seemed strikingly alike in the crude daguerreotypes they liked so much. Some have square, others pointed beards—otherwise, since the old reproductions gave them uniform eyes (except where bush accidents had replaced eyes by the far too frequent sheaths), they all looked brothers. Strapped trousers, blue Crimean shirts, Hessian riding boots and spurs made up their costume, and the city man, of course, noticed their heavy belts with tobacco pouches and pistols, and the crowning structure without which no squatter was complete —the *cabbage-tree* hat, a large, low-crowned, flopping creation, made of plaited leaves of the cabbage tree, laboriously constructed and worth up to 60s. each.

Noisily shouting and whooping down the uneven streets, such men made the Melbourne Club their *rendezvous*, or the Squatters' in Sydney, until the townsmen longed for lambing or shearing to take them up-country again. Fresh from the restraint of their mutton-and-damper existence in the bush, they had their ideas of a city's functions, and nobody was in doubt when the squatters *came to town*. The Squatters' Ball in January, and their March race (especially the steeplechase for gentlemen riders) called them in from the furthest runs; and, in those months, after the clip had gone and before the next year's rush had started, the colonial towns must have seemed peopled by a peculiar race of whiskery Centaurs who whooped the hours away and terrorized another race of pallid beings who appeared to exist in order to minister to their wants.

Of course, every group of squatters included persons who had started off with neither capital nor education and had laboriously worked themselves up. The first Downsmen in Queensland included 'Cocky' Rogers, an earnest part-owner, and 'Tinker' Campbell, a wayside grog-seller, and such men were types to be found everywhere. Foster Fyans, for instance, the Commissioner of Western Victoria, called them 'a kind of shop-boys', who lived in a squalor pronounced even in the comfortless bush, and whose herds increased in marvellous ways. The Commissioner's peevishness (never difficult to arouse at any time) may have been due in this case to finding the leg and part of the hide of a sheep in his mattress : and it was unfair to accuse all of them of revelling in surroundings of rotten sheep-skins and greasy tin dishes. Some of the shepherds and overseers who finally became squatters on their own account were men of decided initiative : indeed, unless they were *duffers* of other men's stock, they could not have survived without organizing ability and attention to their business. Their records belie Foster Fyans's attacks (although strangely few of them succeeded), and the overseer, in particular, was a good type, if he could secure a loan on *thirds*. Some of them, indeed, became Australia's greatest squatters—James Tyson, the king of them all, for example.

His career, however, was in no sense typical—he was the embodiment of all the resource and energy of which his class may have been possessed but which were rarely found in practice. A rough-looking bushman, bearded as his fellows, he commenced as an overseer at Brooks' Point at £30 a year; and later, despite the opposition of his neighbours, took up Gunambil, on the Billabong. From that time, he encountered amazing vicissitudes. He sold one run for a little rum, another for £12—and did not get the money ! Fifteen years later, he casually offered his State a loan of half a million pounds in cold cash ! Going once to Burragorang for a draft of cattle, he had only a shilling at Gundagai and swam the Murrumbidgee to save it. Coming back, after a tedious droving, he met his brother who had hastened to tell him that they no longer possessed a run, because the water had given out. Once more, he had to go back to droving. Finally, he overlanded cattle to the goldfields—a task every bushman had deemed impossible—and killed and auctioned his stock himself. On the way, he had to camp in three feet of water and light his fire on floating logs—but that was little to the man who had built seven different bridges over the different streams of the Murrumbidgee on one trip.

From that time, this modest giant of a man went on from station to station in three States, until his name became a byword. Yet the man who accomplished these superhuman tasks in the bush once ran from a city Bank to secure a friend's aid, because he said the cashier had looked suspiciously at him and made him nervous!

But Tyson was an exception, and, in general, it was not his class that made the Australian squatting movement. In this connection, a peculiar misconception has arisen. Historians assume that these squatters were totally self-made men: one reads of the primitive life in the slab huts and of the eternal mutton-and-damper roughness, and naturally concludes that the squatters rose to affluence like the selectors of a later date—from humble origins. In the majority of cases, this would be false. Indeed, the striking feature about the first squatters was how many of them were men of good birth, education, and capital. The first rush of convicts and expirees peopled the Nineteen Counties, but that was over by the later thirties; and, when the main squatting movement commenced, quite a different class of people took part in it. First were the sons of the successful officials and colonists of the settled parts—the first local-born generation of good stock. Then came the small capitalists who had been caught in the English crises and had been attracted by the Wakefieldian campaign when it emphasized colonies as providing so much scope for men of moderate means. This was especially the case in Scotland, where both the greater distress and the adventurous disposition of the Scotsmen combined to urge them towards the colonies. Lastly, just at this time, the army had been largely reduced and many officers, both at home and in the service of the East India Company, had been thrown into the civil world with small incomes and liberal pensions. These three classes together formed the bulk of the first generation of squatters, and their nature explains why the squatters almost at once became so highly regarded in the life of the colony, despite the crude conditions under which they were forced to live in the bush.

Fortunately, the number of squatters was comparatively limited until the later forties, and sufficient information exists to classify them into divisions. In practically every district—especially in Victoria and Queensland—the historian can almost take an individual census and is not forced to rely upon *outré* types that have survived on record because of their quaintness. The average squatter was more likely to be an educated member of the middle class than a self-made bushman—the contrary would have been strange in a community lacking a progressive proletariat of free working men. With

sheep at anything up to 60s. a head, and with the need for paying
overhead expenses until the year's clip was sold, only capitalists
could enter the movement, even if the credit-institutions would give
up to 66 per cent accommodation. A man needed £5,000 to run a
flock of 1,000 sheep—this in itself was a sufficient selective guarantee. The two classes of dishonest pilferers and overseers set up by city
capital stood outside this, but, in the great majority of cases, the
squatter was possessed of a considerable initial capital.

Any typical group will prove this point. Most would be men of
education and capital, with a large—many would say, predominant
—proportion of Scotsmen and a fair sprinkling of Army Officers.
In Port Phillip, for instance, the western district was noted from the
first for its gentlemanly proprietors from north Britain—among
them, Learmonth of the Barwon, a descendant of Thomas the
Rhymer and the very type of gentleman-pioneer (yet he had named
and pushed past Mt Misery in the search for new stations!): Irvine,
of one of the oldest Deeside families: McKnight of Dunmore, a son
of the church-historian of Scotland (killed while young by a burning
tree): Curdie the botanist: Mitchell of Langi Willi, with his famous
library (where Kingsley wrote *Geoffry Hamlyn*): Hector McLeod,
the Skye man at Benayeo, and his brother at Tahara: the Hope
Brothers at Lake Wallace: Urquhart, who accumulated some 400,000
acres by his Scot tenacity: William Wallace of Elderslie (what could
be more Scotch?): the famous Robertsons of the Coleraine district:
Ballantyne of Newlands, fresh from a Scottish parsonage: and
scores of others.[19] There were Scots of all kinds and stations—from
the capitalist Lachlan Macalister of Myrtle Creek (N.S.W.) to his
rough agent, Angus Macmillan, the discoverer of Gippsland; from
the tantalizingly named 'Black Cameron of Lochiel' in the Wimmera
to such soldier-types as Captain Murchison of the Ross-shire Yeomanry and Captain Donald McLachlan of the Rifle Brigade, two of
the earliest squatters in the north-east. Above all, was the romantic
figure of that Highland chieftain who came with a band of retainers
and some far-famed Scotch cattle to the infant Port Albert—Macdonnell of Glengarry, who made the first stopping-place on the new
road to Gippsland but who was too feudal to succeed as a pastoralist
in that business age. Such emigrants from the Highlands were
probably in the majority, and, as they themselves were wont to say,
those who were neither Scots nor rank outsiders were at least Sas-
senach soldiers. One cannot go far down the list of licensed squatters

---

[19] Hamilton, op. cit., pp. 29-31: Ross in *Victorian Historical Magazine*,
vol., I, 1911.

without finding military men and reading at various times of such men as Captain Bunbury, who, despite one arm left in Navarino Bay, took up Mt William in the Grampians: Kelly of Kamarooka (near Bendigo), famous for his Indian fighting and his pack of hounds: and Major North, who had left the 68th after much campaigning in the Peninsula to take up squatting as a man of over sixty years of age. A few shanty-men and doubtful characters could not exert much influence in a community of such men as these; and any squatters' committee read like the list of members in a regimental reunion in Scotland.

In Queensland the evidence was similar.[20] The first Downsmen who followed Patrick Leslie were typical. Leslie himself was a severely practical Aberdonian, but the next men, the Hodgson brothers, were far more cultured. Arthur Hodgson set up a learned *coterie* at his bachelor Round-table at Eton Vale and fought a winning battle for supremacy in this direction over the less polished squatters of the Burnett. While one of them could be 'a crassly conservative Etonian', there would be such men as Dalrymple, an explorer of quite an unusual degree of learning; H. S. Russell, also an explorer and, to boot, a politician and the author of a delightful book on that early period; 'Macquarie Macdonald of Dungandan', who had exchanged a Scottish regimental mess for damper on the Upper Logan; the lesser luminary rejoicing in the uniqueness of his name—'the Macpherson'; the Honourable Louis Hope, his alternatives omitted 'for short'; and, as before mentioned, a few men like 'Tinker' Campbell and 'Cocky' Rogers. The pastoral kings of the Downs and the Maranoa for long had the reputation of intellectual superiority and were classed as *pure merino squatters*; but, in the outer lands—the Wide Bay and Burnett zones, and even the Dawson River country—the mass of squatters could be compared with the Downsmen, even if the exigencies of existence left them less leisure.

Of course, all over Australia, this life of danger and rich reward attracted strange characters; and there was rarely a squatting district where the ordinary middle-class settlers did not enjoy the spectacle of persons unlike themselves. Mrs Campbell Praed, for instance, writing of her father's run in the forties, recollected a group of cheerful Bohemians round one Lord John, the son of a Marquis, who had introduced art pottery and polo, and water works and prize pigs, as features of bush life; and *Monseer Jacks* of Boompa, who had formerly dallied at house parties at Compiègne. All manner of foreigners were there—from the seven stout Archer brothers, Norse-

[20] Russell's *Genesis of Queensland* tells of these individuals.

men who first went from the Burnett to the Fitzroy, to the de Castellas, Swiss *chasseurs* who settled on the Goulburn and the Yarra, and did much to introduce viniculture to Victoria. Political refugees came from all parts of the Continent, and specialists in the weirdest professions were to be found dotted round the squatting runs of the period.

But, to get back to *the average squatter*, one has to take a given locality at a given time and thus get a cross section of the squatting classes, without distorting the balance by picking out remarkable personalities over a wider space of time. Thus, by arriving at a true evaluation of a representative group, whether in Victoria, South Australia, or Queensland, he would probably be a cross between one of Russell's Downsmen of the Hodgson type, cultured man and explorer, and perhaps a dash of the bush roughness of Sir John R—, *Dingo Jack*, noted for his resource in emergencies and his flow of language. If the mixture is Scotch, somewhat military, and intolerant alike of obstacles and authorities, it is the truer to type: it has to be clad in moleskins and blue shirt, fed on beef and damper and *hyson-skin* tea, and might be reading with equal facility Youatt's treatise on sheep or Virgil in the original. The resultant type was peculiarly of that place and generation—the gentlemanly squatter could triumph over his environment; but his type, as depicted, belongs to the forties and early fifties of last century—he knew no second generation of his own ilk.

VII   The Management and Prospects of a Station

One of the most vexed problems in this squatting period is the question of profits. The squatters themselves were continually bewailing their poverty and their trials; and most who knew them argued that of ten persons who went out into the back country, nine would return broken men, whether from drought or flood or disease, or a thousand other things. Yet there was the spectacle of squatters becoming the richest class in the land and making huge fortunes. How could these two sides be reconciled? Both had some element of truth in them, and one may well ask—what was the outlook of an average stockman, given a reasonable capital and a sound, practical sense?

Many of the early squatters came out with the most absurd hopes. All that they had to argue from were certain optimistic figures in Macarthur's book on Australia, wherein he calculated the highest possible increase in a kind of geometrical progression, and, by ignoring practical set-backs, returned a large fortune for an initial expenditure of a few pounds. Up till 1837, the price of wool was continually rising, and, if lands could be had for nothing, then it stood to reason, argued these theorists, that the results must all be on the credit side. Practically every squatter started with such ideas and had to live through a period of stern disillusion. Even if his flocks did not die, and he could sell his increase, and wool prices remained high—in short, with everything in his favour, the reward was far less than he had anticipated; and it was hard to realize that sheep farming, like most other things, was an industry where returns were slow and labour hard.

Naturally, some fortunes were made comparatively easily, especially in a few years when squatting was at its peak point. Before the financial crisis, those squatters who had bought stock at low prices and obtained nearer lands could scarcely avoid becoming wealthy; and the newcomer could still be successful, even after sheep had soared up to £3 a head and a man had to go further out. Edward Curr was such a successful man, although he started somewhat late in the day (1841), and accordingly had to pay for *a right of station* and take his flocks away up to the northern region of Port Phillip. Moreover, he started under peculiarly disadvantageous conditions, with bad stock and the industry in a general crisis. For the initial £1,500, he took possession of a ragged run near modern Heathcote, and found some 2,100 sheep, of a very low type—650 aged ewes, 650 two, four, or six-tooth ewes, 300 wethers, and 500 weaners of both sexes. This parody of a run could boast nothing else, except some sordid huts—no horses, no drays, no bullocks, no decent rams even. Accordingly, Curr's first year's expenses were:

	£	s.	d.
Wages—Overseer	100	o	o
3 shepherds at £52	156	o	o
Hutkeeper	52	o	o
Bullock-driver	52	o	o
Overseer's servant	40	o	o
Bullock and dray	100	o	o
One mare	75	o	o
One horse	55	o	o
20 rams (the ones there were too scabby)	80	o	o
Rations for 8, with flour at £60 a ton	200	o	o
Licence-fee for run	10	o	o

Assessment on 2,100 sheep	8	15	0
Sheep-washing, shears, wool-packs	23	0	0
Shearing 2,100 sheep	10	0	0
Dressing-materials for scab and footrot	10	0	0
Expenses, travelling, etc.	100	0	0
	£1,071	15	0

Against this, he could only expect two and a half pounds of wool per sheep, at a shilling a pound—a trifle of £262. 1s., leaving a deficit of over £800. This was not taking into account the normal vicissitudes of squatting life, of which Curr had his share—lack of feed made him miss the market for his 300 wethers, and he could not get rid of his scabby sheep, the complaint naturally spreading over the remainder. In all, he had lost £1,000 after his first shearing, but, as compensation, he had a better run and 1,000 lambs worth a shilling each. In the meantime, however, station property had depreciated 50 per cent, and he could not sell his lambs! His way out of the *impasse* was to scour the newer country on the Goulburn until he found a better run—a change at once retrieved his fortunes. Ten years after he started, he was able to retire as a wealthy man. The £1,500 that had been invested in the first bad run of Wolfscrag and the £500 with which he had started the new venture were then producing from £1,000 to £2,500 a year, and, in addition, Curr left 30,000 sheep on the ground in 1851, while his run was of first class quality—capable of depasturing 100,000 sheep with the aid of a few tanks. Yet he had encountered several reverses, his stock had always been of an inferior description, he had never been able to improve them, he could never clip more than two and a half pounds of wool, and prices were low, both for wool and wethers. Such an outcome was not particularly wonderful—it represented the average return a successful squatter might expect over a period of years, if he could survive the spectacular crashes that so frequently obliterated all traces of several years' work.[21]

Curr, it is true, received most of his return after the long crisis: but those squatters who had to live through the four years of crisis had a harder struggle, and, for an average squatter, the figures given in detail by Hodgson would be truer to type.[22] He instanced a squatter on a large scale, at the time before inflation, when both wages and prices were low; and quoted his expenses as follows:

[21] Curr, op. cit., pp. 35-6, 99-100, 449, 450.
[22] Hodgson, *Reminiscences of Australia*, p. 59, *et seq.*

	£	s.	d.
Preliminary—20,000 sheep at 6/-	6,000	0	0
36 bullocks at £7	252	0	0
3 drays at £23	69	0	0
8 horses at £14	112	0	0
Expenses of forming station, huts, woolshed, barn, hurdles, etc.	1,500	0	0
	£7,933	0	0

Annual—Annual expenses for 20,000 sheep—	£	s.	d.
Wages—Superintendent	100	0	0
Overseer	35	0	0
Cook	23	0	0
Storekeeper	25	0	0
2 farm-servants at £20	40	0	0
20 shepherds and watchmen at £20	400	0	0
3 bullock-drivers and 1 mate at £20	80	0	0
Rations for 30 at £12	360	0	0
Wear-and-tear of 3 drays	23	0	0
Loss of bullocks	70	0	0
Licence and assessment on 20,000	83	6	8
Washing—10 men at 5/- for 24 days	60	0	0
Shearing—20,000 at 3/- a score	150	0	0
Pressing—3 men at 5/- a day for 24 days	18	0	0
150 wool-bags at 18/-	135	0	0
4 dozen shears at 3/-	7	4	0
200 hurdles yearly at £7 a 100	14	0	0
6 extra men at lambing-time at 12/- a week for 8 weeks	28	16	0
Decrease of stock, 2%, by accidents	120	0	0
Commission on £3,000, the produce of wool	150	0	0
Freight to Sydney, 150 bales at 10/-	75	0	0
Travelling expenses, household luxuries, grog for shearing, proprietor's time, etc.	200	0	0
Freight home on 40,000 lbs. of wool at 1¼d.	208	6	8
Interest on £7,933 at 8%	632	13	0
	£3,058	6	4

Deducting the interest-charge, this would involve £2,430 a year, against which the squatter in question would have £3,000 for his wool, the money received for the sale of his increase (if the weather and the market were propitious), and the increased value of his run, if the station-values had not become a drug in the market in the interim. The two latter charges would be too uncertain to estimate, but it may be seen how the gains would be cumulative and how the increased flocks every year would enlarge profits all round. With such a commencement, the first year's capital of £11,000 would soon be repaid with good seasons; and it must be remembered that so much loan-money was available in these days before the crisis that probably only £3,000 was the squatter's own capital. All the items on the above account were fairly typical, although the shrinkage seems very low if taken over a period of years, and wages would have been higher in the forties. Drought and disease would have to be taken into account, and, with so large a starting flock, periodical provision would have to be made for new runs. Nevertheless, the squatter in this case would be on a sound financial basis and his ultimate returns would probably rival Curr's.

One other fact emerges from Hodgson's table—that, if regard be paid to the sale of wool alone, expenses and revenue would be very much on a par in a good year. Indeed, that became almost a truism in the squatter's creed, and every man argued on the assumption that his wool would tide him over the seasons, even if no market existed for his increase. This was particularly important in the years of crisis, when sheep-values fell to a few pence and the squatter had no means whatever of selling his unwanted stock. At such times, his fate depended on his wool, and it meant his ultimate survival if he could meet his expenses by his clip. The witnesses before the various *Committees* in the early forties stressed this again and again: one of them, Murray, proved the point for the whole colony, in 1841. His conclusions were as follows—and this table is perhaps the most important document that has survived on the economic side of squatting. In the colony in 1841, the wool sales realized £511,264— the proceeds of two and a quarter pounds of wool at 1s. 4d. a pound, from 3,408,426 sheep. The scarcity of labour had increased the flocks to the average size of seven hundred and fifty (far too high in rough country) and these necessitated 4,544 shepherds and 2,272 watchmen, of whom two-thirds were beyond the boundaries, where wages were higher. The neglect implied in this crowding may be imagined when it is known that expert witnesses wanted 10,000 new shepherds for the flocks as they then stood! But, neglecting this phase of the situation, the expenses for this £511,000 would probably be:

4,544 shepherds at £50	£227,200
2,272 watchmen at £45	102,240
757 overseers at £75	45,420
Shearing at 4/- a score	34,084
Washing at 1/4 a score	11,502
31,954 bales at 10/-	15,977
Carriage at average of 15/- a bale	23,945
Depasturing fee for two-thirds of these sheep	4,733
	£465,101

This takes no account of the purchase of stock, the expenses of establishment, the cost of huts or hurdles, or even such incidentals as curing diseases or commission on sales. Even so, and disregarding both interest on the capital invested and the losses of stock during the year, there would be a profit of only £50,000. This would probably be absorbed in some way or other in running expenses, leaving the increase to pay for interest and net profit. Given a good year, there would thus be some scope for success; but Murray's figures were especially relevant at that time in demonstrating how sheep would just pay their way, with wages so high and wool-prices so low. The crisis could thus be overcome (if no grave droughts took away the wool), and in normal times, when both wool and young stock could be sold, a favourable financial position could be built up.

What made the sheepmen's profit was his increase. M. H. Marsh, of New England, made this clear to the *Immigration Committee* in 1842.[23] Taking the conditions of that moment and estimating sheep at the comparatively high price of £1 a head, he showed how wool would pay for running expenses, and the sales of stock, over and above that, would yield a profit of from 20 per cent to 23 per cent in normal years, not counting increase on capital. A moderately large squatter would buy 15,000 mixed sheep at £1 a head: he would have to invest £1,500 in fixed goods (such as buildings, oxen, drays, horses); and he would have £2,000 in floating capital, to enable him to pay some 13 to 15 months of wages and to buy everything that was needed on the run for current consumption until the wool was disposed of. That is, he needed £18,500—a figure closely approaching Hodgson's, if allowance be made for the different stock values. Of this normal flock of 15,000, about 7,000 would be breeding ewes; and, after allowance for deaths and killing for mutton, there would probably be an increase of 70 per cent, or 5,000 animals. Half of these would be wethers, and, since they were always wanted, their

[23] *Votes and Proceedings*, 1842: Immigration evidence, p. 42.

value did not vary greatly from 10s. The ewes, in a good season, would fetch £1 each, but their value was far more seasonal. That is, the squatter could sell this increase if he pleased, realize £3,750 as annual profit, and still remain in the position he occupied on starting. If, however, he had to pay 10 per cent interest on three-quarters of his commencing capital (and this was the usual position!), his profits would be down to about 13 per cent—a figure that could jump to 20 per cent once he was independent. If he were fortunate enough to strike a run of good seasons, and could absorb most of his increase and thus expand his stature, as it were, he would quickly transform his position and achieve a result like Curr's, which, in a cumulative way, made the return over a period of years appear so large. Naturally, everything depended on the individual, his finances, his run, the seasons, the general financial position of the colony, and the wool sales. With all of them favourable, or even with a majority of them in his favour, a squatter could count on a return of from 10 per cent to 20 per cent in his first few years, and a rapidly increasing reward after that. He was in the position of a company repeatedly watering its stock and always receiving its initial return: the nominal profit would remain constant, but the actual return would be far higher.

Beyond this, one may not go. The balance-sheets quoted show the various conditions that might reasonably be expected, and the observer can only strike an average and say that a squatter could survive in bad seasons and could make larger profits in good years; but that conditions, both natural and artificial, were so uncertain that it all remained a gamble. A score of factors might upset conditions at any time, and a man worth many thousands at one stage might be bankrupt a season later. These early squatters made little attempt to save themselves by *hedging;* they risked everything, both their own money and all they could borrow on any pretext, and either became extremely wealthy or quite bankrupt. There was no moderate living from year to year, with a little saved every season. Moreover, one must close on the opening note—it is almost certain that only a minority survived in the struggle, for either natural conditions or the credit institutions took toll of most. The vagaries of pastoral life were much more pronounced then than now, and, as everybody plunged to his last farthing, there were no safeguards or reserves. Squatting seemed inseparable from boom conditions. *Wool would pay, and wethers were profit,* they argued, and gaily went on to wealth or defeat, according to the way in which the wool and wethers materialized or were absorbed in the drought-lands.

VIII   *Fluctuations and Trials*

Enough has been written to show how extremely uncertain was an average squatter's life, even considering natural difficulties. Droughts and floods and fires made bush life fraught with danger: scab, footrot, and catarrh ravaged the flocks: wild natives and the accidents incidental to any stock-life were always present: and a squatter never knew from which direction the next calamity was to come. A sheepman, irately asserted one of their number in 1852, had far greater risks to encounter and a commensurately less return than any number of merchants or professional men in the towns, because, to the business uncertainties of the latter, were added the myriads of natural obstacles.[24]

Squatting annals were dotted with fatalities due to the bush and the natives, and it was not only in the much-advertised cases like those of the Faithfull party on the Ovens (1838), or the Wills in the Comet country, or the Frazers on the Dawson. These were exceptional in their magnitude and the amount of publicity they received, but rarely a Commissioner's report was handed in without recording the spearing of shepherds or attacks on homesteads. The blacks exacted their toll everywhere. To place a shepherd down, alone and often unarmed, in the bush, eight or nine miles from the nearest out-station was to invite attack; and a marauding party that started by spearing a few cattle often had to complete its work by *waddying* the stockman.

It was quite a feature in the papers of the time for relatives to advertise if anybody had heard of a squatter who had left the out-post of settlement some months before, and just vanished. Sometimes, as with Howey's party, in 1837, a few dray-bullocks would drift back to the old run, and stray sheep would be found across the main overland track: but no sign would be left of the squatter and his men. Perhaps they would disappear without trace, as did Gellibrand and Hesse in the Otway Ranges, the presumption being that the wild Colac blacks had raided them for their horses: perchance, natives would be found with odd leather relics or carbines: or the explanation might be like that on a pitiful cap picked up in the Bungarrabee bush, explaining the fate of a military officer who had tried to settle in Australia—a leather strip with crude letters cut in, *Frederick Hovenden died of hunger*. Whatever the circumstances and the provocation, such episodes were no remote contingencies in this period, but something to be counted on in the daily course of exist-

[24] *Argus*, 7 February 1852: or *Nisbet Papers* (MSS.), p. 184.

ence. The temptation of a lone white man was too great for any gathering of *myall*-natives, and sheep-fat and cattle-steak seemed there for the spearing, so that a stockman always ran the risk of attack, especially if his shepherds interfered with the native women.

More important were the droughts, for, in those days, no safe-guards had been built up. Artificial feeding, water reserves, com-munications to bring water to the distressed zones or the stock to the water, were all lacking. There was no answer to a drought in the forties—a squatter simply had to stand aside and count his losses from time to time. In some cases, he might overland his herds to more favoured sections of country, but very rarely. The land was ready to turn into a parched oven, with every blade of grass shrivelled to a dry stalk, and every creek and claypan without a drop of water. The three-years' drought of '37, '38, '39 was a by-word. Then, the Murrumbidgee ceased to flow in its bed, and there are records of horse races held in the middle of the bed where the river should have flowed. All of the northern part of Port Phillip, des-cribed by Mitchell as perfectly rich, was thus very different country in most seasons: his lushness was the product of unseasonal rains, whereas normally, and especially in drought times, everything was dry. Once the Lachlan was crossed in New South Wales, once the stock passed Mount Remarkable in South Australia, the squatters were in lands where the grassed flats of one season might become baked belts with yawning cracks, brittle and forbidding. Droughts seemed the rule rather than the exception in the outer lands—there '37-'39 were abysmally bad years, then after two fair seasons came the renewed dryness of three years. In other words, most of the years in this survey witnessed droughts in some form or other, astounding conclusion though this seems! The losses, naturally, were enormous, and instances exist of squatters whose flocks sank from 100,000 to 6,000 in a couple of years, and of drought-bound western runs sold for a little rum or tobacco, with the sheep at a few pence a head. In-constancy was the governing law of things Australian, wrote a French visitor (Beauvoir) in this connection: and certainly, the single factor of droughts in itself prevented any squatter planning even a few months ahead.

If it were not droughts, it would be fire or flood. With the plains baked and cracked, and the timber dry as kindling, and the swamps rotten as parchment, the wind would spread a flame over provinces in a night. Black Thursday of 1851 saw the fires range from the Dandenongs and Western Port in a tossing sea of fire over the Wimmera and the Loddon, and for six days, over the great runs of the west and even to Mt Gambier, across the border—and it was only in its spectacular extent that this varied from the myriads of outbreaks that ravaged the runs every year. The flood was equally bad. In 1839, as has been seen, the Murrumbidgee ceased to flow, the Murray was almost dry in its bed, and the western rivers dried up entirely. But, a little later, flood-waters overbanked them—swirling agencies of destruction stained with yellow mud. The Darling might be almost dry one morning; next day, an unheralded burst might sweep a solid column of water down its tunnel-like banks. Such floods would transform the landscape before escape was possible; and many a squatter, without bridges, without boats, and hindered by a mob of frantic sheep, has met his doom. One has only to consider the expedients resorted to in crossing normal rivers to think how such sudden outbursts must have proved annihilatory. Beauvoir, for instance, thought that no more need be said of this atrocious land when, to the 15,000 sheep that perished of thirst on one run in a year, 3,000 had to be sacrificed to a hail-storm the next year, and 4,000 washed away by a flood shortly after.

Any squatter's diary will tell of such risks in unvarnished language. A befingered notebook in the Mitchell Library will give a number of laboriously spelled phrases, boldly narrating trials sufficient to unnerve the most dauntless, and, by their very bareness, reconstructing the struggle of this old life, with its 20 per cent reward. One of the most telling of these documents is the manuscript of a woman, whose scattered entries tell an imaginative observer more than all the Governor's despatches about the Australia of the forties. Mrs McMaugh of the *Pee Dee* station on the Macleay, one of the first Europeans of any sex to be in that Kempsey land, has left a document priceless to Australians of this day—and incidentally, a monument to herself. It is a squatter's saga; and modern feminists may do few things more appropriate than conjure a vision of this first woman in the northern bush performing feats equal to those of any Tyson or John Peter or Henry O'Brien or the other squatters of fable. Her husband was the manager, and then the owner, of the *Pee Dee*, at that time the only station in this area. She continued the run after his death, and often, when the stockmen were away, she would change into men's clothing and fight off the blacks, first by fusillade through the auger-holes bored in her walls, and then by emerging into the open and driving them off at the point of her carbine. On another occasion, she entered a camp of blacks alone to carry off a noted outlaw who had been ravaging her stock, and, almost casually, she relates a chapter of such accidents as her normal course of existence.

The blacks of that timbered region were especially bold, and often the blue-coloured smoke signals would rise from the ridges to gather the tribes. Now wisping up in thin spirals, now damped down to sharp puffs, this bush-telegraph sent orders to scattered hill-tribes, who would come together on the plains and proceed to the homestead, plundering the out-stations *en route*. Mrs McMaugh best tells the story :

The smoke-signals suddenly ceased, but, when several head of cattle were found speared, the Station hands prepared for mischief : all the lead in the place was moulded into bullets, and a sharp lookout was kept. . . . The door was opened cautiously, and before it could be closed again, two spears quivered in it. . . . Through loopholes in the wall prepared for that purpose, it could be seen that the Blacks had set fire to the roofs of the sheds. . . . They began to realize their stock of ammunition was getting short. A volunteer was then called for to crawl out, in the forlorn hope of bringing help before daylight came. . . . Just before the rosy tint of dawn illumined the east, the Blacks suddenly became silent. . . . A few troopers, mounted black police, natives of Queensland, and one or two Settlers galloped up.

That was all, and the pathetic literary figure at the end only heightens the crude strength of it : yet the writer does not see anything extraordinary in the occasion. In the next moment, she would go to succour a calf that had missed a meal, and each incident would be as important from her point of view.

With such interludes as looking for *strays* in a steep gorge, the months passed by until almost regular alternation of floods and fires turned yet another stage. 'The river came down like a torrent,' she wrote in one place, 'sweeping all before it. In the low places, cattle were surrounded with the rushing, surging and mud-stained waters', and the squatter would have to watch the flood-level gradually swirl up to the hill on which the central house stood. Or it might be fire in this catastrophic prodigality of Nature. She told of 'a very dry season when bushfires raged all round, and cattle were perishing for want of grass, and wild apple trees had to be constantly chopped down for food to keep them from starving'. Incidentally, one such fire burnt them out.

We were awakened by the smell of burning timber. . . . The Storeroom held two years' supply of necessaries, with a great stock of Ammunition, guns, saddlery, etc. When the flames reached this, the explosion was terrible. . . . Home was now being fast reduced to a heap of ashes, my poor children homeless, myself alone and unprotected, with a young child in my arms!

And, round her, the curls of smoke from the crags might be mustering-calls for the natives! Or, perhaps, over the dry bottoms where the river usually flowed, a roaring torrent of fire might be coming down to sweep away the few survivors!

Such accumulated misfortunes, spaced by the tedious months of watching stock or waiting for the drought to break, made up the squatter's life: and it is easy to see how the uncertainty and struggle weeded out all save the strongest of the aspirants. The bush was a hard task-master, and the vagaries of the climate almost eliminated the squatter's few chances of survival.

IX   The Labour Problem

CONVICTS

All through this period, both in boom and crisis, the squatter encountered grave labour-difficulties. It was impossible to secure sufficient shepherds. The old days, when shepherds aplenty were available at £15 a year, seemed long past; and supplies were quite inadequate even at the advanced wage of £25 a year and rations. At no single moment after 1835 were shepherds offering as quickly as they could be absorbed. Indeed, at one stage in 1841, a witness before a *Committee* held that 10,000 were needed at that moment in the Central District alone! So bad was their plight that squatters had to mind their own flocks, and it was an ordinary thing to increase the flocks under each shepherd up to 1,000 sheep, and at times 1,500 or 2,000. Run in such large flocks, many sheep became damaged, and even on the Hunter, a comparatively settled zone, the extra travel this necessitated each day so strained the animals that fat sheep practically disappeared as a market item! The wool, too, if not injured in quality was certainly diminished in quantity: and, all in all, the labour shortage was a kind of recurrent plague afflicting the squatters year after year.

The trouble was that life in the bush offered so few attractions. It was intolerably monotonous to take sheep out every morning and drive them in every evening, and live in a slab hut miles from a neighbour, and eat only mutton chops and unleavened damper. *Crawling after sheep* was an occupation no energetic freeman would consider—it involved a certain stigma in those days, and, once a shepherd, a man had consciously lowered himself to a *hatter's* status, far below the stockman or the town mechanic. The irksome monotony of constant contact with sheep day after day for months repelled most men; and all they were offered in return was 10s. a week (oft-times withheld from them by trickery) and a weekly ration of ten pounds of flour, twelve pounds of meat, two pounds of sugar, and some four ounces of tea.[25] They were even forbidden to communicate with their neighbours, eight miles off in the next outstation, lest the separate flocks be mixed!

Even the convicts were loth to go to the back-country, so that the sheepowners had to raise wages once more (even to £50 in the early forties) and accept engagements for much shorter periods than the old yearly contracts. A shepherd could so easily find work that he would not bind himself for more than three months, even in the settled districts, and would break his contract on the slightest pretext. William Lawson of Prospect, for instance, engaged fifty shepherds on an engagement for three years, but all save two took advantage of some legal flaw in their agreements and absconded! Terence Murray, one of the best known figures in the colony, doubled the rations of his men in 1841—they retorted by demanding an increase in wages up to £35 and £40! Little wonder, then, that the squatters turned in despair to Hill-coolies and Chileans: their flocks were rotting for lack of men to shift the hurdles far enough, and their increase died because there were no men to graze them. The lowest class of labourers had the whip hand, especially when the assignment of convicts ceased at the end of 1838—and they knew it. Their wages were doubled, trebled, and more, and their conditions were improved: but still they kept the sheep industry in a chronic state of uncertainty, so that many flocks were left to run wild, and others were known to have as many as four peripatetic shepherds in a single fortnight. All of this naturally implied great damage in an industry that depended so much on regularity over long periods of time, and was the worse, because not all the immigration could get over the difficulty, and because the few thousand shepherds answered better conditions by still wider demands. The position was intolerable, and seemingly irremediable.

Under these conditions, the great majority of the shepherds came to be convicts of a low type. Any settler could obtain assigned convicts until November 1838. He simply had to apply to the Govern-

[25] *Riley Papers* (Mitchell Library), vol. II, pp. 213-17, or *Mollison Papers* (Victorian Historical Society), or *V.D.L. Company's MS Orders* (Burnie), 18 and 19, 1827.

ment, keep the convict, and pay him a small dole; and in return, had his services. In practice, the system meant that a convict-shepherd cost £15 in all, whereas a freeman demanded at least £20 in wages, with as much again for his rations. The squatters, there-fore, steadily maintained a strong agitation for a renewal of convict supplies. Assignment ended in 1838, and transportation itself by an *Order-in-Council* of August 1840, but the squatters refused to take this decision as final and arrayed themselves against the townsmen in preferring convicts to free immigrants. New South Wales had 30,000 convicts at the moment assignment ended, and the squatters took up Benjamin Boyd's cry—*We want 10,000 convicts beyond the boundaries alone!* and continued to press their demands, despite the growing opposition in the towns. They realized that the cheap labour of the past had enabled their industry to establish itself, and that they must have in the future, if not the cheapness of that labour, at least its certainty. They put forward this demand time and again in the forties, and practically every squatter favoured convictism. Gipps, for instance, found the colony in a *furore* in 1838, because assign-ment was doomed and because the sheepmen held that the result had been achieved by misrepresentation at home.[26] No fewer than sixty-seven magistrates and five hundred leading citizens signed a petition for its continuance, and the Council passed a whole series of resolu-tions. Again, next year, Blaxland and Wentworth swayed a huge public meeting in their favour, and from that time, the squatting crisis gave a peculiar emphasis to their demands.[27] Every witness before the *Immigration Committee* of 1841 preferred convicts to the more unstable freemen: and in 1842, the so-called *banditti party* again presented a petition to the Queen praying for renewed trans-portation.

So reiterated were these demands that the Colonial Office had to reconsider its position. The staple of a colony was at stake and the great mass of the prominent citizens were behind the movement. Moreover, it was realized that the members of the Commons *Com-mittee* of 1838, which had decided against assignment, had not been in a position to consider the scope and importance of the new squatting movement—they had avowedly come to a conclusion on imperfect evidence, they had not known the position as it had per-tained at the moment of their decision, and it had changed beyond recognition since that time. It was easy for Glenelg, Normanby, and Lord John Russell to declaim against transportation, but none of

[26] Gipps-Glenelg, 18 July 1838.
[27] *Sydney Herald*, 11 February 1839.

them had proposed any alternative way of giving the colony labour. Every year saw the flocks increase by anything up to 70 per cent and one shepherd could not decently manage more than 1,000 sheep: so that a single mathematical calculation alone posed the problem! The Cabinet had been very concerned with starting Maconochie's *Social System* to pamper the convicts in Norfolk Island, but had not considered the effects either of swamping Van Diemen's Land with convicts or of entirely withdrawing them from New South Wales. They had been led astray by a chimera, but unfortunately, the flocks were increasing at every lambing time, and the position was becoming cumulatively worse.

The Tory, Stanley, was more amenable. As has been seen, he realized the implications of the new squatting movement and was not averse to considering the stockmen's demands. At first, in 1842, he had proposed a theoretical plan of many stages, aimed at really punishing the convicts; but in 1844, after the emergence of the general squatting agitation, he changed his objectives and tried to secure labour for the colonies. In July of that year, came the first suggestion of his system of *Exiles*. Convicts were to be punished at Parkhurst and Pentonville at first, and then, having been reformed from motives partly prudential and partly religious, they would be landed in Australia and allowed to roam where they would. Van Diemen's Land could not absorb its existing convicts, and it was not desirable for the pious Pentonvillians to mix with the debased *canaries* of the island: therefore, argued Stanley, why transport them as convicts at all? If given free pardons, they would offer scope for themselves and labour for the colonies—the best ends of everybody would be attained. He at once sent a preliminary sample on the *Royal George*, proposed a full vessel for Launceston (chosen as the most central point for scattering them over the settled colonies), and even hinted at a completely new settlement on the mainland coast.[28]

The first group were readily absorbed at Port Phillip, where the cry for labour had been especially pronounced, and the squatters eagerly cried for more, despite the protests of a few town papers. The next batch of one hundred and seventy-four who came on the *Sir George Seymour* in March 1845, were absorbed within a fortnight (though one committed suicide when he saw Geelong!); and cries arose for them everywhere—from Melbourne and Yass, Portland Bay and Port Fairy, and especially from the Moreton Bay squatters. The shortage was so acute on the Port Phillip runs that a voluntary

[28] Contrast Stanley's despatches of 25 November 1842, and 27 July 1844.

association had been formed to import Tasmanian convicts without Government aid. The squatters begged for a continuance of the *Exile* scheme, snapping up the fifty-one who came in February 1846, and decrying the Melbourne agitation as the outcry of a minority who neglected the real position of most of the people. Petitions from all directions asked for more convicts. The settled stockholders of the Downs joined those of the new lands to the north, and in 1845, plaints came in from Yass, the Lachlan, and the farthest Murrumbidgee reaches. Their organizations were unanimous on this point, and even the *Patriotic Association*—the political reformers under Wentworth and Bland—were no less convinced.[29]

Therefore, when Gladstone followed Stanley and proposed some modified form of transportation in April 1846, the squatters rejoiced. Behind Gladstone's elaborate tergiversations were the two fixed beliefs that total exclusion was unwise, in view of the chronic labour shortage in the colonies, and that any *regular* supply of convicts could help both public and private works.[30] Wentworth's *Committee* quickly decided to favour the revival, if not less than 5,000 males were sent a year, and if equal numbers of free immigrants were to come. They reported that a majority of the colonists would probably vote against the convicts, but, since New South Wales was to have a felon population to the north and to the south, whether she liked it or not (because Gladstone had already resolved to form a convict settlement in *Northern Australia*), she might as well have the system open and controlled by a half century's experience. The convict colony (the *Buccaneer's Archipelago* of the colonists' skits) soon failed, but the squatters continued to fight for the rest of the plan. As nothing happened, the Council passed a new resolution in 1848, again requesting transportation, but the conditions had changed.

Now that the squatters had locked up the lands, the townsmen were in no mood to allow them to deluge the colony with a corroding mass of criminality, freed from all restraints. Free immigration had set in again, and Robert Lowe was noisily giving coherence to the people's claims. Earl Grey, meanwhile, had received the Council's resolution and had sent out *Exiles* without equivalent free emigrants —an act that completed the organization of the anti-transportation party. Great meetings were held, and the *Hashemy* exiles met with much opposition. The squatters, however, remained obdurate: they eagerly employed the *Hashemy* men in 1849, despite the uproar, and even took them in preference to a thousand freemen who had

[29] Gipps-Stanley, 25 February 1845, 9 April 1845, 2 July 1845.
[30] Gladstone-FitzRoy, 30 April 1846.

come out at the same time. The Queensland stockmen, in particular argued with Earl Grey, both from Australia and in London, and, when convicts were refused, turned to black labourers from every conceivable source.

But the last convicts came to New South Wales in 1850. Distress in England and famine in Ireland were far more telling arguments than all the statistics about sheep increase in Australia. The immigrants were coming—and the squatters no longer represented the colony as they had done ten years before. Indeed, they were in the position of a minority fighting for anti-social rights. The crowd of 5,000 townsmen who met to jeer at the *Hashemy*-exiles represented the new force that was displacing the squatters and their sheep; and the convict-shepherd had to go.

Throughout the period of this book, however, most of the shepherds were still convicts. An average run was managed by *canaries* who had, to this extent, been freed from the hold of the law. There is no general testimony regarding these men. Probably, they were as quiet on their jobs as any other group of some 8,000 mixed human types, for, certainly, the irksome nature of sheep-minding left them little scope for villainy. They generally became strangely subdued and morose (hence the designation *hatters!*), with some petty idiosyncrasy strongly developed. To brew *pennyroyal tea* and sneak off gathering *gum-manna* to supplement sugar rations were their main dissipations—and, perchance, to leave their flocks and seek company at the nearest out-station. Grog was not amiss to them, but opportunities in this direction came only when they received their meagre pay and *knocked it up* at some wayside shanty. Tradition makes of them a race quiet to the point of half-wittedness, and bad mainly in company. Some were strange types—as were their masters—and we read of shepherds who had been at the College of Surgeons in Edinburgh, or lieutenants in the old Ross-shire Buffs, or breeders of blood horses; of French counts and legionaries from the Carlist wars, and cashiered army men; and of numerous quiet old men who went out with haversacks crammed with the latest English magazines and *Reviews*. More frequent are memories of dull, besotted labourers with some little eccentricity—of such as *the Prophet of Khorassan*, who surrounded his cabbage-tree hat with a mosquito net hanging down to his waist—of him who had a dog chained to his waist at each side—of those numerous souls who communed with stones or saw incarnate devils in their sheep, or who suffered a thousand and one melancholic delusions.[31] Usually, however, they were petty criminals, not

[31] For instances, see *Grant Papers* (MSS.), p. 70, or *Améro*, p. 70.

sufficiently strong-minded for open viciousness, innocently deranged from a combination of loneliness and lack of mental stamina, and dangerous only in crowds. There were more small men deported for minor offences than outright criminals or the sweeping of the scums —Curr, for instance, had machine-breakers, drunken marines, petty thieves, horse stealers, and the like, but no major criminals. The deep-dyed villains soon became convicted again, and their havens were the Coal River or Norfolk Island or any of the outer gaols, not the stations of the interior. The average shepherd probably had some pre-disposition to a criminal weakness, either natural or due to the environment of the transport, but, as against this, most were deficient in will power; and they remained weak, lonely men, safeguarded from the defects of their character by their isolated life, and soon becoming pitifully strange. It was no life for a full-witted freeman, the townsmen argued—and, in this, they were correct, because a shepherd had to cope with all the disadvantages of penal isolation, and his mind was inevitably affected. He had, it is true, a fuller diet and less labour than the average English workman, but paid for it in the shaping of his personality. He became a 'crawler after sheep', with the mentality of his charges, and a life little changed from theirs.

It is striking how many squatters have borne testimony as to their desirability. Macarthur, who had one hundred and thirty of them in his employ, held that shepherding gave them regular habits and was in no sense a punishment. Dixon, in manuscript papers referring to the twenties, agreed as to their behaviour and honesty, especially because they had a lively fear of punishment at the Coal River. Grant, also in unpublished manuscript, 'found them faithful, efficient, and often very companionable', and many pieces of evidence exist as to their good conduct on the western runs of Victoria and the Macleay district in New South Wales. Patrick Leslie, overlanding to the Downs, would not have changed his convicts for thrice their number of freemen, and Curr, in northern Victoria, found them more dependable and disciplined than immigrants.

Against this, were the numerous complaints. Mollison, overlanding to Victoria, under similar conditions to Leslie, narrates one long story of mutiny and disaffection, but perhaps the explanation lies, partly at least, in contrasting Leslie's rough *bonhomie* with Mollison's aloof reserve and contempt for his men. Even Curr had, on one occasion, to drive his convicts at carbine point, and the average squatter's diary bristles with entries like those of Hobler, a settler in Van Diemen's Land and western New South Wales:

My two men were sentenced to three years' transportation to a penal settlement (for rioting). . . . Two of my new men, one a boy only, a whip-finisher, the other a Birmingham pot-boy (these are the useful men the Government promised!); the third, who is described as a ploughman, has not yet arrived. . . . He loitered in Hobart Town, got drunk, and was put on the treadwheel for a week. . . . These two men seem to think by the most tantalizing insolence they may get out of a place in which they see plenty of work forward. . . . One was so bad that he was ordered to receive fifty lashes, and the Chief Constable was directed to make a new cat for him (9 tails)—the Magistrate recommended me to stop his tea, sugar, and everything but bread, meat, and water. . . . He let 70 head of cattle I put him in charge of upon the wheat for some hours! (therefore was turned back to Government). He was ordered to receive six months in the gaol-gang. . . . Jem abused and threatened Thomas so grossly that I ordered him to fetch a constable in the morning that he might ruminate Sunday through in the Watch house; he had intimation from Trimmings of the constable's arrival in order to secrete himself— but returned to the hut at night. . . . Took him and Thomas into the Police Officer, and Mr. Mulgrave awarded him fifty lashes, which were laid on this morning—very smartly![32]

Such continued obstruction was by no means unusual, especially in the settled districts, so much so that Governor Arthur told the 1837 *Committee* that convict-shepherds 'involve the settlers in daily trouble, expense, and disappointment'. Similarly, in the *Hogan Papers* in the Mitchell Library, reference is made to one of the first runs of 1833 in the *New Country*, and to the mixed nature of the convicts—some were 'of a malicious and mischievous disposition', while others would somewhat respond to good treatment. But none of them forgot that circumstances favoured them in many ways. As the thirties advanced, they knew that the masters would not return them to Sydney during the labour shortage, and that, with a magistrate perhaps two hundred miles away, they could behave much as they pleased. They could disobey orders, could meet one another clandestinely and thus box the flocks; and, if their rations were stopped, they could keep the sheep penned up or neglect the lambs; while, if they were sent to Court, their services were lost for twenty or thirty days at least, and perhaps altogether, and this at a time when it took anything up to eighteen months to replace a convict through the official channels. A single recalcitrant shepherd could do untold harm to sheep, and it was generally found that it was to the owner's interest to conciliate his men and treat them fairly. Leslie's method was the best for everyone.

[32] *Hobler MSS.* (Mitchell Library), entries 17 August 1826, 15 February 1828.

Nevertheless, despite all of these failings, the squatters were practically unanimous in preferring convicts to free labourers. English shepherds were notoriously unsatisfactory, because the conditions were so different and they had so much to unlearn : while free immigrants would not bind themselves for long periods and despised shepherding too much to do it properly. In 1841, for example, the squatting witnesses before the *Immigration Committee* were emphatic on this point—Hamilton of Cassilis would not have a freeman on his estate at any price and he was supported by many of the largest settlers—Ryrie, William Lawson, and Captain King of the Australian Agricultural Company, to quote a few. Whatever their faults, the convicts made good shepherds if treated tactfully : and the squatters fought for them until the last decisions of the Colonial Office, and even beyond. They may have been insubordinate and crime-tainted, and peculiar to the point of derangement; but they served the squatters' purposes far better than the immigrants, whose very intelligence and ambition made them unsuitable for this most monotonous of employments. But the Government held that 137,000 convicts were sufficient for Australia, and the strange figure of the *hatter*-shepherd, with his handkerchief satchel and his lack-wit expression, soon disappeared from the countryside after the forties.

FREE IMMIGRANTS

The free immigrants enter into this survey much less than would be supposed, because so very few of them became shepherds or stockmen. They affected the labour position, however, because the temporary excess of labourers at the peak periods of emigration (1841 and 1847, for instance) brought down wages and relieved the general pressure. Inversely, the lack of immigrants in most of this period intensified the labour difficulty of the squatters, although such immigrants were in no sense the determining force in the position. Thirty thousand convicts were more important than the four thousand freemen who came on an average in the ten years after 1838, especially when four years elapsed with practically no assisted emigration. Such importance as the emigrants possessed was rather in raising the class of town labourers as a counterpoise to the squatters and their convict servants. As such—although they would not go to the bush to work on runs themselves—they immediately affected the destiny of each squatter. But the cumulative effects of such organization in the towns did not become noticeable until towards the close of this survey; and it would be a great mistake to over-estimate the importance of the immigrants before 1848, and, in particular, to assume that a convoy of 12,000 immigrants, as in 1841, meant an addition of that amount to the labour supplies of the up-country squatters.

Since emigration, however, was ultimately to transform the colony, and since convictism had run its course, this matter attracted more attention in the forties than any other question, except squatting itself: and many were the schemes proposed to accelerate the transfer of labourers across the Wakefield bridge—from the excess of the old countries to the demand of the new. Lord Normanby had given coherence to the movement by his bounties of 1835, and, by Glenelg's time, it was a truism that emigration charges were to be met by the colonial Land Fund. Various *Committees* of Council (under Forbes in 1835 and Snodgrass in 1837) demanded English agricultural labourers—3,000 at least were wanted for the first squatting rush of 1835, and as many afterwards in each year. The 1837 body asserted that it was positively necessary to spend all of the Land Fund on emigration, and that, even then, some hundreds of *Hill-coolies* would be required from India.[33] If nothing were done, 'the consequences will be most fatal to the best interests of the colony', wrote Snodgrass, going much further than the dignified and telling report of Chief Justice Forbes, two years before. In the interim, the demand had gone up to 10,000 workers; and, of course, the abolition of assignment a year later aggravated the shortness over the whole land. The colonists were little troubled over the Home Government's hesitation between the two systems—they did not care whether bounties were paid for every emigrant, or whether the emigration was conducted in Government ships at Government expense: all that they wanted was a regular supply of labour, increasing to keep pace with the movement over the interior. The demand increased year by year, and the supply fell off, because now, to the old objections to *Botany Bay* in England, were added exaggerated reports of the long drought and the high prices of provisions. Nor must it be forgotten that these were just the years when the agents were holding out enticements to go to Texas and New Zealand—an appeal so strong that all the emigrants who came to eastern Australia in the

[33] These two Committees amply tell the story from the colonial point of view. General documents are in the annual *Votes and Proceedings*, and the subject fills the despatches almost in too great detail. A general report on the period, 1837-9, is in Lord John Russell's despatch of 12 February 1840, and Stanley reviews the whole history of emigration in his despatch of 14 October 1846. Modern accounts are in Mills, op. cit., and Roberts, ch. X.

decade after 1838 numbered less than a third of those who went to the United States in any one year! In 1839, the Australian agents could scarcely fill their ships from the distressed regions of the Highlands, while formerly fruitful districts like Kent and Sussex had become quite barren.

To hasten the flow, Gipps and the local Council advocated bounties (as against the system of Government control, wanted by the Colonial Land and Emigration Commissioners at home), but Gipps issued bounty-orders so rapidly that claims for a million pounds were outstanding by 1841. At this, Lord John Russell, who had previously adhered to the bounty system despite his advisers, felt himself obliged to remonstrate, for, even if Gipps had swollen the number of immigrants to 12,000 in 1841, such means were unjustifiable. Yet a Council Committee of 1842, far from being deterred by the prospect of so many immigrants, held that 12,000 were needed every year, even if the colony had to raise a loan to pay for them. But, by this time, Gipps had been ordered to refrain from issuing any more bounty-orders, and the channel of immigration appeared to have dried up, although the colony was crying for labour and there had been little difficulty in absorbing the massed arrivals of 1841.

Such a drastic fall, however, was too salutary a check to improvidence, and, towards the middle of 1843, Stanley contemplated a renewal of emigration—a limited bounty system, for perhaps 5,000 men.[34] In January 1844, the Herald, from Glasgow, was the first ship to arrive under the new scheme, and all of its complement found employment notwithstanding the crisis in the colony. But, for various reasons (especially the weakness of the colonial Land Fund), this effort was practically isolated, and the years passed without any large-scale immigration until 1848, when Earl Grey took a decisive step and advocated a continuous flow of free immigrants, either with or without convicts. The position was as bad as it had been ten years before—New South Wales alone clamoured for 10,000 shepherds for its existing flocks, for, taking Port Phillip into consideration, the seven million sheep needed at least 42,000 labourers to supervise them (even with flocks of 1,000 per man), yet there were only 13,565 at the moment! All the mountains of emphasis in various emigration schemes, all the reams of despatches and reports of Committees, and all the financial expedients had resulted in the tiniest achievement, for, while the flocks had trebled, the only emigrants who arrived (even in Gipps's period of inflation) were:

[34] Stanley-Gipps, 17 September 1843.

	Paid from Colonial Fund (Men and Women)*		Unassisted†
1838	6,102	Cost £101,084	1,328
1839	7,852	139,354	1,983
1840	5,216	116,775	1,301
1841	12,188	194,846	1,598
1842	5,071	72,334	1,534
1843	—	8,778	977
1844	2,726	42,995	485
1845	497	9,166	461
1846	—	873	402
1847	—	951	515
1848	4,376	43,128	651
	44,028	£760,264	11,225

* This was the appropriation from the Colonial Land Fund: there may have been aid from the English end.

† Mainly men of capital, who became squatters or merchants.

Naturally, with such meagre results, the squatting position could be very little affected, except in the period 1841-2. Most of the emigrants stopped in the towns as small artisans, and, even in the peak year, all the effect they had was to reduce the wages of a shepherd from £25 to £20. In general they preferred to starve in the town and be succoured by the Government rather than go into the bush. Thus, Gipps was feeding free immigrants in the Sydney streets even when the squatters were crying for labour of any kind. The emigrants were not sufficiently numerous to affect the situation appreciably and, in addition, refused to aid the squatters: and, in turn, the squatters, though ready to use them, despised the emigrants and preferred *Government men*.

THE ABORIGINES

One other labour supply seemed open to the squatters—the natives. Each pioneer had to solve his relationships with the aboriginal owners of the soil: if he could use them, he had to make an experiment, and, if not, he had to make clear his policy towards them. Numerically, the aborigines were never very strong—Victoria had only 7,000 at the outset—but the isolation necessitated by squatting existence placed an altogether disproportionate power of evil in their hands.[35]

[35] This is an important topic, crying for some general treatment. No history of European relationships with the natives has been attempted, despite the obvious gap.

Their history is a sordid one from beginning to end, a tale that sickens in the reiteration. For long, nothing whatever was done for them—only £51,800 was appropriated for native welfare in the whole of Australia's first half century.[36] Isolated missions received a few hundreds a year, and some blankets and rations were distributed: but there, Government action stopped. Gipps, indeed, was anxious to change this inertia and set up an elaborate system of *Protectorates*. Head protectors were installed at Sydney and Melbourne, and various assistants were scattered throughout the country. The Protectors, usually clergymen who expected to do religious work, were placed on the Commission of the Peace and ordered to patrol their districts and perform executive functions, in much the same way as Commissioners of Crown Lands. They were to be local governors rather than parsons or teachers. As most of them were inoffensive bookish men, the result can be imagined. They were retiring clerics who had brought their families with them, and expected ready-made manses; whereas, instead, they were given a single dray, curtly told that their wives and children had no official existence, and ordered to go over impassible tracts into the plains or mountains of the interior and earn their £200 a year by keeping a huge district in order and, in particular, checking the squatters. Not unnaturally, the results were quite negative. Prevented from doing their proper work, the Protectors achieved nothing; and, year by year, Gipps was forced to report on the system as a costly absurdity, scheme of his own though it was.

Even the missionaries admitted the failure. A few natives came to them as long as free rations were to be obtained, but religion without food had no charms for them, and oft-times the Wellington Valley establishment had not a single native there. 'Their only concern is about eating', wrote a Mission Inspector, and in general, the blacks mistrusted the missions and disliked sending their children to them. The great majority were migratory, and, after seeming to respond to treatment for a period of months, would suddenly pack off without any reason. Indeed, they appeared to use the missions— certainly at Wellington Valley—as a centre for getting into touch with stockmen for immoral purposes. The missions therefore dwindled. Wellington Valley came down to one consumptive, and the next year's report said that even he had *gone bush!* Their products reverted to savagery, a great commotion being caused by two supposedly religious natives who left the mission after eleven years

---

[36] An important paper on aborigines is in *Votes and Proceedings*, 1843— 68 pages of documents.

to kill two sailors at Western Port. Failure succeeded failure, until
Lord Stanley recommended the abolition of the entire scheme
(1842).[37] Both missions and protectorate had broken down, partly
because of the unsuitable *personnel*, but mainly because of the
nature of the natives. By the end of 1842, then, New South Wales
was without any native policy—Gipps and Stanley were even past
the promulgation of new theories! The natives were left, a disorganized and drifting mass, to adjust themselves to squatting conditions. Missionaries and Commissioners continued to send in reports
on the various districts, but even the philanthropically inclined
had to join in the long tale of native faults—of their thoughtlessness,
ingratitude, debauchery, want of effort, infanticide, and outrages.
The aborigines would not work, and only abandoned themselves to
fighting and selling their *gins* to shepherds for tobacco or spirits. In
the wake of these evils, came the inevitable venereal disease, consumption, and an appallingly rapid depopulation.

All that Gipps could now do was to enforce the law against
aggressors on both sides and trust that the more energetic natives
could be absorbed on the squatting runs. Unfortunately, both of
these expedients were out of the question. Gipps was a hard man, and
a theory, once in his mind, acquired all the force of an obsession. He
thus conceived it his duty to wage war on the squatters in favour
of what he viewed as oppressed aborigines. Looking upon himself as
their *Proconsul-Protector*, he usually attributed aggression to the
squatters and their shepherds, and would not listen to the tales of
native provocations and marauding habits. To him, blacks were
innocent and unsophisticated children of nature. He said that
squatters forced natives to labour and did not pay them, that lonely
shepherds plundered their womenfolk, and that the natives were
forcibly despoiled of their traditional hunting-grounds. He saw himself as a revered *White Father* at Sydney, whose edict was to go
forth and be admired by the dusky natives and implicitly obeyed by
the sheepmen.

He pursued this policy to the point of intolerance, and met the
arguments of practical settlers with his customary brusqueness. He
instituted a *Border Police* to keep order, incidentally taxing the
squatters for its maintenance: he insisted that every native killed
should have the same form of inquest as a European, and ignored the
hundreds of miles that made absurd any comparison between a crime
in George Street and a murder in the outer bush. In particular, he
harried white aggressors to the gallows, and told a squatter who pro-

[37] Long enclosures in Gipps-Lord John Russell, 7 May 1840.

tested that his flocks were laid open to depredation that, *if he
defended himself against myall or wild natives, by God he would
hang him!*

The terrible affair of *Myall Creek* gave point to his assertions and
defined the attitude he adopted towards the squatters' difficulties.
Under particularly revolting circumstances, certain convict-shepherds
had deliberately shot and burnt twenty-eight innocent natives in the
cattle-country on the Big River, irrespective of age or sex. Gipps at
once put eleven of the criminals on trial for murder, but, horrid as
was the outrage, such a step shook the colony to its foundations. The
colonists had not deemed it possible to try white men for killing
natives, and now the Governor was actually trying and re-trying
them, and in the end, executing seven of them.[38] It would be difficult
to exaggerate the stir this caused in the squatting ranks, for it
changed one of the basic assumptions of life in the bush. Next year,
Gipps called two special sessions of the Executive Council to consider
the punishment of Major Nunn, of the Mounted Police, who had
killed too many natives in the execution of his duty.[39] True, he had
to delay this latter inquiry for months, because the public were still
too excited about the Myall Creek case, and he had to stop the actual
Nunn trial, because any jury would have acquitted at that moment
and because he was afraid the Mounted Police—volunteers—would
resign *en masse*. He was even compelled to give way to the public
ferment and withhold his contemplated notices on protecting the
natives, since rarely a month passed, either in the South or the
North, without reports of some new depredations. Nunn had been
ordered north to clear the Namoi lands, or 'we may have them
presently within the Counties', asserted Acting-Governor Snodgrass
—and this represented the prevailing opinion. The Governor found
himself in a minority on the native question, opposed by squatters
and townsmen alike.

What happened was that the Governor's attitude had spread like
wildfire over the interior, and the natives, with that peculiar *bush
telegraphy* by which the Governor's simple-sons-of-the-soil kept informed of the latest events at Sydney, heard that they could do anything they pleased and not be punished. *Bullock* (as they called beef)
was to be had for the spearing : they could go where they wished,
stations or no stations : they could say and do what they liked : and,
if any shepherd or squatter remonstrated with them, they would

[38] See page 87. Gipps-Glenelg, 19 December 1838.
[39] The full evidence is in Gipps-Glenelg, 22 July 1839.

threaten him with the vengeance of the troopers. They could even decorate him then and there with the ugly square gashes of their tomahawks and, if he fired in return, the black troopers would come, haul the aggressor to Sydney, judge him according to the strange white's man's law, and hang him as high as the gallows-post in public view of all whites and natives who chose to attend. Quantities were as nothing to *Massa Gubna*, for had he not hanged seven of the Myall Creek shepherds all at once, and said that he would so dispose of all the squatters in a given district if they repeated the offence? On the other hand, if they themselves were apprehended, all that they had to do was to profess ignorance and say nothing; and they would get a free trip far away to the white man's towns, and depart laden with the Governor's presents, and perhaps even a uniform? If they were very lucky, they would be placed in the Governor's stronghouses, and receive much for doing absolutely nothing, as well as white man's wonderful shelter!

Facts were on their side in this argument, for, in Gipps's first six years, he found only ten natives guilty of crime, and, despite the multitude of outrages, punished the perpetrators of no more than seven murders. Most were discharged by proclamation and sent back to their tribes. The results were soon evident to the squatters. The natives became unbearably impudent, and no longer were flocks or even human life safe. Seven or eight years of virtual terror set in after 1837—aggravated because this was just the period when the stockmen were overrunning Port Phillip, Moreton Bay, and the West. Practically every squatter had to reckon on the hostility of the natives. It was quite useless to treat them fairly, because they were completely amoral and usually incapable of sincere and prolonged gratitude. They could see no wrong in demanding supplies at the point of the tomahawk or by the pressure of numbers, or in spearing cattle for the sake of a single strip of meat, or sheep for a fragment of kidney-fat, or in hitting sheep on the head if they were refused tobacco or damper in absurd quantities, or even for killing lonely whites for no reason at all save their isolation! The grievance so much stressed by Gipps (that the blacks objected to the attacks on their women) was not a pressing one in reality. Even the missionaries admitted that their charges would offer their women for sticks of tobacco or for nothing at all, since promiscuous sexual intercourse irked them not at all, as long as the mixture was outside certain native totem-groupings. Their grievances, on the other hand, were usually the result of their own ungovernable dispositions and their failure to see any sense in the white man's laws of property. Two vitally different ideas were clashing, and harmony was impossible under the given conditions.

For the moment, all that the blacks saw was that the white men were held back and punished if they offended them—La Trobe, for instance, pursuing certain shepherds of Port Fairy for eighteen months for murdering native women.[40] Life became almost unbearable on the outer stations. A native of Portland Bay, cutting a single steak from a living bullock, said when caught in the act, '*If you touch me, the Gubbna will hang you!*' According to returns submitted to the House of Commons, such aggressions became so common that, in the one small district of Port Fairy (and conditions were usually worse in the more northerly parts of Port Phillip, and especially away towards Moreton Bay), twelve white men were either killed or severely wounded in two months of 1842, and at least 3,500 sheep driven off. Scarcely a station was exempt from outrages or menace: one was attacked four times, and flock after flock, sometimes four at once, were taken. Most were ruthlessly speared and left as sheer carrion—a wanton waste.

From the time Faithfull's party were massacred on the Ovens (1838), the tracks became worse every year. The west of Port Phillip had a particularly bad name at this time: then, in 1840, the northern rivers became unsafe, and blacks attacked Mackay's station on the Ovens with firearms: and, all through 1842 and 1843, the West and the new overland route to Adelaide were terrorized. Then, the stage shifted to Moreton Bay—to the newer country, where natural conditions made retaliation practically impossible; and observers spoke without hesitation of a menaced border, of guerilla action so widespread as to merit the name of native insurrection. Responding, the community seemed panic-stricken, and frantic queries were bandied down the stock-routes:

What safety could the squatters have now that the Myall Creek executions had removed the blacks' timorousness? Had not seven of Faithfull's overlanders been slain in 1838, and forty stockmen in all of Port Phillip? Were not fifteen shepherds killed on the Liverpool Plains alone in 1838? Were not the new pasture-grounds of Moreton Bay notoriously unsafe, and what was being done to prevent terrorism by armed natives in western Port Phillip?

With such a state of public opinion—and it was perfectly justified from the pioneers' point of view—it was very difficult to solve the

[40] Gipps-Stanley, 11 September 1843.

problem. Outrage, real or imaginary, was met by outrage, and Europeans killed natives on the slightest pretext. When shepherds came together, it was not unusual to *potshot* natives in exactly the same way that pigeons are shot at shooting-meets. Some shepherds sought for notoriety as heartless killers, one overseer in the Grampians having an unenviable priority in this regard, until a particularly cruel outrage forced him to flee to the *North Countree*. It is recorded that 130 natives were killed in the first few years of Port Phillip, and it must be known that these were the cases officially known to the authorities and substantiated by them. In reality, the actual number must have been huge, for it was no unusual sight to come across heaps of the bones of murdered natives. Curr relates how his convict-shepherds, meeting two blacks in the bush, begged him to allow them to shoot—to save trouble later! The Myall Creek and Port Fairy massacres were not the only ones of their kind, and it may be imagined how criminals, living the awful loneliness of a shepherd's or hutkeeper's existence, would treat the surrounding natives. Indeed, the whole colony was at one on this matter. It was believed that the natives had either to be driven back when the flocks approached, or, at least, taught their place and made to hearken to the law of the carbine. Scattering shot was to be their portion if they came close, except when sought out; and, if they transgressed this code, ball-cartridges would be bitten! Some facts, a general fear, and a common emotional argument combined to put any other case out of court, and the squatters held that they had reduced the native problem to essentials.

Oddly enough, very little effort was made to utilize native labour on the squatting runs. It was assumed that the aborigines were unsuited for the continuous work of shepherding, and this belief lasted throughout the squatting period. Gipps, indeed, had tried to induce settlers to employ natives, thinking that money-payments would civilize them, but the general mass of squatters passed over his arguments. One man, the Reverend J. Docker, certainly answered the perennial labour-shortage by handing over his 7,000 sheep to some 36 native shepherds, and for a time found them 'excellent shepherds, faithful and honest', but he was an exception. The *Immigration Committee* of 1841 sent a circular letter to the squatters, seeking information on this point, but received depressing replies. Only one Commissioner, Bingham of the Tumut, favoured them, and even Docker had to admit that his men absconded without reason. The Bligh Commissioner declared them idle and worthless, doing less than a third of a convict's work, and held that no settler would trust them with a flock. Some squatters, like Ryrie of Yering (Port Phillip), Walker of Castlereagh, and Rouse of Mudgee, had experimented with them, but they were too undependable in every case, and would readily desert their flocks for any chance excursion in the bush. The Australian Agricultural Company, which had twenty-two of them permanently employed, found them far too volatile and temperamental, and quite unable to resist the many calls of the bush, of the tribe, and of nomadic instincts in general. They might be useful for cutting bark, but would work neither hard nor steadily. Five-sixths of the squatting witnesses were certain of this point, and the rest wavered, only one of them, John Peter of Yass, espousing their cause unreservedly. None of these squatters, however, paid wages to the natives—only a few rations; and it may not be irrelevant to argue from this that the blacks had no incentive for remaining on the stations.

At a slightly later date, the Queensland natives were used to a greater extent, especially on horse- and cattle-stations. Such labour appeared to accord more with their desire for change and movement than the irksome repetition of driving out sheep, and the results were correspondingly greater. On the Lachlan, for instance, it was found that they would round up stock and perform the more exciting tasks such as sheep-washing, but would flee from general shepherding. Similarly, in the northern districts, if they were not tied down too closely and if variety was introduced into their life, they could be used. By this newer toleration, the squatters of the Liverpool Plains were employing 150 aborigines as stockkeepers in 1851, and further north, various Downsmen, especially on the Macintyre and the Burnett, were using them even as shepherds.

In general, however, the natives scorned the minding of sheep, and could not be looked upon as a dependable labour-supply. Unfortunately, they were a menace and a trouble, and in scarcely any sense an aid to the squatters. Even Gipps had to come round to this opinion, and, in his last few years, realized that all he could do was to enlist aborigines in his mounted *Border Police*, as Dana was doing in Port Phillip. Beyond this, the natives appeared useless to the squatters. If they did not spear sheep or run off cattle, and menace the out-stations, they suborned the shepherds (one missionary reported that, 'upon almost every station, Aboriginal females are living with European men'), and were a general nuisance, diseased and demoralizing. A few squatters might indulge in the whimsy of employing blacks, much as others might read Thucydides or carve pipes or grow flowers, but, even after the excitement of the early forties died down, no average squatter viewed the natives as serious labourers. Squatting life certainly impinged on native existence, but the interaction was as between landowner and raiders and very rarely took the form of employer and labourer.

COOLIES AND KANAKAS

The uselessness of the natives and the lack of emigrants turned the attention of squatters throughout this period to a veritable world-hunt for labour-supplies. The colony was being starved for lack of labour, and the sheep were trampled or rotted in their neglect. Convicts belonged to the past, freemen were dwindling, Europeans found no countenance with the administration: so that there remained only the coolie-classes of the Oriental countries. Many schemes were formulated by the squatters to bring in these semi-slave emigrants, and scarcely a year passed without a new stage in the campaign.

The first real move was when the *Immigration Committee* of 1837, under Snodgrass, in a somewhat panicky report, spoke of the colony crumbling into an abyss if some 10,000 labourers were not soon forthcoming. Though disapproving of a permanent class of coloured servants, they were forced by the demands of the situation to recommend from three to five hundred coolies as a temporary relief of the distress. One John Mackay, formerly an indigo-planter and merchant of Bengal, had been a very earnest advocate of Indian labour for Australia and drew up several *Memoranda* for Bourke in this year, especially mentioning their success on the sugar-plantations of Mauritius. He particularly wanted the *Dhangars* or Hill-coolies, the natives of the mountains north of Calcutta, because, being neither Moslems nor Hindus, they had no religious or caste prejudices, and, since they were accustomed to labour in the indigo-factories up to their waists in water, they could probably stand the coldness of New South Wales. Mackay, carrying his theory into effect, actually brought in forty-one coolies, having each approved by the Medical Officers of the Indian government, and scattering them amongst the other settlers, such as John Lord and William Lawson.

The results were entirely satisfactory, because each coolie, passage included, cost only £18. 8s. a year, as against the £41. 8s. of a freeman. Even an assigned convict had cost his employer £16. 7s. 4d., so that this was almost a substitute for transportation, in so far as the squatters were concerned. All that they needed was 10s. a month and a few clothes. A blanket, two wrappers, a chintz jacket, and a lascar's cap satisfied their modest demands; and their rations cost only sixpence a day. A little rice, some *dhall* and *ghee*, and a pinch of salt filled the bill; or, if these were unobtainable, some 10½ pounds of flour and a third as much beef, with a few chillies or ginger to flavour. With maintenance-costs down to this level, it was estimated that the squatter could save 4½d. on every pound of wool he produced—a tremendous reduction in his running-expenses. As for their work, James Macarthur held, after 4½ years' experience, that 'the experiment has equalled and surpassed their most sanguine expectations'; and Mackay asserted that he would willingly take a hundred of them at any time. There was thus no doubt about the economic side of the coolie-labour.[41]

The authorities, however, frowned on the scheme, despite both the Council's recommendation and the petition of the flockmasters in 1837. They refused to pay Mackay any bounty for his Indians, and induced the Government of India to prevent further migration. Lord Glenelg, the Secretary of State, violently objected to the permanent introduction of an inferior and servile element into the population; but the argument he emphasized most was that the coolies would discourage English migration by associating agricultural labour with a certain degradation. Elliot, the Agent-General for Emigration, also deprecated 'introducing Indian Blood into their Population, or Indian Habits into their Industry', and Gipps, looking far into the future, rightly claimed that a continued immigration of such classes 'would be fraught, in my opinion, with evils of the highest magnitude'. Later, the all-powerful Colonial Lands and Emigration Commissioners, in one of their first acts, joined the weight of their opposition, so that all official opinion opposed the coolies.

Such objections, however, merely whetted the colonists' discontent. If the convicts were withdrawn, they must have some labour or perish. The papers waxed righteously indignant at the claim that coolie-labour was a thinly-veiled form of slavery—the man who calls out 'Slavery!' in this connection, said the *Sydney Herald*, would have cried 'Fire!' in the Deluge! If the Indian Government is suborned in the matter and stops the migration, carry the case to the Bengal Supreme Court! 'What right have canting hypocrites to interfere in the matter? What right have they to assume that the settlers will not fulfil any contract into which they may enter?'

[41] Evidence before 1837 and 1841 *Immigration Committee*. An original indenture is in the *Agricultural Papers* (MSS.), Mitchell Library. For colonial viewpoint, see *Sydney Herald*, 7, 14 January 1839. See Appendix VI below.

Either the coolies were British subjects or not. If they were, they could move at will from one part of the Empire to another: while, if they were not, 'Parliament has no more right to legislate in matters affecting them than it has in the case of Prester John's subjects, wherever that functionary may be.' The *Herald*, in its long campaign for them, wanted to know if those who spoke of incipient slavery could compare the condition of the coolies on John Lord's farm at Williams River with that of their fellows in the famine-stricken areas of Bengal. If liberty meant the right to starve, then well-fed slavery was preferable.

The colony thus continued the fight. The great meeting of February 1839, in favour of transportation, coupled coolies with convicts in its recommendations; and, in 1841, the Council discussed Macarthur's motion for three hours and was not averse to their introduction, though conditions made that moment unpropitious. Next year, a voluntary association was formed to bring in hill-coolies (though some followed Major Lockyer in wanting the sturdier Mahrattas), and the matter was once more carried to the Colonial Office. The organized working-men of Sydney had presented a petition denying the right of the squatters to bring quasi-slave classes into a democracy, to which the squatters retorted by carrying the argument into the enemy's camp and asserting that most of the migrant-labourers of the last few years had themselves become employers of labour and had thus intensified the crisis. Some 686 persons, including the great majority of the squatters and a third of the magistrates, signed this petition of May 1843; but the curt refusal of Lord Stanley ended the agitation. The Government of India firmly declined to sanction any renewed migration to Australia, and the door seemed closed on the coolies, thoroughly favourable though the experiment had been. The Queensland squatters, taking up the cudgels again, formed an *Indian Labour Association* in 1848, and odd coolies came; but, in its wider form, the scheme was finished. A desirable economic measure met its doom on wider social grounds, for it was held that the temporary crisis of the squatters should not be met by measures that would imperil the straightforward social progress of the community in the after-years.

In no sense quelled, the squatters simply diverted their quest into other directions, and, for a time, Chileans absorbed their attention. Various enterprising sheepmen had met the long crisis by sending off sheep to Valparaiso and bringing back Chilean labourers in return. By 1841, between three and four hundred South Americans had been thus engaged, and it was no unusual sight to see the

Chilean muleteers of the Australian Agricultural Company thread-
ing their way down the coastal ranges to the sea, or to hear the love-
lilts of some Spanish *hacienda* ringing through the she-oaks and
casuarina on an Australian sheep-run. William Lawson of Prospect
told the *Immigration Committee* in 1841 that he had engaged
twenty-six Chileans in place of his fifty free labourers who had
absconded: he paid £10 for their passage, £20 in wages, and rations
of only meat and flour. But the squatters who had dabbled in this
form of labour found the South Americans far too turbulent. If left
to horse-breaking or handling mules, they were eminently desirable;
but they were too wandering and independent for anything else,
especially for the monotony of shepherding. They were too high-
spirited, too prone to invoke the law of the knife, to succeed in New
South Wales, and the squatters had to renew their quest afresh.

This time, it was in the direction of China. Captain King, of the
Australian Agricultural Company, had been corresponding with
Chinese merchants on this matter even before 1841, and was placing
the scheme on a sound foundation when the Chinese War abruptly
put an end to his planning. As with the Indians, the general con-
sensus of opinion was that the colony would not welcome Cantonese
coolies but would take them as a remedy for the existing distress.
The Government had previously wanted Chinese for the Port Essing-
ton settlement, and, even in 1844, Lord Stanley had given orders to
encourage the introduction of coolies there. Stimulated by this, the
squatters thought that no serious objections would be raised against
Chinese shepherds, and arranged with local headmen to send coolies
in large numbers, on five-yearly indentures. The Foreign Office at
once entered into negotiations with the Colonial Office (1848), and
expressed grave concern that such a trade should be springing up.[42]
Earl Grey could only respond that the migration was not in itself
illegal, and that it would be very difficult to stop it, however much
its suppression might be desired. He had before him proposals to
introduce a hundred coolies and twenty-one *boys* at salaries of 2½
dollars and rations; but he could do nothing beyond expressing his
disapproval to Governor FitzRoy, urging him to stop the movement
if he could.

FitzRoy, however, could do little, and the coolies began to trickle
into Australia. The first shipment came from Amoy in the *Nimrod*
towards the close of 1848, but the movement did not swell to

[42] Foreign Office to Colonial Office, 30 December 1846 (P.R.O.), no. 1169.
Grey-FitzRoy, 27 February 1849. An indenture is in the Mitchell Library. See
Appendix VI below.

thousands a year until the gold discoveries three years later. Usually they came from ports outside consular control like Swatow, but, from two consular ports alone, 2,100 came in nine months of 1854. But these arrived after the period of this book, and, throughout the forties, the squatters had only a few hundred low-grade coolies from Amoy to help them out of their difficulties. The Chinese immigration, even more than the Indian, remained an agitation rather than an accomplished fact; and the coolies proved unreliable and took the first opportunity of absconding to the diggings.

Much more significant was the fight to tap the labour-resources of the adjacent Pacific Islands, where thousands of Kanakas could be secured simply for the *blackbirding* (kidnapping) at only a few days' sail from Sydney. The direct cause of the turn to the Islands was the veto on Indian labour and the rejection of the Council's proposals for English immigrants in 1845-6. Benjamin Boyd, the magnate of Monaro, failing in his scheme to entice freemen to the isolated plateaux of the south and offer them the choice between a £10 wage or the long tramp back to Sydney, sent a steamer to the New Hebrides. By devious means, the island Melanesians—one of the most primitive of human types—affixed their marks to a contract in these terms.

I,...................., a native of.................., in the Pacific Ocean, have this day engaged with Captain........................ on the part of Mr. Benjamin Boyd, of the city of Sydney, N.S.W., to serve the said Benjamin Boyd in the capacity of a seaman in any of his ships, or as a whaler either on board or on shore, or as a shepherd or other labourer in any part of the Colony of New South Wales, and to make myself generally useful for the term of five years.

In return, they were to receive 26s. a year, and a weekly ration of ten pounds of meat, seven pounds of wheat, maize, or flour, and various slop-clothes.

Boyd sent his vessel, the *Velocity*, quite openly, and distributed his sixty-two islanders over the Murray and Monaro runs. His instructions to his manager he published, because, as he said, the experiment was so vital to the colony, and the eyes of every squatter and townsman were on it. He especially prevented bullying by *the old hands*, and kept the natives in bands of ten or twelve, both to prevent such bullying and to safeguard against loneliness and pining. Each group was under a trusted old shepherd, and Boyd informed all of his stockmen that any man annoying these Kanakas was to be instantly discharged. Feed them well, he wrote, and always have plenty of potato on hand, but (remembering those principles on which he had amassed his riches) there is no need to bother over tea or sugar, since these were omitted from the agreement. Boyd hoped by these means to reduce the keep of his sheep to fourpence a head, thus, by inference, raising the value of every ewe in the colony to £1.[43]

At once, the opposition in the Council commenced its outcry. By this time (October 1847), the townsmen had become organized, and Lowe had deserted the squatters for their cause. It was his biting tongue, therefore, that moved the resolution to stop this traffic. If this was not slavery, he asserted in one of his best speeches, it was criminal misrepresentation. What idea had ignorant New Hebrideans of Mr Benjamin Boyd? And what would people who had never seen a sheep-station know of the occupation of shepherding, or tropical natives of whales? How did they know what five years meant, when probably, like the Cherokees, to go beyond three meant something like the mass of the hairs on their head? Did they know what ten pounds of meat represented, or what meal meant, or moleskin trousers, or woollen shirts, or the crowning item in that absurd contract—one Kilmarnock cap? 'As for killing, he had no doubt the new importations understood that fairly well; but, though neither a cannibal nor a native of Tanna himself, he must say that he was utterly unacquainted with the meaning of a Kilmarnock cap.' What Lowe doubted—and his flashing mane of snowy hair shook with the indignation he felt or simulated—was whether the Kanakas were told that they were to be dumped down on the snow-pastures of Monaro, the coldest in New South Wales, and left to die there, with one shirt and one blanket to protect them in the long months of winter? It may not technically have been slave-trade but, at least, it was inhuman and open to a thousand times more objections than the coolie-trade of Bengal. There, at least, the Government supervised, but here was only raiding by low sailing-crews.

The definition of a slave, as given by Aristotle, and asserted by the jurists of his time, was that he was an animated instrument, and so were these parties; and it would not be more absurd to say that Mr. Boyd had entered into a contract with chests of tea or bags of sugar, than it was to imagine he could contract fairly and in good faith with these savages!

Cowper seconded this searing irony, and then Robinson—a representative of Port Phillip and Boyd's man-of-all-work—arose to put

[43] A full report of the Council enquiry is in *Sydney Morning Herald*, 2 October 1847.

the squatters' case. He denied that either force or fraud was used, and said that precisely similar methods were employed to man the whalers in the last few years. 'On the contrary, hundreds and thousands of them were ready and anxious to come, and the chiefs of the Islands had sent word to that effect.' The experiment had been frank and open at every stage, and Robinson challenged Lowe to show how the islanders were any worse off than the Indians at Bourbon. Wentworth, advocating a cause that appeared strange to a tribune of the people, upheld Boyd and reprimanded Lowe for this motion, a motion that could not be followed by any enquiry and that could serve only to terrify the old women of Exeter Hall! Islanders had come to Sydney Town in whalers before that date, and their fellows thus had some notion of the lands beyond the sea: and, moreover, how were these natives, well-clothed and amply fed, and freed from the uncertain terrors of savage existence, any worse off than unpaid apprentices in trades? Since they would be of no use for three or four years, he went on, why pay them at all, when their subsistence is ample recompense?

Beyond these weak and contradictory arguments, the squatters could offer nothing, because their case was so weak. While it was true, as the Colonial Secretary admitted at home and as Governor FitzRoy reported in December 1847, that the islanders were not kidnapped, it could not be denied that the system was open to all manner of abuses and was very akin to slavery if carried on without official supervision. Fortunately, the natives could not resist the cold climate, and, by the time FitzRoy made his official enquiry, it was evident that the immigration was not a sound speculation. No sane squatter would have followed in Boyd's footsteps, and the survivors of this early band of sixty-six male and four female Kanakas, after parading the Sydney streets almost naked and with savage arms in hand, gradually drifted back to the islands. The scheme was not revived until Towns' proposals for the Queensland sugar-plantations some years later; but, for some time, the picture of Boyd's Kanakas, shivering with their *Kilmarnock caps* on the Monaro plateaux, was a telling argument in the armoury of the squatters' enemies.

All of the squatters' plans for cheap coloured labour thus failed— the successful Indians because the Government intervened; the Chinese because they absconded; and the Kanakas because of climatic conditions and Lowe's bitter ridicule. All of them would have involved grave social and economic problems for the future: and a colony, newly emergent from the morass of convictism and with a town-population now clearly articulate, found itself in no mood to fill the country districts with an indentured class of blacks. The squatters were thus faced with the fact that they had either to rely on English freemen or adjust the conditions of their industry. Anything on a slave-basis, anything that made the squatters independent of the towns, and anything that complicated the colony's problems was out of the question. By the end of the forties, the stockmen had realized this, and the later years knew none of the agitation for yellow and black men that characterized every year of the forties. On this note the decade closed, and fortunately, the renewal of British immigration after 1847 clinched the point and secured some solution of the squatters' immediate difficulties as well as allowing the townsmen to maintain their social arguments. Boyd himself was slain on the sands of Malekula—a not inept termination to the unhealthy strivings of the squatters to obtain cheap labour.

X   *From Station to Stapler*

Having overcome these various difficulties of nature and the labour-supply, and having safely pressed his wool into the bulging square bundles of some three hundredweights each, the squatters were confronted by one of the most difficult of their tasks—getting the wool to the port and selling it. They knew that they were at a disadvantage in this. They were as untaught in the wiles of city-business as a bank clerk would have been as a station jackeroo; they knew nothing of markets and conditions on the other side of the world; and their ignorance and isolation were increased by the concerted action of the buyers.

From the first, therefore, even from Macarthur's time, the problem of selling their wool occupied much of the growers' attention—so much so, indeed, that the history of squatting could be narrated in terms of wool-sales. Macarthur himself realized that the conduct of the sales determined whether the sheepman was to secure the full advantages from his product, or whether he should be permanently ground down, with the intermediaries—the wool-buyers—taking all the profits. He set the fashion of being his own agent and sending his clip directly to London for sale, but this was possible only when the output was a few bales or where the sellers leagued together.

It was not long before some order sprang up in the colonies. Ordinary sheepmen could not afford to send their wool direct to London. They could not spare the time to make the arrangements in Sydney, they could not come to terms with London agents, and—more important still—they could not wait for their money during the eight months which elapsed in the passage to England and back. They needed prompt returns in order to carry on their ordinary station-activities. Hence, general merchants in Sydney adopted the practice of advancing money to squatters on the security of their wool-clip: and, from this, it was but a short step to speculators and organized wool-buying. By the thirties (that is, just at the time of the grazing boom), Sydney had professional wool-buyers, who bought the squatters' bales outright and then sold them in London as they pleased. The squatter's part ended when he was paid the price agreed upon by the local buyer. The middleman had entered, and the squatter's activities were limited to those of a producer: the disposal of the wool was now a matter for professional outsiders.

By this time, then, the rival buyers bought up as much wool as they could, the curious feature for long being that the demand was much greater than the supply—or, if not quite precisely this, that too many speculators had entered the new trade and all could not get a living, the result being a largely artificial but none the less eager local competition. The merchants were anxious to secure wool to exchange for the goods they were bringing out from London, because, at this time, the only other colonial product was whale-oil, and so great was the rush of imports to the new colonies that ships frequently had to make the return journey with empty bottoms. The colony exported no wheat and little timber; oil did not take much room, and there were no manufactures—so that everybody cried for the wool-packs, everybody besieged the drays that gradually approached the great trunk-roads from Parramatta, Liverpool, and the South.

So keen was the demand that the Sydney-men could scarcely wait until the drays arrived. The tedious delay was the last irritation and was so intolerable that merchants enlisted men who had handled wool in Yorkshire and sent them out along the roads to seek out the incoming teams and pounce on the bales. Wool-buyers on fast ponies raced along the roads from Sydney to intercept growers at strategic points, at *the Black Huts* on the southern road, or the inn-yards along the Parramatta road. Many a tale was told, many a bargain clinched, and many an argument of defeated buyer or disappointed squatter took place in those old hostelries. *The Farmer's Home*, the *Square and Compass*, and the old *Woolpack* saw such meetings and clashes, while a yet more famous spot was the corner of the Liverpool and Parramatta roads, where two main tracks converged on *Old Jack Ireland's*.

The story is not difficult to reconstruct. The buyers, at the due season, raced for the country in a spirit of sporting rivalry, and took up their position at the given vantage-points. Hours passed while each ear strained for the creaking of the ungreased hubs of over-loaded waggons, and perchance the teamsters' oaths and the crack of the long bullock-whips. Then, by fair means or foul, a buyer pounced on the incoming overseer or squatter, and, according to the type of individual, bargained over Bengal rum, or perhaps by a tersely economic process, or even by deceit. He cut a slash in an ordinary bale, took out a handful of wool and bid for it, trusting to his luck in having chosen a representative sample. Locks and pieces were sold, in this rough-and-ready stage, at half the price of the fleece-wool; and, the deal concluded or rejected, the party moved to the inn-yard proper and celebrated their business.

Such a system may appear to place a premium on deceit, and would seem to leave the relatively unsophisticated bushmen at a disadvantage. As a matter of fact, however, it did not work badly in practice. The squatters, in the enforced loneliness of the bush, had had months of thinking and knew what price was needed to cover their expenses. They knew, too, that there was no need to sell to the first buyer they met on the road, and that, by being obdurate and going on to the first inn-yard, they could meet a whole group of representatives. It was not unheard-of, of course, for buyers to co-operate and appear to boycott obstinate sheepmen : nor was it rare for groups to conspire to beat down the growers by meeting them at various points and, by uniform tales of depressed markets, secure the wool at too low a price. They brought into play every device capable of being used by co-operating city-men working with country-settlers out of all touch with the practical world. But usually, the growers obtained a fair price, because the competition was so keen and the element of personal integrity began to enter as the competition increased— growers went year after year to buyers whom they could trust for 'giving them a fair deal'. The early *Roadside Dealing Era* was by its nature a passing anomaly—made possible only by the excess of shipping accommodation and by the disorganized state of buying agencies in Sydney. Once the wool-sales had become a profession, the old racing-ponies and cajoling buyers in the inn-yards had to go; and, with their exit, commenced an era of trading on sound business lines and by more and more reputable firms.

Picturesque though the early stage was, it clearly pertained to a period of origins. The very magnitude of the trade after the squatting rush of the thirties made new and organized methods necessary;

and wool-sales shifted from the roadside and inn-yards to commercial buildings specially set aside for that purpose.

It was not very long before this system was seen. The old haphazard methods had everywhere to go when more regular supplies of colonial wool began to reach London. At first, methods were very lax when stray bales of the historic J.Mc.A. wool came in, and even when the total Australian clip amounted to thousands of bales. The bales were gathered at Garraway's famous coffee-house in Change Alley, Cornhill—and there—where Pickwick had sent his telegram to Mrs Bardell—the sale occupied an hour. Lots usually consisted of a single bale, Australian and foreign wools being mixed indiscriminately. The bale in question was exposed, a guttering candle lit, and bids were received before it had flickered or run down to the next inch-mark. But the vast increase in Australian exports changed all this. When two million pounds came in from New South Wales and Van Diemen's Land in 1830, and when the figure jumped to four millions five years later, such a system was absurd.

At this juncture, came regular sales of colonial wool by itself. Its staple qualities were so different from German and Barbary wool that it was unreasonable to sell them all together. Hereafter, a London middleman could attend sales where only colonial wools would be put up. This meant the abandonment of Garraway's (1843), which had for long been out of date, and a change to the Hall of Commerce in the Royal Exchange.

At the same time, a further change had been taking place in the colonies. The old system of bartering directly with the growers—the traditional American plan—had, first in part, and then wholly, given way to auction within the colony. Even in the hey-day of the roadside era, odd lines of wool had gone to the block with other goods, when some general trader's stock was being realized—thus opening the way for regular wool-auctions. By the early forties, over seventeen million pounds were sent away every year, so that naturally there was a wide scope for sales in Melbourne and Sydney. The first auction-sales of wool alone were those of Thomas Sutcliffe Mort in 1843. This Lancashire man had come to Australia five years previously as an ordinary salesman and had set up as an independent auctioneer, specializing in wool, when his firm was caught in the great colonial crash of 1843. Auctioneers, at this time, usually offered a few lots of wool, but Mort was the first to see the possibilities of concentration. He was especially supported by the small growers who were at a disadvantage in bartering with private capitalists, but who now received the same treatment as the squatting magnate. The first wool-shed was a primitive erection on the banks of the dirty Tank Stream which flowed through the centre of Sydney, and later a shabby low building on Sydney Cove.

Everything was free and easy. The auctioneer took his place in this dingy and smelling atmosphere, grasped a formidable knife with which to rip open the bales, and, instead of simply calling the number of each lot, as at present, dealt in flowery language with the peculiar merits of each—talking like an American bagman about to swindle small farmers, and incidentally wasting much time.

A few years later, Melbourne entered the field. Richard Goldsbrough had come to Australia from Shipley in the West Riding of Yorkshire in 1847, after carefully studying Australian wools while working for twelve years as a wool-stapler in Bradford. Unlike his Sydney predecessor, he was a practical wool-buyer and sorter, not simply a general auctioneer, so that his success was already assured when he started in Flinders Street in 1848. Soon afterwards, Melbourne ousted Sydney as the main selling-centre in Australia, though, when the Riverina trade opened in the seventies, the fight had to be reopened.

Here matters rested for decades. Mort kept his low two-storied buildings on Sydney Quay, Goldsbrough erected the finest warehouses in the South; but, with both, large stores and systematic methods came very slowly. Though wool was Australia's staple, buyers had to go from store to store, until a combined salesroom was acquired at the Royal Exchange in Sydney decades later—and at last (just when Sydney had again defeated Melbourne in the supremacy of wool-sales) a wool-exchange in Macquarie Street (1892). But this was almost fifty years too late, and many stout fights had taken place in the interim, both for Australian sales and the priority of London. At one stage, even Antwerp entered the fray, but the amazing feature was how little the basic system changed and how any move towards co-ordinated buying or selling had to encounter almost insurmountable difficulties.

In the forties, London was chiefly concerned with checking the irruption of a new set of middlemen by the growth of the Goldsbroughs and Morts in the colony. Such a move seemed to them entirely subversive of the principles behind colonial trade—almost an analogy of that administrative bugbear, responsible government for the colonies. All through the thirties, the London buyers had waged a similar campaign against those speculators who bought up the wool and thus interfered with the natural course of allowing it to be sold at London auctions. 'Manoeuvres and combinations', complained a London house in 1833, 'are practised among the Purchasers, to the detriments of the Proprietors of Colonial Wool', and an idyllic picture was painted in circular letters to the Australian graziers of the fair competition offered in London by the presence of manufacturers' representatives. To the contrary, it was asserted, by selling locally, a man disposed of his produce when the world-parity was unknown to him—and to some local speculator who was probably a low fellow—perchance an emancipist! Some of the larger graziers, like Alexander Riley (the first man to import Saxon merinos in numbers) clung to the old direct method, but most sold in the colony.

But the evil was done: the colonial houses had entirely usurped the position. At Bakewell's in the Melbourne of 1847, for instance, everything was done. The wool was sorted into the two classes of combing and clothing; then, each species was run out into five qualities, ranging from the coarsest Leicester to the specially classed *Super* lots; and thence, after sorting, handwashing, and scouring (the three operations together costing only 1¾d. a pound), the wool, now uniformly arranged, classed and cleaned, was auctioned.

The final blow to London came when even Continental buyers deserted the Old World and began to buy directly at the fountain-head of wool-supplies. They found it quicker to go to Sydney or Melbourne and to take advantage of the wider selection offering there. The end was already in sight, and soon London left the lists. Sydney and Melbourne entirely replaced London as the disseminating centre, and what had been construed as an impudent colonial growth, of necessity bound to shrivel up through inanition, had become an entirely new organism supplanting the parent. First the racing wool-buyers on horseback had gone; then the low-roofed auction-sheds had tried to compete with London; and finally the warehouses of the South had not only ousted London, but become cosmopolitan in a way that London had never been. The hubbub and din of a modern wool-sale in Melbourne, with its sprinkling of every nationality under the sun, seems far from the *Crown and Anchor* inn-yard of the thirties: but the story is one of constant development and sums up no little portion of Australia's history, with wool running through it all, and giving meaning to the strange development.

THE TRANSFORMATION OF THE SQUATTERS

I *The Squatters' Rivals*

ABOUT THE TIME the squatters obtained security of tenure, their whole position changed—not only in itself, but in relation to the other elements in the community! They themselves had obtained a practical monopoly over the lands of Australia and were swept on to prosperity; but now classes had arisen against them—farmers and city-dwellers: and these were the classes that were to triumph in the long run.

With the farmers, the amazing feature was how slow they were in emerging. All through the period of this book, farming was incredibly backward for such a temperate country. In a primarily agricultural country, half the proceeds of the wool-clip were going for foreign grain! The local millers had to pay seven or eight shillings a bushel for Australian grain, at a time when foreign supplies might come in at any moment for 3s. cheaper. Farming barely paid on the rich Hunter lands at this price, yet the East Indies offered supplies at 3s. 6d.! As late as 1845, it could be said that the colony had never raised enough wheat for its own consumption: only in three of the previous ten years had colonial production met the demand. Usually, grain and barley and flour came in in huge quantities—half a million pounds were paid in hard cash in 1839-40, for instance.[1] Indeed, the position was so clear that it had become an accepted part of colonial economy. Nobody expected the colony to keep itself afoot in this connection: even Gipps (an extreme Free-Trader) held that imports of corn should be facilitated from every possible source and that any protective duty would have been erroneous. He reported in January 1844:

I feel it my duty distinctly to state to Your Lordship that, looking at the precarious nature of its climate, the unfitness of its soil (except in favoured localities) for the production of Wheat, and the distance of every other Market (except Van Diemen's Land) from which the colony can obtain grain, it seems to me that there is not on the face of the Globe any country

[1] *Australian*, 2 September 1841.

in which a free-trade in Corn is so absolutely necessary, in order to guard against dearth.

Stray voices, like the *Australian*, might say that this was 'an act of deliberate suicide' in a non-manufacturing country, and the Council might fight for a genuinely protective duty: but the general opinion was that wool sufficed for Australia, and that the people could be fed on the cheaply-produced corn of China and South America. The idea that wool belonged to the outer lands and wheat for the belts nearer the towns was simply non-existent throughout this period.

Agriculture was at best a hazardous investment, usually a means of severing fools from their money. Farmers were decried as visionaries, and everywhere the emphasis was on wool. In all of New England, only three settlers grew enough wheat for their own consumption in 1842: and when the hickory-flats of Port Albert were opened in 1845, they were described as 'in a locality, *one of the few in New South Wales* where agricultural results may be considered certain'. The current expression of improbable contingencies was to refer to a time 'when wheat shall grow on the Darling Downs', and what foreign observers most noticed was the entire absence of cultivation on the stations. 'Not a trace of culture,' wrote a Frenchman, Fauchery, 'nothing except sheep and bullocks!'

It was scandalous that this state of affairs should have persisted for so long, but gradually a new tendency emerged in the forties. The menace of actual starvation in the early years of that decade and memories of the time when Gipps had to store grain in rock-silos to feed the people, dramatically showed in which direction the colony was going: and, just at that moment, the renewal of small-scale immigration introduced thousands of men who were not wealthy enough to become squatters and yet who would not become bush-shepherds for £20 a year. Then, too, the refusal of the Commons in 1844-5 to help Australian wheat, and the ban of Gipps and Stanley on a protective duty within Australia, roused the ire of the colonists, at a time when they welcomed opposition to England.[2] The growers wanted both to keep Valparaiso wheat out of Australia and to have facilities for exporting their produce to England (though the latter was surely premature!), and were infuriated when they were checked on both points. Lastly, the organization of smaller men against the squatters was going on apace, and an agitation commenced for small agricultural blocks near the towns. The success of small farming in Van Diemen's Land and South Australia clinched the point, and a new era dawned for Australian farming when

[2] Stanley-Gipps, 27 August 1843.

Governor Grey of South Australia announced in 1845 that his farmers could make wheat remunerative at 2s. 6d. a bushel and could compete on the English market while facing a duty of 1s. Before the Corn Laws were repealed, the London *Bankers' Circular* predicted the entry of a million quarters of Australian wheat into England before five years should have passed; and, if the rapid increase of population in Australia itself prevented this from materializing, at least the argument held good.[3]

In the colony, first Sir Thomas Mitchell and then Robert Lowe fought the monopolists. Small men demanded holdings in the Clarence, the Moruya, and the McLeay districts, and *Regulations* of 1848 allowed the occupation of tiny farms. The *cockatoo-farmer*—the *cockie*, had entered Australian life.

> O'im going to be married
> To what is termed a Cockatoo—
> Which manes a farmer

ran an early song, and the term was symbolical. The squatters used it as aptly describing the small farmers who occupied land, likening them to the white-coated, yellow-crested screamers that perched on the edge of the clearings. The old wooden-ploughs and the reaping-hooks had entered upon their heritage, and marvellous changes soon came. The old spades and hoes and flails (which had sufficed until the forties) were replaced by ploughs, and news filtered through of the wonderful new stripper that Ridley had invented in South Australia, and that had made the harvest of 1842-3 such an event. All through the fifties, the farmers consolidated their position and even challenged the squatters, while, after the free-selection laws of 1861, they claimed—and secured—the right of picking farms anywhere on the squatters' runs. And all of this was implicit in the first *Regulations* of 1848, and in the first fights of Lowe. The force had emerged that was finally to assert its rights over any land that could be tilled: it was to have priority and to oust the squatters into what was already a second place. The hegemony of the wool-king was broken by the first outward move of the selectors, who arrived when emigration was renewed in 1847: and henceforth the squatter had to share his patrimony.

Exactly similar arguments applied to the townsmen, except that, with them, the menace was not so much to the squatter' lands as to the influence they exerted in the community. Here again, the first

[3] *Atlas,* 11 October 1845.

notes of change were heard in the late forties. Prior to that, the convicts had been too powerful, and the balance of power could not be changed until the large emigration of this decade. But, from that time, it became clear that freemen were no longer content to be viewed as labour-supplies for the squatters and to isolate themselves in the bush for a mere pittance: they began to organize and to demand a settled life in the cities, with interests apart from the squatters and even, if need be, opposed to them. The rumbling of new forces was to be heard on the horizon by persons of discernment. The *Australian Society of Compositors*, for instance, proposed a strike in 1839—an unheard-of-thing in a community that was as despotically ruled as Australia. Next year, meetings were held against the punishments visited on workers for breach of contract, and mere 'operatives' presided. Free labourers objected to being treated as criminals, and soon showed how ambitious were their claims. In 1843, they formed a political league to secure suitable members of Council, and several of their number gave evidence before two *Committees* of the Council, on immigration and the relief of distress. They were demanding expression, and there were several signs that the organized working class—the concerted proletariat—was making itself felt. Thus, Gipps forwarded a petition from 4,129 workers to Lord Stanley, against the proposed importation of coolies for the squatters; and the 40,000 British immigrants were asserting that the squatters had to suffer pecuniarily, if the future of the colony could thereby benefit. The political reforms of 1843, with a franchise that was relatively low, offered them a wider scope; and, by 1850, one reads of tumultuous elections and programmes that were frankly directed against the squatters. When petitions spoke of the capitalists suffering 'from extravagant expenditure, over-speculation, and efforts to monopolize all the land and stock of the colony' the change had gone far: and the cession of responsible government in 1851 gave such classes power to make their demands effective.

The change came so rapidly as to be almost cataclysmic; and it needed only a large influx of population to make the new elements supreme and to place the squatters in the position of a landed aristocracy who were seeking to monopolize the lands that belonged to the people in general. That final change was presaged one day early in May 1851, when an old Californian digger, Hargraves, made public the news of his gold-discoveries. Before the month was out, thousands of men were panning mullock at Bathurst and Ophir: in June, the Turon burst, and attracted 15,000 men within two months; and, on 26 September, the overland mail from Melbourne drew in with news of Ballarat, down amongst the western runs of Port Phillip. In that wonder-month of September, the entire population of Australia was delirious with the yellow-fever, and field after field was tapped. In October, the poor, rocky land round Mt Alexander was shown to be rich gold-country, and, one day in November, the escort carried away half a ton of solid gold from it! Bendigo, to the north, came into the field the next April, and was at its height in June, with carriage from the city £100 a ton. By March 1852, £2,000,000 of gold was exported from the country. The magic news had by this time spread throughout England. Captain Bloomfield, of the *Mazeppa*, had brought the first tidings on 28 August 1851, and *The Times* devoted an article to it five days later. The dull month of September, always a bane to the press, was thus miraculously tided over, when an Australian goldfield came in with the first partridges!

The response was immediate. When £21,000,000 was shipped from Victoria in golden bars by the end of 1853, the most arrant pessimist could not survive, and ships hastened from all ends of the earth. Over 1,300 vessels arrived in Hobson's Bay in the first eight months of 1853, and Victoria's population increased from 77,000 in March 1851, to 236,000 three years later.

The upshot of all this was to give a sudden impetus to the move- ments that had been quietly emerging to change the squatters' position. The normal development of decades was attained in a few years. The squatters, to meet the new demand for food, found a temporary prosperity (how could they avoid it with beef at fivepence a pound?); but it was clear to all that the days of their absolute rule were gone forever. In Victoria, for instance, their numbers remained practically constant while the population increased seven-fold be- tween 1851 and 1859—while the number of small farmers went up more than tenfold. They were being swamped by the vast additions to the ranks of the city-dwellers and the farmers, and by the intro- duction of the new and noisily insistent class of gold diggers, who were not inclined to allow a few sheepmen to rule the country. The squatters, their hands included, were a tenth of the population at the moment gold was discovered: six years later, they were less than a fortieth, and in that solitary change lies the whole history of their submergence! In 1851, new factors were emerging that would ultimately have come to rival them; but, almost at a blow, the gold discoveries had changed the slow tendencies into an accom- plished fact—and the squatters at once had to commence their fight to hold the good lands. They were now on the defensive, struggling hopelessly against the ranks of the diggers, the farmers, and the townsmen.

II Changes in Squatting Methods

At the same time, the old methods of the squatters—methods that, a few years before, had seemed implanted for ever—began to change; and, in this direction too, the very essentials on which they had built their existence seemed to be swept away in these years of transformation. Indeed, the gold rush again appeared the immediate cause of the change. Early in 1851, every squatter in the land would have sworn that the existence of Australia depended on its 14,000,000 sheep, and that these sheep, in turn, depended on being shepherded in flocks of from 400 to 1,000 at a time: but, a few months later, this position was challenged. The flocks remained, but it was practically impossible to secure hands to look after them. Every shepherd and hutkeeper was off to Mt Alexander or the Turon, and not a man but thought the eight square feet of auriferous land preferable to *tailing* after a few hundred sheep, day after day. Corn waited for the sickle uncut, and the shearing season drew near—and still the men absconded. The first clip of 1851 was not so bad, but, once the main Victorian diggings boomed, the squatters' position appeared hopeless, unless they were content simply to sell their flocks for meat.

In consequence, many of the flocks were left to manage themselves, and—*here entered the miracle*—they appeared little the worse for their unrestricted wanderings! The harassed owners of the Grampians left their sheep to go leg-free, when their men *sloped* to the diggings, and the MacLeods first turned out their sheep in Gippsland to roam like cattle—and both lots prospered! With that realization, a revolution was at hand in the sheep industry; and the whole basis of squatting economy was seized with change. If the flocks could roam unrestrained, then logically, shepherds, watchmen, hurdles, and settled bases could all go. Once confine the area within which the sheep could forage for themselves, and all of the old structure of driving sheep out, and watching them all day, and confining them at night, was a useless and expensive irrelevancy and could be cleared away. The import of such a tremendous change needs no explanation: suffice to say that the change, which was bound to come some time or other, was hastened at this crucial juncture.

In the earliest days, the squatter merely fenced his homestead and branding-paddock, and sometimes scarcely that. Later, log fences replaced moveable hurdles, and the sheep were herded at night into log compartments. But this was simply a matter of convenience— to obviate the use of nightwatchmen: and it did not extend to the run itself, because nobody would waste time or money in fencing, when the boundaries were so uncertain and the law recognized no permanent tenure. When, however, some acceptance of the squatters' claims came with the fifties (especially after Newcastle's despatch of 1853), it was agreed that, partly in equity and partly in law, they were permanently settled on their holdings. With this acceptance, and with the experience that sheep could survive without shepherds, came fences.

The first fences in the fifties—as Wright, the son of a Namoi squatter, tells the story in manuscript—were either of logs or split rails set in posts. Logs would be felled and slewed into place, contrivances called *doglegs* built over them, and the so-called fence or obstruction completed by a smaller log or sapling. This was the crude form that survived until 1870, when wires became universal; but it served its purpose.[4]

The results were immediate. Up to 1850, there were no fences at all—a state of affairs which meant that much labour was wasted on sheep and that cattle were continually straying. Cattle-*lifting*, boundary disputes, and chronic uncertainty were inevitable accompaniments of the system of *the open range*. But enclosed runs changed all this, and ended the disputes and the *duffing*. Chances for dishonesty were reduced to a minimum, and working expenses vastly cut down. Instead of two shepherds and a hutkeeper for every thousand sheep, several thousand animals could now graze at will in the big paddocks, and all the help needed was to have a boundary rider see that the fences were kept in good order. In Wright's case, he allotted three men to each fifty-six miles of fencing, each riding about ten miles a day, and the owner himself went round all the fences twice a year to see that all was well and to give bonuses to the most careful boundary riders. There was no longer any of the tiresome business of folding sheep every night, no more difficulty over recalcitrant shepherds, no more of the waste and uncertainty. The sheep, too— free to roam and not getting footrot by being cooped up every night —improved in carcase and wool, and, until the degeneration following over-stocking, paid their masters better. While the loss and

[4] Wright and Nisbet MSS., best tell the change, though all the works quoted mention it in various ways.

decrease were, of course, greater than when hand-shepherded, the improvement in condition and fleece counteracted this. *The more they are out of yards and hurdles, the better they become*, ran the slogan of the new sheepman. Their wool was better-grown, cleaner, and mellower to the touch; and these qualities survived even when overstocking considerably reduced the weight of the animals. A fleece of seven pounds was good in the old shepherding days: now, merino lambs might very well average from nine to twelve pounds, and of a type much easier to handle. So obvious were the benefits that, even in the fifties, some enterprising squatters were replacing wooden fences by wire—Wright had wire on the Namoi in 1855, and Lloyd in the Liverpool Plains in 1856—probably the first in New South Wales.[5] The shepherds had gone for ever: in place of the two shepherds and hutkeeper at £25 a year, were the boundary rider and his wife, at £35 a year and rations for two (and the introduction of family life to the outposts was no little thing). And the alluring figures worked out at 25 per cent more fleece, 25 per cent less expense; and 50 per cent more sheep could be run! Truly, with meat prices soaring on the goldfields and a phenomenally sudden rise of wool values in Europe, the stockmen were flourishing—economically, at any rate!

Coincidently with this, the new generation of squatters began to change. Squatting had become a capitalistic venture—large resources were needed to stand against the new selectors and to create the improvements necessitated by the new methods. The old-style squatter probably ran no more than 30,000 sheep, but larger areas and better stocks were needed in the newer regions of western New South Wales and Queensland. Squatting had become an industry, it was being capitalized, and methods were becoming more intensive. Accordingly, the new type of run came to follow the Riverina model, where a typically good holding ran to 130,000 acres (with the selectors on 10,000 acres in various positions), divided into twelve large and twenty-four small paddocks. All would be fenced and well-watered, either by tanks or creeks, and there would be 50,000 sheep (one to three acres was the rule), good seasons or bad. To look after them would be four boundary riders (three of them married), and some Sydney banking institution would be backing the whole venture. Some, like Sir Sam McCaughey at Toorale, might have three and a quarter million acres with 280 miles of river frontage, and shear 180,000 sheep: but this, of course, was an exception. The normal squatting holding, however, was a far cry from the slab huts

[5] *Namoi Independent*, 11 June 1814, article by Lloyd.

of the thirties, with a few thousand sheep and some low-grade shepherds and hutkeepers!

Squatters now were speaking of specialization in wool growing, of the much-abused American merinos, of *reconstructing the merino*, of bores, of frozen meat, of scouring and shearing machinery, and of runs that were largely freehold. Squatting was no longer the hand-to-mouth jumble it had been in the forties, or even the rush of frenzied profits it had been in the gold-days, but a large-scale industry, with capital infinitely greater than was needed earlier, and with efficiency-systems reminiscent of the most specialized factories. Everything had changed, and the painful readjustments after the sixties left few of the features of the original runs. The pioneer had become an industrialist, and, in some sense, a monopolist. His claims had to be adjusted to those of the newer classes in the community, and his own methods transformed to meet the new conditions. The more haphazard early days had ended. The romance of pioneer life had changed, it would appear—almost gone: but the strain of mystery will always run through the story. The ceaseless romance is there, if it can be sought out, just as it has been from the day the first flock-masters crossed the mountain-trail to the west. It is the tale of Australia—the tale of

> How they're shearing on Belalie
> Or the Cootaburra's dry;
> How the border's red with ruin,
> From the rabbits and the drought,
> How the floods have filled the Tuen,
> From the big rains further out.

APPENDIX I

POSITION AT BEGINNING OF THIS SURVEY, 1836

	New South Wales and Port Phillip	Van Diemen's Land
Population	77,096	43,895
Population—Free	49,265	26,234
Population—Bond	27,831	17,661
Total Revenue	£315,621	£127,961
Total Expenditure	£195,271	£137,533
Land Revenue	£132,403	£33,916
Imports	£1,237,406	£558,240
Exports	£748,624	£420,123
Acres Cultivated	87,432	89,528
Wool Exports	3,693,241 lbs.	1,710,000 lbs.
Value of Wool	£369,324	£171,009

APPENDIX II

ANNUAL WOOL EXPORTS (AND TABLES FOR COMPARISON)

	Wool Exports lbs.	Value of Wool £	Total Exports £
1836	3,693,000	369,324	748,624
1837	4,448,000	332,000	760,000
1838	5,749,000	405,000	802,000
1839	7,213,000	442,000	948,000
1840	8,610,000	566,000	1,399,000
1841	8,390,000	517,000	1,023,000
1842	9,428,000	595,000	1,067,000
1843	12,704,000	685,000	1,172,000
1844	13,542,000	645,000	1,128,000

Compare with this growth—

	Population	Land Revenue	Acres Cultivated
1836	77,096	£132,000	77,432
1837	85,267	128,000	92,125
1838	97,912	125,000	92,912
1839	114,386	172,000	95,913
1840	129,463	354,000	126,116
1841	149,669	117,000	115,130
1842	159,889	63,149	126,874
1843	165,541	47,742	145,653
1844	173,377	44,288	144,095

Note the increasingly important place of wool in these tables, despite the numerous years of crisis.

APPENDIX III

POSITION AFTER THE GREAT EXPANSION, 1840-1841

(In the midst of this survey)

(1) SQUATTING POSITION (New South Wales, including modern Victoria)

Beyond the boundaries—

352,126 cattle
1,204,470 sheep
£4,796 13 6 assessment
3,999 free persons (including 636 women)
2,695 convicts (including 23 women)

Distributed thus—

District	Squatters	Acres Cultivated
Port Macquarie	22	590
New England	66	361
Liverpool Plains	121	292
Bligh	44	218
Wellington	56	433
Lachlan	84	1,943
Murrumbidgee	147	1,795
Maneroo (running to Port Phillip)	133	1,031
	673	6,663

Note the shortage of women outside the counties, the small assessment paid for the use of so much country, the great proportion of convicts, the relatively large number of stations in 'The New Country' to the south of the Lachlan, and (above all) the practical absence of agriculture.

(2) POPULATION POSITION (1841 CENSUS)

Total population of New South Wales and Port Phillip—130,856 (87,298 men, 43,558 women).

Distributed thus—

4,477 Landed proprietors, merchants, professional
1,774 Shopkeepers
10,715 Mechanics and artificers
9,825 Domestics
72,317 Unclassified (but of lower grades, and mainly convicts)

Of the free persons, 14,819 males and 14,630 females were born in the colony, 30,745 and 22,158 arrived free, and 15,760 and 3,637 became free by servitude.

Of the male prisoners, 5,843 had tickets-of-leave, 6,658 were in Government employment, and 11,343 were assigned to private individuals, forming the bulk of the squatters' labour supply. Of the female convicts, the corresponding numbers were 316, 979, and 1,838.

Of all the males in the colony, 53,381 were adults between the ages of 21 and 45, and 7,212 were between 45 and 60, the corresponding numbers of females being 19,513 and 2,175.

APPENDIX IV

POSITION IN THE FIRST ELECTED LEGISLATIVE COUNCIL, 1843
(The body that fought the squatters' cause)

	Number of Electors	Member	Occupation
Sydney City	3,319	W. C. Wentworth	Barrister, Squatter
		W. Bland	Journalist
Parramatta Town	279	H. H. Macarthur	Squatter
Cumberland Boroughs	287	W. Bowman	Settler
Northumberland B'ghs	270	D'Arcy Wentworth	Retired Major
Cumberland County	1,391	C. Cowper	Settler, ex-Official
		W. Lawson	Settler
Northumberland	352	W. Foster	Barrister
Argyle	133	W. Bradley	Settler, Brewer
St Vincent and Auckland	73	J. Coghill	Settler, ex-Merchant-captain
Murray, King and Georgiana	154	T. A. Murray	Settler
Roxburgh, Phillip, and Wellington	133	W. Suttor	Settler
Bathurst	172	Francis Lord	Settler
Brisbane, Bligh, Hunter	212	W. Dumaresq	Settler, ex-Captain in Staff Corps
Durham	353	R. Windeyer	Barrister
Gloucester, Macquarie, and Stanley	244	A. M'Leay	Ex-Colonial Secretary
Cook and Westmoreland	249	J. Panton	Settler
Camden	365	R. Therry	Commissioner of Court of Requests
Melbourne Town	859	H. Condell	Brewer, Mayor of Melbourne
		C. H. Ebden	Squatter
		T. Walker	Sydney Merchant
Port Phillip District	470	C. Nicholson	Sydney Physician
		A. Thomson	Squatter, ex-Surgeon
		J. D. Lang	Described by Gipps as 'a Presbyterian Minister, but deposed by the Synod'.

In addition to these were the official members, but the elected members formed a solid body of squatting-advocates, and, constituting themselves into a permanent opposition, dominated the Council. They were, in effect, the Council-of-war which directed the campaign against Gipps.

APPENDIX V

POSITION AT END OF THIS SURVEY, 1848-1849

	New South Wales (proper)	Port Phillip
Number of squatters	1,041	824
Area of runs, sq. miles	54,821	30,304
Average area of a run	34,000 acres	24,000 acres
Sheep depastured	2,358,000	3,146,000
Cattle depastured	644,000	244,000
Licences paid	£18,812	£13,009
Average per sq. mile	8/10	8/7
Average annual cost of depasturing each sheep	1½d.	1d.

ANALYSIS OF HOLDINGS (END OF 1848)

Area	Number of Persons	Number of Licences	Area (acres)
Middle District (New South Wales Proper)			
Under 25,000 acres	451	464	5,844,000
25,000 to 50,000	267	362	9,372,000
50,000 to 100,000	195	355	13,375,000
100,000 to 150,000	40	113	4,764,000
150,000 to 200,000	17	81	2,748,000
200,000 to 250,000	9	34	1,957,000
250,000 to 300,000	10	43	2,632,000
300,000 to 350,000	3	15	979,000
350,000 to 400,000	1	4	391,000
400,000 to 450,000	1	9	420,800
550,000 to 600,000	1	5	595,760
800,000 to 850,000	1	6	814,560
Quantities not given	23	29	—
	1,019	1,520	43,896,232
Port Phillip			
Under 25,000 acres	339	347	4,599,000
25,000 to 50,000	153	180	5,302,000
50,000 to 100,000	103	162	7,141,000
100,000 to 150,000	33	52	3,996,000
150,000 to 200,000	16	31	2,666,000
200,000 to 250,000	5	16	1,094,000
250,000 to 300,000	4	11	1,064,000
350,000 to 400,000	3	10	1,079,000
400,000 to 450,000	1	5	408,583
600,000 to 650,000	2	5	1,272,000

800,000 to 850,000	1	1	845,600
Quantities not given	6	7	
	666	827	29,464,240

Note that Port Phillip had the biggest station of all, and three of the four largest. Three-quarters of the whole of Port Phillip was held under squatting-licence.

APPENDIX VI

INDENTURES OF LABOURERS IMPORTED FOR SQUATTERS

I—INDIAN (all hand-printed)

'I, *Madhoo*, engage to serve John Mackay, Esquire, or such person as I may be transferred to by him as a Free Labourer, by mutual consent to be declared before a Public Officer, for the period of five years from this contract, on a monthly salary of Company's Rupees five (5), and food and clothing as follows, viz.:

Rice, 14 Chittacks		One blanket	
Dhall, 2 Chittacks	Daily	Two dhoties	Yearly
Ghee, ¼ Chittack		One chintz jacket	
Salt, ¼ Chittack		One lascar's cap	
		One wooden bowl	

Also one *lota* or brass-cup between four persons, and medical attendance when required, and to be sent back to Calcutta at the expiration of my term of service, free of all expense to myself should such be my wishes, subject to the terms of my general agreement, dated this the eighteenth day of August.

Calcutta, 1837

Madhoo, his mark

Endorsed—Indian Labourer's Permit, No. 49. Signed by Superintendent
On Back—Transferred to S. Lord, Esquire, by J. Mackay
On Second Page—Height, 5 feet 4 inches
                    Age, 25 years
                    Colour, black
                    Particular marks, none
                    Caste, Dhangar Hazareebung (?).

'I hereby certify that this Memorandum of Contract has been inspected by me, and the contents thereof fully explained to the within-named.'
Calcutta, 22nd August, 1837

H. M. Bell,
Supt., Calcutta Police

On the *Peter Proctor*, Captain Barlow.
Passed and vaccinated by surgeon.

II—CHINESE (on printed form, English on front, and Chinese on back)

'MEMORANDUM OF AGREEMENT made and entered into this Eleventh Day of October in the year of our Lord One Thousand Eight Hundred and Fifty-one between *Yap Hai*, a native of China, on the one part, and Thomas Beckford Simpson, of Sydney, in the Territory of New South Wales, on the other part: *Witnesseth* that the said Yap Hai agrees to serve the said T. B. Simpson, and such person or persons whom he may place in charge over the said Yap Hai, in the capacity of Shepherd, Farm and General Servant, and Labourer, in the said Territory, for the term of Five Years, to commence from the date of the arrival of the said Yap Hai in the said Territory, and to obey all his lawful orders, and the orders of such persons as may be placed over him. *And* the said T. B. Simpson agrees to pay the said Yap Hai at the end of every three months, wages at the rate of Three Dollars per Month, the said amount to be paid in Sterling British Money at the rate of Exchange of 4/- per Dollar. *And* to provide the following Weekly rations, namely—

> 1 lb. of Sugar
> 8 lbs. of flour
> 9 lbs. of meat
> 2 ozs. of tea

And the said Yap Hai agrees to pay to the said T. B. Simpson out of the first Moneys or Wages to be received by him, by four equal monthly payments, the sum of Six Dollars now advanced to him.

Witness of signature and
payment of advance.
Jno. Condly.

XXXX (Yap Hai).
T. B. Simpson.

SELECT BIBLIOGRAPHY

WITH SPECIAL REFERENCE TO EARLY SQUATTING

This bibliography is strictly selective. Some quite unimportant works are given, because of the local colour they afford to the student of squatting conditions, and far more important books on the period passed over, if they lack that emphasis. The more general works, however, should be considered as having afforded the background. For a more detailed survey, see the Bibliography in author's *History of Australian Land Settlement*, 1924.

I *OFFICIAL SOURCES*

1 BRITISH PARLIAMENTARY PAPERS

1828—Lords Committee on the Wool Industry—401 pages of important evidence. Compare survey by J. Luccock, 1809, for district by district.

1834, Nos. 82, 614, 616, 617—Correspondence on Transportation, Emigration, and Aborigines.

1836, No. 512—Committee on Land Sales.

1836, No. 76—Emigration Correspondence.

1836, No. 538, and 1837, No. 425—Two reports of Committee on Aborigines.

1837-8, Vol. 40, p. 186—Squatting in Western Australia.

1837, No. 518, and 1838, No. 669—Two reports of Committee on Transportation.

1837, No. 358; 1838, No. 389; 1839, No. 536—Emigration.

1839, No. 526—Trial of Aborigines (important).

1839, Nos. 76, 582—Transportation Papers. Also 152 of 1840, and 412 of 1841.

1840, Nos. 509, 511, 559—Waste Lands. Also 1843, No. 71.

1840, No. 612—Committee on Emigration.

1841, Nos. 81, 241, 308—Papers on Emigration. Also 1843, Nos. 109, 323.

1842, No. 105; 1845, No. 318; 1846, Nos. 206, 276—Crown Lands Bills.

1844, No. 180—Squatting Papers. Also No. 505 for crisis.

1847, No. 114—The Squatting Order-in-Council (fundamental).

1847-8, Vol. 23—Despatches re Crown Lands.

1850, Vol. 9—Statistics for period 1832-1848 (all the period dealt with in this book).

2 DESPATCHES, incoming and outgoing, for New South Wales, South Australia, Van Diemen's Land, and Western Australia. Also correspondence of Lieutenant-Governor of Port Phillip with Sydney.

Historical Records of Australia, series 1, vol. XVIII on, give all up to 1847.

Mitchell Library, Sydney, has all for New South Wales and Victoria up to 1853.

State Library of Victoria has despatches relating to Port Phillip, 1835, and 1851 on.

Tasmanian Archives have all despatches relating to Van Diemen's Land up to 1856.

South Australian Archives have copies of despatches between Governors of South Australia, the Colonial Office, and the Colonization Commissioners (the latter for period 1836-40).

Chief Secretary's Office, Melbourne, has Letter-books of Lonsdale and La Trobe (now under supervision of State Library of Victoria).

Mitchell Library has all despatches relating to Queensland between 1820 and 1860.

Add to these despatches the reports of the Crown Lands and Emigration Commissioners—annual after 1840.

3 VOTES AND PROCEEDINGS OF N.S.W. LEGISLATIVE COUNCIL

(Full of relevant documents—should be used to counteract the view presented in the despatches.) Important papers are in:

1835—Police Committee (for first squatting).

1839—Committees on Squatting, Police, Emigration.

1840, 1841—Immigration Committees.

1842—Land correspondence and important evidence of Immigration Committee.

1843—Immigration Committee: Distress Committee: Important papers on Aborigines (compare Westgarth's pamphlet): Windeyer's Committee on Monetary Confusion (documents on crisis).

1844, Vol. I—All correspondence on land up to 1844.

1844, Vol. II—Cowper's Committee on Crown Lands—fundamental report on squatting conditions, the most important single source for this subject. But an opposition document.

1845—Immigration Committee.

1847—Lowe's Committee on land matters.

4 LESSER DOCUMENTS

V. a'Beckett, *Reserved Judgments of the Supreme Court of N.S.W.—Port Phillip district*—in yearly volumes, 1847-50, for squatting cases.

T. Callaghan, *Acts and Ordinances of the Governor and Council of N.S.W.*, 1827-44—documents with notes.

II NEWSPAPERS

New South Wales

Sydney Gazette, to 1842—The official organ until March 1832.

Australian, 14 October 1824 to 1848—The most important opposition paper.

Monitor, 1816-42—Opposition weekly.

Colonist, 1835-40—Lang's opposition paper, especially against Bourke.

Sydney Herald (later *Sydney Morning Herald*)—Mildly official, but later turned against Gipps (18 April 1831 on).

Atlas, 1844-8—Lowe's weekly, the most literary of all, but of uncertain principles. Formed to fight the squatting cause, but later turned to the people.

South Australia

South Australian Register, June 1836 on.

South Australian Record, November 1837 on.

Victoria

Port Phillip Gazette, 27 October 1838 on.

Port Phillip Patriot, 6 February 1839 on.

Herald, 3 January 1840 on.

III MANUSCRIPTS OF SQUATTERS

In Mitchell Library unless otherwise stated.

Hobler Manuscripts, 1825 to 1856. The most detailed reminiscences of a squatter having experience in various parts of Australia. He was the first squatter to push to the Lachlan-Darling junction in 1844, and gives a full account of forming a station at Paika. Good for conditions of assignment in Van Diemen's Land, the crisis of 1841-4, and Port Phillip conditions in 1848-50 (10 volumes).

Riley Papers. Managing a station in the thirties, by one of the first men to import Saxon merinos.

Hogan Papers, 1830-4. Conduct of a station before the squatting rush of the mid-thirties. Letters and instructions from an absentee-owner to his manager on the Goulburn Plains—a luminous account. Compare *Suttor's Diary*, 1831-40.

Gardiner Manuscripts. Basic source for the occupation of the various wards of New England. Gardiner was a well-read man, tutor to various squatters at the time.

McMaugh Papers. Early Settlement of the Macleay River. Days of Yore: Macleay River. Vivid tales of pioneer life, from 1843 on, especially of its vicissitudes. Compare with this G. B. White's manuscript letters on the district, 1839-42.

Lloyd Papers, Vol. II. Gives an account of the squatters of the Liverpool Plains, and of squatting methods before the great changes. Lloyd had much to do with the introduction of Shropshire sheep.

Nisbet Manuscripts. Pioneering Days in Queensland. Squatting on the Dawson, and conditions on the Lower Thomson. Encloses a valuable memo. by Jesse Gregson on fences and the changes of methods in the sixties and seventies.

Wright Papers. A good account of running a mountain-station and of various sidelights of Queensland squatting life, especially for the change to fences. By the son of an early run-appraiser in the Namoi district.

Grant Papers. Early Station Life in Queensland. The best of the surviving squatting journals, though referring to life in northern Queensland in the sixties.

Holt Papers. The Life of an Etonian in Australia, 1844-1921. Account of a Queensland cattle-station, especially useful for overlanding.

Mollison Manuscripts (Royal Historical Society of Victoria). For the occupation of central Victoria.

Collie, Shaw and Wollaston Papers. For the settlement of Western Australia to 1844.

South Australian Public Library has *Journal* of Joseph Hawdon (the overlander), and diaries of various settlers (Watson, 1839; Stuart, 1833-43; J. B. Hack, 1836-9; May, 1839; Everard, 1838-48; Davies, 1839-76; Dr Duncan, 1839-42). Add to these the Reports of the South Australian Company, 1836-49, and the annual reports of the South Australian Commissioners, 1836-40.

Frew Papers. A general account to 1842, for the mercantile side of crops and wool by a South Australian settler and merchant.

Roderick Mitchell Letters. A Commissioner of Crown Lands' account of conditions on the Barwon and the Gwydir in the forties.

Gisborne Diary (Office of Commissioner of Police, Melbourne). By the first Victorian Commissioner of Crown Lands.

Macarthur Family Papers. A wide-ranging source of the highest importance.

Wentworth Papers.

South Australian Manuscripts. Diary of John Brown, 1834 to the middle of 1836, for the founding of the new colony. Volume III gives details of the first public meetings, especially re pasturage. Also has long accounts of the negotiations re the relation of master and man, and a long report by Brown on the condition of the colony in April 1837. Brown's letters (which are practically diaries) give the best account of the first years of South Australia.

IV   PUBLISHED REMINISCENCES OF SQUATTERS

D. L. Waugh, *Three Years' Experience of a Settler in N.S.W.* (1838).

A. Harris, *Settlers and Convicts* (1847; re-issued, 1964). By an emigrant-mechanic who became a cedar-splitter and a squatter for sixteen years. An excellent account of life outback in the thirties and forties, very good for local colour.

C. W. Brown, *Overlanding in Australia* (n.d.). Excellent.

C. Hodgson (ed.), *Reminiscences of Australia* (1846). One of the best of the contemporary accounts, with very useful statistics of stock-life.

T. F. Bride, *Letters from Victorian Pioneers* (1898). The answers of the squatters to La Trobe's circular of 1853, giving accounts of the formation of the first runs. This is the invaluable basis for all of Victoria.

E. M. Curr, *Recollections of Squatting in Victoria* (1883). Account by a cultured squatter of the first settlements on the Goulburn, 1841-51. May be taken as a type of the life of a successful squatter.

J. C. Hamilton, *Pioneering Days in Western Victoria* (1913). A sane and balanced account of station-life in the forties.

J. W. Bull, *Early Experiences of Life in South Australia* (1884). For the occupation of the north of South Australia. Compare Dutton's account of 1846.

H. S. Russell, *Genesis of Queensland*. A detailed account of the occupation of South Queensland, by one of the first Downsmen. Very well written.

Mrs Campbell Praed, *My Australian Girlhood* (1904). For squatting in northern Queensland—a most living account of the forties by a daughter of Murray-Prior.

J. Gormly, *Exploration and Settlement in Australia* (1922). Reprinted articles of one of the earliest pioneers of the Murrumbidgee. Rather mixed, but full of good information. Compare Yeo in *Yass Evening Tribune*, 1921-2.

J. Lewis, *Reminiscences* (1922). By one of the earliest men in the north of South Australia.

H. de Castella, *Les Squatters Australiens* (1861). Also translated into German. A eulogistic account of early squatting on the Goulburn and at Yering. A rather naïve foreigner's outlook.

R. Boldrewood, *Old Melbourne Memories* (1899). An intimate account of squatting in western Port Phillip in the forties, before the West was filled.

R. D. Barton, *Reminiscences of an Australian Pioneer*. The vicissitudes of sixty years of squatting, especially ch. 2 : 11. Somewhat embittered.

W. A. Brodribb, *Recollections of an Australian Squatter* (1883). For western Gippsland.

C. Fetherstonhaugh, *After Many Days* (1917). Account of squatting in three States by a member of Gordon's *côterie*.

E. Palmer, *Early Days in North Queensland* (1903), For the occupation of the Flinders.

P. L. Brown (ed.), *The Clyde Company Papers*, Vols. II-IV (1952-9).

A. Joyce, *A Homestead History* (ed. G. F. James, 1942).

V   OTHER WORKS

For conditions in the Colonial Office, see

Sir H. Taylor, *Autobiography* (2 vols., 1885). Account of the successive Secretaries of State in this period by a permanent official.

Melbourne Papers (edited by Sanders, 1889), for Glenelg.

Spencer Walpole, *Lord John Russell*, Vol. I, for Glenelg and Russell.

John Morley, *Life of Gladstone*, Vol. I, for chapter on Gladstone at Colonial Office.

W. P. Morrell, *British Colonial Policy in the Age of Peel and Russell* (1930).

Henry George, 3rd Earl Grey, *Colonial Policy of Lord John Russell's Administration* (2 vols., 1853). Grey's apologia, well reasoned.

For conditions in Australia, see

S. H. Roberts, *History of Australian Land Settlement, 1788-1920* (1924).

S. J. Butlin. *Foundations of the Australian Monetary System, 1788-1851* (1953). Another interpretation of the slump of the 1840s.

R. M. Hartwell, *The Economic Development of Van Diemen's Land, 1820-1850* (1954).

B. Fitzpatrick, *The British Empire in Australia. An Economic History, 1834-1939* (1949).

D. S. Macmillan, *The Debtor's War* (1960).

For general problems of squatting, see for various aspects

J. Bischoff, *Wool Question Considered* (1828). A pamphlet against the wool-tax, full of important facts. Compare an anonymous pamphlet *On the Wool-Trade* (1829), or Earl Stanhope's pamphlet of 1828.

Catalogue of the first large shipment of Australian wool to England, 1821, is in *N.S.W. Agricultural Gazette*, January 1901.

T. B. Southey, *Observations Addressed to the Woolgrowers of Australia and Tasmania*, 1830, 1831, urging better packing, etc.

J. Macarthur, *New South Wales: Its Present State and Future Prospects* (1837). For the growth of squatting. Valuable appendices on emigration.

J. Mudie, *The Felonry of New South Wales* (1837). By one of the magistrates discharged by Bourke, and thus strongly oppositionist. But shows the abuses, especially of the land position.

R. Therry, *Reminiscences of Thirty Years' Residence in New South Wales and Victoria* (1863). The suppressed edition. A lively but biased history from Bourke onwards.

E. Macarthur, *Colonial Policy of 1840-1841*. For land laws.

R. Flanagan, *History of New South Wales* (2 vols., 1861). A lifeless chronology, but useful for the facts of every year.

R. M. Martin, *The British Colonies* (1852), Vol. II on Australia. For valuable documents and statistics. Compare his long work of 1839.

S. Sidney, *The Three Colonies of Australia* (2nd edn., 1853). Good account of history and problems, but occasionally *pirates* paragraphs.

T. Southey, *The Rise, Progress, and Present State of Colonial Wools* (1848). A good account and statistics by a London wool-broker.

W. Campbell, *The Crown Lands of Australia* (1855). Documents and arguments for the squatters' point of view after the Order-in-Council. Biased, but a good collection of documentary appendices.

A. P. Martin, *Life and Letters of the Hon. R. Lowe* (2 vols., 1893). A good documentary account in vol. I, though overstating Lowe's importance in Australia. Hogan's *Robert Lowe* (1893) is livelier.

J. Bonwick, *Port Phillip Settlement* (1883). For the occupation of a State by squatters, in the face of an official ban.

G. Ranken, Three pamphlets on the land question, 1876-7, especially for the squatting changes.

1870 *Committee on the Sales of Australian Wools in London* (compare Brodribb's pamphlet).

J. B. Graham, *Treatise on the Australian Merino* (1872).

U.S. Statistics Bureau, *Australasian Sheep and Wool* (1892).

R. M. Mackenzie, *Among the Pastoralists and Producers*. Series of articles published in *Maitland Mercury*, 1895-6. Account of the Hunter and Goulburn squatters in detail, with historical accounts of the runs. Much scattered information.

G. R. Nichols, *Notes on Sheep and Wool in New South Wales* (MS., Mitchell Library). Articles in Sydney *Daily Telegraph*, especially on the history of wool, settlement of Queensland and the West, and the romance of wool-selling.

F. W. Holder, *Our Pastoral Industry* (1892). A squatter's analysis of the changes in South Australia.

R.J.W., Series of important articles in *Daily Telegraph*, 1912-13, on the history of the wool-trade in Australia. Compare J. Bonwick, *Romance of the Wool-Trade* (1887).

Some Early Records of the Macarthurs of Camden (ed. S. Macarthur-Onslow, 1914). Documents for the founding of the wool industry. Compare accounts by Burfitt (1907), or *Historical Records of Australia*, series I, Vol. V, or W. S. Campbell (1912).

A. Hawkesworth, *Australian Sheep and Wool* (1906).

H. B. Smith, *Sheep and Wool Industry of Australia* (1914).

Pastoral Homes of Australia, 1910-14. For the results of the squatting efforts.

J. Collier, *The Pastoral Age in Australasia* (1911).

M. Bassett, *The Hentys: an Australian Colonial Tapestry* (1954). Fascinating account of a remarkable family.

A. Barnard, *The Australian Wool Market, 1840-1900* (1958).

────── (ed.), *The Simple Fleece: Studies in the Australian Wool Industry* (1962).

M. Kiddle, *Men of Yesterday, A Social History of the Western District of Victoria 1834-1890* (1961). An important book using many new sources.

K. Buckley, 'Gipps and the Graziers of New South Wales, 1841-1846', Parts I and II. *Historical Studies, Australia and New Zealand: Selected Articles* (1964).

Articles in *Journal of the Royal Australian Historical Society, Victorian Historical Magazine, Journal of Royal Geographical Society (South Australia), Journal of Queensland Historical Society*, and *Journal of Queensland Geographical Society* (esp. 1902). Every student of the early squatters must go through these periodicals, both for the colour of the period, and for the numerous articles on the occupation of particular districts. Those by Greig, Daley, Kenyon, Andrews, and Campbell are particularly good.

The squatter himself would probably read Youatt's book *The Sheep*, or A. Blacklock, *Treatise on Sheep* (1841), or, later, T. Shaw, *Practical Treatise on Sheep-breeding and Wool-growing* (1860), and J. C. Jordan, *Management of Sheep and Stations* (1867). A glossary of squatting terms and first usages is in E. E. Morris, *Austral-English* (1898). Full of documentary and historical value.

Various documents are in the Mitchell Library collections, entitled *Immigration Papers* (for manuscript returns, 1838-52), and *Agricultural Papers* (for original Indian and Chinese indentures, calculations of labour-costs, MS. stock-returns, and a long sketch on agriculture in New South Wales during Brisbane's time).

Reports of the Australian Agricultural Company, 1824 to 1876, are often useful.

Excellent documentary and descriptive material is in the books of R. V. Billis and A. S. Kenyon, *Pastures New: An Account of the Pastoral Occupation of Port Phillip* (1930), and *Pastoral Pioneers of Port Phillip* (1932).

INDEX

Aborigines, 87 et seq., 89, 91, 101, 157, 159, 217, 314 et seq., 316 et seq., 329 et seq.
Agriculture, see Farming
Armidale, 142
Assignment, convict, 15 et seq., 19, 93, 100, 121, 320
Australian Agricultural Company, 3, 4, 18, 73, 138 et seq., 326, 340

Banks, effect of, on crisis, 188 et seq., 191, 193 et seq., 195, 200, 201, 207, 208, 210-11
Bathurst, 2, 3, 4, 52, 59, 95, 131, 132, 133, 217, 237, 246, 279
Bathurst, Lake, 134
Bathurst, Lord, 74, 75
Batman, John, 5, 50, 158 et seq., 290
Blaxland, John, 28, 30, 89, 97, 129, 131, 222
Blue Mountains, 50, 51, 129, 137
Boiling down, 204 et seq.
Border Police, 89 et seq., 214, 243, 248, 259 et seq., 284, 285, 298, 317, 331, 332, 336
Bourke, Sir Richard, 9 et seq., 12, 17, 18, 19 et seq., 22, 95, 96, 141, 147 et seq., 163, 186, 194, 196, 221, 226, 276
    and convict system, 17 et seq., 22, 23 et seq., 26 et seq.
    opposition to Bourke, 24 et seq., 31 et seq., 86 et seq.
    and Council, 28 et seq., 102 et seq.
    and Constitution, 29 et seq.
    resignation of, 32 et seq.
    latter days of, 34
    attitude to squatters, 50, 65 et seq., 75 et seq., 83 et seq., 92
    and the Colonial Office, 71 et seq.
Bounty-orders, 116 et seq., 124, 190, 198, 328
Bowman, William, 156, 157, 164, 211, 361
Boyd, Archibald, 250 et seq., 255

Boyd, Benjamin, 180, 235, 236, 245, 250 et seq., 252, 253, 270, 320, 341 et seq., 344
Brisbane, Sir Thomas, 2, 13, 74, 133
Broughton, Bishop, 97, 102, 114, 116, 123, 244, 253, 270
Bulwer, H. Lytton, 29
Burton, Sir William, 19, 20, 25, 26, 85 et seq., 88, 205
Burton's Purge, 205

Cattle-station, 294 et seq.
Chinese immigration, 340 et seq., 343 et seq., 364
Clarke, W. J. T., 155, 163, 164
Clyde Company, 160
Cockatoo-farmers, 185, 352
Colonial Land and Emigration Commissioners, 105 et seq., 110, 116, 122, 172n., 217, 264 et seq., 270, 338
Colonial Office, 69 et seq., 86, 100, 102 et seq., 106 et seq., 115 et seq., 118, 166, 195, 207, 223, 255, 256 et seq., 262, 264 et seq., 271, 321, 338, 340
Commissioners of Crown Lands, 80 et seq., 85, 87 et seq., 90, 177, 214, 238, 239, 259 et seq., 284 et seq., 331, 335
Committees:
    Wool Values (1828), 35 et seq.
    Emigration (1831), 12
    Immigration (1835), 12, 327
    Police and Gaols (1835), 19, 55 et seq., 64, 66, 77, 78
    Crown Lands (1836), 69
    Immigration (1837), 327, 337, 338n.
    Transportation (1838), 16, 18, 24, 210, 320, 325
    Lands Bill (1839), 88
    Debenture Bill (1841), 107
    Immigration (1841), 320, 326, 335, 338n.
    South Australia (1841), 110

373

Immigration (1842), 200, 215, 312, 328

Monetary Confusion (1843), 195, 200, 202, 208, 229

Squatting (1844), 248, 252, 253, 256, 266, 287

Constitution, changes in, 29 *et seq.*, 125, 217 *et seq.*, 353

Constitution Act, 30, 97, 103, 125, 218

Convicts, 9 *et seq.*, 13 *et seq.*, 23 *et seq.*, 29, 96, 175, 318 *et seq.*

Coolies:
Indian, 121, 227, 319, 327, 337 *et seq.*
Chinese, 340 *et seq.*

Corn Laws, 352

Council, Legislative, nominated, 97, 101 *et seq.*, 121, 123 *et seq.*, 199, 206, 209, 211 *et seq.*, 217 *et seq.*
first elected, 220, 256
opposes Gipps, 221 *et seq.*, 236, 247 *et seq.*
protests in England, 251 *et seq.*
rejects Squatting Act, 257
is prorogued, 259
and Kanaka labour, 342
and town-workers, 353

Cowper, Sir Charles, 235 *et seq.*, 248, 342 *et seq.*, 361

Crisis, the Great (1841), 186 *et seq.*
course of, 189 *et seq.*
causes of, 194 *et seq.*, 200 *et seq.*
is accelerated by Government, 196
recovery from, 203 *et seq.*, 211 *et seq.*

Cumberland, county, 2, 4, 14, 129, 134

Cunningham, Allan, 4, 138, 142, 143, 144, 173 *et seq.*, 175

Curr, Edward, 192, 281, 288, 308 *et seq.*, 324

Darling, Sir Ralph, 9, 10, 13, 20 *et seq.*, 22, 23, 24 *et seq.*, 31, 50, 75, 136, 221, 226

Darling Downs, 46, 91, 145, 167, 176 *et seq.*, 278, 306, 322, 336

Darling River, 91, 180 *et seq.*, 227, 316

Deas Thomson, Sir Edward, 220, 222, 235, 236, 261

Debentures, 121

Depasturing Regulations, *see* Occupation Regulations

Droughts, 315

Ebden, C. H., 153, 155, 156, 361

Education, 114, 238, 275, 276

Emancipists, 10, 13, 21, 23 *et seq.*, 30, 31, 210, 218

Exiles, 321 *et seq.*

Eyre, Captain E. J., 168 *et seq.*

Faithfull, George, 156 *et seq.*, 314, 334

Farmers, rise of, 171, 185, 274, 350 *et seq.*

Fencing, 356

FitzRoy, Sir Charles, 181, 257, 270, 340, 343

Forbes, Sir Francis, 21, 23, 30, 327

Forster, William, 236, 261

Fyans, Foster, 286n., 288, 303

Gipps, Sir George, 30, 93, 98 *et seq.*
attitude towards squatters, 67, 85 *et seq.*, 91, 92, 173, 177, 183, 214 *et seq.*, 236 *et seq.*, 244 *et seq.*
opposition to, 85, 87, 101 *et seq.*, 214 *et seq.*, 220 *et seq.*, 236, 244 *et seq.*, 249 *et seq.*, 254 *et seq.*, 257 *et seq.*
and Colonial Office, 86, 103, 105 *et seq.*, 110, 214 *et seq.*, 241, 247, 254, 255 *et seq.*, 257, 264
and natives, 87, 330 *et seq.*, 335
passes Second Squatting Act, 88 *et seq.*
early policy of, 93 *et seq.*, 236 *et seq.*
and Legislative Council, 97, 101 *et seq.*, 121 *et seq.*, 199, 206, 209, 211 *et seq.*, 217 *et seq.*
and Wakefield theory, 107 *et seq.*, 214, 237
and the Great Crisis, 110 *et seq.*, 186 *et seq.*, 198 *et seq.*, 205 *et seq.*
and immigration, 116 *et seq.*, 124, 189 *et seq.*, 198, 199, 327 *et seq.*
is censured by Russell, 118 *et seq.*, 122, 190, 198, 328
is censured by Stanley, 120, 126, 223

visits Moreton Bay, 177
and old Legislative Council, 97,
101 *et seq.*, 121, 123 *et seq.*, 199,
206, 209, 211, 217 *et seq.*
and new Legislative Council
(1843), 220 *et seq.*, 244 *et seq.*,
247, 257 *et seq.*, 260
character of, 223 *et seq.*, 262
is betrayed by Robert Lowe, 222,
223, 231 *et seq.*
evolution of ideas on squatting,
236 *et seq.*
proposes 1844 Regulations, 239 *et
seq.*, 256
criticism of, 243, 252, 260, 261
last fights with the squatters, 244
et seq., 252 *et seq.*, 257 *et seq.*
final views on squatting, 253 *et
seq.*, 257
recall of, 255
prorogues Council, 259
leaves Australia, 260 *et seq.*
latter days of, 262
vindication of, by Grey, 262
opposes squatting leases, 268
favours free trade, 350
Gippsland, 181 *et seq.*, 215, 300, 355
Gladstone, W. E., 251, 256, 263, 268,
322
Glenelg, Baron (Charles Grant), 19,
29, 32 *et seq.*, 34, 50, 69, 70 *et
seq.*, 81, 82, 83, 84, 98, 100, 101,
103, 104, 107, 320, 327, 338
Goderich, *see* Ripon, Earl of
Gold discoveries, 227, 253 *et seq.*
Goldsbrough, Richard, 348
Goulburn, 3, 4, 58, 246
Goulburn Plains, 3, 135, 153, 280
Goulburn River, 153, 155, 281
Grey, Earl, 12, 262, 269, 271, 322 *et
seq.*, 328, 340
Grey, Sir George, 170, 352

Hawdon, Joseph, 150, 152, 156, 160,
168 *et seq.*
Henty brothers, 5, 95, 147, 148, 162
et seq., 169, 184, 290 *et seq.*
Hepburn, Captain, 150, 156, 164
Hodgson, Sir Arthur, 176, 306, 307
Hobler, 179, 180, 193n., 227n., 324,
325n.

Howey, Henry, 153 *et seq.*, 155, 160,
162, 314
Hume, Hamilton, 3, 5, 135, 145, 146
Hunter River, 3, 4, 10, 14, 18, 19,
51, 52, 54, 59, 78, 95, 133 *et seq.*,
138, 141, 276

Immigration, annual figures of, 329
Immigration, free, 6, 9, 10, 11 *et
seq.*, 34, 93, 96, 116 *et seq.*, 121,
122, 190, 199 *et seq.*, 322 *et seq.*,
352, 355
Indian, 121, 327, 337 *et seq.*, 363
Pacific Islands, *see* Kanakas
Chinese, 340 *et seq.*, 364
India, 112, 113, 121, 201, 337 *et seq.*,
363

Kanakas, 250, 341 *et seq.*

Lachlan River, 3, 132, 134, 135, 136,
179, 184, 315, 336
district, 91
Lang, Dr J. D., 11, 12, 15, 24, 99,
199n., 235, 246, 361
La Trobe, C. J., 216, 267, 334
Lawson, William, 337, 340, 361
Leases, squatting, 255, 256 *et seq.*,
265 *et seq.*, 267 *et seq.*
Leslie, Patrick, 115, 144 *et seq.*, 173
et seq., 290, 306, 324, 325
Lien-on-Wool Act, 206 *et seq.*, 212
Liverpool Plains, 27, 73, 89, 91, 133,
134, 140, 141, 176, 336
Liverpool Ranges, 4, 136, 137
Lowe, Robert, 222, 223, 224, 229 *et
seq.*, 246, 247, 250, 256, 257, 259,
260, 270, 342 *et seq.*
need for new estimate of work in
Australia, 230
character sketch of, 231 *et seq.*
betrays Gipps, 232 *et seq.*
changes principles, 233 *et seq.*, 270
et seq.
fights for the people, 270 *et seq.*,
322, 342 *et seq.*, 352
writes song of the squatters, 289

M'Leay, Alexander, 10, 22, 23, 24,
25, 31, 33, 55n., 56, 221, 224, 361
Macarthur, Hannibal, 211, 361
Macarthur, James, 28, 64, 78, 89, 123,
147, 307, 324, 338, 339

Macarthur, John, 10, 40, 41, 53, 65, 129, 347
Macdermott, Alderman, 345 *et seq.*, 270
Mackay, John, 337 *et seq.*
Macmillan, Angus, 183, 305
Macquarie, Lachlan, 2, 22, 50, 129, 131, 132, 134 *et seq.*
Maitland, 134, 141, 246
Major's Line, 95, 149, 150, 152, 153, 165, 281, 291
Mallee, Victorian, 181, 183
Melanesian immigration, 341 *et seq.*
Melbourne, 5, 117, 150, 152, 157 *et seq.*, 159, 163, 187, 192, 218
Mitchell, Sir Thomas, 3, 5, 6, 52, 73, 137, 138, 140, 147, 148 *et seq.*, 152 *et seq.*, 162, 178, 181, 278, 315, 352
Merinos, 35, 37
Mollison, Alexander, 154 *et seq.*, 324
Moreton Bay, 46, 87, 91, 138, 172 *et seq.*, 177, 183, 215, 321, 334
Mort, Thomas, 347, 348
Murray River, 76, 89, 148, 149, 151, 152, 153, 155, 156, 157, 179, 316
Murrumbidgee River, 4, 5, 27, 46, 52, 57, 73, 76, 87, 91, 95, 106, 111, 135, 137, 145 *et seq.*, 149, 150, 152, 155, 164, 173, 178 *et seq.*, 277, 278, 303, 316
Mustering, cattle, 296 *et seq.*
Myall Creek trial, 87, 332 *et seq.*, 334, 335

Native policy, *see* Aborigines
Navigation Acts, 112
New England, 4, 5, 6, 34, 46, 52, 69, 91, 137 *et seq.*, 144, 145, 149, 172, 173, 175, 215, 277, 278, 299, 312
Nineteen Counties, 3 *et seq.*, 7, 34, 50, 51, 55, 65, 72, 79, 109, 128 *et seq.*, 136 *et seq.*, 145, 184, 215, 218, 304

O'Brien, Henry, 77, 137, 146, 204, 316
Occupation Regulations, 239 *et seq.*, 244 *et seq.*, 248 *et seq.*, 252, 255, 256, 264 *et seq.*, 267
Order-in-Council (1847), 262, 271
Overlanding, 149, 155 *et seq.*, 168 *et seq.*, 185

Oxley, John, 2, 3, 4, 52, 75 *et seq.*, 132, 133, 134, 137, 138, 142, 172
Pastoral Association, 232, 239, 246, 248, 253
Patriotic Association, 97, 322
Pentonvillians, 321
Perth, 7
Port Phillip, 6, 27, 34, 46, 52, 67, 69, 72, 89, 90, 91, 95, 106, 109, 110, 111, 114, 115, 116, 118, 137, 147 *et seq.*, 156 *et seq.*, 163, 164, 165, 176, 186, 187, 218, 246, 252, 305, 308, 321, 334, 335, 354
Port Phillip Association, 158 *et seq.*, 160
Portland, 5, 71, 91, 109, 147, 148, 162, 163, 215, 321, 334
Pre-emptive right, 216, 217, 240 *et seq.*, 254, 256 *et seq.*
Protectors, native, 330 *et seq.*
Purchase Regulations (1844), 239, 243, 248, 252, 255, 256, 265 *et seq.*, 267

Queensland (Moreton Bay), 95, 115, 144, 165, 172 *et seq.*, 299, 300, 306, 323, 339

Riddell, Treasurer, 97, 235, 236
Ripon, Earl of, 11, 12, 71
Riverina, 178 *et seq.*
Rivoli Bay, 170 *et seq.*, 178
Russell, Lord John, 19, 83, 103, 105 *et seq.*, 107, 109, 110, 114, 115 *et seq.*, 118 *et seq.*, 122, 190, 198, 214, 216, 218, 263, 320, 328

Sales Regulations, *see* Purchase Regulations
Saxon merinos, 8, 40, 41, 44, 50, 141, 282, 349
Scott, Francis, 251, 252, 268
Shearing, 293 *et seq.*
Sheep-run, 291 *et seq.*
Shepherds, life of, 276, 282, 292, 318 *et seq.*, 323 *et seq.*, 332
displacement of, 355 *et seq.*
South America, labour from, 340 *et seq.*
South Australia, 46, 69, 77, 82, 87, 104, 108, 109, 165 *et seq.*, 351, 352
Squatters:
first meaning of term, 53 *et seq.*, 62 *et seq.*, 301 *et seq.*

the original convict type of, 55 *et seq.*

changed social status of, 62 *et seq.*, 67

under First Act (1836), 83 *et seq.*

under Second Act (1839), 88 *et seq.*, 90 *et seq.*

tracks of, 127 *et seq.*

pass the Boundaries, 137

occupy New England, 137 *et seq.*

occupy the Murrumbidgee, 145 *et seq.*, 178 *et seq.*

occupy Port Phillip, 147 *et seq.*, 181

occupy South Australia, 165 *et seq.*, 184

occupy Queensland, 172 *et seq.*, 184

are challenged by farmers, 185, 350 *et seq.*

and the Great Crisis, 186 *et seq.*

attitude of Banks to, 186 *et seq.*

and the franchise, 218 *et seq.*

dominate first elected Council, 219 *et seq.*

fight Gipps, 220 *et seq.*, 236, 244 *et seq.*

organize protests in England, 247, 249 *et seq.*, 268

obtain leases, 256 *et seq.*, 265, 269 *et seq.*, 271

lock up the land, 271, 353

life of, 272 *et seq.*

types of, 301 *et seq.*

large proportion of Scotsmen amongst, 305, 307

military types amongst, 306

foreigners amongst, 306 *et seq.*

average type of, 307

financial returns of, 307 *et seq.*

labour supplies of, 318 *et seq.*

and convicts, 319 *et seq.*, 323 *et seq.*

and free immigrants, 326 *et seq.*

and aborigines, 329 *et seq.*

and coolies, 337 *et seq.*

and Chinese, 340 *et seq.*

and Kanakas, 341 *et seq.*

rise of new classes against, 343 *et seq.*, 350 *et seq.*, 353 *et seq.*

and problem of selling wool, 344 *et seq.*

transformation of, 350 *et seq.*, 355 *et seq.*

Squatting:

origin of, 5, 9, 34, 49 *et seq.*

first opposition to, 54 *et seq.*

changed nature of, 65 *et seq.*, 67 *et seq.*, 238, 271

regulation of, 66 *et seq.*, 69 *et seq.*, 77 *et seq.*, 83 *et seq.*, 88, 237 *et seq.*

districts proclaimed, 91, 178

legal position of, 92, 171, 215, 216 *et seq.*, 287

expansion of, 127 *et seq.*, 215

and challenge of farmers, 185, 350 *et seq.*

profits from, 308 *et seq.*

balance-sheet of, for whole colony, 311 *et seq.*

principles of finance, 312 *et seq.*

transformation of bases of, 350 *et seq.*

is challenged by agriculture, 351 *et seq.*

changes in methods of, 355 *et seq.*

industrialization of, 357

Squatting Act:

First (1836), 77 *et seq.*, 83 *et seq.*, 284

Second (1839), 88 *et seq.*, 104, 237, 241, 245, 257 *et seq.*, 267

Squatting life:

nature of, 272 *et seq.*

difficulties of, 277, 284 *et seq.*, 308 *et seq.*, 314 *et seq.*

on a sheep-run, 291 *et seq.*

on a cattle-station, 294 *et seq.*

transformation of, in fifties, 350 *et seq.*

and gold discoveries, 353 *et seq.*

Stanley, Lord (Earl of Derby), 69, 81, 103, 110, 113, 120, 124, 125, 195, 207, 211, 223, 251 *et seq.*, 254, 255 *et seq.*, 257, 258, 260, 263, 264 *et seq.*, 267, 268, 321 *et seq.*, 328, 331, 339, 340, 351, 353

Stephen, James, 75, 82, 83 *et seq.*, 242, 264

Sturt, Charles, 145, 148, 168

Swan River, 6, 7, 70, 184

Sydney, life in, 272 *et seq.*

Tallow, 204 *et seq.*
Tasmania, *see* Van Diemen's Land
Therry, Roger, 25, 27, 32, 65, 199, 361
Town workers, 274 *et seq.*, 322 *et seq.*, 339, 343 *et seq.*, 350, 352 *et seq.*
Throsby, Charles, 2, 132, 135, 211
Trades union, 353
Trial at bar, 211
Tyson, James, 179, 279, 303 *et seq.*

Van Diemen's Land, 5, 6, 16, 42, 46, 50, 61, 106, 111, 112, 150, 157, 321, 347, 351
Victoria, *see* Port Phillip

Wakefield theorists, 13, 22, 49, 50, 69 *et seq.*, 71, 82, 104, 106, 107 *et seq.*, 165 *et seq.*, 187, 249, 264, 265, 269, 304, 327
Wardell, Robert, 25, 225
Wentworth, William Charles, 28, 53, 203, 234, 235
  opposes Darling, 23
  helps Bourke, 24
  joins Patriotic Association, 97
  tries to grab New Zealand, 114, 226

opposes Gipps, 123, 223, 224, 227, 233, 245, 247 *et seq.*, 259
  services of, 129, 206 *et seq.*, 224, 228
  speculates in runs, 179, 180, 226
  and the Great Crisis, 193, 206 *et seq.*, 209
  is caught in Bank failure, 211
  opposes Lowe, 223, 228 *et seq.*, 231, 270
  character of, 224 *et seq.*, 228, 235
  change to conservatism of, 226, 228
  faults of, 225 *et seq.*, 227 *et seq.*
  opposes free immigrants, 227
  great mistake of, 228
  favours convicts, 322
Western Australia, *see* Swan River
Wheat, 96, 112, 121, 122, 201, 212, 350
Windeyer, Richard, 202, 208 *et seq.*, 231, 235, 248, 259, 260, 361
Wool:
  decline of English, 35 *et seq.*
  growth of Australian, 40 *et seq.*, 92
  decline of German, 43 *et seq.*
Wool sales, 344 *et seq.*